Bound With Love

Letters Home From China 1935-1945

EDITED BY AUDREY SALTERS

First published 2007
by Agequod Publications
Vine Cottage, St Andrews, KY16 9UH

www.boundwithlove.co.uk

Grateful thanks are given to the following:

The Baptist Missionary Society,
for permission to reprint material under their copyright;

The Carnegie Trust for the Universities of Scotland,
for financial assistance towards research costs;

The Trustees of the Imperial War Museum, London,
for allowing access to their collection and for permission to reproduce photographs under their copyright.

While every effort has been made to trace copyright holders, we shall be glad to learn of any instances where acknowledgement is due.

ISBN: 978-0-9557536-0-2

British Library Cataloguing in Publication Data.
A catalogue record for this book is available from the British Library.

Cover design by The Puffin Room, www.thepuffinroom.co.uk
Cover calligraphy by Zheng Zhao Li

Printed and bound in Great Britain by
Anthony Rowe Ltd, Chippenham, Wiltshire

Dedicated to the memory of

Wu Shi Rong (Wu Shi Fu),
Gao Yun Ren (Kao Ta Ko)
and the two Wang Ta Saos

with affection and gratitude

谨以此书献给
吴世荣
高允仁
及两位王氏大嫂
永志谢忱

CONTENTS

INTRODUCTION

One winter evening more than forty years ago, I sat down with my mother in the dining room of our home in Leeds. Between us was a giant cardboard box, stuffed with small square blue airmail envelopes, containing almost a thousand letters written from China between 1935 and 1945. My mother, Gwyneth, was in her early fifties, a comparatively young woman, and the events recounted in those letters were fresh in her memory. The family stories woven around those events were well known to me, and it did not occur to me that there was much for me to discover by examining the letters in detail.

I was anxious to help my mother with a chore which I knew had been bothering her for some time, and together we sorted the piles of letters sent to members of her family in Cambridge, and a second set of letters sent to my father's family in Ilkley. We arranged them carefully in date order and packed them into the file folders which were no longer needed for my GCE 'A level' notes - two files each for 1935, 1936 and 1937, one each for 1938, 1939, 1940 and 1941, and then a final file for the years 1942 to 1945.

Many years were to pass before I retrieved the box of files from its shelf in the large storage cupboard on our landing. It was spring 2000 and I was getting ready for a visit to China. I thought there might be information in the box which would help me plan my journey, and better understand the places I visited. I was unprepared for the treasure trove I uncovered.

Sheets of blue airmail paper, folded down the middle and written on four sides in blue ink. Closely covered typing paper, indistinct carbon copies. Rust spots and tattered edges, betraying the freshness of my parents' neat handwriting and the spontaneity and urgency of the post scripts and pre scripts. My grandmother's careful numbering at the top of some of the letters. Spidery Chinese characters scattered occasionally amongst the handwriting. Pen and ink sketches, meticulous drawings of rooms and furniture layout.

Here and there within the files a faded scrap of flowered cotton, another of heavy blue linen, a wad of photographic negatives, a tiny hand rolled spool of thread. A breakfast menu for the P & O ship SS Chitral, August 1935, showing roast lamb and three different types of potato available alongside the stewed prunes and buckwheat cakes. An ageing programme for The Peking Pavilion, November 1935, promising 'Three Shows daily' of 'Max Reinhardt's first motion picture production of A

Midsummer Night's Dream, accompanied by the immortal music of Felix Mendelssohn'.

In the final files, striking a very different note, a red cloth armband, grubby and wellworn, inscribed in black lettering 'B2576', and a bundle of short poignant messages sent 'prisoner of war post' through the offices of the international Red Cross. A scrap of crayonned paper, with a dozen pencilled signatures, proclaiming 'Merry Christmas 1944'. The remains of a 1945 ration book and Utility furniture dockets.

I found the letters themselves teeming with family, friends and colleagues; with doctors and nurses, teachers and preachers; with servants and soldiers and little children. Above all, they reflected the strength and warmth of the relationship between my parents and their own parents, John and May in Cambridge, and William and Elizabeth in Ilkley. 'Mummy dear' or 'Mummy dearest' wrote Gwyneth affectionately to May, or 'My dears' to the wider family. My father, Ronald, was both more formal and more effusive, opening his own letters, 'My ever dear Mother and Father' or 'Dear ones all'.

The place names looked different from those on the new map of China I had bought for my journey, being spelt in the old Wade Giles system of romanization current at the time the letters were written. What was written 'Tsinan' is now 'Jinan', 'Shantung' is 'Shandong', and so on. I could not find my way around China using the names found in the letters, but for me those earlier names opened the door into an almost forgotten world.

As I began to read, I found myself engrossed in the story which started to unfold, a story in which I found that I myself had a part.

PART ONE

CHINA BOUND
August 1935 – July 1937

Gwyneth to Cambridge[1]

P&O S.S. Chitral
16th August 1935

We can scarcely believe we are really on our way at last, but here we are in berths 219 and 220. Ronald is unpacking his trunk and I'm sitting on my bed. I've done some of my unpacking and will do the rest when he's finished, or after dinner.

Although it's such a short time since we left, I feel as though I could write all night. Mr and Mrs Still and Mr Ewing met us at Liverpool Street. Uncle Jack, Marion, Carol, Hilda (Ron's cousin) and various BMS[2] folk farewelled us. I behaved beautifully, not a tear at all after Cambridge – well, perhaps just one! Anyway, we got off quite comfortably and reached the dock. There the ship's men took our bags on board and we followed suit. Mr and Mrs Still and Mr Ewing came but were too late to come aboard, so for nearly an hour we waved to them!

It's quite a nice boat as far as we've seen it so far. Our cabin we think is as good as we could desire. The porthole overlooks the sea, which is good, and I'm sure we shall be quite comfy. We had tea at 4.15, not with the other mishes[3], but we have been booked to sit with them in future. It's quite obvious which they are – they need no introduction. There is quite a number going under other societies including half a dozen Salvationists with a sweet baby. There seem to be some lovely children on the boat.

We had to parade out in our life belts this evening. Everyone looked, and apparently felt, very foolish, but of course it's a necessary procedure. We are somewhere in the English Channel now and can see lights all along. Every now and again there is a gaily lighted pier. It's a

[1] Letters written to the whole family, rather than to Gwyneth or Ronald's parents specifically, are headed 'To Cambridge' or 'To Ilkley', and were intended to be read by the wider family unless otherwise indicated.
[2] Baptist Missionary Society
[3] Gwyneth's usual abbreviation for 'missionaries'.

lovely calm evening and there's a fresh breeze – it's really very nice and so far fairly smooth and we've eaten well! We both feel as though we cannot realise we are really on the way – it's all so strange.

Counting the mail bag and other letters, we've sixty eight letters and twelve telegrams, so we feel just a wee bit neglected – but I suppose we can't expect too much! People have really been wonderfully good to us all the time, haven't they? What with the wedding and now this. It was lovely to have a note from you, Mummy, in with the budget of letters. I hope you found the things I left on the table in the bedroom.

9.10 a.m. Saturday We've just had brekker. The menu made me feel sick, about a mile long and the thought of fried stuff at breakfast upsets me as you know. However, by sticking to booze and toast I feel O.K.

We awoke at 6 a.m, beds quite comfy. As we arose we found we were just being piloted into Southampton. It was rather fun watching it from bed! We're apparently on the hot side of the boat, but of course that hasn't worried us yet. The Winchester Castle is in dock next to us. It's a huge boat – didn't Auntie B. go on it once? I seem to remember someone did. We were rather thrilled last night to see Dover Castle floodlit.

Perhaps you'll let Dray and Polly see this and Auntie N.[4] and anyone you think is old enough. Take care of yourselves. I hope everyone wept over you at Chapel – it does so much to cheer you up I always think and it's a pity to miss a good cry, isn't it?

I loved the little white rose, it is still fairly fresh.

P&O SS Chitral

[4] Auntie Nellie, Gwyneth's aunt and May Johnson's sister.

Ronald Still, and his wife Gwyneth were aged just 27 and 29 years old when they set off from Tilbury at the start of the long sea voyage to Shanghai. Loaded deep in the hold of the ship were twenty one trunks and crates closely packed with their wedding presents, some still in their original wrapping, and with all the other things they expected to need during their time abroad. They did not expect to return to England for at least seven years. As it turned out, it was more than ten years before they saw any of their family again.

Ronald's father, William Knapman Still, was a minister, a Baptist, serving at that time the small Baptist congregation in the Yorkshire town of Ilkley. His mother, Elizabeth, was a trained primary school teacher and herself a keen church worker. Throughout his adult life, Ronald maintained close and important relationships with his parents and with his two older brothers, Will and Reg, and their wives, Florence and Phyllis.

As a boy Ronald had attended Leeds Grammar School. In 1927 he went from there to Magdalene College, Cambridge, where he had been awarded a scholarship to read Classics, intending to become a teacher. Early in his second year at Cambridge, he experienced the overwhelming conviction that God was calling him to go as a medical missionary to China. In the final year of his Classics degree, therefore, he also undertook accelerated first and second year studies in medicine. He graduated in Classics in 1930 and qualified as a doctor in 1933.

Gwyneth had been brought up in Cambridge. Her father, John Johnson, owned the family bookseller and stationer's shop in St Andrew's Street, Harry Johnson and Nephew, and Gwyneth had worked in the shop with her father before her marriage. John and his wife, May, had three other daughters, Kathleen (Kay), Olive (Polly), and Audrey (Dray). They were an old established Cambridge family who for years had been active members of St Andrew's Street Baptist Church.

John and May were in the habit of inviting undergraduates to their home after church services on Sundays, and it was in this way that they first got to know Ronald, while he was in his first year at university. Gwyneth and Ronald became engaged in 1931, and in due course Ronald made application to the Baptist Missionary Society (BMS) for acceptance as a medical missionary.

At that time it was the policy of the Society not to allow young applicants to marry before going abroad, in the belief that too comfortable a domestic life would be a distraction from the rigours of language learning to which all new recruits had to apply themselves in the first years overseas. On being faced with this rigid policy, Ronald showed the independence and determination which was to stand him in such good stead during his years in China. He made it clear that his offer to serve in China was conditional on him going out as a married man. His application to be accepted for service was considered by the Candidates' Sub-Committee on 11 December 1934. The Society accepted his stipulation, while making the point that no precedents had been set, and Ronald and Gwyneth were married on 30 May 1935.

Ronald to Ilkley[5] and Cambridge

18th August 1935
Sunday 5.15 p.m.

I'm writing this as we sail through the ill-famed Bay of Biscay, but be reassured at once – the Bay is behaving itself beautifully. The sun is shining brightly, the sea is a glorious blue, there is a pleasant breeze and we are neither too cold nor too hot. We expect to post this at Tangiers, our next port of call, and after that I imagine we should have calm seas through the Mediterranean.

We posted our last notes to you at Southampton. Kay came down to the docks to see us and arrived about 11 a.m. She looked round the boat with us for a little while, and then we went ashore. We were just departing for the town, when Guy (Gwyneth's friend from Felixstowe, who is on holiday on the Isle of Wight) jumped off a bus and met us, after having flown over from the island! Apparently the whole journey had only taken about half an hour, and he had been provided with motor transport from door to door. The whole thing had only cost 16/6![6] We thought that quite reasonably cheap, and we have visions of being able to fly home from China when our time comes.

We went into the town with Kay and Guy and had some lunch, paid a visit to the post-office, then went back to the boat. We were due to sail at 4.00 p.m. so we had a nice long time before they had to leave us. There were plenty of interesting things to see on board, watching the great cranes loading cases into the holds. Not all the cases were labelled outside, but we noticed those that were contained "Cognac" and "Muscat", so if they are leaving the country I think it is just as well that missionaries should be going too!

---

[5] See footnote 1 above
[6] around 82p

Gwyneth & Ronald
seen through their porthole

We learn that our porthole looks out on the starboard side of the ship, and Guy was able to take some snaps of us peeping through, and we tried to get a snap of them from our side. We waved them "Goodbye" about 4 p.m. and then the tugs started us on our journey down the Solent.

It was a fine sunny afternoon, and we had a good view of the Isle of Wight as we passed, and the Needles and the Needles' lighthouse make a fine picture. Just past the Needles we dropped our Pilot and he waved us Goodbye and we felt that now we were fairly started on our long voyage. We wondered if we should catch a glimpse of the Lizard to remind us of our honeymoon, but if it was to be seen we didn't see it, and gradually the land faded in the distance and the twilight, and when we woke up this morning there was no land to be seen.

The ship's rules are that people should stick to the same places at dinner, but may sit where they like for other meals. In practice, it turns out that people only change their places for tea, so that is our only meal-time opportunity for getting to know other people. We personally think it is a mistake for the missionary passengers to stick together at meals. They can easily get in touch with each other at other times, and the meals would give them an opportunity of talking with the other passengers. Anyway, I think that the missionary passengers have too strong a tendency to be cliquey. At our first meal, being newcomers, we fell in with the suggestion of our party leaders, and now all the places are allotted, so that we cannot change, but I do feel it would have been wiser to split up at mealtimes.

This morning I read a little medicine. I would like to read my textbook through once on my voyage out, so I read my first thirty pages this morning. This afternoon we had a lazy time, reading and knitting and playing deck quoits with some of the other men passengers. It was the first time I had played, but I'm glad to say my partner and I won all our five games. We mustn't let these Army and business people think that missionaries are no good!

Time to change for dinner now. Gwyneth is just changing, and although the majority of the 2nd class passengers do not put on dinner jackets for dinner, yet I do not think that my shorts are quite the thing so I'd better change.

Gwyneth to Cambridge

21st August 1935

Ronald is up in the music room, supposed to be working, so I thought I would try our new typewriter. There is so much to say that I feel almost hopeless, but I'll do the best I can in the time.

Every time that land is sighted, people all flock to the side of the ship where it is on view. It's quite exciting. Tonight we are supposed to be seeing the Balearic Islands and later on Majorca. Some of these places are quite fresh to me. My geography seems to have been sadly neglected, but I am learning a lot on this trip and doubtless shall learn a lot more before I see you all again.

We are keeping very early hours and get excellent nights in spite of the noise of the engines and the sea. We are having great fun with our watches. The first three nights we had to put them on twenty minutes to bring them into line with the ones at Gibraltar, and then last night we had to put them on half an hour in preparation for putting in at Marseilles tomorrow.

Most people play cards or dance in the evening. We have the dance band one evening and the 1st class has it the other. On the night when we have no band we have the wireless, but no one seems to like that as well for dancing. It seems funny to hear the Children's Hour come through. Most of the children on the boat are either too young or else too old to appreciate it, but the grown ups seem to like it.

We have thought a lot about you all. How is the Broadstairs holiday going? I wonder what you think of that part of the country? I think that Ronald has told you that we take it in turns to dip into the mailbag[7]. He usually does it at brekker and I at tea. We are the envy of everyone else who has to wait till we reach port for a letter. Yesterday we read Olive's first letter, and I think I told you how beautifully illustrated it was.

Last night the Bridge was open for inspection and we had a look round. Some of the passengers were steering the ship but we were too late to do that, though we had a good look at the wheel and saw how to steer. Apparently summer arrives on the ship the day we reach Gibraltar. On the morning we were due there, the stewards, who had been wearing trousers and navy and white striped blouses, appeared in all white rig-

---

[7] Because of the difficulty of sending and receiving mail while at sea, Ronald and Gwyneth's family and friends had put together a mailbag of letters before they set off, to be opened at intervals during the journey.

outs, and the chairs in the music room were all covered in white loose-covers. We felt it was time for us to don our summer attire, too. Ronald is now sporting his khaki-shorts and seems to find them nice and cool. So far I have not appeared in beach pyjamas or even in shorts, though some of the ladies look very ravishing in their backless garments.

The deck chairs we bought are quite decent, far superior to the P&O ones. The sunshade which we bought in London and said we wanted on board never turned up with our other things, but we got it from the office yesterday. The sun hasn't been sufficient yet for me to need it.

Gwyneth to Cambridge

Marseilles
23rd August 1935

We arrived here at 3 p.m. yesterday and leave again 3 a.m. tonight. It's an awful place, so very dirty and so noisy, golly, the traffic is the last word. Of course it keeps - or is supposed to keep - to the right of the road, but it seems to dash madly along and cars just go where there's room, regardless of other traffic. The police seem to have no control. They blow whistles and wave batons, but it seems of little use. There are not only horns but also bells, so there's a terrific din all the time. You'd loathe it.

This afternoon we started off at 2 p.m. with an elderly lady, a Mrs Williamson. She must be about 70. She's travelling alone to join her son who is living in Hong Kong. She seemed to have no one to take her ashore, so we took her to see Notre Dame de la Garde and then had tea. Then we had a thrilling trip to Chateau d'If. It's the island where the Count of Monte Cristo was imprisoned. We went in a little boat and the sea was rather choppy, so we went up and down a lot, but I liked it.

The island is a most depressing place and the prison even worse. It's exciting to see it, but I can't bear to think of the prisoners. I wonder they didn't die straight away, the dungeons and cells are terrible, almost pitch dark, just a tiny slot of light coming in through barred windows. I wonder if Daddy would send me a copy of the Count of Monte Cristo? A 2/- edition I should think – something with fairly decent type, but not expensive. Perhaps he'll charge it up, we're sure to have other things and will pay for them all together.

We think of going in again tonight to the flicks, it may be our last chance for months. Everyone seems to have umpteen frocks. Mine aren't in it, even the mishes have stacks – and some of the evening ones are too grand for words. I've not got my wedding one out yet, I think perhaps it's a bit too much.

We were very amused today. Mrs Williamson, who came with us to the Chateau d'If, didn't know we were mishes and when we told her she said she wouldn't have come with us had she known! She said they usually embarrass you so by trying to force their religion on you. She said she had thought Ronald an engineer, but she did just wonder about me because she noticed I didn't paint or make up at all! So you see, even without my mish's hat I give the game away!

Every passenger liner travelling east before World War II carried its contingent of missionaries, along with its army officers and colonial service personnel. Missionaries had been going to Africa and Asia from Europe and America since the late eighteenth century, at a time when China had closed its doors to Westerners.

Christians from Syria and from Europe had had a presence in China since the 7th century but an edict issued in 1724 had prohibited the entry of foreigners and had proscribed the teaching of Christianity. Following the two 'Opium Wars' (1839-42 and 1856-60), new treaties were negotiated between Britain and China, allowing British subjects to live and trade in a number of Chinese ports. The second of these, the Treaty of Tientsin, allowed foreigners to travel inland, permitted the preaching of Christianity throughout the Chinese Empire, and guaranteed protection to foreign missionaries. By 1935 there were about 3,500 Protestant missionaries of all denominations in China, including ministers, teachers, doctors and nurses. Of these, just over a hundred were employed by the Baptist Missionary Society.

Ronald and Gwyneth continued their journey eastwards, through Port Said and the Suez Canal, Aden, Bombay, Colombo, Penang, Singapore and Hong Kong. In Ceylon they visited the mission station at Nugegoda where Ronald's uncle and aunt, John and Ethel Ewing, had worked before they retired. Later, they visited one of Ronald's contemporaries from medical school who was working as House Surgeon at the Singapore General Hospital. 'He holds his appointment', wrote Ronald, 'under the colonial medical service at what seems to me the princely salary of £700 a year. He has a very smart little Singer sports car, and it was a very refreshing drive to the hospital with the hood down and the wind blowing about us.' They went on to have dinner and a swim at Singapore Swimming Club, novel experiences of luxury living for Ronald and Gwyneth. 'The water is so clear that you can see the bottom perfectly at the deep end. It really looks as though it would be perfectly fit to drink, and it has a glorious blue green colour. The club keeps open until late at night and the pool is lit by electric light at night. The water is delightfully warm and it is possible to stay in for a long time and not feel cold.'

Much as they enjoyed all the new experiences of the journey, they were eager to reach their destination. From Hong Kong Ronald wrote, 'We are glad and thankful to have come so far and are looking forward eagerly to landing in the land of our adoption. When next I write it will be from Chinese soil.'

Gwyneth and Ronald to Ilkley

Missionary Home, Shanghai
23rd September 1935

At last we can say we are really in China! You will realise a little how thrilled we feel now we are actually in the country of which we have thought so much during the last few months.

On Saturday evening at about ten o'clock, we turned into the mouth of the river by Wusun, and then waited until early morning to sail up to Shanghai. Ronald and I had finished our packing over-night so we were all ready on Sunday and were up on deck early to see all we could. All the luggage and cargo had to be unloaded before any passengers were allowed ashore, and in this part of the world all that sort of thing is done in a very leisurely fashion with a tremendous amount of shouting over it all. The coolies carry huge loads - they have a stick across their backs and a big cabin trunk on each end of the stick and they seem to get on quite well with such a load. We stood by the rail trying to count our many boxes and goods of all sorts, but as we had 21 in all, it was rather a job. At last all the luggage was off and we were allowed to land. We felt that the Chitral was our last little bit of home and in some ways were sorry to leave it, but we said all our au revoirs and proceeded to the customs office.

Mr Black [8] met us with two of the Chinese men from the missionary home and they were able to help with getting our things through the customs. This was in a big shed sort of place with benches all

[8] Adam Black, associate missionary with the Baptist Missionary Society, was based in Shanghai and responsible for banking, salary and administrative arrangements for several missionary societies all over China.

round and letters over them. We went up to the section labelled 'S' and tried to see what there was of ours. The customs man opened several suitcases and one trunk but passed the others without bothering to open them. The typewriter he passed with no trouble! We heaved a sigh of relief, and again when my brand new sewing machine[9] was ignored in spite of the fact that we had declared it. The wooden packing cases all have to be opened, but the man just read our list of the contents and then poked a little way down at the sides and passed it. Ronald had declared the microscope and after much discussion, which was all carried on in a very friendly manner, he had to pay something on it and also on the mercury vapour lamp which we brought for the hospital. It amounted to about two pounds in all, and as everything else was passed quite easily we really felt that we were fortunate. Of course our cases of wedding presents have not yet got through so we may have more trouble with them.

Everyone else had left the place long before we were ready, but the missionary home man brought us up in a taxi. On the way we passed our luggage tied together and put on small hand carts - there was quite a long procession of them all piled high with our baggage. It looked so funny, but there seem to be lots of things here which strike us as looking very funny!

We arrived here at about 12.15 and until lunch read our letters and looked around. Our room is quite comfy. It is clean but very old fashioned and we think it would be very depressing to stay here long, but for these two days it is quite all right. The home is run as a guest house for mishes who are passing through, but they seem to take other people too when there is room. There are texts all over everywhere, and until recently everyone was expected to say a text every morning, but that is now abolished and we just went into prayers. It lasted about ten minutes this morning and quarter of an hour this evening.

Yesterday morning, we started off about nine o'clock in rickshaws to visit Mr Black in his office. You would have laughed if you could have seen us, I'm sure. We all felt very silly, perched up in the rickshaws. We were in a procession and every now and again one man took it into his head to get in front, so he did a little spurt, and then another would do the same, until finally they were back in the original order. The rickshaws are not specially clean, though they vary a lot and they are all right for a short distance. The men are very poor looking, they just wear blue trousers, very torn or patched, no shoes, at least a

[9] a hand operated Singer, a wedding present to Gwyneth from her sisters.

good many wear none, some wear sort of bedroom slippers! And up top some wear very loose blue magyar shaped coats while others wear nothing. I think it is their headgear that amuses me most. Some are bald and hatless, others have lots of black hair standing straight up on end. Some wear old cloth caps of all sorts, some very antique felt hats and other various types of straw things. I suppose they are or were hats but they have quite lost any shape they ever had and look very funny.

Mr. Black is the Treasurer of several missionary societies and deals with all our money matters out here and he made various arrangements with us. We found him very helpful in every way and very charming too. The currency is very complicated, and I can see that it is going to make keeping accounts a positive nightmare! The unit is the Mexican dollar, and that undergoes almost daily fluctuations in value. Then, as an extra complication, they have what they call “big money” and “small money”. “Big money” is represented by notes, whereas “small money” is in coins. You get 100 cents big money for the dollar, but you get about 140 cents small money for the dollar, and this figure varies from time to time. Besides having dollars and cents, they still have “cash”. Three cash are the equivalent of one cent small money, and one cent is therefore worth about 1/24 of a penny. When you’ve got your money changed into cash and silver dollars, which are nearly as big as a 5/- piece, you need a cabin trunk to put it all in, even when you’re getting only a poor missionary’s salary!

Well, dears, it’s now Tuesday evening and I am continuing the letter which Gwyneth has started. I’m typing this in the dining car of the Shanghai Express, so you can guess how excited we all are. It’s about 5.15 p.m. We expect to arrive at Tsinan at 8.15 p.m. tomorrow, then Gwyneth and I are going straight on to Chouts’un.

The meals on the train are good. We had a good eight course dinner last night for $1.50, not quite so well served as on the English trains, but well cooked and good. As I write this we are stopping in a small Chinese town that I imagine will be very like Chouts’un. The sun is shining brightly out of a blue sky. The fields all round are brown and apparently baked hard. Here and there by the side of the railway the Chinese have cut up the mud from the river bottom into squares and have laid them out in rows to dry in the sun for bricks. The houses are almost all made of these mud bricks with thatched roofs, but here and there occasionally there are more modern houses of bricks and tiles.

Gwyneth to her mother

Shanghai to Peking Express
24th September 1935

The train is nothing like as dirty or uncomfy as we'd been led to expect. Our carriage has four bunks, but it's quite comfy for sitting. I slept very well from 1 a.m. – 7.30 a.m. We couldn't get off earlier although we were all in bed, lights out by 9.00. The whistle isn't anything like those at home. It's like the loudest hooter shrieking down your ear and several times in the night we were awakened by it and felt scared to death!

At Nanking, where we stopped at about 11 p.m., there were lots of people getting on and off and then a lot of noise while we crossed the river. The train goes over on a huge ferry. It is divided into three portions and they stand side by side on the ferry and then are joined up again the other side. When we were on the ferry Mary (Miss King)[10] and I walked about in the corridor in our pyjamas and kimonos to get the air and we slept much better afterwards. She is really a *very* nice girl and I get on well with her. This a.m. we've all been playing Lexicon and dominoes and the time has passed very quickly.

As yet we can't get accustomed to seeing spittoons all over the train nor to seeing and hearing them used! It's decidedly unpleasant! I only tell you this so that you don't have a shock when you come to visit us out here. Apart from that we're very happy! At the small country stations people peer at us as if we were curios! There are several armed police on the train who parade up and down and we've seen a number of soldiers.

The floods must have been awful and in some parts quite near the flood area we have seen rivers quite dried up. Isn't it strange? The country for the most part is just like the Fens around Ely, except that every inch of it is cultivated. There are no hedges or walls, I suppose they have their own way of knowing where their property begins and ends. The villages seem to be mostly composed of mud houses and we all feel now that we can picture the background of Pearl Buck's "Good Earth". We have not yet seen one road, just dusty tracks, not wide enough for a car. We've just crossed another empty river bed - there must be dozens quite dried up and the earth all round is parched.

---

[10] Mary King, a nurse, was another new BMS missionary, who had travelled out to China with Gwyneth and Ronald on the Chitral.

The waiters and stewards on the train, understand English fairly well and are very obliging and pleasant. We have found most of the Chinese friendly and both think we are going to like them, though the more we see and hear of the language the more hopeless we feel about it!

We can scarcely realise we'll be at journey's end tonight. After hearing and thinking so much about Chouts'un we are longing to get there. Mrs Flowers said in her letter that there is a pile of letters for us, so perhaps there'll be one from you – we hope so. I'm always trying to think what you'll be doing. It's now 2.30 here, so I suppose it's about 6.30 in which case you'll still be in bed! Already I can easily feel violently homesick, only don't tell anyone! I'm happy and all the rest of it, but it's all so different from home. We'll feel better when we get settled down.

Chouts'un, at last! We arrived safely and I'm sure we'll like being here. Will write as soon as I can. Lovely pile of letters, for which many thanks to everyone.

China in 1935 was a poor country. For hundreds of years, the Chinese had led the world in artistic creativity and technological innovation, but the prosperity China had enjoyed in the 18th century had been undermined by almost a hundred years of corrupt and inept government, and economic exploitation by foreign powers. Following the overthrow of the Manchu Empire in 1911, the country had been plunged into almost twenty years of social and political ferment, when the 'warlords' (independent military governors) fought amongst each other for dominance. The hardships of the country people were increased by the presence of their roving armies, who lived off the countryside, looting and extorting payment from the local peasantry.

Devastating natural disasters, including both drought and floods, compounded the difficulties. In Shantung, the northern province to which Ronald and Gwyneth were bound, 1935 had been a year of most unusual rains, with calamitous results. The Huang Ho, the great Yellow River, as it was known to Westerners, had overflowed its banks in several places, flooding hundreds of miles of fertile territory, destroying many towns and villages and causing the loss of more than 500,000 lives.

Chouts'un, a walled town of over 100,000 inhabitants in inland Shantung some four hundred miles north of Shanghai, was a thriving market town and commercial centre. Its silk markets were the largest in North China and it had connections by rail with the extensive colliery and pottery districts nearby. The flat agricultural land round about produced crops of wheat and millet, yellow beans and sesame, sweet potatoes, sunflowers and cabbage. There were orchards, too, of cherries, peaches, plums, pears, apples, apricots and walnuts. Baptist missionaries had settled there in the late 1880s, building the original mission compound to the west of the town, outside the town wall. It was a substantial compound and included residences for missionaries, school buildings and a small church. In 1912 permission was secured to open church buildings within the town itself, including a large assembly hall, with adjoining reading rooms and classrooms and accommodation for visitors coming from a distance.

Later, land was also purchased to the east of the town, near the newly opened railway station, with a view to initiating medical work. A hospital was opened there in 1915 and named after the Foster family of Cambridge, who had supplied most of the funding for it.

Ronald to Ilkley and Cambridge

The Foster Hospital,
Chouts'un
26th September 1935

You will see by the address that we have at last reached our destination, and what we hope is to be our future home. We're very thankful and all our first impressions are good ones and we have had no disappointments.

We arrived at Tsinan promptly at about 8.10 on Wednesday night. It was dark when we got there and we could only see the lights of the city as we approached. Dr Flowers was at the station to meet us and took us by car to Dr Ingle's home in the Cheeloo[11] grounds. We had supper with the Ingles and Flowers, and were able to stay about an hour before we had to go to catch the 10 p.m. train and then we had a two-hour journey down to Chouts'un. Of course we couldn't see anything of the countryside and we were all very tired and glad when our journey came to an end. Some of the hospital compound servants came down to meet us at the station and helped us with our luggage.

It was pitch dark and there were no lights on the road so we had to pick our way by the light of electric torches that Flowers and the

[11] Cheeloo University, formerly Shantung Christian University, brought together the work of several British and American missionary societies. It was formed in 1917 by uniting the Arts and Science College at Weihsien, the Theological College at Tsingchow and the Medical College at Tsinan.

servant carried. Some people carried lanterns, and I was surprised to see that the 'Chinese lanterns' that I thought were only used for ornaments at Christmas parties are actually used here to light the way at night on the roads. After about five or ten minutes' walk we saw a light at a gate and some people at the gate waiting and we realised that we had arrived at our journey's end, at long last after nearly six weeks of travelling, and I think that in our hearts we both heaved a big sigh of thankfulness.

Waiting for us were Mrs Flowers and Nurse Logan and Nurse Wheal. As it was so late we did not stay to talk, but Mrs. Flowers took us with her to their house. We soon had a hot drink (the nights are already quite cool here) and did not stay up long as it was late, but in the short time that we had, we saw something of Mrs Flowers and enough to let us know that we should both like her very much indeed. As they are to be our next door neighbours and our closest colleagues in the next six years and perhaps for much longer, it means a great deal to us.

After breakfast next morning Flowers took me round the hospital. I was introduced to the two Chinese doctors. One of them has been at the hospital four years and has just recently been married. His name is Hsu. Dr and Mrs Hsu and Dr Chang (pronounced Jong) are all Christians. The Hsus speak English quite well and he seems to be a very capable doctor and is a very pleasant and cultured man and will make a very good colleague, I'm sure. Dr Chang has been here a year since qualifying at Cheeloo. He is very nice and friendly and we shall get on well together, I'm sure.

The whole compound is surrounded by a wall and has a gate which is locked at night. There are a nice lot of trees and two tennis courts, one for the doctors and one for the nurses. Inside are two main wards, one for men and one for women, and several small side wards. The operating theatre is a big light room and they say that it is one of the best in the mission hospitals in China. The x-ray plant too seems very efficient and I have seen some very good pictures taken by it. There is a well equipped dispensary, good laboratory, offices for Dr Flowers and Nurse Logan and the business manager. The most primitive thing about the hospital is the water supply. There is no running water, and the difficulty is met by having enclosed tanks of water which are filled daily. We saw all round the premises, the boiler house, the laundry, the kitchens, the outpatient department, everything, including the hospital gates and their keeper.

The hospital is not full at present: it is harvest time here just now and most of the Chinese are working night and day in the fields getting in their harvests, and only the very urgent cases come to hospital. For all that there are plenty of bad cases. The thing that struck me most was the number of cases of tuberculosis, and still more cases of venereal disease. The verandahs were full of patients with tuberculosis of some part, spine, joints, glands or lungs. Another remarkable thing is that the patients here often have not one single uncomplicated disease, but frequently have more than one disease at the same time. One patient has diabetes and syphilis and cataract as well, another tuberculosis of the lungs and dysentery, and so on.

We are going to Tsinan this afternoon and Gwyneth and I are going to stay with Dr and Mrs Ingle until Friday evening when we go to Peiping by the evening train, arriving in Peiping about 11 a.m.

Gwyneth to Cambridge and Ilkley

Chouts'un
27th September 1935

Oh there's so very much to tell you and I've so little time. Please excuse hurry. It's very quiet here, except for trains which run near, but so seldom that they trouble people very little.

The European population in Chouts'un just now is composed of, Dr and Mrs Flowers and Ian and Michael. We both feel that we could not have better colleagues. Mrs is really very charming and she's going to be a tremendous help to me, at first. Ian, who will be six next month is a tall slim boy and Michael, aged two and two months, is very wide. He has lovely fat firm arms and legs and his father thinks he'll have to be a footballer. They are friendly and behave very well and it will be lovely to have them near.

Then the two nurses. Nurse Logan has been out years and is coming home for good next year. Nurse Wheal is the youngest of everyone except the Flowers. She's very friendly and jolly and I think we shall get on very well with her. The evangelists, Miss Manger and Miss Wood, have three more years before their retirement – they are quite friendly. The school mistress, Miss Smurthwaite, is younger than the two above and I think we shall like her too, and Miss Thomas (who is shared by a station in the north) seems to be very nice. Mrs Flowers says she's wonderful. That was the whole community, till we came.

I wish I could describe Chouts'un to you, perhaps I shall be able to later on. The population is 90,000 and the place isn't very big so you can guess how closely they all live. It's utterly Chinese, all the houses and shops are made of mud or at the best a few bricks and oddments of wood. It all looks very primitive. The people all sit around everywhere.

They so seldom see white people that they all stared and many giggled as we went through the streets. The streets are *ghastly* – the dust is inches deep and filthy and it flies all over the place. Many of the shops have open fronts and the shop keepers sit on the doorstep or on the ground outside. There are no such things as cars, just a few bicycles and rickshaws. There are big ruts in the streets and the rickshaws bump about terribly, but the boys just tear along in a daring manner. I kept expecting to land on my head at every fresh jolt! But it was all rather fun.

It's funny, but we both feel quite at home among so many Chinese, though of course they think we're absolute flukes. Miss King is very tall and they stare at her utterly amazed, they're all so short and dark. She has such pretty curly hair – which reminds me that I'm told everyone loses all signs of a wave and all the men go bald out here! Cheery, isn't it?

Besides the hospital there seem to be the school, the houses for the men and women nurses, the bungalow for the two English nurses, two houses for the Chinese doctors, the house where Miss Wood and Miss Manger live, the Flowers' house and ours. All the gardens have a few flowers. The Nurses had some violets in theirs and there are dahlias, hollyhocks, asters and enormous sunflowers, far taller than Ronald. The gardens are a good size and everyone is rather keen on them. Our gardening book was warmly welcomed.

We're very glad we bought our electric torch. There are no street lights and you need a lamp just for going about the compound at night.

Mrs Flowers has made her house very nice. They haven't been extravagant and have only added gradually. It's bigger than ours, has an extra room, but of course with the children they're glad of it. Apparently Dr Bethell[12] was very keen on keeping everything in good condition. Consequently all the hospital property is in a fairly good state of repair and our house is quite well kept.

Mrs Flowers has engaged the cook and table boy who were with the Harris'[13]. They are said to be honest and they look quite decent, but they both came out with yards and yards of gabble which of course we couldn't understand at all. The cook cooks temporarily for Miss Wood and we went to lunch yesterday and the meal was quite well cooked, so I

---

[12] Dr S E Bethell had been senior doctor at Chouts'un, and at that time was on furlough in England, pending retirement. On Dr Bethell's departure, Dr Flowers had been promoted to senior doctor and Ronald was appointed to fill the vacancy left by Dr Flowers.

[13] Mr and Mrs Harris were the only members of the Chouts'un mission who were absent when Ronald and Gwyneth first arrived, being at home in England on furlough.

feel hopeful. I'd like to do my own extra things, so if you find any new dainties, sweets, cakes and things like that please let me have the recipes.

By the way, please note that what I put in my letters for the family is *not* to be broadcast! Of course ordinary things you can tell, but I don't want things repeated everywhere, because if it is, it will mean that I can only write home in a very careful manner, without telling you half the little things I'd like to tell you.

Will everyone please accept grateful thanks for their letters? I loved reading them all. I hope to write to you all individually some day, but there isn't time yet.

After only four days in Chouts'un, Ronald and Gwyneth left to embark on their Chinese language learning at the College of Chinese Studies, Peking. This was a demanding and stimulating experience for both of them as the teaching was very intensive and a high standard was required to pass the exams at the end of each term. The teaching was all done in Chinese by native Chinese speakers, and both Ronald and Gwyneth developed a great admiration for their skill. Many of the other students at the college were also missionaries, but working for several different missionary societies and from several different countries. Extra curricular events were organised mostly by the Americans, who were in the majority, and Ronald and Gwyneth commented on more than one occasion on the differences in outlook and lifestyle between the Americans and the British. As well as enjoying some sightseeing in the area, Ronald took advantage of the opportunity of their time in Peking to make contact with staff at Peking Union Medical College (PUMC) [14]*, and spent part of his free time observing operations there. A number of lifelong friendships were forged with their fellow students and with members of the medical and Christian community in Peking.*

Most language students stayed for one or two years, but the BMS had decided that Ronald and Gwyneth should go to their mission station after only one term. The plan was for them to continue their language study with a teacher there, while at the same time Ronald gradually familiarised himself with medical work in the hospital. Consequently,

---

[14] In 1900, three American and two British missionary societies combined to establish a medical school in Peking, known as Peking Union Medical College. The hospital and medical college were rebuilt in 1915 on a much larger scale with funds from the Rockefeller Foundation. This institution subsequently came under the control of the China Medical Board and in the 1930s was widely considered one of the finest hospitals in the world. See E R Hughes, *The Invasion of China by the Western World*, 1937

they returned to Chouts'un at the end of one term at Language School, arriving in time to spend their first Christmas in China

Gwyneth to her mother and father

Chouts'un
27th December 1935

Many thanks for all the letters and papers, also for the beautiful Times Calendar. We're not looking ahead at the pictures, so we'll have a really new one each week. We shall love them. Then the magazines and weekly Sketch are very welcome and all the papers. I'm all on the look out for furnishing schemes now, so even the adverts come in useful. Will you tell Auntie Nellie we're very glad to have the Illustrated London News?

On our arrival we had thirty letters including ones from Miss Smith, Polly, Dray, Carol[15] (a real long one full of helpful ideas for housewarmings and parties), Miss Songer, Guy, Eleanor, two from Mummy and lots of Ilkley ones. Then we had seventy three Christmas cards, about six calendars and quite a lot of presents.

I'm sorry my writing is even worse than usual, but this pen won't go right since I dropped it. I must have another shot at straightening the nib. I wish I had Daddy's pliers here, or better still Daddy himself to put it right.

I think we posted our last letters from Peking on Wednesday. Friday morning we had our character writing exam. We're hoping that all our results will be good. We're very keen to prove that a married couple *can* work at the Language School! Of course we're more than ever convinced that it was right for us to be married when we were. We've found no shadow of any disadvantage.

We had a hectic time finishing off our packing. As usual our goods were too many, so we had to buy another case. This time a wicker basket affair, only cost about 3/- and will be useful. Eventually we squeezed all our odds into bags and said our farewells. Quite a little crowd came to the gates to farewell us! Everyone seemed sorry we were leaving and of course we were sorry too, we'd made some good friends. The taxi only just held us and all our pieces and we'd sent three trunks on ahead! A Language School boy came to see to our luggage - for a very

[15] A cousin of Gwyneth's on her father's side.

small tip you can get plenty of helpers from the School and you know they're reliable.

We had a three hour journey to Tientsin quite comfy. The 2nd class is well-heated and we were quite happy. Mr and Mrs Mould[16] met us at Tientsin. We left six of our twelve bits of luggage at the cloakroom and they took the rest up to their house with us in their car. They gave us a very happy time. They've a very nice home, so comfy and warm and they were very kind in every way. After a good dinner we went to see "Escape me Never" at the Flicks. A good picture – I think you'd like it.

Early the next morning, Mrs Mould drove us around Tientsin and we saw some very good shops. Tientsin is a western modern town[17]. You'd never know you were in China as far as streets and shops and houses go. We tried several second hand pianos. We didn't decide on one, but we liked a Broadwood and are waiting to hear about the price. We bought a chesterfield and two easy chairs, covered in a blue velvety looking material. They aren't first class quality, but they're comfy and look quite nice and only cost $50. That is about 65/- and then there will be about £1 for carriage I expect. So the whole thing won't be more than £4. It's very cheap isn't it?

In the afternoon we all four went to the Tientsin Country Club. I've never felt a colder wind. Our east winds at home are nothing compared with these north ones, but I don't feel cold in myself, except for my feet. The Club is a marvellous place, much what I imagine big clubs are at home, a beautiful restaurant, big ballroom, badminton hall, swimming pool – everything on a very grand scale. Most of the members are English, I think, army and business people. After tea Mr Mould and Ronald played billiards and we watched. Then back home for a real Christmas dinner. Turkey and plum pudding, which needless to say we thoroughly enjoyed!

Then at 10 p.m. they drove us down to the station and saw us and all our goods safely onto the train. We had booked berths for sleeping, so although it was crowded our places were reserved, Ronald in a compartment with three Chinese men. I think he had rather a bad night,

---

[16] Family friends of Gwyneth's parents, in business in Tientsin

[17] Tientsin was a walled city, eighty miles south of Peking and thirty five miles from the sea. At the northern terminus of the Grand Canal, it had been for centuries a place of commercial and strategic importance and a strong military base. It was opened to British and French subjects for trade and residence following the Treaty of 1858, and in the early 20th century rivalled Shanghai as a centre of commerce and society. By 1935 it had a population of 1½ million, of whom about 10,000 were foreigners, including British, French, German, Russian, Japanese, Italian and Belgian.

the others all snored so violently. The compartments are like ours at home, only instead of the ordinary seat they have a wider one which forms the lower berth and another above that. I prefer to sleep up top, out of the way.

I was quite comfy, in with three Chinese women. The old dear opposite me looked about seventy and had tiny bound feet, and smoked nearly all night! Every time I awakened she seemed to be lighting up another cigarette. The ladies below made frequent use of the spittoon. That's one reason why I prefer a top berth – I've not yet met anyone who does it upwards! They were all most interested in me of course and although I couldn't follow all they were saying I knew they were discussing me at great length! After a little time I aired my Chinese and we had a somewhat stunted conversation. It's great fun being among people who know no English, because then you just have to try out what Chinese you have. I fell asleep at about midnight and slept fairly soundly till 7.00.

At Tsinan Dr Ingle met us and again we parked our spare bags at the station and then went on to their house. Mrs Ingle welcomed us and after a good wash, we had tea and then she and I sat by the fire and talked till lunch. In the evening we went to church and nearly died of cold. It's a stone building badly heated – gosh, it was awful!

We had to leave on Monday morning and were relieved when we and all our baggage were safely packed in the train for Chouts'un. Dr and Mrs Flowers and Ian met us and we came up here. It was lovely to be here and feel we can stay a while after all our travels. We're just longing to get unpacked. Every time we look at "our" house we get more thrilled. It really does look lovely. It's awful to be so near and not able to move in.

The next day, we spent most of our day reading our letters, looking at cards, helping to put up Christmas decorations and being lazy. In the evening the four of us went and sang carols outside the other houses on the compound. It was very cold, but I wore my heavy tweed coat on top of another coat and Ronald wrapped up well, so we survived. It was fun and I think everyone appreciated it - they all said they did.

Christmas morning, we got down to find a table piled high with presents, quite a lot of packages for us and lots for the children. After we had looked at these, we had breakfast and then all went to the Hospital. The nurses had made all the decorations, lovely flowers, butterflies, all very cleverly done. The men went into the Men's Ward for the Service there and we went to the women's service. After that the Ward was cleared and Father Christmas appeared with a big sack. He had presents for everyone – Mrs Flowers and I each had a box of stationery. Afterwards Father Christmas came to the Men's Ward and everyone there, all the coolies and so on, had gifts. The two English nurses had wrapped them all up and as there were about a hundred and fifty altogether they must have worked very hard at it. Ronald had a nice loofah.

After this was over, Ronald and I went to the Service in the church with Miss Smurthwaite. The Church is about ten minutes walk from here, inside the city. It's a biggish building and like most out here has a stone floor, so that your feet just die of cold, but the Chinese don't seem to feel cold, they wear very thickly padded garments which must be nice and warm. The Church was packed, the Chinese pastor led, and the business manager of the hospital and his wife and four of his children sang a hymn together. Then about a dozen men from a silk factory sang a hymn and they all kept their trilby hats on – it did look funny!

The two things I enjoyed most were two little action songs by two Primary schools. They looked so sweet with their big brown eyes and they acted so well and sang together so sweetly. The children really are marvellously attractive, and if they smile they look so saucy. They were in their Sunday best, which in most cases meant that they had on such thickly padded coats that they found it difficult to bend and sit down! They did their songs beautifully, kept in time and sang clearly and did their actions very prettily. I'd love to have a moving picture of them!

In the evening we went to the Hospital again, the nurses did some plays in the wards. It was very good, but I got sleepy – it's tiring listening to Chinese and not understanding. It was a very good Christmas Day, quite unlike any we've ever had before.

I'm longing to hear how you spent Christmas. I'm afraid none of the girls were with you. We thought about you all very often, and didn't I just wish I could come along and be with you!

Gwyneth to Cambridge

Chouts'un
9th January 1936

Many thanks for your lovely long letter dated December 16. Louie doesn't seem to be such a joy as at first hoped. I'll have to send you a "Yu Li"! In spite of grumbles, as far as I can see most people's boys out here seem pretty good. Thank you for sending our public letters around. Everyone seems to appreciate them. Have you read about the

China and Japan[18] troubles? I expect there has been a lot in all the papers.

This week we have been busy again. We worked hard at Chinese morning and afternoon on Tuesday and most of the evening, with a ¾ hour interval for tennis. We want to do that every day, it's the only exercise we get. Dr Flowers and I play Ronald and Mrs Flowers and we're just about even. Sometimes they beat us 6-5 and then we beat them 6-5 next set. I'm glad we are well matched, otherwise we couldn't get such a good game. Our left hands get cold, but otherwise we keep very warm.

In the evening, Dr Hsu and his wife came in to say goodbye. They're going to his home and hers in the South for a couple of months. There is the possibility that he will be leaving for good in July. His contract is up then and his father is dead against him staying here. He wants him to go into private practice and make plenty of money. Out here parental authority is a big thing, and very few can stand against it. They are really a charming couple. He is so very quick and active and so keen on everything in the hospital and so thoroughly trustworthy and capable. Her English isn't as good as his and she talks Chinese to help me. I hate trying out my Chinese when foreigners are about, but don't mind at all with the Chinese – it's queer, I don't feel half so reluctant and shy over it as I thought I would. In fact I like trying it out! And the Chinese are all so very thrilled when we try! But they are terrible flatterers, all the time saying how wonderfully well we speak, when we know well enough it doesn't sound a bit right.

Last night there was a committee of all the BMS here, ten of us. We were officially welcomed to the station – everyone has been most kind to us. In fact I keep sort of wondering if it's real, they are all so nice! The business was chiefly concerning the property at the west side of the city. There are buildings over there which the BMS will not require in future for the English staff and the question is what shall be done with them. The policy of the BMS is to leave Shantung to the Chinese in the next ten years, gradually withdrawing the missionaries and handing over the work to the Chinese to carry, so that there will be no one to live in the houses over the other side. The medical side of the

[18] There had been several tense incidents in North China during the past week, including one in which Chinese soldiers guarding one of the entrances to Peking exchanged shots with a party of Japanese soldiers who arrived after the gates had closed for the night. The Chinese insisted that the Japanese, exasperated at being kept waiting at the gate, were the aggressors while the Japanese blamed the Chinese. Japanese troops based in Manchukuo had occupied border districts in Chahar, and were demanding their cession to Japan.

work will be carried on by foreigners even when all the rest has been handed over, so we shall perhaps be left to hold the fort alone in years to come!

On Friday afternoon we walked over to the West side to see the buildings again so that when the matter is discussed we shall know just what they are talking about. We went outside the city wall, then came back through the city. There is no green like the English fields and hedges. We feel hungry for that freshness which we see everywhere in the country at home, but the country here is very much better than we had expected, and there are one or two good walks. It is very flat but at least we can walk outside the compound for a change sometimes. There are some very lovely hills away in the distance. We love them more every time we see them. They look so beautiful with the snow on them, and at about 4.30 when the sun is setting behind them.

Oh, I forgot to tell you that we've got in a ton of coal, so we feel we're getting on, and I ordered household stores from the coast. I'll enclose a copy of my order if I remember – you'd probably be amused to see it. It was very thrilling to feel we are really starting housekeeping at last, and I loved making out the order. Mrs Flowers gave me advice about the various brands as they all seem different from the ones we have at home. We can get some fruit, all our vegetables, meat and rice on the street, but nearly all the other things have to come up from Tsingtao by rail. So we have to order enough to last some time, but everyone shares round if someone runs short of anything. We have goats' milk. The hospital goats supply that and it seems very good, but in case there is not enough some days we have to keep a little tinned in stock. I have mostly ordered the brands that Mrs Flowers has, and can try others later on. I expect I've forgotten some important items, if so, I'll go round and borrow. When you have to wait at least a week for supplies, it's inevitable that sometimes you get landed.

Today we undid the box containing our stationery. I just revelled in bringing out boxes of good paper. I'm almost afraid to use it!

Your letters have just arrived, I'm so thrilled to have them. Will you please thank Daddy for his lovely long one. I'm heartbroken about those stamps[19]. I put on one of every sort and they looked so very nice. I haven't been able to get hold of any of the new issue yet. I am glad you

[19] Gwyneth's father and sister Kay were both keen stamp collectors, as was Ronald's brother, Will. Whenever possible, Ronald and Gwyneth made a point of sending them interesting additions for their collections. On this occasion, they had evidently been cut from Gwyneth's envelope before it was delivered.

had such pretty cards. We like to hear about them all, and about the presents too.

We feel so envious of Ian. He can chatter away in Chinese to the servants as easily as anything. Michael still mixes English and Chinese – he'll say Pu yao porridge (don't want porridge) and such-like things, it's priceless.

Ronald to Ilkley

Chouts'un
20th January 1936

This is the first letter I have written from our new home! We moved in today! Can you guess how glad and excited we are? This is the first time we have had our own home since we were married, and it's lovely to be in it. We must wait until later to give you a full description but I can tell you now that we like it already very much, and I feel sure we shall like it more when we have got it more in order. We have our dining room and bedroom in order, and the little study in which we shall have our lessons with our Chinese teacher. The others we will try to get in order later, as soon as we can.

We had our first meal here at lunch time today, and we are very pleased with what we have seen so far of our cook and table-boy, but more about them too later on.

Ronald to Ilkley

Chouts'un
22nd January 1936

Today's paper says that at Tsinan yesterday the minimum temperature was 17.3 degrees below zero Fahrenheit or 49.3 degrees of frost. Of course, you can guess how pleased we are to be able to write home and record such low temperatures!

An ordinary coal grate fire isn't really enough to warm a whole room, and a good many people have stoves in their rooms. Others have an ordinary fire in the rooms and have a stove in the hall. It's really quite amusing when you go out to people's houses to listen to other people's plans and devices for keeping warm. It forms a regular topic of conversation, much more than the weather, which is not sufficiently variable to form an interesting topic of conversation. Unfortunately, at present our hall stove is out of order. We are just managing to keep warm by stoking up fires in the dining room and study and in the bedroom at night, and hugging the fires as closely as we can. This is the coldest part of the year, and people say that it soon gets much warmer. At present it's cold!

Since we came into our own home, Gwyneth and I have been having prayers together every morning. We read a little from Weymouth's version of John and then have prayers and we remember you then, and of course many many times during the day. I hope we may be able to keep on the custom we have started, and we would like to be able to remember your needs and things you would want us to pray for.

Our Chinese teacher has arrived and we are very pleased with him so far. He is a young man of about twenty three years old. He was born in Peiping and speaks the Peiping accent, but he has spent a good deal of his time lately in Shantung. We have lessons with him every day from 9 a.m. until 12.15 p.m. and from 2 p.m. until 4 p.m. More about our lessons later. Our teacher's name is Chao (pronounced Jow as in 'jowl'). He is a Christian and has quite an attractive disposition, and we both like him.

Now this for Father – we must start our games of chess, mustn't we? I think we shall be able to manage quite well, only we must be careful about certain points or we shall get into a muddle. I will send on a separate sheet my move Number 1 in Game Number 1, and then in next week's letter I will send move Number 1 in Game Number 2, and I will begin a new game each week until I get your reply to this letter. In this way we should be able to carry on about five or six games without difficulty. Points to be careful about:

(1) Each of us should keep a complete list of the moves of each game in a safe place.
(2) Every time we send a move take care to number the game and the move.
(3) When two pieces can both move to the same square, be careful to say which of the pieces makes the move
(4) Be very careful to give correct notation for each move, otherwise we shall get in a mess.
(5) No consulting with Uncle Harold before you move!!!!!

More power to your elbow!

Before I close I must tell you the result of our language exams which we have just had from Peiping. Gwyneth was given 'A' and I was given 'A-'. We haven't had any more detailed results, but of course we are delighted that Gwyneth has done so well, though of course I knew she would, and I am glad I have done no worse. Now for the next exam, which we are to take at the end of a year's work, somewhere about the beginning of October I expect.

Gwyneth to her mother and father

Chouts'un
26th January 1936

Mummy and Daddy dears, this is the first letter I have written to you from our own home. I feel quite thrilled about it – I do so wish you could all see it. That's the only thing that disappoints me about it. It's so awfully nice and all our things we brought out look so lovely and we're so thrilled with everything. We long to show it and share it with you all. We couldn't have had a lovelier home anywhere (except that a modern smallest room in the house and bathroom would be an improvement, but the boy is so good that we have no shortage of hot water and it's really quite nice).

By the way, other people, Ilkley and elsewhere, make no complaints about stamps being torn off and letters open, so I think it must be Cambridge people who do it. I'm furious that our Christmas card was missing. Of course it was the nicest we bought, a lovely little photograph of Peiping. I'm so sorry you didn't get it.

We were very interested to hear all about your Christmas. You seem to have had quite a good time on your own, but still I hope one or more of the girls will be with you next year. I'm glad people have remembered you. You always made out it was because of us, but evidently a few people like you for your own sake! I'm very interested always in all the news about Cambridge people, even though I don't always have time to reply. When we get settled down there won't be so much new news and I'll hope to be able to write better letters.

Thank you very much for the watch ribbon. Mrs Flowers used the first piece as hers was broken, but there's enough left for me to last six months or more.

I'm so glad you got the flowers, Mummy. I had to do it through Kay because of the money and also to get the right day. From here it's so uncertain. I'm almost envious of you having spring flowers!

Isn't it awful about the King[20]? It gave me a nasty shock when I got the news. There is no foreign paper available here, Flowers has one up from Shanghai, and we're thinking of having one from Tientsin when we get settled in.

---

[20] George V died on 21st January, after a brief and unexpected illness.

Will you please tell Barretts[21], Daddy, how well everything travelled? Considering the amount of fragile glass, it's marvellous. I'm just thrilled with everything. Kao seems a careful lad, so we hope he won't smash the lot just yet! His name is pronounced 'Gow' (the ow part like the end of cow) and the cook is Wu (pronounced Woo). We call Kao "Kao ta ko"[22] pronounced Gow der gore, as near as I can tell you, and Wu is "Wu shih fu"[23] (Woo sher foo). We like them both *very* much so far.

I like it Mummy when you tell me how you spend the day, like telling me you clear the breakfast things etc. It brings you nearer. I think the material for your frock is very nice and it's not expensive. Tons of love to you both and to the girls.

Gwyneth to Cambridge

Chouts'un
2nd February 1936

To give you an idea of the enormous expense involved in sending you a letter – we pay 50 cents for two letters and for 52 cents we can buy a nice little chicken! They're very cheap now and eggs are at their dearest, which is forty for $1 = 1/2½d! But they're smaller than English ones and there is usually a fair proportion of bad ones I think in each lot.

I expected your letter today, but it may come this afternoon. You see, even when they're actually in Chouts'un, it may be hours before they arrive. The postman is very old and he usually takes four times as long as a younger man who occasionally does his round. And what's more, he doesn't like carrying much, so he brings a few letters and leaves the others until another time!

This week has been another busy one. All our boxes are now neatly stored away and the room is swept and clean and the bathroom is clean and nice, ready for the bath when it comes. At present we're "bathing" in a tiny enamel basin, a delightful occupation in this weather I can assure you!

We are having great thrills using our cutlery etc. We are very pleased with our dinner service. It's white with a deep sort of saxe blue rim and a little gold on it. We use it for breakfast (we had cups and saucers to match), lunch and supper and usually for tea. Auntie Winnie's

---

[21] Cambridge department store which had despatched their wedding presents
[22] Pinyin = Gao da ge, ie Big Brother Kao
[23] Pinyin = Wu shi fu, ie Master Craftsman Wu

set is too exclusive for everyday use – I'm going to trot it out some day soon in triumph.

The furniture still hasn't come, but it's really on the way and Kao goes up to the station every day to see if it's there. The boys are quite thrilled with us having new things and, what is more, without being told or shown they know exactly where I keep everything! They were priceless over the Pyrex. They were terrified of using *glass* dishes – they'd never seen them before and were awfully nervous. I thought they'd drop them, they looked so scared, but they seem to be overcoming their nerves and are using them now.

Miss Mack's fireside companion is in constant use in the dining room. The other one is in the sitting room and will be used more next year. You know it's chromium plated? Well, young Ian simply gazed in amazement when he saw me unpack it, and he said he'd never seen a *silver* one before. He's terribly impressed.

People have all been awfully good in lending and giving us things. These last two weeks the shops have mostly been shut[24], so we couldn't buy a thing and I'd not thought to bring clothes line, pegs, bread tins and such like things. We have no fire guard and as we have to keep such a big fire, we feel a bit nervous when we're out, especially as this coal has a habit of spitting. We're hoping to get one made this week.

Kao really is a marvel. He doesn't need to be told anything twice and he never slacks off, but finds jobs to do. They both get up terribly early, do the fires and clean out the dining room and study, bring our cup of tea (or rather mine) and hot water at 7.15. Breakfast laid next. We eat about 7.45 – he brings in the porridge etc. and wears a white sort of gown which he had made for him. He waits at table very quietly and well. After our brekker is cleared, they have theirs and then Wu goes on the street to shop or cooks or something and Kao does the bedroom and landing, stairs and hall. Everywhere we have polished wood floors, so they are easy to mop over.

So far there has been special cleaning every day, so he hasn't got into a regular routine, but he seems to know his work well and is very willing and, what is most important, he's most bright in understanding my Chinese! You'd laugh at the way I stand in the dining room planning out a sentence, then pluck up courage and go to the kitchen and of course when I get there I forget it all and end by blurting out "Use this - that – here – no – yes – won't do – don't understand …" and with the aid of pointing get my meaning across.

---

[24] For Chinese Spring Festival

I haven't told you yet how we manage without modern conveniences and as I trust this letter will only be read by suitable people (to be picked by Mummy using her Doughty[25] discretion), I'll tell you now. We nearly always have hot water on the stove, so we needn't wash in cold. Of course, we have to be careful with it as the boys have a long way to carry it and we don't want to give them more work than necessary. As for our smallest room in the house, you soon get used to it. We have a little wooden contrivance with an earthenware jar below and at the back is a sort of trap-door into the back garden. Then there's a bloke who comes round, takes away the jar, empties the contents into his buckets and returns the jar. He gets no pay for this pleasant pastime but seems to regard his collection as sufficient remuneration! At present we don't use the upstairs place as it means him coming upstairs. Of course he uses the back ones but even so we prefer not to have him in the house. Flowers seems to think it possible that in two or three years we may have running water here. Of course it would be a great help in the hospital, so much time and energy are spent carrying it.

We have a break in lessons 10.30 - 10.45 and drink ginger and eat biscuits - Wu makes very nice ginger ones – then we have lunch at 12.30. After they've cleared that the boys have theirs and then are more or less free till supper, except that Kao comes in to get us our tea and of course Wu comes in to prepare supper. As they get up at about 5 a.m. they mostly sleep in the afternoon. There is a row of rooms in the back yard and they each have one. They just have wooden plank beds and a table – it's very bare, but they seem quite content.

We have supper at 7 p.m. and they go off for good after that, unless we want them specially. They work hard all day, Kao especially, because he fetches most of the water and the well is the other end of the garden, so he has to carry it a good way. They both attend the Christian church and seem very keen, though I didn't feel surprised to see Kao was taking forty winks there this a.m. I'm not really sure, of course he *may* have been just meditating!

I am gradually getting through the jobs in the house, though I still don't feel inclined to spend long tidying and sorting upstairs. It's so terribly cold.

[25] Doughty was May Johnson's maiden name.

Gwyneth to Ilkley

Chouts'un
9th February 1936

I don't know where to begin – there seems to have been so many things happening this week. First of all our furniture arriving, that caused quite a stir and then we produced the vacuum. We hadn't previously mentioned its existence, so the others were all very interested and we have been giving demonstrations and at the moment it's round at the Flowers. It seems to work very well and is absolutely no trouble, and so light and easy to carry about. I think everyone will find it very useful. The boys having never seen anything like it were quite excited over it and were longing to use it. If they are as careful always as they seem now, we shall probably let them later on.

We're thinking of hiring it out at 10 cents a day and putting it to the Samaritan fund. People may not like to ask for it if we just lend it, but if they pay they won't mind so much. The Samaritan Fund is run by the nurses and is used for extras, such as clothing for patients who are leaving the hospital and have nothing to wear. Now there are all these flood refugees there are heavy demands on this fund. The flood conditions are appalling. In spite of all the efforts at relief work, millions of people have been rendered destitute and thousands have died and are dying of exposure and starvation. The Yellow River floods cover 4,000 square miles and the Yangtze floods 10,000. The relief committees are trying to deal with about 300,000 people, but of course it's impossible to do it adequately. They are housed in old temples, camps and billeted in villages on people almost as destitute as they themselves.

This week our bath has arrived. It's a zinc one, quite a good size with a high back. Flowers seemed to think that an advantage, said it was cool in summer and kept out draughts in winter. Anyway, it will be satisfactory I think and cost us $8, which isn't bad (that's about 10/-).

We have had electricians in too and are feeling very pleased with our arrangements in that line. We had no light in the lobby, so they put one there. There's no question of taking up boards and knocking the walls about, they just run the flex up the wall. Then we've had plugs in the dining room and sitting room and study just by the fireplaces for using our lamp and also the vacuum. The electricians came on three different occasions. Each time different lads came, obviously to look around. Our house is palatial compared with the best Chinese ones here, and the lads have just stared open-mouthed at everything. They're all very nice and friendly and love to chat. Of course we only understand a hundredth of what they say, but that's a detail. One lad, almost as soon as he came, asked Ronald how much over 30 he was! And then having ascertained his age proceeded to enquire the price of everything in the room!

The carpenter has been in repairing our chairs and measuring up for the tables we want made, and, as it has been rather muddy under foot this week, poor Kao has been running round sweeping up after these workmen all day. He's a wonderful good lad, so thoughtful and careful, we think we're very fortunate.

Another really big thrill this week has been the arrival of a piano! You'll guess how excited we have been over that. It's second hand but a very good piano, a Moutrie, made in Shanghai. You know I can't play much, but I can manage the hymns when I have Ian's Sunday School and I hope to practise so that I can play for our foreign service if necessary. I love trying to play when there's no one around, and of course you all know Ronald will love to have it. We both feel very thrilled at having a piano of our own.

Today I did the 'suan chang' with Wu shih fu myself, the first time I've done it alone. I couldn't understand one or two items, but eventually I got it all clear. He starts off by telling me how much he had in hand at the beginning of the week and then proceeds to tell me each item bought during the week. Sometimes if I fail to understand even his descriptive actions, he departs to the kitchen and returns with a broom, or a basin, or a cloth or a poker or whatever it is he's been buying, and then of course I can pass the item. It's really quite amusing. Eggs have gone down now, instead of being $1.00 for 40, they are 80c for 45. At present we're not getting enough goats' milk to last the day, so we have Carnation with our porridge. We get it with the rest of our groceries from Tsingtao.

Well, I haven't mentioned the most important event today, the arrival of home mail and letters from M and F. Many thanks to you both. Whatever I'm doing when the mail arrives I leave off and peep into the Ilkley and Cambridge letters. It's lovely to feel we can keep in such close touch – and we do feel close to you, even though we're so far away.

We were of course very sorry about the King, but glad that his passing was peaceful, and interested in all you told us about it. The MG[26] has arrived, Father, but only just and we haven't looked at it, but I know we shall be glad to read it. I'm awfully glad you've a good map of

[26] Manchester Guardian

Shantung. The hills you mention are the ones we can see to the west. They're lovely. We love watching the sunset beyond them.

Ronald is busy now studying a book on surgery ready for tomorrow. It seems so long since he did any that I think he is rather anxious.

Ronald to Ilkley

Chouts'un
15th February 1936

The hospital is beginning to get busier again after the Chinese New Year celebrations. The Chinese do not like to be in Hospital for 'Kuo Nien' any more than we would like to be in hospital for Christmas, so the wards are usually pretty empty round about the end of January and the beginning of February and the attendances at outpatients fall off a good deal. Dr Flowers usually takes the opportunity of getting the wards cleaned, and this year we have had them painted and they look quite smart. The lower half of the walls is a kind of terra-cotta, and the upper part white.

I think I told you about the operations done on Tuesday. It was quite a change for me to be doing some surgery – it's eight months since I wielded a scalpel. The first one was to remove the extra fingers and toes from a man who had been born with six digits on each hand and foot. One of them was just a wee one but the other three were quite well-formed ones, though not any use to him and the toes were painful through making his foot so broad. He looks quite normal again now and seems pleased with himself.

Then there was the man with the gun-shot wound of his thigh which had smashed his femur. Apparently he had been trying to steal a donkey, but the donkey's owner had objected and had shot him in the leg. This of course was a compound fracture and had to have a metal calliper fixed on to apply the necessary traction. The leg seems to be in a fairly good position and I hope he will be able to keep a useful leg – and won't use it to help him to steal donkeys any more. He'll be with us for another six weeks or so yet, so he'll have time to reflect a bit, won't he?

While I was doing this, Dr Chang came up from outpatients and told me that he had just admitted a four-day old baby boy, whom Mother Nature had forgotten to provide with the usual apparatus for getting rid of waste products. Four days is a long time to go without this bit of apparatus, and the poor mite was almost moribund when he arrived, with a great distended tummy and haemorrhages into his skin, and vomiting faecal material. I wasn't sure what was the best thing to do for him. It was certain that if nothing was done for him he was going to die soon. The question was whether to try to provide him with his opening in its usual place (a procedure which might turn out to be difficult, since there was no means of knowing how far I should have to go before I could find his lower bowel), or whether to give him a temporary opening in his tummy, and look for the lower end later on.

Flowers advised the former since it would probably involve less shock for the baby, so I operated at the site of the usual opening. I had to make a hole about 1½ inches deep before I came upon the lower end of the bowel, and I was able to give him an opening and wash out the bowel gently and give him satisfactory drainage. But it did not avail anything, because the little man died about two hours later. I did not blame myself for operating, because I knew that if he had been left the result would have been just the same. I longed very much to have been able to save his life, but I think that it was impossible. The parents were not upset that he had died after the operation – the father realised that he was dying and pressed us to operate even if the chance of recovery was very small.

We had another disappointment the next day. About 2.30 p.m. a little boy about seven years old was brought in having just been run over by a coal truck on the railway line. The poor little lad was a horrible sight when he was brought in. The skin had been torn off him from his umbilicus down to his left knee, and he died from shock about three hours later. I had hoped that it might be possible to do something for him too, but the shock was too great and after recovering a little at first, he soon relapsed and died.

Not all the cases were disappointments, though. On Thursday I had to operate on a woman who had had a baby about four months ago. She had had a difficult labour, and had suffered some severe lacerations at the time (the baby was born in her own home, and she had not been seen by us before) and in the process of healing the parts had joined together, and the opening to the passage had been almost obliterated. I gave her a spinal anaesthetic and it worked very satisfactorily, and I was able to put things right for her, and I think she will be satisfied and grateful.

The Nursing School term here starts tomorrow, and so we shall be going across to the hospital every morning at 8.30 a.m. for morning prayers. Did I tell you that Gwyneth and I have undertaken to take one of the English classes each week? Gwyneth has five of the women nurses in her class, and I have six of the men nurses in my class. We start this week. Some of the nurses know a little English but not much.

Ronald to Ilkley

Chouts'un
23rd February 1936

Gwyneth and I have just come back from our Sunday evening service at the Nurses' home, and I have about three-quarters of an hour before we have our supper. Perhaps you would like to know something about the patients who are in the hospital at present. First I'd better tell you something about the general layout of the hospital itself.

The inpatient block consists of a big long straight building, facing north and south. It is divided into two by a staircase-hall, which has a door on both the north and the south sides. To the west of this hall are the two main wards, the men's ward on the ground floor, and the women's ward on the first floor. To the east of the hall are small side-wards which can be used as isolation rooms and rooms for patients who do not want to be in the main wards and are willing to pay more for their accommodation. So you see we are quite up-to-date at Chouts'un, and have our private and semi-private rooms even before they have them at Leeds Infirmary! There are a few private rooms to the west of the entrance hall, too, between the hall and the big wards. The accommodation of the hospital is for between seventy and eighty patients.

Foster Hospital main building

The hall and the wards are connected by a corridor, which has to be used as extra space for beds when we are crowded. It is not really a bad spot, warm and light and airy and roomy, so it serves very well, I think.

Outside the wards on the south side are broad verandas, which are enclosed by wire mosquito nets, and these are very useful for about eight months in the year. They enable us to put up ten or twelve extra beds, and they are especially useful for the tuberculous patients, whom we have to treat at present in the general wards along with the other patients in the winter. Not an ideal arrangement, of course, but in the summer they can be put out on the verandas, and that is much better both for themselves and for the rest of the patients.

In the men's ward, as you go in you come to

- a man who has burned his foot rather badly. The foot is healing fairly well, but in the course of the routine investigations that we make on all patients entering the hospital, we found that he also has syphilis, and so he is being treated for this too. The treatment (by intravenous injections) is expensive, and we ask patients to pay for the treatment if they are able. If they are unable and the case is an urgent one, we try to provide free treatment.
- a man with a hernia, treated by operation (successfully, we hope!) but his disease too is complicated by a discharge from both his ears which is being treated while he is in hospital.
- a man of about 50 who has a disease of his arteries which is causing commencing gangrene of his foot. This is a common disease here, and a painful one. When you go into the ward at night, most of the patients are asleep but you will usually see the ones who have this disease sitting up in bed and holding their toes because of the pain. We are treating this man with injections at present in an attempt, which I am afraid will be of no avail, to save the foot.
- a young man of about 30 who came with a swelling on one side of his jaw bigger than a hen's egg, which proved to be an abscess in the jaw-bone due to a septic tooth. This is now drained and I hope that he will do well.
- a poor old man who has this same disease of the arteries, and whom Gwyneth saw dragging himself into hospital on all fours the other day. He has gangrene of both feet, and has had to have one foot amputated, and I think the other will have to be amputated too. He pleads with us to take it off.
- a man with a septic hand now settling down
- a lad with a hare-lip, who hopes to leave hospital more beautiful than when he came in.

- another lad with necrosis of the jaw
- one with subacute nephritis
- two with cirrhosis of the liver
- the man who tried to steal the donkey and got a bullet in his leg in the attempt. His leg has become infected, and he is having a stormy convalescence.
- two young lads with osteomyelitis, now recovering and waiting for their wounds to heal up.

We are back at the door again, after having walked round the ward, and there is a poor young fellow who is riddled with tuberculosis – lungs, glands and bones and joints, and I am afraid there is not much hope for him, nor much that we can do. In the side wards there are more cases of tuberculosis, one of the spine, one of the lungs, and various others; one with trachoma[27], which is so very prevalent and so very infectious and so very damaging out here; one with blast mycosis, a fungus infection of the skin; the man whose extra fingers I took away, and a young lad who has symptoms like those of gastric ulcer, but who has syphilis, and whose symptoms may be due to that.

Upstairs in the women's ward there is a woman with a breast abscess and an old lady with inflammation of the tear-sac; a still older lady with chronic rheumatism who is a little better since she came in, and is disproportionately grateful; a woman with scabies and a tuberculous spine who is trying to get rid of the scabies before she is started on the treatment for her spine.

Another woman who had to have her leg amputated for tuberculous knee joint, not doing very well; a TB chest, and an old lady with acute trachoma, and another young girl almost blind with chronic trachoma, who has gone out of hospital today, able to count fingers two feet away from her since the operation on her eyes; then another TB spine and hip – a bright patient girl, who always smiles when Dr Hsu asks how she is, and says 'Quite well, thank you'. Next to her, the most pathetic patient in the hospital, I think, a girl of about my own age, who is an opium addict, has tuberculosis of the chest and larynx, and syphilis into the bargain.

There are three little boys in the hospital at present with kala-azar[28], a disease which I hadn't seen before I came to China but which is

---

[27] Trachoma remained a major public health problem in China up to the late 1950s when more than half the population was estimated to have been affected.

[28] Also known as Leishmaniasis – prevalent north of the Yangtze River, especially among children, well into the 1950s.

common enough out here. It is one of the encouraging diseases which we have to deal with, because you know that if they are left untreated, 95% of them die in about a year, but with present day treatment (which Baptist medical missionaries have helped to discover) the majority of them are cured, and instead of the poor pale anaemic wasted little fellows that come into hospital, they go out fat and rosy-cheeked and smiling. The three who are in at present are sweet little lads and I know you would love them if you could see them. Two of them are up here in the women's ward. One of the needs of the hospital is for better accommodation for the children – perhaps we shall be able to do something in that line after we have got the new X-Ray building up, which Flowers hopes to put up this spring.

Gwyneth and I are sitting in front of the fire in our dining room as I type this. Gwyneth is getting on with the Gospel of John which we are just starting in Chinese, and she is already ahead of me, so I must stop and try to catch her up!

The prevalence of eye disease was one of the first things which prompted the early missionaries in China to become involved in the provision of medical care. The young English doctor who opened the Macao Ophthalmic Hospital in 1827 was deeply affected by 'the pathetic helplessness of the blind – the old man tapping his way along with his stick, the procession of beggars guiding one another's footsteps, the children clinging to the shadows to avoid the painful glare of the strong eastern sun'[29]

The Chinese had studied disease and practised the art of healing for many hundreds of years before the arrival of westerners. Four thousand years earlier they had been able to identify accurately the symptoms of cholera. Inoculation against smallpox was practised in China seven hundred years before it was adopted in the west. There were no hospitals, however, in pre-missionary days, only hostels or inns where the patient could be looked after by friends while attending a doctor. Each doctor practised independently. His job, if called upon, was to make a diagnosis and suggest a remedy. He did not see it as his responsibility to see the patient through to recovery. If his prescription was ineffective, the patient or his family could try someone else.

The decision to develop medical work at a professional level gave rise initially to some controversy within the missionary societies. Some

---

[29] Balm, Harold, *China and Modern Medicine*, London 1921

believed that every missionary's first duty was as a preacher and evangelist, and only incidentally as a healer. William Brown, of Edinburgh, offered himself to the BMS specifically as a medical missionary and went out to China in 1870, but after only four years he was recalled by the Home Committee because he insisted on devoting himself wholly to medical work. There was also disagreement about the kind of training required by the prospective practitioner. Did he require full medical qualifications or simply some medical knowledge and experience with which to tackle straightforward problems? And if a candidate was going out as a doctor, rather than as a preacher, was there any need for him to learn the language?

A clear voice on this was heard from the Rev Alfred G Jones, who arrived in Shantung in 1877. He was a man of exceptional vision and organisational ability, whose foresight contributed enormously to the development of the Baptist mission in Shantung. Writing to mission headquarters in 1886 to request that several medical missionaries be recruited, he insisted that they must be 'fully qualified' and devote themselves only to medicine. 'It is impossible to mix the two things – preaching and medicine. I would rather see a man do one thing well than two things ill. As to language, . . . I know nothing more perplexing than the terms in which the poor describe their symptoms and the history of their cases. Life after life depends on the understanding of those descriptions.'[30]

By the time the Medical Missionary Auxiliary of the BMS was set up in 1901 the mission had resolved these questions. Medical work was an essential part of the Christian calling. It was quite wrong to regard it as some kind of bait to attract people to the church. The responsibility of the mission was to provide the best possible buildings and equipment, and the best qualified doctors, nurses, pharmacists and hospital technicians it could obtain. In an organisation funded by individual subscriptions, financial constraints inevitably came into play, but the choice made by the mission was to limit the number of institutions to which it aspired, rather than lower the standards for those institutions to which it was committed. Of the 500 hospitals registered in China in 1935, 214 were mission hospitals.

Initially, Chinese students were sent to Europe or America for education in Western medicine – the first Chinese student sent to Edinburgh graduated with distinction in 1857. The first Western medical

[30] A G Jones to A H Baynes, *Letters written by missionaries concerning the consolidation and development of work in Shantung,* pub. Shanghai 1886, Angus Library, Oxford

school opened in China in Tientsin in 1881. By 1935, thirteen mission run medical schools were in existence. The Nursing School at Chouts'un was part of the drive to transfer professional skills and responsibility into the hands of the Chinese themselves.

Gwyneth to Cambridge

Chouts'un
23rd February 1936

This morning Su and Ronald and I went to the Chinese church. It's a biggish stone building, with stone floor, there are just wooden forms (with backs). About five years ago they were all smashed to bits and everything was torn down and the windows smashed, in a Communistic and anti-foreign row. Today there was quite a good attendance and, although we arrived ten minutes before the time to start, they were well on the way through the first hymn. If they happen to have a crowd there in good time they usually start. They have no organ, but just sing without music. Today one of the hymns was sung to our tune for "Auld Lang Syne".

The men sit on forms down the centre, mostly keep their hats on. Then at one side is the Ming Tao School (Su's school), about fifty girls all dressed in neat blue jackets. They all sing very lustily. We usually sit with them now. The other side are old women and a few young ones, with various babes, toddlers and in arms. The old women all wear short padded coats and padded trousers and nearly all have bound feet. The infants are allowed to run about and talk and eat buns or peanuts and even adults just come in and out as they like. I admire people who can get up and talk to a crowd like that. We still follow very little of the sermon, but can understand some of the hymns, and sing heartily inserting la, la or de de, when we don't recognise characters. The men usually wear those little round black sort of skull caps with a red or black button on top and long blue gowns, buttoning down the right side. It's not quite so cold now, but I still wear my little woolly sockees and heavy shoes for church because the stone floors are chillsome.

This week Su and I have been out through the fields most afternoons for half an hour and on Thursday we went to see a kindergarten, run on the church premises. The room is bare and dark, but the children love it. It's clean and has a few pictures on the walls and the children have sweet little stools and forms. They all wear their hats and padded coats in school. They're all very poor. There are about twenty, nice little things. They were in the playground playing a round game and seemed very happy. Su has the oversight of the school, and also of another kindergarten on the west side of Chouts'un. We took some snaps of them, which of course we'll let you see if we get them out OK.

It's five years tomorrow since we became engaged! And we've been married nine months, so we feel real old stagers now! For tomorrow night's supper I've made a pudding, the nearest I could to a Christmas one and we're having roast beef, roast potatoes, Yorkshire pudding and gravy and then the pudding. Will you send me your Christmas pudding recipe some time please, Mummy? Wu can't understand us having a special pudding and not having visitors to share it, but he was quite thrilled because I said that we wouldn't tell Ronald what we were having so that he'd be surprised and pleased, as it was his favourite dinner.

Ronald to Will and Florence

Chouts'un

Sunday 8th March 1936

Another welcome batch of mail today, including yours dated February 11th. There seems to have been some delay on the line recently and the last lot of letters has taken twenty six days to get here. The Siberian route doesn't seem to try to make a name for itself for regularity, but considering what sort of political conditions it has to come through, I suppose that's not surprising. If you have anything of importance to send, and if you don't mind it taking six weeks to get here, send it by sea. If the relationship between Japan and Russia gets worse, it is quite possible that the mail service will be held up entirely – it remains to be seen.

This last week the water in one of our large enamel jugs in the bedroom froze absolutely solid and cracked all the enamel off the jug. We thought it had cracked the iron too, but it still holds water. But since then we have had one or two warm days, so I think we shall soon be having spring. Spring here, they say, is a time of strong winds – and winds bring (1) dusts and (2) kites, and plenty of both. Hope you didn't have any trouble with burst pipes – we are spared any anxieties about that, because we have no running water and therefore no pipes.

Running water is one of the big needs of the hospital at present, and I think that when the new X-Ray building is finished, as I hope it will be this spring, the next objective will be to put running water in. At present we manage with an apparatus that has a definitely Heath

Robinson appearance, but which is quite effective. It consists of a water container, holding about three or four gallons, fixed in a wooden box and fastened to the wall at a height of about six feet. It has a hole at the bottom and to this hole is attached a rubber tube: this rubber tube passes through a kind of trap, the trap being operated by means of your foot pressing on a wooden lever on the ground. A system of levers causes the rubber outlet pipe to be compressed or released so as to hold the water in or let it out. It is fairly convenient. When scrubbing up for an operation you don't need to turn on or off any taps, but operate the apparatus with one foot, but it means extra work carrying water for the coolies. If we get running water, we shall have to take great care not to have burst pipes in the winter. So far as I know there isn't a plumber in Chouts'un, so we should have to look after our own bursts!

Ronald to Ilkley

Chouts'un
Sunday 22nd March 1936

Last Sunday Gwyneth and I and Miss Wheal and Miss Smurthwaite went over to the little church at the other side of Chouts'un for the morning service there. There is no settled minister, but there is a kind of 'plan' of preachers for each Sunday, there being several preachers who go round to the various churches in the district each Sunday. Last Sunday the preacher was Mr Yin, the minister of the City church. They had about fifty there.

It was a very warm morning, and I was too hot in an overcoat and scarf by the time we got there. The walk made us realise what a blessing the spring must be to the Chinese. When so many of them are living so near to extreme poverty, it must mean a lot to them when they can sit out in the sun without feeling cold. Of course the shops on the street were open as usual on Sunday morning, and round about the spot where the stream runs through the town, there was a market in progress. It seemed to be a carrot and turnip market, because that was all that was being sold, except for one or two people who were selling leeks. The sellers come into town from outside with their big baskets of vegetables, and then just sit down by the roadside, with their baskets by their sides, displaying their goods. Near the west side, a good many of the places manufacture silk goods and as we passed some of them the doors were open and we could see the silk being worked on their home-made machines.

Building the new X-ray block has begun, and it's very interesting to watch. They digged about four feet deep for the foundations, and for the last day or two they have been filling in the lower two feet with earth mixed with lime and have been ramming it down hard. Their ram consists of several flat stones about a foot square fastened together with two poles as handles. Two men stand in the trench and hold these poles, and six men stand on top, three on each side and have ropes that pass underneath the stones by which they can lift them. Then they work to music – the leader sings a song and the rest of the gang join in the chorus lines. The words of the verses are impromptu, we are told, the leader just making up words as he goes along, and the rest singing the chorus, and they bang down the ram in time with the music. They sing very lustily and it almost seems as though they put more energy into the singing than they do into the ramming!

Yesterday the wood for the building arrived, about a thousand pieces of Oregon pine, and it all had to be counted and checked, so that kept me busy for part of the morning. The foundations are almost ready for the first stones to be laid, and after that the building will soon shoot up, I expect. It's important to get the roof on before the heavy rains come about July.

We're still not quite out of winter weather. It froze again hard one night this week, and when we woke up on Friday morning we were surprised to find snow on the ground once again. But there are signs that spring isn't far off now, one of them being that most of the men servants on the compound have had their heads shaved bare! The days are gradually getting warmer too. The snow was gone by midday and there are some green shoots in the garden. When you go out of the compound it almost seems as though a miracle has happened, because instead of the bare brown earth that was there a week ago, there is now quite a mass of green where the wheat is coming up. And the Chinese are beginning to come out and fly their kites. Last night I went to the gate with Flowers and saw some of them flying kites. It seemed as though there was hardly a breath of air, and yet they were flying kites high up in the sky, so high that they were almost out of sight.

We recently ordered some seeds from the Nanking University Agricultural School, and also two Bartlett pear trees, and the two pear trees arrived on Friday and we put them in on yesterday. We carefully followed the directions in the 'All about gardening' that we brought with us. Kao digged the holes for us, using a Chinese spade for the purpose. The Chinese don't dig as we do – they dig towards themselves instead of away, using a heavy weapon like a great big hoe bent at a right angle.

We wrapped up our pear trees in straw overnight in case there should be any more frosts. Everyone tells us that we shall never eat any pears off the trees even if they produce them, because they will disappear mysteriously, as they used to do at Meltham[31], but anyway I think it is worthwhile planting them. It seems a shame, when all the rest of China is so carefully cultivated, so that not an inch of ground should be wasted, that we should have a good sized garden not producing things – and the pear blossom should be pretty, too.

A lot of things may happen before these trees bear fruit, but we thought that we might as well plant as early as possible if we were to get any results at all for our efforts.

Gwyneth to her mother and father

Chouts'un

Sunday 22nd March 1936

Well, this time I've two letters to answer! You must spend nearly all your days writing to the four of us. You ought to start typing and send duplicate copies! I always make time to read my letters, whatever I'm doing I always stop and read your letter. When I tell Kao it's from my 'mu chin' (mother) he gets quite girlish and says 'shih mang te mu'chin p'ing an',[32] in other words he hopes you're O.K.

As usual I was very interested in all the news, Mother. The Borneo talk at W.O. must have been interesting. I think when I come home I'll find it difficult to know what sort of things to tell people about, so if you have any ideas please hang onto them. When you've been 'out here' a few months you get so used to things that you find it hard to think of what other people would like to hear about. I hope you thought my letter to the Work Party was suitable, I couldn't think what to say, because I didn't feel free to write as I should to a less mixed crowd. I felt that things that Mrs. Cole and M. Nutter would like would quickly send others to stop their BMS subscriptions!

The fact that M. Nutter's clock keeps good time isn't really much help, because the hospital time keeper often pushes that clock on ten minutes if he wants to get prayers over quickly! So we have several times gone in good time and arrived to find the service was in progress. That happened today, probably because it was a nice day and people felt in good spirits and got there early.

Our kitchen is whitewashed, has a few shelves, no cupboard, two tables with drawers, where they keep their etceteras, knives and so on.

---

[31] Meltham, Yorkshire, where Ronald's father was minister 1902 - 1909

[32] Pinyin = shi mang de muqin ping an

There is one big wooden chair and then two huge earthenware jars, like your bread bin only much bigger. The bigger holds all the water as it is drawn from the well, the smaller is where they empty dirty water and rubbish. Then they have odd bowls about, containing vegetables, and oil tins for coal. The stove is something like the old kitcheners we used to have before the Ideal boiler, but it seems very effective. Wu cooks very well with it.

The crockery is usually washed very clean and nice – the boys have to fetch eight buckets (big ones, bigger than our scullery pails) to fill the jar once. For our bath we have one bucket cold and two boiling and it's really very hot and quite pleasant and, as we don't have the bother of carrying it up and emptying it out, it's no bother. There's no waste pipe, but the boys bale the dirty water out quite cheerily. Yes, the washing is hard on clothes. I'm trying to do woollies and specials myself, but I don't get much time – this language study is a full-time job. No, I don't wish I'd brought more warm nighties, am very pleased with all I brought. Two nighties and one pair of pyjamas have shrunk, and are rather short, but I can wear them all right.

The house is fairly well built, the windows fit well and most of the doors. The distemper easily knocks off and some of the floor boards are uneven, so that the tables wobble a bit, but it's far nicer than I ever expected – everything is – so once again I needn't have been pessimistic.

I am reading (many times), answering (eventually) and then burning all the letters I receive. It's no good storing things here. Mrs Flowers kept all the letters she had from her M and F and sister the first four years she was out. But I think it's daft. What do you think? The three girls continue to send us marvellous epistles – I just long to sit and reply at length, but it just can't be done.

I brought some twigs of jasmine in on Tuesday and put them in water and today the yellow buds look just ready to burst. Do you remember when Dray used to go out looking for 'signs of activity and growth'!? I think I'm getting that way inclined now – probably it's just old age creeping on.

Ronald to his father and mother

Chouts'un
30th March 1936

I've just finished a letter to Mr and Mrs W.[33] The parcel arrived quite safely on Saturday night – it contained seven pairs of pyjamas as I think you said. The parcel had travelled very well indeed, thanks to good packing, and the things were in excellent condition.

I have thanked Mr and Mrs W very much in the letter, but there are some things that I haven't said about the parcel that I want to say to you. I know that Mr W in sending the parcel would send it with the idea of its being used by the Chinese patients, but both Miss Logan here and Miss Wheal, who are in charge of the linen arrangements, think that the pyjamas are not very suitable for use by the patients. They think that the material is too good – the Chinese patients would not like to wear such good materials as these for sleeping in and the colours too are not very suitable. The Chinese, they say, do not like bright colours for clothes except for children, and for brides, and so they would not like to wear the bright reds, and broad obvious stripes are unsuitable. I'm sorry that I wasn't able to tell you this before.

For future guidance, this is the advice we have had from the nurses – pyjamas are very welcome. Material: flannelette especially is useful, as the biggest need is for warm night clothing for the winter months. Cotton is also useful, but the better and more expensive materials are not really suitable. Styles: avoid too bright colours, simple blues are acceptable, and simple patterns (e.g. stripes) that are not too obvious or loud, but plain colours and patterns are the safest.

In my letter to the Ws I have said that I knew that the parcel will be of great service and that I will write later and tell them what use we have made of the pyjamas. The nurses think that the way that the parcel would help the hospital most would be for the pyjamas to be bought by any of the English people here who are needing pyjamas, and for the money to be used for the provision of necessary bed and other linen for the hospital. Dr Flowers would be quite glad to have some of the pyjamas, and I could quite well do with two pairs. My only anxiety is that Mr. W should not be disappointed with the way in which his gift is used. I will try to see to it that a fair and good price is given for the pyjamas when they are sold.

---

[33] Members of the Ilkley church congregation

The nurses were saying that they are greatly in need of a sewing machine. There are two sewing women and only one sewing machine at present. If the money from the sale of the pyjamas went towards buying another sewing machine I think it would be well spent. What do you think?

I do not know what you will think best to tell Mr and Mrs W. At any rate I won't write to them again until I hear from you. I'm sorry to take up so much of this letter talking about the pyjamas, but it is such a valuable parcel, and I know it would mean a good deal to the Ws to send it and I do not want them to feel disappointed at its reception.

I had a disappointment last week – a little child on whom I operated for tuberculous glands of the neck died the day after operation. There was nothing untoward in the operation, and Dr Flowers thinks, as do I, that the death was due to anaesthetic shock, which could not have been foreseen or prevented, but it was very sad.

The story of the pyjamas illustrates the crucial role played in maintaining the missions by their supporters at home. From the outset, the whole missionary enterprise had been based on the commitment and practical support of individuals who believed in it. There was no public funding.

The BMS was in a true sense a co-operative society, made up of individuals who pooled their funds in order to secure a common goal. At its launch in 1792, thirteen Northamptonshire Baptist ministers, none of them wealthy men, each pledged an annual subscription to ensure that the worldwide work of mission, spreading the good news about Jesus Christ to every corner of the globe, might be undertaken. It was on the basis of these individual pledges that the Society was founded. Securing financial support from individual church members was a continuing necessity if the Society was to be able to pay salaries to its workers overseas, pay for passages to and from Britain, maintain Mission buildings and cover administrative overheads.

Gifts in kind provided an important part of this practical support. Scrapbooks made by Sunday School children, garments knitted or bandages rolled by members of church 'work parties', invariably women, were sent out regularly and put to good use. Ronald's painstaking explanations about the proposed arrangements for the pyjamas was based both on his personal sensitivity to the feelings of the donors, and on his awareness of the importance of this kind of support.

Ronald to his father and mother

Chouts'un
20th April 1936

I don't know about sending bulbs out here, Mother – we shall have to try to tell you when we know more about the garden. We have just opened our packet of Sutton's seeds[34] and hope to be planting them tomorrow and during the next few days. I do wish you could see our garden now, it is a glorious mass of colour. Nearly all the trees are in blossom. The purple lilac is out – glorious blossoms - and the Golden Bell, the Judas tree (a kind of magenta blossom, very bright) and the quince are all out, and make the garden look lovely. The two pear trees which we planted seem to be taking and I hope they will live and bear fruit in two or three years.

The question of 'supporting beds' is in some ways a difficult one. It is apparently impossible for the Mission House to send the money that is ear-marked to the place for which it is ear-marked in every case. For example, if all the money that is contributed by bed-supporters to the Chouts'un Hospital were to come to us, we should get a much bigger allocation than we are getting at present. This may be right from the point of view of Mission policy, but it creates awkward situations for missionaries sometimes – but this in confidence of course, and I'll talk to you about it more fully later.

Our chess games are a good substitute for the real thing, aren't they? I could see you putting the Bishop on K2 when I got the last letter! We shall be in the exciting stage soon!

I'm very glad that you went to the Infirmary and had the blood test done, Father. It was a wise thing to do, and I hope that the result will be reassuring. It should give you a good idea of the true state of affairs – and remember, most of all, that God's medicine is "In ***nothing*** be anxious".

---

[34] Suttons, the seed merchants, had for a number of years made a practice of sending a set of seed packets each year to every mission station overseas where Baptist missionaries were based. This generous and thoughtful gesture was a source of great pleasure as well as a real practical help.

Gwyneth to her mother and father

Chouts'un
3rd May 1936

Fancy we've been married nearly a year – the time has flown. Your letters came today so we can answer them now, it's nice when they come on Sunday. It's disappointing Easter weather was so bad. As you'll have heard, it was nice here and today it's raining and we're thrilled because we're longing to see our seeds shooting up. We get thrilled over the garden and walk round nearly every day to watch progress and yesterday we both weeded for about an hour. The boys are working hard and really it's beginning to look very nice. Yesterday morning there was one white iris out and now there are eighty to a hundred in full bloom!

The insects are starting on their summer excursions now and we've found various unpleasant beasts about. I still haven't finished putting woollies away, it's an awful business, everything has to be gone over, then sunned, then gone over and packed away. Blankets and big coats are O.K. It's vests and socks and gloves etc. that are such a blight. However I hope to finish this week. The woollies we keep out to wear in the summer have to be put into cotton bags.

Olive and Audrey's letters one week were missing and have never arrived and I know they wrote, because they both said so in their next. I was sorry because it was about their Sunday together and I was keen to hear about it. However, I suppose we're lucky to hear as regularly as we do.

By the way, if ever you're sending a parcel out, with that material or anything, I've a great craving for that nice cheese we have in portions and I'm sure it ought to travel all right in those boxes – if ever you feel like sending some, send small portions, to make it last longer! And if you could send me a fresh crisp lettuce salad I'd be delighted! And a pot of nice thick cream too! I'm afraid I'm a greedy girl! Although the food here is really very good, I do crave for things like that sometimes, but you know I always was rather keen on a good meal!

You wouldn't believe how strange it is never to look into shop windows. I don't touch money at all, it's very queer. I pay by cheque for things from the coast and Ronald just gives me what I need for Wu each week and I have my collection on Sunday. There's no use having cash because I couldn't use it – I never go anywhere. Wu does all the shopping, it's not wise to leave money about and it saves me carrying a purse all day. I believe our boys are both perfectly honest as far as our possessions and cash are concerned, but I don't think it's fair to leave money about, especially as we so often seem to have workmen in for something or other.

We've had all our vases full of Japanese lilac this week, the blossom is similar to ordinary lilac, but rather more feathery in effect and is a slightly deeper colour. It looks very pretty. I've been putting it in the Maypole marmalade jar in the fireplace to help to cover the grate until we get our railway poster screens made.

Have just heard from Mr Drake, our examiner, that he thinks it an excellent idea to do the exam in June[35]. It will have to be on the 15th or 16th, so we've not quite six weeks and we still have quite a lot of the syllabus to get through. So will you please excuse very short notes and explain to the others. I shall have to slog all the time. It's worth it, if I can get through because it will mean that I needn't work much or worry at all about the exam during the hottest weather. It will be a marvellous relief and will make all the difference to our holiday.

I've lots of letters of Dray's I haven't answered. I'm awfully sorry. Tell her, if only she can keep up her courage another couple of months she'll have her reward.

Gwyneth to Cambridge

Chouts'un
16th May 1936

Your letter came while we were over in prayers this morning, with one from Polly and others from Ilkley and Bradford, also the Times Weekly which Ronald seems to have read from cover to cover. I used to enjoy a squint at papers at home, but now I read all the adverts as well as the news! You see we never or so rarely meet anyone from outside and we get so tired of always hearing about local affairs, that it's a great joy to have papers.

People are awfully good. Daisy sends Needlewoman and Good Needlework. Both contain good patterns and ideas and will be useful to keep. Carol sends odd magazines, My Home etc. - very nice! Please tell her how I enjoy them. Miss Hield, a Leeds Baptist, sends me Modern Woman every month – she has also written a very nice letter introducing herself. Ronald has the BMJ[36] and the Lancet Weekly. Reg sends us the

[35] Their first year language exam was due to be held in September, but Ronald and Gwyneth had asked if it might be put forward so they could get it behind them before going off on holiday.

[36] British Medical Journal

Children's Newspaper[37]. A Baptist in Leeds sends the Baptist Times, another Baptist sends us the M.G. Weekly, Auntie N. sometimes sends the Banner or a Christian Herald, Doris Coulson the Listener (and she marks the bits she likes, which is useful). Then there's the Times and the Sketch, not to mention the Missionary Herald and other oddments. We always try to sit for about twenty minutes after lunch and supper and we read then, and we pass most of them round to the rest of the folk. It's a good selection, isn't it?

We've worked hard nearly all the time this week and we feel we are getting on fairly well, though we feel we need every minute available for study. Apparently it's unheard of for anyone to ask to take the exam early and we're going to try it in eight months instead of twelve. There are days when we feel quite hopeful, and others when we don't seem to know any Chinese at all. We have to write four hundred characters – I know about three hundred. We have to recognise over a thousand[38] and be able to give romanisation, tone and meaning. It's fairly easy to recognise them in a sentence, but when given to you separately with no context, it's sometimes very confusing, so many just differ in one or two strokes.

I'm so envious of Kay being at home. Although I don't say so often, I get very hungry longings for you all often, but it's no good thinking about it. You can never feel absolutely free with people out here. They don't know and usually aren't interested in your home (at home) which is what you would like to talk about, and you must everlastingly weigh your words on most subjects, because in a small community everyone knows everyone else. I can't think how single people can stick living abroad. We're very happy, but having each other makes all the difference in the world.

I am sorry about the maid or lack of maid. How I wish you could have Kao, I'm sure you'd like him. Wu has gone home for a couple of days, and Kao is nipping round and cooking quite nicely and so terribly proud as he produces things at meals. You'd laugh – sometimes when I am in the kitchen and mention in excellent (?!) Chinese a certain article and Wu doesn't understand, Kao, with his eyes half popping out of his head, will say very shyly, 'Shih niang ti I ssu'[39] (the mistress' meaning

[37] Arthur Mee's paper, published weekly from 1919 to 1965. Like his Children's Encyclopaedia, it was designed for children but was also read widely by adults for its verve, clarity and editorial balance.

[38] There are more than 50,000 Chinese characters in existence, of which around 4,000 are required for basic literacy.

[39] Pinyin = shi niang de yisi

is) 'shih Banana'. He brings out the English word so nicely and is so proud of himself – he really knows lots of English words and of course I feel terribly small, but he does it just to help. Wu's English is worse than his Chinese, except for one word, he adores to use and which sends me into fits. It's 'salad', which he pronounces 'SALAAAARD' in a priceless way.

But to return to the maid – I do wish you would get someone. I really and truly feel quite homesick for your nice scullery and would like to do a wash up after a big meal – for the joy of using hot water from a tap in a nice sink! And being able to let the water run away – all ours in the kitchen has to be emptied into a bucket and then outside. I don't know what Kao would think of your kitchen and the oven. They always cook on coal fires, and do jolly well too.

I hope Auntie N duly appreciated the teapot. If she likes it as much as we like all our things, it will be O.K. We were lucky weren't we? Everything fits in so well together. Hurry up and save your pennies to come and see them before they're all smashed. You can get here in sixteen days for £30 hard[40] class – so that's not bad. You must really think about it seriously. Miss Manger's mother (now about 86) has been out to see her three times, so you had better follow suit. There's nothing for you to do here, but look at the house and garden and talk to me, but if you'd like that, I should.

I should like a Cambridge cream cheese! – goats milk here has to be boiled first and it's most uninteresting. You see being a Mrs Mish has not cured my craving for good food! Or for trying on frocks. (The other morning I tried on six before brekker! Hush!).

Gwyneth to Cambridge

Chouts'un
7th June 1936

At last the heat has begun to arrive! It's reached the stage when we keep all our doors and windows shut all day to shut out the heat and open them if the evening is at all cool. The air is just like an oven and the sun terrifically hot. It's quite different from the heat at home. It takes away most of our energy and makes us very heavy and sleepy.

Today we had peas from our garden. Of course they were delicious. They're still quite small but that made them all the nicer. This

---

[40] Accommodation on Chinese trains is divided into 'hard' and 'soft' class – referring to the provision of wooden or upholstered seating.

week we've had mutton for the first time since we've been housekeeping, so you guess how thrilled I was. Today we had it cold with mint sauce (home grown mint) and lettuce and radishes (home grown, though the lettuces are only a few inches long and not crisp). Cherries are in now – they're small but quite a good flavour. We've bottled 6 lbs. and they look lovely. I hope they'll keep because we get so tired of apples in the winter. We're hoping to make some strawberry jam this week – I've ordered twelve pounds to come by rail. Think I'll make about ten pounds into jam and use the rest to eat now. They have to be washed in various sterilisers if you eat them uncooked and I've no time for that this week, so we'll probably stew them.

Thanks for the cuttings and the snaps of Kay's room. I think I shall want to sleep in it and let the tap run all night – to make up for being without running water so long!

The ants here are enormous, at least ½" long and fat, thousands of them too. So far we haven't met any scorpions, though they're fairly common but there are all sorts of creepy, crawly creatures that Kay would love.

This last week the wind has been from the south and the noise from the station has been very clear, especially at night when the doors and windows are open. The Chinese trains have a ghastly whistle – it lasts for ages and is more piercing than any I've ever heard. Luckily the morning train which used to wake me at five has been made later, and now goes at five to six, so it's an hour more sleep. It doesn't really wake me properly, but I always sort of hear it. Or, before I'm quite fast off, Kao usually carpet sweeps in the room below, which hasn't the soothing effect desired! Anyway, now it's so hot I don't mind getting up and am glad to start with Chao at 7.00.

Tsinan, to which Ronald and Gwyneth travelled to take their first year language exam in the summer of 1936, was provincial headquarters of the Baptist Missionary Society and about fifty miles south west of Chouts'un. Their chief examiner, Fred Drake, was an old China hand. His father, S B Drake, had been one of the pioneer missionaries in China between 1886 and 1910. Fred himself had learned Chinese as a child and had worked in China since 1914.

The city of Tsinan had been the provincial capital of Shantung from the 14th century. It was known especially for its numerous and abundant natural springs. The flat plain to the north of the city extended almost all the way to Peking. To the south, hills reached almost to the town gates. Looking across the city from the top of these hills, you could see the Yellow River four miles to the north. To the south could be seen, on clear days, the sacred mountain of Shantung, Taishan, fifty miles away.

Benevolent and forward looking city Governors during the late 19th and early 20th century had introduced civic improvements and administrative reforms in Tsinan, as well as opening numerous schools and colleges. By 1900 the central streets had been paved over with solid stone blocks, a street cleaning system had been introduced, and a telephone system, electric light and street lighting installed. In 1901 a branch of the Chinese Post Office was opened.

The coming of the railways had an immediate impact on the town. The German-built Shantung Railway from Tsingtao on the east coast to Tsinan was opened in 1904 and the north-south railway, from Tientsin to Tsinan, in 1910. The population, 150,000 in the mid 19th century, grew to around 250,000 by 1911 and 427,000 in 1933. The foreign community in 1900 had consisted of only fifty individuals, including children. By 1935 there were three hundred Europeans, numbers of Americans and two thousand or more Japanese.

The property belonging to the Baptist Missionary Society was in the south suburb of the city, between the massive inner 14th century city wall and the outer wall, built in the 1860s.

Gwyneth to Cambridge

At Tsinan
14th June 1936

We came up here yesterday, left Chouts'un at 12.24 and arrived at 3.30. There were lots of soldiers on the train – a cheery crowd. They all took off their coats and sat in their shirts and it seemed very funny to us to see them sitting there using fans! Everyone out here uses them now it's hot and these last few days have been really hot. Our teacher has sat gently fanning himself all the time lately, and although I was scornful at first, I really begin to find it's rather pleasant. It helps to keep your face dry. The rickshaws have little cotton shades, but the poor boys were just dripping all over the place. Ronald's especially, because, to begin with, Ronald is no featherweight, and then he had the case with him and it was like a ton weight as he had brought up a huge bundle of magazines to be bound.

We had a very warm welcome, in more ways than one! On our arrival Mr Drake welcomed us and then took us and introduced us to our Chinese examiner, a perfectly charming person, perhaps about sixty years old, but I find it hopeless to try guessing Chinese ages. He is tall and very comfortably covered, a round happy face, and had on a long white thin silk gown and carried a white fan and looked very dignified. Mr Drake had kindly provided Chinese tea so we all sipped at that. It is quite different from our tea. I like ours to drink straight off, but Chinese tea you just enjoy sitting and drinking and talking in a leisurely style.

The oral really wasn't a bit alarming. We were not even taken separately so it seemed much more like a friendly chat. After a few preliminary polite remarks the Chinese gentleman, Mr Sun, told Ronald a story, then Ronald told it back in English to Mr Drake. I was thankful it wasn't my turn, as I missed the point. However, Ronald got it and Mr Drake said 'excellent' to his version. Then I had my turn and mercifully I followed easily and was able to reproduce it. I forgot to tell the end of the story but that was not because I didn't understand, but just that I forgot it in English, so Mr Drake told me in Chinese and I remembered at once and he seemed quite satisfied. (By the way, Ronald missed the point of my story, so it was a blessing we had them the way we did.) Then we talked a little about various things. Ronald did awfully well and then I read two passages from John – luckily I knew them well. At first I got scared and stumbled a bit, but when I got going I think it was all right. I think Ronald's passages were harder, but he managed them well. Then I had to read two lesson sheets. After Ronald had read, we talked a bit more in Chinese and then Mr. Drake told us about the rest of the exams.

Mr. Drake is very nice as an examiner, very fair and most thoughtful. Mr Sun was very smiling and charming but we don't know what he thought of our Chinese.

We feel rather bucked to be able to tell you that we did the oral in a temperature of 104 degrees in the shade! It really adds to your feeling of importance, you know! The night was pretty awful. We had very comfy beds, there was a slight breeze and I think we should have slept well if we hadn't been reciting Chinese all night. We both got one or two sentences on the brain and kept saying them over and over again.

Before I forget, will you please let me have your recipe for that nice yellow pickle (piccalilli or whatever it's called), also for tomato or any other nice chutney you know.

Gwyneth to Ilkley

Chouts'un
19th June 1936

We do hope this will be in time for July 6th[41], but if it is late please forgive us, and understand that we shall be thinking of you on the day. We hope that it will be a lovely time for you both and that you'll be able to make it a real holiday. Perhaps you'll be able to go out for the day. If you do, we shall love to hear all about it. Of course we hope you'll have many happy returns of the day and that we shall be able to celebrate July 6 together again before so very long – one year has nearly gone.

I haven't thanked you yet, Mother, for the pattern. I do like it, it was a lovely idea sending it and I've always wanted to try a Buttericks[42], but never have. Everyone says they are such a great help. I want to thank you for that and for your loving thoughts and for the material which is on the way. We think the little pattern of it is very pretty and I am sure it will look nice made up.

This morning (Sunday), Su and I, went to the Chapel. There was a baptismal service and I was greatly impressed. I had heard that they were very noisy and showy out here, but it was carried out very reverently I thought. To prevent noisy inquisitive outsiders they have to close the main doors and we entered by a little side door. There weren't many there besides those receiving baptism, and a few interested in them and officials of the church. The service was like an ordinary Sunday one, except that the hymns, reading and sermon all referred to baptism, or dedication. Then at the end, the names were read out and each candidate said, 'Tao', meaning 'Here'. Then they filed out to change and we waited. They just wore old garments and some of them, poor souls, were very poor.

There were eleven men and between twenty and thirty women. The men were mostly under thirty, or even twenty five, except one who might have been sixty or more. The young lads looked as if they were very much in earnest, and when you realise how much harder it is for them than it is for us at home, it makes you feel very thankful for their courage. Two of our men nurses and one woman were baptised. I was more impressed almost by the women. Some of them were so very poor

---

[41] Elizabeth Still and Gwyneth shared a birthday on July 6th

[42] It seems surprising that Gwyneth, a keen seamstress, had never tried a Butterick dressmaking pattern. They had been around a good many years, having been first made in 1863.

and old and shrivelled, but they looked very glad and proud. You know the majority had most likely never been wet all over before, and although the water had been slightly warmed they were terrified of catching cold and were so frightened going into the water. The minister was very good – he held their arms and told them not to fear. The physical part alone is a terrible ordeal for these country people, and many of them are bound to be persecuted in all sorts of awful ways, because they belong to un-Christian families. Apart from one or two babies who cried when their mothers left them to be baptised, the service was very quiet.

Gwyneth to Cambridge

Chouts'un
28th June 1936

Well, I've had a lovely week! The exam being over, I've done no Chinese except two hours a day with Chao. We've started on St Luke – done fifteen chapters, only reading through quickly of course. In the rest of the time I have written a few letters and read. Such a joy to be free to read without feeling guilty because I'm not reading Chinese! Every afternoon I've reckoned to read till about 2.30 and then gone to bed and read till I fell asleep, then get up for tea at 3.30. After tea I feel absolutely fine. I like tea early because I feel sleepy till I've had it and once we've had it then I can get on again.

On Wednesday the Conference[43] at the West side of Chouts'un opened and we all went over in rickshaws to the welcome meeting and sang a song and the nurses did a play. There were about fifteen of us returning in rickshaws, counting nurses. It was quite dark, except for a very few shop lights and one or two street lamps – a rough road, the rickshaws mostly had no lamps. It was really a weird feeling, being pulled along in the dark, just the rickshaw boys shouting to each other and to people to clear out of the way. It was a hot night and we passed many people sleeping on the paths, some on the ground, others on mats, most of the men just wearing trousers. Then there were several women with two or three quite naked children asleep on their mat. Often the mother and children sleep in the street. They've no yards or gardens and their houses are dark and scruffy. The children are tied to the mother so that they shouldn't wander off if they wake, or be pinched in the night!

---

[43] The Annual Summer School of the Shantung branch of the Church of Christ in China.

On Thursday the rain started. Dr Williamson[44] arrived at 3.30 and went over to the meeting in the evening – got soaked coming back. Friday was wet, a steady downpour which has been marvellously cooling and good for the crops, but very inconvenient for those who wish to get from here to the Conference at the other side. It's a good 2½ miles and the road is un-made most of the way, just big ruts of mud and slosh, almost impossible. Dr Williamson went to a meeting in the morning and spoke in the evening, coming back here for meals. We went with him in the evening. On the way back it poured with rain. The roads were ghastly, just pools of mud. The rickshaw boys were slipping about and they'd not a light between them. Luckily we'd taken our torches. You learn to carry them everywhere here and so we shone them on the road as best we could and got home safely, but several times I felt sure we'd be pitched head first out and into the mud and filth.

If you feel sorry for the rickshaw boys having to be in the rain and mud and wade through it yourself, then you are doing them out of their only means of making a living - and they surround you and nearly push you into their rickshaws. Sometimes at stations you have to fight to get through the crowd of boys begging you to ride. They prefer foreigners because we always pay nearly double what the Chinese pay. I much prefer to walk usually, but sometimes it is convenient to ride and cars are more or less unknown here.

I find our thermos flask and jug most useful when we go out in the evening. You see we don't want the boys to keep the fire in after supper (it burns a heap of coal and besides they're really off duty) so we can tell them to fill the things with boiling water and have a nice hot drink of ginger wine or lemonade when we get in. We make both from stuff from the dispensary and they're quite good. We can't buy lemons here and if you send away they cost about 3 1/2d for a tiny one.

Mrs Flowers and Ian and Michael went off to Tsingtao on the midnight train Friday. They'll be there till the end of August. We miss hearing the children, because they nearly always play in the garden or on the verandah.

[44] H R Williamson had been with the BMS in China since 1908. In 1936 he was acting as BMS China Secretary with responsibility for all important correspondence with the Home Committee, and for co-ordinating the work of the various mission enterprises within China.

Ronald to his father and mother

Chouts'un
12th July 1936

This is only a very tiny note, but it comes to bring you some good news. We are hoping that by the end of November or the beginning of December you may have another grandson, or granddaughter (or perhaps even both!) Isn't that good news? We are both very well and happy and we'll try to write again for the next post.

Ronald to Ilkley

Chouts'un
19th July 1936

When we came back from Tsinan after the exam, the Christian community in Chouts'un was all astir with the various conferences that were being held in the Mission premises the other side of the town. Three conferences have been held there during the last few weeks – first, a general conference of the Church of Christ in China, a body which is seeking to unify as far as possible all the Christian churches in China; then, second, the annual business meeting of the Shantung Synod of the Church of Christ in China; and finally there was the summer school of our own Shantung Baptist Union, which was for the leaders of our Shantung Baptist churches. Altogether they had nearly two hundred people staying in Chouts'un for the meetings, both Chinese and foreign.

The three conferences held in Chouts'un in the summer of 1936 give some idea of the organisational background within the Baptist community and within the Chinese church at that time.

The Baptist Union of Shantung, covering an area larger than England and Wales, had been formed in 1910, at which time complete responsibility for church organisation and finance had been transferred from the Mission Board to the local churches. The Baptist belief that every local church has the right to be self-governing, answerable to no authority but Jesus Christ, does not preclude joining voluntarily with other Baptist churches to facilitate common action. Such voluntary liaisons include local Associations, at neighbourhood or district level; Baptist Unions, at provincial or national level; and, at international level, the Baptist World Alliance.

As well as the Baptist summer school, Chouts'un was host that summer to two gatherings of the Church of Christ in China - the local synod and the nationally constituted General Assembly.

Many different denominations and missionary societies initiated work in China in the years after 1840 when China first opened its doors to the West. For most of the 19th century the different societies continued to work on denominational lines, making pragmatic arrangements about the geographical distribution of their efforts. China was a vast country and there was more than enough work for all. Missionaries from many different societies were, however, thrown together in the general evacuation occasioned by the Boxer rising in 1900 and this experience led to a number of co-operative, interdenominational initiatives.

Amongst the Chinese themselves, improvements in communication and transport at the beginning of the 20th century raised awareness of developments at a national level, and this was accentuated by the new national aspirations which resulted from the founding of the Republic in 1911. These factors, along with practical, theological and cultural considerations, encouraged Chinese Christians to want to move towards a more united Christian community. 'It is surprising to us who have been brought up in a denominational atmosphere,' wrote Henry Payne, somewhat laconically, 'to see how little the Chinese care for these distinctions'.[45]

A federation of Protestant churches committed to an agreed declaration of faith was, therefore, formed, under the name 'the Church of Christ in China'. 'To join a church that starts out by saying that men and women, Chinese and foreigners, ministers and laymen, shall all have equal rights within the organisation must mean, sooner or later, a right view of the purpose of the Kingdom of God in the world', wrote Rev A G Castleton,[46] *when the Shantung Baptist churches decided to affiliate with the new body. The first properly constituted General Assembly was held in October 1927. The Assembly held in Chouts'un in 1936 was its fourth national gathering.*

None of those attending the meetings in Chouts'un that summer could have known that the next full meeting of the Church of Christ in China would not take place until the autumn of 1948. Meanwhile, China – and the Chinese church – was to endure twelve years of hardship, turmoil and bloodshed.

---

[45] Payne, H, *The Chinese Church Holds On*, Missionary Herald 1928, p32
[46] Castleton, A G, *A letter from China*, Missionary Herald 1928, p60

While the meetings were in progress, we were kept quite busy entertaining. We had Dr Williamson and Mr Emmott staying with us and quite a number of the delegates came here for meals. We had some good games of tennis while Dr Williamson and Mr Emmott were here. Dr Williamson plays a splendid game. He has a very gracious and cheerful personality[47] – plenty of cheery conversation, full of enthusiasm for his work, ready to try out any idea that may benefit the work, always puts work first, but is still very keen on taking exercise and on encouraging others to keep fit too. It was really a great pleasure to have him stay with us as our guest. Mrs Williamson is just as nice too.

Flowers left for Tsingtao on July 1st. Our new Dr Chang (fresh from Tsinan) started here then, so we have four doctors on the staff here, Dr Hsu, the two Drs. Chang, and I. Flowers left Dr Hsu in charge of the medical work of the hospital, and he certainly is very capable, much more capable at his medical work than I am. He is a very quick thinker, a keen student, a good operator, and has a very attractive, cheerful personality. We shall all be extremely sorry to lose him when he leaves in about a month's time.

I am now taking two outpatient days a week, Tuesdays and Thursdays. The duties consist of attending to all the outpatients who attend on those days, and being responsible for the treatment of all the patients who are admitted to the hospital wards on those two days. My Chinese is still a long way from being adequate for the job, but we are doing our best. At present I just know about enough to ask the questions I want to know, but not enough to understand the answers! I sometimes used to have some difficulty in understanding a really broad Yorkshire dialect at Leeds and Bradford, and it is worse here. Sometimes when the patients come from the country districts I really wonder if they are speaking Chinese at all. It all sounds so very different from anything I have been taught and I'm sure the patients, or some of them, don't think that I am trying to speak their own mother tongue. So I have to talk my best Chinese to the nurse, who interprets into the local equivalent of 'Eh, lass, Ah'm fair capped'! and we manage to understand each other. And a syphilitic ulcer or a tuberculosis bacillus doesn't need to be translated

[47] Brian Stanley, in his *History of the Baptist Missionary Society 1792 – 1992* writes of H R Williamson's enormous popularity with the Chinese, his qualities as a Chinese scholar and linguist (confirmed by the offer, in 1936, of the Chair of Chinese in the University of London, which Williamson declined) and his important impact on the life of the church in China during the 1930s. 'To Williamson must belong much of the credit for the fact that relationships between the BMS and the Chinese church were so generally free of tension amidst the turbulent changes of the 1930s.'

into English or Chinese – it speaks in its own language, which he who has ears to hear can hear.

I've not had many very spectacular cases so far. The most dramatic of them was a young woman with an extensive ulcer of the arm which she had had for many months. I thought it was syphilitic and the blood test that we took supported me. It was a very dirty ulcer when she came in, extending well up the arm and down the forearm, and now there is only an area about the size of a 3d piece that hasn't healed up, and I expect that will heal completely this week.

Other patients have included a man with a gunshot wound of the back. He was riding his bicycle when he was attacked by robbers who stole his bicycle; when he protested, they tied him to a tree and shot him. Fortunately for him their aim can't have been very good, for the bullet entered his back and passed through the subcutaneous tissues and came out through his arm, without doing any serious damage, so I hope that he will do well.

There is a little girl in the hospital at present with fairly bad bronchiectasis, a lung disease which makes her constantly cough and bring up large quantities of offensive sputum. She is a cheerful little girl and I usually spend some time with her each day. She is learning to recognise the English alphabet and is very thrilled about it, and sometimes she reads to me from one of her Chinese books. It is one published by the Christian Literature Society in Shanghai. The CLS is putting out some very attractive little books just now, like the ones we used to like when we were small, with a picture on one page and the text on the opposite page. The pictures are in colour, and the paper and print and pictures are all very good. This little book tells the story of the parable of the sower in an attractive modern way, and is very good. This little girl likes it very much.

If you know of anybody who would like to send a small subscription out, this would be a splendid idea. Our Chinese pastors are none of them wealthy and it is not easy for them to find as much literature as they would like to help them in their work. A subscription of about six shillings would provide a year's supply of literature which would be a big help to some of our pastors. I'll try to send you a copy of one of these little books so that you can see how they are turned out.

Last night I had my first game of Chinese Chess. Mr Ma, our dispenser, came in to supper and after supper we had a game of Chinese Chess. It is a bit difficult to follow at first. I'll try to send you a detailed account later.

Gwyneth to Cambridge

Chouts'un
25th July 1936

We had a lovely surprise one day this week. I had a parcel by registered post – a box of lovely chocolates from Kisslings, the best known firm up here, Germans. It was from Mr Christian, the American who came here with the chicken bone, wasn't it nice of him?[48] He had given a subscription to the hospital too, although we couldn't help him much. Still we put him in touch with Tsinan where they removed the bone. It's the first chocolates we've had, so we have enjoyed them.

We plan to leave here at 4 p.m. on the 31st and arrive in Peitaiho at 6.30 p.m. on August 1. Dr Williamson kindly booked our tickets and berths in Tsinan for us and arranged for a China Travel Service man to meet us. They're excellent, they see to all the luggage and help you changing stations and book berths etc. Our Chinese still isn't up to dealing with all emergencies. We can get on moderately well, but booking berths and bagging them when the train arrives is quite a business. So often Chinese are in them and won't budge without a bother and in such cases a travel service man takes all the responsibility.

I'm so thrilled today. Chao has gone home and I've no lessons. Although I really enjoy them, it is so nice to feel I can potter about and enjoy my house. I have started tidying up ready for going away, but haven't started packing. Kao has just put the trunk on the veranda to be sunned and I have told him to give it a brushing later on, so I feel I have got a beginning.

Many thanks for your recipes – they'll all be most useful. What on earth is turmeric? By now we've made our apricot jam, only 3 lbs. It's expensive buying jars – all the jam we've bought has been in tins so we have to buy jars and they cost 6d small and 9d large. However, it's only this year. We now have about 9lbs of bottled cherries, 15lbs bottled apricots, 10lbs strawberry jam, 3lbs apricot. I wanted to do plum but have no jars and don't want to pay carriage on them and as there's nothing else I need till after the holiday, I shall leave it. I want to have

[48] Gwyneth had written earlier of the unexpected visit of Mr Christian, the North China manager of an American tobacco company. He had swallowed a chicken bone while on business in Chouts'un and had come to the hospital for help. As there were no appropriate instruments in Chouts'un for the necessary operation, Ronald had advised him to go to Cheeloo Hospital in Tsinan for it, and Mr Christian had spent four hours in Ronald and Gwyneth's home while waiting for the train to Tsinan.

our stores as low as possible. If the house is burgled or anything, they may as well have as little as possible!

Was glad to hear about Nellie and so very glad you're still pleased with her. I feel a little less guilty at having Wu and Kao now I know you are having help! Yesterday I had to have a long somewhat difficult interview with Wu, over one or two things - nothing serious, only some things he'd been 'trying out' knowing our newness to life out here. It all ended happily I think, though I've not seen him today, but he poured out torrents of Chinese faster and faster, till I had to tell him I didn't understand a word and made him slow down a bit. Anyway, there was one amusing thing he said – I think his meaning was of the best, but the literal translation is this: He and Kao knew indeed that the mistress' p'i ch'i (disposition or temperament) was excellent and the doctor's also 'wasn't bad'. In Chinese 'not bad' doesn't really have the slightly doubtful meaning it has in English. It really means very good, but I always translate it as not bad and it just tickled me when he said that about our tempers!

I suppose Polly is in Germany now. I do hope she enjoys it all. She's been so thrilled about it. I'd rather be there than in Spain, it's ghastly there, isn't it?

Glad you saw David Copperfield [49]– I'd like to see it. Glad you take M out sometimes, Daddy. You must keep up these little tricks, or when we come home she'll be so used to staying in, she won't want to come out with us. Tell it not, but I'm longing to see a flick when we're away.

Bus jams sound very odd. Rickshaw crushes I can understand, but buses - my dear, how old fashioned – and cars!

Ronald and Gwyneth were fortunate to be able to spend their first holiday in China at the well-known resort of Peitaiho, with its six miles of fine sandy beaches. Its popularity with the foreign community went back to the 1890s when it provided a welcome summer escape for British railway engineers building the line to Tientsin and Moukden. At one time the entire staff of the foreign embassies in Peking moved to Peitaiho for three months each summer. By 1935 there were nearly six hundred holiday villas strung along the shore and on the low lying hills behind it.

Situated about two hundred miles north east of Peking, Peitaiho was a long journey from Chouts'un. It involved first an overnight train

[49] Made in 1935 with W C Fields as Micawber.

ride to Tientsin, 'hot and dirty, but bearable. The night was terribly sticky and the Chinese girl in with me wouldn't have even a ventilator open'. Ronald and Gwyneth spent a few hours in Tientsin, where Gwyneth relished a proper wash ('hot water from taps and a really nice white basin!') and Ronald took the opportunity to see round the hospital run by the London Missionary Society, the Mackenzie Memorial Hospital. Thereafter another four or five hours in the train took them to their destination, 'a day and a half nearer home,' as Gwyneth wrote, 'we can get to London from here in thirteen days! This is on the direct route to the Siberian railway.'

Gwyneth to Cambridge

August 1936
c/o Mr Drake, 44 K'angho Road, Peitaiho

Well, here we are safely established in our summer resort and a lovely place it is. We are lucky to be able to come to such a delightful spot. The air is so refreshing after being in Chouts'un. We felt sort of stifled all the time there, but here it is warm and the sun is brilliant, but it is bracing and there seems to be a lovely sort of cool breeze all the time – you'd love it.

We are an hour's walk from the station. No cars are allowed here, bikes, donkeys and rickshaws being the only mode of travel. We aren't donkeying this time, though it looks good fun, but have used rickshaws a bit. From the station here we pass through the town, just a few Chinese shops and one or two small foreign ones, which are opened just for the summer season, and then we come along a sandy coloured road with trees on both sides and lovely views of the sea and mountains. There is no crowding, no rows of houses like at home, all the houses or bungalows are separated from their neighbours by gardens or large patches of grass or quite big sort of 'downs', every house seems to have grand views. The whole place stretches about six miles and there are really very few houses, so it's lovely and free.

This end nearly all the people are mishes, but they are from all over China, some even from Hong Kong. There are some lovely children. They're all such a lovely brown and look so nice in their scanty clothing. After seeing so few children all the year, it's a joy to see so many now. At the other end is the 'business' community, quite a lot of Russians and really it's an education to go and see them. People like Mummy Davies and larger appear in skimpy shorts and an even skimpier brassiere (Daddy had better not read this, or he'll be dashing off by the next boat). I've not taken to shorts yet, but feel quite out of it up that end of the town!

We've met lots of Language School people – they're a cheery crowd. It's a terrible place for meals out, nearly every meal someone comes in or we shall be out it seems. Tonight we are taking our supper on the rocks and going to cook sausages down there. The rocks have all sorts of suitable places for a fire and the cooks are thrilled to do it out of doors. We don't get sausages inland, so it's a change to have them here. It's full moon now and glorious every evening. We haven't bathed by moonlight yet, but want to soon. We've only oil lamps so we don't do much at night. It's lovely to have such a lazy time.

On Monday evening we went to see 'The lives of a Bengal lancer'. It's a good film. There's no proper cinema, just a put up thing for summer – no roof and matting walls – canvas seats. We hear David Copperfield is coming and hope to see that. The flick is a long way from here, but we can go in a rickshaw and it waits and brings us home. It costs about 1/- each and the flicks are 10d, so it's not very expensive.

All day long men come round here with things for sale. They all have a long pole over their shoulder and a bundle or basket of goods tied to each end. There is fruit, cloth, embroidery, silk, cotton wool, flowers etc. etc. I've bought two pieces of sort of silk cotton wool. It's like cotton wool only silk and very light. They're the size for single bed eiderdowns and I'm going to have them covered for our spare room. They only cost $3.30 the two, about 4/-. They're almost featherweight and yet beautifully warm and I can buy cheap material for covers, as I shall put them under the bedspreads so they won't fade.

Did I tell you Mr and Mrs Drake have one little boy, Bernard, aged 5½, a nice little chap? He has two lovely kittens, sandy, very much like the C E Brock variety[50]. They're sort of pedigree ones and not allowed out. You can't let them get out and mix with the dirty ones, but these are really very clean and nice and play together so prettily.

The colours are glorious, the sky such a perfect clear blue and the sea the deepest of blues and the sand and grass so clean and fresh. The rocks are mostly a light fawny colour and clean-looking.

On Sunday at church we were introduced to crowds of folk and, after Chouts'un where some days I don't speak to anyone but Ronald and the two boys, it was overwhelming. All night I dreamed I was being

[50] C E Brock, one of the famous family of Cambridge artists, was a family friend of May and John Johnson.

introduced to folk! However, we sleep all night and about two hours in the afternoons and we eat enormous meals, and both feel wonderfully fit.

Gwyneth to Ronald's mother and father

Peitaiho
20th August 1936

It's lovely of you to promise us a shawl. You just couldn't make anything more acceptable and, strange to say, I'm still English enough to prefer a white one[51]! When we think of how cold we were last winter, we wonder how we shall ever keep our wee baby warm, but of course are making all sorts of plans, including a stove of some sort in the little bedroom. Our bedrooms are really like ice-boxes. Having doors onto the veranda is nice in the hot weather, but makes it very cold in the winter. But, well wrapped in the shawl from our Ilkley Granny, I'm sure baby will be safe from all the draughts.

Mrs Flowers has offered me her cot, so we shall be using that. I don't know about blankets – if we need them from home, we'll be letting you know. At present we're waiting to see what we can buy in Tientsin, but it's a great help to know we've someone to do any shopping that needs to be done at home. It's very exciting getting things ready, but it's so long since we saw a small English baby that we almost forget what it needs. However, I think we've remembered all the necessities.

Don't worry about me. I really feel marvellously well and have been able to do everything as usual and am enjoying the walking and bathing here. We're just having a real holiday, sleeping and eating being the chief items on our programme!

It's a great comfort to have Ronald. I feel sorry for folk in lonely stations without a doctor. We're very fortunate too, in having Dr King, the only BMS man who specialises in obstetrics in China, in Tsinan. He's not only excellent at his job, but also an exceptionally nice man. As he's so near, Ronald thinks it wise to let him see me. We may as well have the best doctor available, so I shall be going to him some time later on. Ronald also thinks of getting Dr Moss the heart specialist in Tsinan to examine me. This is not because he has any fears about me, but after the doubts raised at home[52], he feels it a wise precaution. So you see I

---

[51] White is the Chinese colour signifying death and mourning, and so was avoided as a colour for clothes.

[52] This refers to the questions raised about Gwyneth's health by the BMS prior to her acceptance for mission work in China. Her heart showed scarring, probably caused by childhood diphtheria.

shall have just as good advice as if I were at home, so there's no need for you to worry. Ronald says if he were in England he would not find a man he'd trust more than Gordon King, so you'll realise how highly he regards him.

I've had such fun at Chouts'un, the last month, since I started my knitting. I didn't want anyone to see it, so every time Kao or Wu came along I had to hide it and had some narrow escapes. I got quite good at arranging the cushions over it quickly and so on, but now we've told Flowers everyone will know and I can knit in public. I have tried to get on quickly so that when I get back I can work hard at Chinese. I'll be missing time later and am keen not to get left too far behind Ronald. I want to take the next exam when he does.

We feel as though living in this large community of foreigners has blown away quite a lot of our cobwebs – we felt real 'country cousins' in Chouts'un. It's great meeting missionaries from all over China and Manchuria and missionaries of various nationalities too. Mr Drake seems to have a very clear outlook on the whole of the BMS work in China and we find it a great help to get him talking to us about it. Up till now our outlook has been very confined. We hope that some day we may have an opportunity to visit the stations in the other Provinces, and, now that the railway is extended, there's more hope of it.

Ronald to his father and mother

Chouts'un
3rd September 1936

Hope you did manage to go to the pictures on the 12th, Mother. When we were at the CIM home in Tientsin[53] we went to see "A Midsummer Night's Dream" and enjoyed it very much indeed[54]. There was a lady staying there with her daughter who had just left school at Chefoo[55]. We thought the girl would like to go to see the film with us, so we asked her Mother if she might come. Evidently the Mother did not approve of picture going, and afterwards the daughter came to us and said if we would excuse her she would rather not go (though she herself would have liked to have gone, I think). We were sorry she couldn't

[53] Ronald and Gwyneth spent three days at the home for missionaries run by the China Inland Mission in Tientsin on their return to Chouts'un from Peitaiho.

[54] This Warner Bros film, with James Cagney as Bottom and Olivia de Havilland as Hermione, won numerous awards when it came out in 1935.

[55] The boarding school at Chefoo, run by the China Inland Mission primarily for the children of missionaries.

come with us, because I'm sure she would have really enjoyed the film, but we were glad that she had said 'no' when she felt it was right. But it was a good film, and I think you would like it too if you could see it.

Ronald to Will and Florence

Chouts'un
5th September 1936

Thank you, Will, for those splendid plans of the house, and also for the photographs, which are splendid too. They all give a fine idea of the house, and with the wall-paper patterns too I think we could find our way about easily. You seem to have a nice big kitchen, Florence, and it will be nice to have the evening sun and the sunsets in the drawing-room. Is Geoffrey[56] sleeping in the back bedroom now? I like the little window in the spare bedroom. Of course we are delighted to have the photos. We were amazed at the difference we saw in Geoffrey. He is growing quite tall, isn't he? It is a lovely photo of you too, Florence.

Thank you again for your letter and all its enclosures. I think the article about the Russo-Sino-Japanese situation was a fair statement. There have been a lot of sparks flying in various places lately – incidents of Japanese residents in China being murdered - and these may possibly set light to the explosives, of which there is a big quantity lying around. Things have been comparatively peaceful in our district for some time. So as far as I can see there is no immediate likelihood of any change, though it is impossible to predict accurately when so much news is suppressed, and there must be a tremendous lot happening behind the scenes that we never hear of.

The English days are still longer than ours, Will. It's dark here now by 7 p.m., though it never stays light later than about 8.30 p.m. at any time of year. Do you know anything about the other end of the day?! I do about China! I was up soon after 5 a.m. one day this week and can vouch for the fact that it is just coming light then. The occasion for the early rise was a visit to Tsouping[57], a place about fifteen miles to the north west of Chouts'un; a public health conference was being held there, to discuss methods by which rural public health and preventive medicine could be assisted, so I went over last Wednesday and Flowers went over

---

[56] Will and Florence's four year old son.

[57] One of the first centres of BMS work in Shantung, Tsouping had at one time had its own mission hospital. This closed in 1914 when the decision was made to centre medical work in Chouts'un. The money raised by the sale of the property covered part of the cost of the new Foster Hospital.

on Thursday. This summer there has been a big move towards better public health measures in China and this conference is an attempt to enable the church, the hospitals, the government to cooperate to produce a public health and preventive medicine programme. I don't know whether we shall be adopting any Public Health measures in Chouts'un just yet. There is room for plenty to be done. The important question is, can we afford to start work on new lines, or will it result in inefficiency of the work already being done? It is a question of finance and staffing – we shall have to see what can be done.

Things are getting pretty busy here again now and we are full of preparations for autumn and winter. Our nursing school term starts tomorrow and we have six new girl probationers, all looking very shy in the wards! Did I tell you that we have stopped taking any more men nurses, and intend to have almost the whole of the nursing done by women nurses? It involves certain difficulties in the transition period, but it's the right thing to do, I'm sure, and I think will work out well in the end[58].

Although busy and very much fulfilled in their lives in China, Ronald and Gwyneth continued to feel and express a warm interest in the lives of their family and friends elsewhere. Ronald's two brothers, Will and Reg, and Gwyneth's sisters, Kay, Polly and Dray, all wrote to them regularly and went to considerable pains to find imaginative ways of involving them in affairs at home. The photos, house plans, wallpaper samples and news cuttings to which Ronald refers in his letter to Will are one small example of their efforts in this regard.

This edited version of their letters does not do justice to this aspect of the correspondence. Most of the detailed comments which Ronald and Gwyneth made on news they received from home has been omitted in the interests of brevity and coherence, and this leaves an unfortunately restricted view of their friendships and interests.

As well as writing fully and regularly to their parents throughout their time abroad, Gwyneth particularly kept up a prolific and affectionate correspondence with a very large number of friends and family members. It is no accident that Ronald's father refers admiringly

---

[58] The first nurses trained in mission hospitals in China were all men, in accordance with the Chinese practice of having a man friend accompany anyone attending the doctor, to assist with practical needs. It would not have been thought suitable for a woman to take on this role. The proposed change to an all female nursing staff in Chouts'un is likely to have been met with anxiety, if not opposition, from some quarters.

at one point to 'the flow of correspondence from Gwyneth's delightfully facile pen'.

Gwyneth to members of St Andrew's Street Baptist Church

Chouts'un
6th September 1936

I think you may be interested to hear about a day I spent in the country. Four of us set out at 7.30 a.m. in rickshaws on our way to Tsouping where there was a big annual fair. The people gather for a religious festival, and climb a mountain to burn incense in a Temple at the top. Most of them come from a distance and have to stay a night or two, so it is made into a great occasion for buying and selling, and all sorts of merriment. We were about half an hour going through the walled part of Chouts'un. As we went out through the last gate the air was so fresh and the country looked so clean after the dirt of the city, the crops and the trees were green, and in the distance we could see the bluish grey hills.

Most of the way the views reminded me very much of Cambridgeshire, and I felt we must suddenly catch a glimpse of the Granta or Cam, but nothing so good turned up! There had been rain a few days earlier and the road all the way was deep in mud. The rickshaws kept mostly to a little narrow footpath at the edge of the fields. We met and passed many people on our way, pedestrians, cyclists (usually without brakes or bells and with very little idea of how to control their machine, so that several times our rickshaws were knocked into, but after a joke or two the cyclist went on quite happily), some folk were on donkeys, others on very squeaky barrows, and we met a few large farm carts drawn by oxen, laden with a dozen or more people laughing and talking. It reminded me of my earliest Sunday School Treats when we used to go to Cantelupe in wagonettes!

We passed many old women hobbling painfully on bound feet, but none were too busy or in too much of a hurry to stop and stare at the rare sight of four foreigners. We heard many remarks about the odd shape of our noses and more on our very huge feet. Most of the villages through which we passed were quite picturesque and in the fields the workers looked attractive in their blue coats and big straw hats. We passed one or two large shady trees which made good resting places and there enterprising people had set up stalls and were selling tea, sweets, etc. There were salesmen of all sorts on the road, mostly carrying their wares in two bundles or baskets, one at each end of a long stick which they had over their shoulder. All over the place we saw Levers soaps advertised in English and Chinese and we felt that it would be a good thing if a little more of it were used.

We arrived at Tsouping at about 10.30 and after going to the Mission House, which is used by our women evangelists when they are in the district, we went into the town. The leaders of the church always take the opportunity of preaching to the crowds gathered for this fair, and some of our Bible School girls go and talk to the women. We visited the church first, but as there was a service on, we did not go in. If we had, all the people would have stopped listening and stared at us. Outside there were several of the church workers calling to the passers-by urging them to listen to the good news, and quite a number were going in to see what it was all about. We went on to the Preaching Tent, it was just off the main street and many weary pilgrims were glad to go in to rest, and we hope that they learnt something too. Some of them seemed very interested and were looking at the gospels which were being handed round. The trouble is that so many of them cannot read.

At first all the attention was centred on us. It is not often that those country folk have the opportunity of seeing anything as funny as four foreign women, and they like to make the most of the chance when it comes. Some of the bolder ones came up and felt our dresses and looked us up and down very closely. Meanwhile the preaching was going on. Chinese evangelists seem able to carry on whatever interruptions they have, and after a time the attention went back to the speaker. We thought our Bible School girls did wonderfully well, they were mostly young, about eighteen or twenty, but they were keeping the crowd interested. They started off by showing a picture and then told the story it represented. Some of these pictures were bought with some of the money sent by Miss Hart's Bible Class, and they are a big help in the work in the country.

We spent a little time in the streets afterwards. They were crowded with people, all obviously out to enjoy themselves and see their old friends, and the children begging money for sweets and toys. On our way home through the town, rickshaws had a job to get along, the crowds were so thick and when people caught sight of us they pressed as close as they could so as not to miss anything. Again they remarked particularly on our ugly big feet, but they were all very friendly and smiled back when we smiled at them and I enjoyed watching them as much as they enjoyed watching me.

We are both very happy to be out here. There is something very attractive about the people, and we have been treated most kindly everywhere. The Chinese all seem to have a great sense of humour and if you can make a joke it is greatly appreciated. The poverty of the people is appalling, but they seem to keep very bright in spite of all their difficulties. Rickshaw coolies, pulling heavy loads along a road with ankle deep mud, on a dark rainy night, will often be laughing and talking as if they had not a care in the world.

Gwyneth to her mother

Chouts'un
6th September 1936

You just can't guess (I expect you can really!) how thrilled I am about the parcel. I shall get terribly impatient till it comes. I don't mind paying on it as long as it arrives safely. There's something so exciting in parcels from away and especially from home and this will be extra special. You must have spent ages getting the things together and thinking about it all. I'm so thankful to you, I can't imagine what on earth I'd have done otherwise.

By the way, I'd be glad if you'd send a rubber sheet. I think the safest way would be via Siberia, as it's less hot. The best way to pack it would be on a cardboard roll – roll the rubber sheet and a piece of paper together round the cardboard roll, the paper would prevent the rubber sticking to itself. I can't think of a better way, Daddy may be able to.

I can't remember if I told you what we think about baby's arrival? We feel now that it would probably be best for me to go to the Tsinan Hospital. We both loathe the idea of separation. I'd have to stay up there a week or two in readiness and Ronald would be down here all the time. He might be able to come up once baby came to see me, but he would be here most of the time and it might involve Christmas away from home, if the child came late. Even so, at present we favour Tsinan for various reasons. Ronald feels that Gordon King is absolutely the best man I could have and we feel that with him so near it is only right to make the most of him if we are able. Apart from fares, there will be extra hospital fees and my board while I'm waiting and for a few days after till I'm fit to travel, but the difference in price won't be enormous.

Mrs Flowers is selling me her pram. It's the chair type, but large enough for a babe to lie flat. Also her mattress for the crib and Michael's big cot. Also a wooden screen which I shall cover with cretonne. It will be lovely for draughty days and I may as well buy hers as have a new one made. I've decided to use a basket, and probably shall use the one we bought in Peiping for our luggage! It's flat and the top fits over the bottom. Of course if it's twins we shall be able to use top and bottom! I think it'll do and I'll cover the inside with silk as some of the wicker is a bit rough.

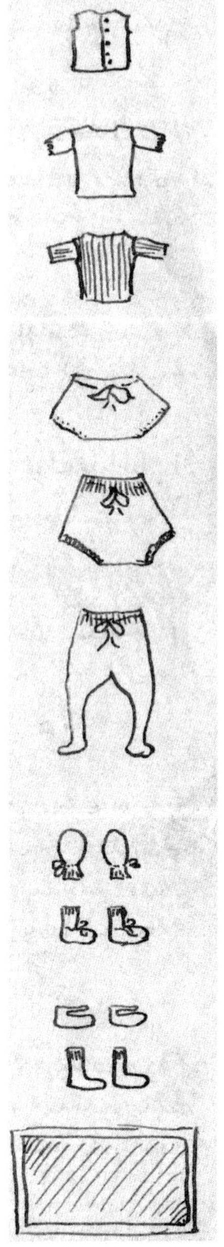
Gwyneth's sketches of the baby's clothes

Gwyneth to her mother

Chouts'un
13th September 1936

It was so exciting having that big registered envelope last night. I'm sorry it didn't arrive in the morning so I could have acknowledged it by last night's mail, but that couldn't be helped. I'm thrilled with the nightie. It's the first thing I've had apart from what I've made and it's so exciting. You've made it beautifully, much daintier than I could have done. I keep taking it out of the drawer to admire it! I think the infant will most likely fall out whatever its size – it doesn't matter. It's a good thing to have it big enough to last a while.

I'm so crazy for the parcel. I think the earliest it could reach us is about October 9th, that's if it caught a boat almost at once. But already I sort of look for a PO note. When parcels come they aren't delivered – we get a paper slip which we have to sign and then Wu takes it to the PO and gets the parcel and if there's duty he has to pay. We pay 25 cents (about 4d) on all parcels.

This week I have planned the lining for the bassinette affair and hope to do it this next day or two and I've made the curtains for the room. No trimmings on them yet, they'll do for a while as they are - and I've done the screen. It looks very nice. I'm awfully pleased with it. This next week I hope to make a dozen thin nappies to save the others a bit – shall buy material off the street. I don't suppose the babe will come very early, but I want to be all ready, so that if it does, I've nothing to worry about.

Wu has bottled some more tomatoes and next week I hope he'll do some chutney and perhaps marrow and plum jams, and apple jelly. We tried your famous treacle pudding and I was thrilled, absolutely scraped the dish as of old, poor Ronald didn't get a look in!

I've got to prepare two services now - that's rather a trial. I'm doing them as early as I can. Ian started Sunday School again today[59] so my Sundays are as busy as ever now. Luckily I'm fairly well up with my letters, scarcely owe any which is a relief. I'm trying to do four hours Chinese a day now, but it's an effort when I'm wanting to sew.

I do so wish you could see all the things and be here to talk everything over. I'm afraid I can think of little else! I'm not making any bonnets. At first a shawl will be necessary, and then later I can make a cap.

By now your Folkestone visit if you had it will be over. I do hope you managed it. Shall hope to hear all about it. Did you tell Auntie that you hope to be a granny almost as soon as she is? Don't forget to tell me who you've told. Thank you for the heather. It's so pretty, I'd love to see it growing again. There are lots of English things I'd like to see!

The official language exam results came this week, I'll enclose a copy. Everyone here seems awfully pleased and says we're a credit to Shantung[60]. Ronald really spent a great deal more time on it all along than I and also he gets more practice than I in hospital. He really has done well though and we're awfully bucked. I don't feel so hopeful of my second year work, but I must do it somehow.

Dray's little mitts and bootees arrived this a.m. Aren't they sweet? And Polly's breeches have come too. They are marvellously neat and will be

[59] Gwyneth had been taking Ian Flowers for a Sunday School class each Sunday morning since she arrived in Chouts'un.

[60] Both Ronald and Gwyneth had scores of 90% for their oral exams. Ronald's average for the written papers was 92.4% and Gwyneth's 84.4%. The examiners commented, 'Dr and Mrs Still have done very good papers indeed, and the papers give evidence of intelligent and thorough work. To have done the papers so quickly (i.e three months before they were due) and so thoroughly is a great credit to them both.'

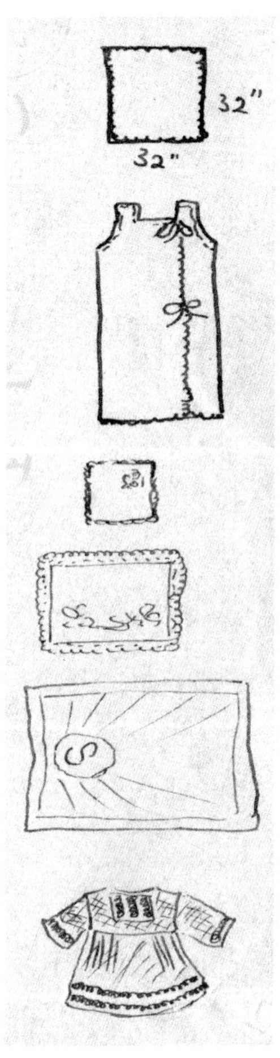

most useful. Oh, it is so exciting having parcels! It helps a lot to make up for not having you all near. Ronald likes to know all about the clothes and all the things I am getting ready and if he didn't I would go mad, because I must share them with someone and I just can't with anyone else, but he is marvellous. He is on call today and at present is opening up a man who just came in having been gored by a bull! Most unpleasant.

Just because the things mostly have blue trimmings people all seem to think we have set our hearts on a boy! Aren't they cracked, as if we'd prefer a colour for that reason! We will be glad whichever it is. If it was girl triplets I wouldn't change the trimmings to pink for anyone, though I think some pink is lovely.

Did I tell you that when ordering the baby's bath (in Chinese) I said I wanted it 30 feet long and 16 feet wide and when Wu said that would be bigger than the bath we already had I couldn't make out what he meant. Luckily they didn't follow my instructions!

No, we don't really worry over money, so don't you worry about us. We want to make the best use of what we have, that's all.

Ronald to Ilkley and Cambridge

Chouts'un
27th September 1936

The new nursing school term has started, and has a full programme of lectures which keeps both the nurses and the doctors well occupied. Miss Smurthwaite's Girls' Bible School has started its new term too, and her fifty pupils fill one side of the chapel at the Sunday services, so that the place now seems quite full again. Miss Smurthwaite is constantly having applications from people who want their girls to be admitted as pupils to her school, so since the holiday she has had a new dormitory built to accommodate ten more girls. Miss Manger and Miss Wood are back from their holiday, and are making preparations to go out into the country again, to visit the various villages round here where there are branches of the church.

The present time is one of the two slack periods of the year in hospital. It is harvest time, and everybody who can possibly work is needed for the work of cutting the crops, and winnowing and grinding the grain. The crops have been fairly good this year[61], so it is to be hoped that when there has been time for some of them to be sold, there will be not so much distress in our area, and money will be a little freer. The Chinese soil is very productive, partly owing to a careful system of rotation of crops. Wheat is planted in the late autumn, and begins to grow with the early spring and is ripe by the end of spring. Then while the wheat is growing, the tall grain kaoliang[62] and maize and millet are planted (and in some places rice and cotton and tobacco) and in between the rows of kaoliang big quantities of soya beans. The kaoliang and maize and millet are just harvested now, and the grains are being ground. The beans are not quite ripe yet, but soon will be. Then after they are harvested, the whole of the land will be emptied (except for the hidden wheat seeds) and will take on the brown aspect that it will keep all through the winter, except for the times when there is snow.

This week I was very proud and pleased to be able to assist my first Chinese baby to make her debut, which she did without any mishap either to herself or her mother, so we are all very pleased. Then another mother came in to have her baby in hospital. She had previously had two babies, but they had both died of what the Chinese call "Five Days Wind", or "Seven Days Wind", which really means that they got tetanus of the new born through either deliberate or accidental soiling of the umbilical cord. Her little girl has now safely passed the critical fifth day and so she is very pleased too.

When I got so far, it being my Sunday on duty, I was called away to see a patient who had just been brought to hospital. He was a man of about fifty who had been gored in the abdomen by a bull about three days ago. He looked as though he might have some bowel injury, so we admitted him, and this afternoon Dr Flowers helped me to operate on him. When we got inside we found that sure enough the bull's horn had perforated a loop of small intestine, and this loop was protruding from the hole in the abdominal wall and was pouring its contents in between the layers of the abdominal wall. We stitched up the hole in the intestine and repaired the hole in the abdominal wall, and now it remains to be

---

[61] 1936 and 1937 were both bumper harvests – the best in nearly 20 years.
[62] Pinyin = gaoliang, ie sorghum

seen whether he can survive after having had a ruptured bowel for so long a time. His condition is fairly good at present and I hope very much that he may pull through.

Another interesting patient arrived this afternoon too. She is the daughter of the station master at a place called Chih-Chuan, between here and Tsingchoufu, where we have a small Christian church. She has a huge ovarian cyst which fills her whole abdomen. Our woman evangelist from Chouts'un has just been down to Chih-chuan, and has told her that she knows of several people who have had big lumps successfully removed at the Foster Hospital and so she has decided to come here for the operation. I hope that it may be successful. She is only twenty three.

So much for patients. Here's another bit of news which I find exciting! You know that it is just a year this week since we arrived in China? Well, to celebrate the anniversary, I conducted a service in Chinese for the first time! We have a set series of topics for the ward services, taken from Luke's gospel, so I could choose my own subject from these topics, and I chose the Parable of the Sower. Whether or not, and how much, the patients understood of what I said, I shall never know, I suppose, but anyway, I got through without breaking down, and found when I got to the end that I had been speaking for a quarter of an hour! At any rate, I have made a start and that is better than not having made a start, isn't it?

Ronald to his father and mother

Chouts'un
19th October 1936

Thank you for sending the other page of the Lancet proof, father. I'm very pleased and thrilled that the Lancet are publishing the article[63]. I don't think I've written to you since the proofs arrived. They arrived on a day when I wasn't especially cheerful, but when I came home in the evening Gwyneth greeted me with the news that you had sent the proofs and that cheered me up for the whole evening! I felt as though I *was* worth something after all!

My lady who had the cancer of the breast removed is doing splendidly and she is very bright and cheerful – stitches out tomorrow. I'm sorry to say, the patient who was gored by the bull died two weeks

---

[63] Ronald's article was published in the Lancet on 31st October 1936, under the title *'Mortality and later results of sub-total Gastrectomy'*. It was based on a study of gastrectomies performed in Bradford between 1925 and 1935 by Basil Hughes, the surgeon with whom Ronald had worked as a houseman.

ago. It seemed that it was seven or eight days since the accident. I'm very sorry we couldn't save him. I wish we could have done but we did our best.

A good many of my other patients have gun-shot wounds, some of them inflicted by armed robbers in the country districts, but a good many of them self-inflicted, by accident, or accidentally inflicted by 'friends' while they have been playing with their guns. They are often very dirty wounds and get badly infected and take a long time to heal up.

Then there is a little boy of about six with kala-azar. He comes from a village some miles from here, where live several patients who have already been treated here for the disease, so he and his parents know all about the disease, and that it is able to be cured. The treatment is expensive, about £1 for each patient, but if anyone wants to invest in Medical missions, I don't know of a more satisfactory investment. Most of the people from the kala-azar districts know what the hospital charges for the treatment, and when they come to the hospital they are usually prepared to pay. But sometimes, with the usual Chinese love of bargaining, they plead poverty and try to get let off some of the price. Of course sometimes the plea of poverty is a genuine one, and then we have to leave it to Mr Huang, our Business Manager, to decide that the people really cannot afford the treatment, and in such cases we are glad to try to meet the expense ourselves, or to use gifts from other people for the purpose, because we feel that it is a really worthwhile piece of work.

Gwyneth to her mother

Chouts'un,
6th November 1936

Yes, I do feel decidedly like saying 'I can't hardly wait!' but the time is flying and I have still plenty to do before I go to Tsinan. Once I am there the sooner baby arrives the better pleased I will be, though I will be there seventeen days before the day expected. Oh, I do hope it's early, so I can get back home to Ronald! I don't think I shall find the journey bad. The trains will be heated by then and Ronald will travel with me, so I will have no trouble over luggage. In Tsinan we can have a taxi, and here a rickshaw, and we will be home in two minutes, so don't you worry about that.

Of course it would be much simpler to stay here – no bother packing, taking nappies and all the things I will need for the few days after hospital, and Ronald with me right up to the last minute and able to look in often. On the other hand, we really feel much happier having

Gordon King. He does nothing but women and babes all the year and, although we don't anticipate any trouble, we feel absolutely confident in him.

By the time my next letter arrives you may have had a cable!

Mr Harris is back and he has no intention of taking Wu or Kao[64], anyway for two or three years. If, later on, his wife returns it is possible they might like them back or if he were ill and had to give up eating Chinese food, he might need a cook, but he says we needn't worry at all. So I am very thankful and I don't think they will want to leave us, unless anything unexpected occurs. They were with the Harris family thirteen or fourteen years.

The Allens (from Shansi) are coming down to Tsingchoufu this week. Mr Allen's health has not been too good at high altitude and it is hoped he will be better here. She was Connie Greening before her marriage.

We feel quite cheered by Mr Harris. He really is most amusing, full of humour and yet not too overwhelming, very keen on his work and very anxious not to be any trouble. He will miss his wife terribly I think and the children. They have five, and they all stayed out here at school. Kao loves to talk about them, he is crazy on children. Mr Harris is a real family sort of man so it will be hard for him, but Mrs Harris felt she ought to stay at home a bit and see the children settled. That is the big problem – it is hard whichever way you decide. He is full of stories of past days and tells them all in such a humorous style.

We are determined to get our house warmer. I would be scared to have a babe in a house as cold as ours was last year. Of course coal is an awful item, but it can't be helped. We still don't really need fires till after tea. If we open the windows and let the sun in it is quite warmish, but today being Sunday I have lit the sitting room one and am on the couch near it. It is not a de Freville[65] or an Ilkley fire by any means, but it is quite cosy.

I have decided to go to Mrs Drake in Tsinan. She will make me very comfy, and Mr Drake is exceedingly thoughtful and considerate. As soon as I go into hospital Mr Drake will wire Ronald and he will come up by the first possible train so as to be there to welcome the babe. He will probably just stay a day or two to see all is OK and then return till I am ready to go home and then he will fetch me.

---

[64] Wu and Kao had worked for Mr and Mrs Harris before the family's return to England for furlough in August 1935.

[65] 8 de Freville Avenue was Gwyneth's family home in Cambridge.

My dear, what do you think? Our Dray actually admits she is thrilled! So we have achieved something, haven't we? She goes on to say she is fed up with me for having the babe in China, but I feel very bucked at getting her to such a pitch as to acknowledge a thrill of any sort!

Gwyneth to Cambridge

C/o Mrs F S Drake
Cheeloo University, Tsinan
17th November 1936

Well, we came up here yesterday. The journey didn't worry me in the very least, though it was a bit hot for a heavy coat. We came straight here for tea and then back to the hospital at once. Dr King was all ready and saw me straight away. Everything is still quite satisfactory and he seemed to have no anxieties about me. I am to go again on Thursday. It is only ten minutes walk from here and I could have a rickshaw if I needed, but I like walking. If the weather gets bad and the babe hasn't come, I shall probably sleep in hospital to prevent turning out in the night.

Mr and Mrs Drake gave me a very warm welcome. They are both most thoughtful and hospitable. I shall be as happy here as possible away from home, but I am just longing to get back to Ronald. He could easily come up for a weekend without missing any work as he is off duty the next three Sundays and Saturday afternoons and he could be back by 9.30 on Monday. Weekend jaunts are frowned on in Chouts'un, though everyone here expects him to come. People in small stations get such an exaggerated idea of things, I think. However, as you know, Ronald is quite good at getting away when he wants to see me, so I have hopes. He can travel up and back by 3rd class for $2.80 = 3/-. We usually travel 2nd when we have luggage because 3rd is packed, but he would come third if he was on his own I guess. It is really not bad, especially in cool weather – the dust and smells are less noticeable. Really I don't think you (Mummy) would ever like China – the smells and dust are just too, too! And the publicity of things English folk keep private would upset you somewhat, I fear.

You don't wish any more than I do that you could see all the baby things, I've had such joy over them and Ronald has, too. They're all so very dainty and sweet and I'd love you and the girls to be able to rave over them. Ronald really is a perfect joy – he shares them all so nicely, and really ***is*** interested. So few men seem to be, Mr Drake is one of the few. He loves to know all about things, and one of the ones who regards babies as absolutely 'holy'. He really is a most awfully nice man, so exceedingly thoughtful.

The hospital here is huge, very up to date in every way and a big staff of highly qualified men and women. It is quite one of the best hospitals in China and Ronald feels sure I will be as well cared for as I could be anywhere at home. It is funny people thinking of a small hospital with Dr Ingle in charge, because it is so big and modern, people would be amazed. No, the Chouts'un medicals aren't hurt. I think they all feel glad to be free of responsibility of their own colleague.

Cheeloo Hospital, Tsinan

I'm tired of being told what a small baby it must be, because I'm so thin. What do I care about its size as long as it's normal? And what advantage is it to me or anyone else to keep harping on the size? I can't make it swell to order. Really, out here people do get potty on such subjects. Last night I had my palm read and was told I'd live to 80, so I think I'll come through December 4th or whenever it is without pegging out! Everyone looks me up and down and says, 'Are you ***still*** keeping well?' as though they almost wish I wasn't!

I do wish there was someone out here with whom I could 'play silly'. I am so afraid I will get too horribly dull and entirely lacking in humour. Ronald is a dear and really we have great fun out of things together, but no one else seems to share my sort of humour. People really are most awfully kind and hospitable and nice, but we do long for you and the girls. I want to be silly sometimes! No offence meant!

Perhaps you will be granny, grandpa and aunties when you read this! What thrills for you all!

Ronald to his father and mother

Chouts'un
1st December 1936

Well, Rosemary was born at 8.25 a.m. on Monday November 30th and I saw Gwyneth several times on Monday (yesterday) and again today just before I came back here. She was splendidly well, though a little bit weary, and we are hoping that she will soon be strong and well again and that we shall be able to have Christmas together in our own home.

And as for Rosemary, I wonder if you'll believe me if I tell you that she is the loveliest little child you ever saw! Oh, but she ***is*** lovely, and she's so good and well-behaved. She has such a lovely complexion, and her eyes are dark, a sort of dark blue-grey, and her cheeks are a lovely pink, and her hair, though she hasn't very much, is sort of brunette at present, and she gives little smiles, and just lies quietly and peeps out at the room and is very patient and good.

Gwyneth has a very nice private room to herself in the new building at the Cheeloo Hospital and I think she likes it and will be happy there. She has Chinese nurses attending to her. She likes them all very much and says how gentle and patient and thoughtful they have been and I think she is very happy and thankful that she decided to go to Tsinan. Of course she is able to speak to the nurses in Chinese and tell them of things she needs.

Now I think I mustn't write any more. It is after midnight and I still have my ward round to do. I wonder if you would mind letting mother and father in Ilkley see this when you have finished it? I haven't been able to write to them by this mail and I know they will want to know.

Gwyneth to Cambridge

Cheeloo University Hospital, Tsinan
5th December 1936

Here I am propped up in bed, trying to look a pathetic sight but feeling very flourishing and pleased with life. It is surprising what a difference a few days can make, isn't it? I feel almost as usual now, though I quite think once I try to get up I will find I am not quite as bright as I imagine!

Well, to start off on the topic of conversation, which will fill all my letters from now on, Rosemary (I hope you approve of her name) has just been in and had a good meal. She is, you will need no telling, quite the most beautiful baby who ever appeared on the face of the earth, so I won't spoil it by saying she is the image of me or Ron or any of her relations, though at times when she is being superior and pretending that milk holds no interest for her, she reminds me very much of her good Aunt Dray! She has just her superior expression then!

Her hair is 'olive-oiled' every day here, so it looks darker than it really is, but I think it is about the colour of the darkest of mine. Her face is round and she has fat cheeks – pink, not raw beef shade either. Her ears look all right to me, about the same size as each other and so on. Her eyes are deep blue and when she deigns to open them, which isn't often, they seem perfectly normal, not crossed or anything funny, and she looks rather surprised but that's probably because she thinks what a queer looking specimen I am and wonders how on earth she could choose me as her mother. Her mouth is elegantly shaped, but opens wide at times to allow a nice little red tongue to pop out. She is quite a good length, but not fat, though she is not skinny at all. Her fingers and toes are all there, much to my relief, and they all seem full of energy. So really I think all is well with her.

I expect Ronald told you she was 6lbs 11oz. I am glad she is no bigger, she is so sweet as she is.

The nurses in this ward are all State registered, most of them trained in big hospitals in Shanghai, Hankow etc. and with good experience. They couldn't be nicer than they have been to me. They are all slim little things, but so energetic and find nothing too much bother and they are awfully gentle and thoughtful. I had heard that Chinese nurses were rough with patients, but I have nothing but praise for all I have had here. Once or twice others have come in to help and they too have been very good.

I couldn't possibly complain of anything, except my lack of Chinese! I get so tied up sometimes trying to understand their questions and explain my symptoms – am reduced to saying such things as 'This place pain violent', 'That thing not comfortable', 'Want turn over;' and so on and they accept it all meekly. Some of them know quite a lot of English words, but have no idea of putting them into sentences. So they talk half in Chinese and throw in an English word such as 'operation', 'anaesthetic'. It's quite fun.

In the ordinary maternity ward here the mothers are all in one ward and the babies in a little room. They are in wee hanging cots in two rows one above the other. I am thankful mine is the only foreign baby in now or it might be getting moved. I think at least I would know that if they gave me a Chinese one to feed it was a mistake. They distinguish them all by their foot-prints, which is rather cute.

I am hoping to be out on the 14th and stay a week at Mrs Drake's, going home a day or two before Christmas. Dr King seems quite satisfied with me so far. I can't tell you how good he has been to us since he first saw me in October. Although he is about the busiest man I know, he is up till midnight most nights and yet he visits this ward at 6 a.m.! He is never too busy to help anyone and he talks to everyone as though he had all the time in the world to spare for them. He has actually written to Ronald every day too, to report on me, which is awfully good of him.

This ought, with luck, to arrive just in time to wish you all a Happy Christmas. I am longing to hear how many of you get home for it and so on. We are thrilled at the thought that Rosemary has arrived in time to be with us when we have our first Christmas in our own home.

I have loved all the extra letters you have written, Mother, and thanks to Dad for the view of Queens[66] and the CWN.[67] I expect Ronald told you how thrilling it was to have your cable. I wonder what time you had the news? I hope you aren't all fed up at yet another girl in the family. Although of course I would have loved a boy, I think I am really glad to have a girl (for a first anyway!) and I believe Ronald is almost more pleased than if it had been a boy. We couldn't be more thrilled than we are if we had had 'quin' boys! But I am glad we didn't!

Gwyneth to Cambridge

Tsinan
18th December 1936

Once more a few lines to report on the family. Today is Friday and tomorrow I hope Ronald will be here. I can't say how excited I am, but no doubt you can guess.

Well, I'll hastily tell you what's happened since I wrote. Mrs Drake and the car were to arrive at hospital at 3.30 so I got up at 2.30 and dressed. It felt very queer after living in pyjamas for two and a half weeks, but I looked so elegant and slim that I had quite a shock when I looked in a mirror! At 3.15 we dressed Rosemary in her new Viyella nightie made by her Grannie. On top she wore the matinee coat made by Auntie Dray and the mittens and bonnet which match. She looked too sweet for anything, sleeping peacefully all the time, displaying none of

[66] Queens' College, Cambridge
[67] Cambridge Weekly News

the modern girl's craving for new clothes. Then when Mrs Drake came we wrapped the old shawl round and the padded cape on top. In the taxi she still slept on, not in the least interested in her first ride. Oh, I do wish you could see her in the posh clothes, she looks such a darling.

I'm longing for Ron to come, so I can talk about what a nice baby she is! I daren't to anyone else, and of course she is nice! Oh yes, you'd all love her. We'll get a snap as soon as ever we can. Her first train journey is going to be through snow covered country, I think. It's everywhere today and there's no chance of a thaw, maybe more snow. As long as Ronald gets here I don't mind. I'd be wild if he was snowed up in Chouts'un and I was ditto here, but I don't think we'll have all that much in the next twenty four hours. Though when it starts to snow here it's wonderful how quickly it comes. The view from this window is beautiful, the hills and mountains all snow clad.

We plan to go home on Monday. It will be hot in the train and I'll wrap Rosemary up well so it ought to be all right. I shall be pretty busy getting settled in, seeing folk and getting ready for Christmas and resting, so don't expect a long letter.

Gwyneth to Cambridge

Chouts'un
27th December 1936

Well, Rosemary is outside on the veranda fast asleep. At least she gurgled a few minutes ago, but I think she is asleep. Oh, she is adorable, I do keep wishing you could all see her. She has changed a lot already. She seems contented and sleeps and eats well and has nice firm little limbs. I just love bathing her! She is getting to enjoy it now, at first she wasn't quite sure what to make of it, but she doesn't cry now. And she loves having her hair brushed.

Of course I never realised a baby could be half as thrilling. I go nearly crazy telling her how lovely she is! This last week she has discovered what a delightful flavour her fingers have, and now spends most of her waking moments sucking them. Oh, and she thinks the little coat her auntie Dray made has a too, too delicious taste and just loves to chew it. She looks priceless in her bonnet. It is a bit too big and she wriggles around till it is all skew whiff and then she falls asleep, looking completely à la.

On Christmas day Ronald was out at hospital and church all morning, so after I had bathed Rosemary and fed her I sat by the fire and mooned. Then we had duck and plum pudding (we had Wu's after all, as he seemed so keen and I knew you would understand, but we're looking forward to yours). The duck was small, but very tasty. Then, after I fed baby, we looked at our parcels. We had saved everything, we have been ever so lucky – lots of lovely things.

I love Daddy's calendar. Ronald and I are both freshly amazed at the clearness of his photos and also at the cute way he has of getting just the right things. I do wish he could come and use his camera here, though he couldn't take people much, as so many are still terrified of having their photo taken. I think of all the pictures the one I am most bucked to have is the Common[68]. I like it because the chestnuts were all out like that when I went along it to be married, and also because I always used to love cycling across there on Spring and frosty mornings.

While Ron was in Tsinan with us last weekend, Wu and Kao and our teacher, Chao, bought and put up in the dining room a beautiful Chinese scroll affair. It is red silk with two big pink paper flowers at the top. Down the centre, in green characters edged with gold and decorated with pink and yellow paper flowers, are characters meaning "God has given a 'talented' daughter". 'Talented' isn't quite the word, but we can't think how else to translate it. The whole thing is about eight feet high and one and a half feet wide. Everyone is surprised at them doing such a thing for a girl baby, as they never take any notice of girls usually, so we feel greatly honoured.

One of our Christmas gifts was from the Chinese business manager and is an idea for Daddy for next Christmas. Wu brought it in – a live fish with a piece of string fastened to his fins. It is a fat carp, or rather it was. We had it to eat Christmas Eve. We nearly always buy our fish alive and keep it in a big jar of water, otherwise you can't be sure it is fresh, but we hadn't had such a present before and it just amused me. Then two of the nurses gave us two tiny pairs of embroidered silk shoes for Rosemary, one scarlet and one green, and one of the Chinese doctors gave her a woolly cap in dark red. It will do when she is bigger.

Ronald to his father and mother

Chouts'un
30th December 1936

All day yesterday and all my spare time today so far I have been going through the hospital accounts for Flowers. It was my first experience of dealing with accounts of any size, but eventually I

[68] Midsummer Common, Cambridge

understood them, and was able to find four or five mistakes in the entries and additions and when these were accounted for the accounts balanced properly. So I feel that I have really done a piece of good work! When the accounts are finished I shall have to help, I expect, with the analysis of the year's work, inpatient and outpatient and operations statistics and so on, in preparation for the publication of the hospital annual report, so we are likely to be busy for some time.

I expect your papers will have told you the news of General Chiang Kai-shek's release by now. All China is jubilant about it and it really is a great mercy. Humanly speaking, he is China's greatest hope at the present time.

Of course we were all upset by the change of reigns at home[69]. But I agree with you, Father, that in the circumstances the best course has been taken and everything done with dignity. Edward ought to have made the decision to give Mrs S up long before he became king.

While Ronald and Gwyneth's energies had been absorbed in getting to grips with their life in Chouts'un, the intricacies of the Chinese language and the arrival of their baby daughter, events were taking place elsewhere in China which were to have an important impact on their own lives and the lives of millions of others. Threatened from outside by the expansionist ambitions of Japan, and from inside by power struggles amongst the various military factions, China during the 1930s was never far from major conflict. In the autumn of 1936, matters were coming to a head.

Japan's attempts, since the outbreak of World War, to extend its control over Chinese territory had culminated in the invasion of Manchuria in 1931, and in the establishment of the puppet state of Manchukuo. Shortly afterwards, the Japanese launched a vicious but ultimately unsuccessful attack on Shanghai.

Meanwhile, General Chiang Kai-shek had emerged as the most powerful amongst the warring Chinese generals, and had set his sights on uniting the whole country under his control. On his rise to power, he had shown himself willing to overlook or acquiesce in Japanese advances. Now, in the autumn of 1936, recognising the strength of anti-Japanese feeling throughout China, Chiang had agreed not to concede to any further encroachments by Japan.

---

[69] A reference to Edward VIII's abdication on 10 December 1936

He was still determined, though, to subdue the 30,000 strong Communist army, located in the north west corner of Shensi province. In early December he flew north to instruct General Chang Hsueh Liang, commander of the largest northern army and formerly Governor of Manchuria, to initiate an offensive against the Communists. General Chang had already entered into an agreement with the Communists to act with them against Japan and refused to obey Chiang's order. To Chiang's threats of coercion, Chang responded by staging a dawn raid on Chiang's quarters, killing most of his bodyguards and capturing and imprisoning Chiang.

News of the dramatic kidnapping spread immediately throughout China and the threat of civil war seemed imminent. The threat was averted, however, when on the morning of December 25th Chiang pledged himself to join with the Communists in a united front against Japan. The whole country erupted in relieved celebrations.

Ronald to Cambridge and Ilkley

Chouts'un
24th January 1937

I expect by the time you get this that you will know that our Shensi missionaries have had to evacuate the province. Quite a number of them have already arrived in Tsinan and we are hoping before long to see some of them down here in Chouts'un. The revolt in Shensi was not settled by the release of General Chiang Kai-shek. After his departure, the rebellious General Chang Hsueh-liang's troops (who were not satisfied with the result of the negotiations) joined up with the Communists, and now there are about 250,000 of them surrounding Sian. There have been no actual hostilities up to the present, but it seems as though they are unavoidable. In the circumstances, the foreign embassies' attachés advised all foreign residents to evacuate, and both sides agreed to allow foreigners to leave the city unmolested.

So last week all our Shensi missionaries, with the exception of four, left the province. We hear from the papers that four have refused to follow the attachés' advice, but we do not know for certain at present who these four are. Most of the rest of them are in Tsinan at present. Some have gone to Shanghai as some of them are almost due for furlough. The rest intend to remain in Shantung until such time as they are able to return to Shensi.

We had a station meeting on Friday morning to talk over the situation, and invited some of them down here. We hope that we may be able to have Mary King (who came out with us, you will remember, and was at the L.anguage School with us) and Nurse Natten, who is a year senior to Mary, to stay with us. We should be ever so pleased if Mary could come and stay with us. She and Gwyneth get on very well together.

I hope that things may still be settled peacefully in Shensi, and that there will be no fighting, though the outlook at present is not very good. There has been very little anti-foreign feeling in the present evacuation, and our friends do not seem to have been molested in any way, though there is no telling what will happen to the property they have had to leave behind if a civil war should break out.

Ian is going away to Chefoo to school on Tuesday[70]. Of course this is the first time he will have been away from home by himself, so it is quite an exciting occasion for him and for the rest of the family. He was seven last October, and seems to be very young in some ways but grown up in others But I think it will do him a lot of good to go away and to be able to mix with other children, though Michael will miss him very much as a playmate. Mrs Flowers will be taking him as far as Tsingtao and there putting him on the special boat that the CIM charters for the school children from Tsingtao to Chefoo.

Rosemary makes us more and more glad every day. She gained another five ounces last week, and really isn't causing us any anxiety at all. Photographs still not ready – please be patient a little longer!

Gwyneth to Cambridge

Chouts'un
14th February 1937

Well, more news - Ronald has just started off on a journey up to Taiyuan. It will take two and a half days if he catches all his connections, and goodness only knows when he will come back. So that's cheery, isn't it?

On Thursday morning Dr Williamson came down from Tsinan and said he'd been worried that the doctor in Taiyuan, Dr Wyatt, was down with typhus and as his colleague Dr Bloom is on furlough they felt we ought to lend a hand. So they had a committee and all decided Ronald was the man to send. Dr Bloom is due back in Shanghai April

[70] The China Inland Mission school at Chefoo.

18, so it looks as if Ronald is up there till the end of April. Of course he is glad of the chance to see the work there and so on, but it is vile being separated, especially so soon after our last separation, and I hate him to miss all this time of baby. She changes so much and he is so thrilled with her all the time.

A lady doctor, Dr Tait, is coming here, and will live with me. Everyone thinks it will be so nice. Well, so it will, but I prefer Ronald! She is coming tomorrow and someone else insists on sleeping here tonight, though I really don't mind being alone at all, for a night or two.

These last days have of course been upset, sending telegrams and so on, and Mary King has been staying here and her colleague, Winifred Natten, so I have been fairly busy. Mary really is a nice person. I just loved having her here. Mary loves babies and was sweet with Rosemary. Having Mary and Winifred here, I felt quite sort of young and skittish again. They are both so jolly and I felt so free to talk to them. I wished they could stay when Ronald goes, but they have had to return to Tsinan. Mary stayed three days and Winifred one, so it wasn't long, but it has done me a lot of good!

Ronald's last job was to vaccinate Rosemary! There was no vaccine earlier. We didn't do her arm because of her frocks without sleeves, and we did it high up so she could wear shorts! To cheer me up, I dressed her in a new nightie today (she had only worn one of yours) and she looks such a love in it.

Wu was home last week, but Kao did marvels. We had these two people here and a lot of extra, but he just nipped around, got up at 5.00 to light all the stoves and did extras just to show how much he could do. He cooked all sorts of things that weren't exactly necessary. Did them jolly well too! He didn't finish till after 9 p.m. but never complained and was as bright as anything. I am hoping he will be able to go home next week when Dr Tait has been here and got settled in. I think Wu can manage. They are both being very sweet to me – Ronald told them to look after me well! I am awfully lucky having them.

By the way, next time you see Bea Smart tell her there's a circular letter coming to her soon, as we feel no Mish is complete without, and also tell her Ronald has really started his itinerations! Taiyuan is very high. It is supposed to be in lovely country and the journey very interesting. If we had not had baby I would have gone too but it is too cold to risk taking her, especially as we don't really know the facts of the case yet. All news came by telegram.

PS: A wire to say Ronald arrived safely, Dr Wyatt improving.

Gwyneth to Ilkley and Cambridge

Chouts'un
21st February 1937

There is as yet no further news from Ronald since the telegram I told you about in my last letter, but I am told it often takes a week to get letters from Taiyuan, so it is nearly as bad as waiting for ones from you! But as I heard that he arrived safely I am not worrying. We are wondering so many things, at least I am, how Dr Wyatt is, how Ronald is settling in and so on.

The Shensi situation is still very unsettled. The Shensi folk are all very keen to get back, but we hear today that the situation is worse and an early return is not advised. In the meantime we are enjoying their company. On Tuesday night Miss Watson, who came out with us in 1935 after her furlough, stayed with me. She is very musical so we had a grand time. All the station came in here for coffee, twelve of them, and then we had a sort of musical evening. It was rather a squash as we are a bit crowded in the dining room now that we have the piano as well. However we managed to fit them all in and I think they all enjoyed it. Of course I was wishing all the time that Ronald was here, and he would have loved the music. Miss Watson played nearly all the time and had no music. She also recited one or two very funny recitations with a broad Lancashire accent.

Rosemary does not seem very troubled by her vaccination. She seems quite happy and Dr Tait says it is going on nicely and that today is the worst, so she is doing well. Dr Tait seems very impressed by how well she behaves. She is so contented. If she is not asleep she very rarely cries but rests in her pram looking round with great interest. Of course I miss Ronald's help, but Dr Tait does all she can, and insists on staying in so that I can get out for a breath of fresh air occasionally. She really is so thoughtful, without being fussy and no trouble in the house. I could not have had anyone I would like better.

Last night we all went in to the Flowers' after supper and I took our records and gramophone. Everyone has started a craze for knitting. I used to be the only one who ever knitted but now they have all started, and last night it was really funny to see everyone but the two men and Dr Tait knitting away.

Ian has had flu and been in the school hospital a few days, but Mrs Flowers has had a letter from him and he does not sound too bad, though he says he will not go back to school after this term! We think he will change his mind when he gets back into lessons again.

Ronald to his father and mother

Schofield Memorial Men's Hospital, Taiyuan
21st February 1937

I little thought when I wrote last that my next letter to you would be written from Taiyuan, but here I am! I left Chouts'un at midday on Sunday and reached Taiyuan last Tuesday evening at 5.15 p.m., travelling by way of Tsinan, Tientsin, Peking and a place called Shih chia chuang on the Peiping-Hankow line. Of course it wasn't very nice leaving Gwyneth and Rosemary behind, and harder still for them to be left.

I believe today for the first time since Wyatt became ill we can really say he is improving. After the febrile part of his illness was over he developed heart complications and the weekend before I arrived Clow[71] didn't think he was going to pull through[72]. For the last week his pulse has been very weak and he hasn't been out of danger, but yesterday and today his pulse has come down a little and I really believe he has turned the corner now. It will be a big relief when I feel that he is really better again.

Now that Clow has gone I am left in charge here. I am staying with Mr Price (Mrs Price is just on the way home with their daughter to make a home for themselves and their three boys). He lives just across the road from the men's hospital and very convenient for me.

Taiyuan lies in a fertile basin, in the valley formed by the Fen River in central Shansi. In 1937 it was a fine old walled city, with massive gate towers, built facing north, south, east and west, after the style of Peiping. The streets themselves ran north-south, and east-west, so that, as Ronald wrote, ' it becomes easy to say that you keep your socks in the north drawer on the west side of the room, and even, as one of our patients did recently, to say that you have a pain in the west leg!'

Shansi itself is protected on the north and east by high masses of barren mountains, and bounded on the south and west by the Yellow River. It was one of the earliest centres of Chinese civilization, the land cultivated continuously for four thousand years and the place where the art of making pottery had first been developed. Once the political and

[71] Dr J Menzies Clow, normally stationed in Sian but temporarily trapped, with his family, in Taiyuanfu, because of the troubles in Shensi.
[72] A number of BMS doctors in China had died from typhus earlier in the century and typhus continued to be a major killer.

cultural centre of China, it had formed an important defensive boundary between the Han peoples and the nomadic tribes in the north.

English Baptists had first come there in the autumn of 1877, when the International Famine Relief Committee in Shanghai invited Timothy Richards of the Shantung mission to undertake relief work in the province. Persistent drought in north China from 1876 had caused widespread famine, and Shansi was particularly acutely affected. The death toll for the whole of north China during the years 1876-8 is estimated to have been at least 15 million and Richards, working along with two other Baptist colleagues in horrific conditions, is thought to have saved upwards of 70,000 Shansi people from starvation and death. The opening of the first Baptist church was as a direct result of this work.

Hospital work in Taiyuan had been initiated in 1880 by Dr Harold Schofield of the China Inland Mission. He died tragically of typhoid fever after only three years' service, and it was in his memory that the Baptist hospital in the city was named.

Ronald to his father and mother

Taiyuan
9th March 1937

I think this is the longest time I have been without writing to you, though I know you will understand. I have been busier than at Chouts'un and seem to have been on my feet almost the whole day except for meal times. The hospital here is a little bigger than the Chouts'un one and its layout doesn't make for as easy running as at Chouts'un. Then there is only one trained Chinese doctor here, so the outpatient burden is rather heavy. And of course, with Dart, the business manager, going away on Monday, and handing on the business side as well to me, I am having quite a lively time.

You will be glad to know that Dr Wyatt is now sufficiently well to have been able to go home. I still go to see him every day, but it is just a 'friendly' visit now! He sits out of bed in his chair about three hours a day now and is really making splendid progress. They are hoping to go away for a month at the end of this month, he and Mrs Wyatt. They have four children, one away at Chefoo, the other three at home.

I am getting some good opportunities for surgery. There is as much tuberculosis here as in Shantung, if not more. A lot of the TB joints are so far gone that amputation is the only thing and I have had several amputations to do since I came, through the thigh or the leg or feet or arm. Dr Clow[73] has been very good in letting me do operations with her assistance at the women's hospital and I have been specially glad to have the opportunity of doing some Caesarean sections. There is a lot of a bone disease called ostermalacia here in Shansi, which results in some very crippling deformities which make a Caesarean section necessary as a life-saving measure. The first one I did with Dr T'ang's assistance, as Dr Clow was out when the patient came in. I managed to do it without any difficulties or trouble and both the mother and her little daughter are doing well.

I am very glad indeed of the opportunity of coming here. It helps us to put all our Chouts'un ideas in a more correct perspective, and especially since I have the opportunity of finding out things both about the medical and business side of the work. They are making me feel very much at home here and very happy, and it is just possible that Gwyneth may be able to get up here with Rosemary towards the end of this month, so as to be able to have about a fortnight here before we have to go back. It will be lovely if she can – I would like her to have the opportunity of seeing Taiyuan and the people here.

Coming to Taiyuan has made me value more than ever the work that the Ilkley folk are doing in winding such good bandages. Perhaps this ought not to be spread abroad, but I know you will understand if I tell you that our bandages at Chouts'un are very much better than the ones that are being used here and the sight of the ones they use here makes me more than ever grateful for the good quality of the material that was used for the Chouts'un ones. You have no idea what a difference it makes from everybody's point of view, patients' nurses' and doctors'.

Chess moves will have to wait until I am back in Chouts'un, Father – haven't my board and the games here. Old Mr Turner[74] (Mrs Lewis' father) here, used to be very keen on chess and played a lot, but he is 82 now and I am afraid he is past playing though he talks about having a game with me.

[73] Dr Ellen Clow, (sister to Dr J Menzies Clow)

[74] Rev. J J Turner, served with the BMS in China from 1883 to his retirement in 1920. He continued to live in Taiyuanfu until his death later in 1937. His daughter, Nellie, had been married to Dr John Lewis, and, after his premature death in 1918, had continued mission work in her own right, first in Taiyuan and later in Shantung.

Gwyneth to Cambridge

Chouts'un
12th March 1937

First of all, Mummy, thank you for the sweet wee nightie. That is the material I love, it is so soft and wears so nicely. I will certainly be honest about anything you send, don't worry. I have no complaints at all. She looks lovely in everything you have sent, the matinee coats, nighties and all.

Oh, I go nearly mad with wishing you could see her. She is so firm and fat and so dimpled everywhere and she has such a saucy smile these days - her chin is double if not treble! She gets so excited now if when she is lying awake I go up to her. She knows me and makes little excited noises and waves her arms and kicks her legs so furiously

Today I took her to the station to meet Miss Thomas and she kept wide awake all the time, evidently felt it wasn't the thing to be asleep when welcoming a person straight from home. The people on the platform were very intrigued. Kao came with me and got my platform ticket (you have to queue for ages and with the pram I couldn't, it is so crowded and stuffy). So I hurried onto the platform and Kao waited to get the tickets. Then when the train came he minded the pram, while I ran across to the other platform to welcome Miss Thomas. Then he helped me down the steps again – there are six or seven stone steps up to the station from the street. He really is a good lad.

Kao ta Ko *(left)* and Wu shi fu

Tonight he came to the CE and came home with me. I made the excuse that I wanted someone to hold a lamp, because you can't push the pram over the steps in the dark and I needed help. Also I preferred company coming into the empty house, but I didn't tell him that! He is so thrilled when Rosemary looks at him, and so is Wu. They are both good-hearted lads we think and really try to look after me now Ronald is away. I have not met two boys in any house in China who I find as good as they, though on the whole most of our mission boys are nice lads.

One great advantage with Wu and Kao is that they are such excellent friends. You never hear the slightest disagreement and they share the work so nicely, helping each other. Some men squabble and swear at each other and won't do a thing that they don't consider their job, but these two share it all. When we have fires, Kao has to do them, so Wu will help with the dusting or getting tea which is Kao's job really. The cook reckons to prepare brekker, lunch and supper but the table boy gets mid morning drinks and tea. Ronald doesn't like the cooking anywhere else as much as here. Neither do I and we have never had anything dished up that we couldn't eat – if he has failures we never know it.

Gwyneth to Cambridge

Taiyuan
25th March 1937

Well dears, here we are in Taiyuan, all safe and sound. Rosemary is celebrating her arrival by a good long sleep, but she was awake when we got here and gave her Daddy a lovely smile. When he left us, she had not learned to smile very much, but she is making up for it now.

On Monday afternoon, we had an easy trip to Tsinan, only two and a half hours. Rosemary slept some of the time, but stared round with interest most of the way. In Tsinan I stayed with Miss Hickson of the BMS and she made us very comfortable. I took baby's basket and sleeping things, so soon had her fed and in her bed asleep. All the way she has kept to her feeds quite regularly and I've tried not to pick her up more than necessary. On Tuesday I had luncheon with the Pailings and tea with Mrs Williamson, and saw all the other people – all came and admired Rosemary!

Then Tuesday evening I caught a train for Tientsin. Got to Tsinan station at 7.45 and was told it would be late. So Miss Hickson went home and I sat in the waiting room, in the only comfy seat, until the train came at 10 p.m.! The Travel Service man helped us on the train and to my joy I found I'd a four berth coupé to myself, so I soon gave Rosemary her 10 o'clock feed, put her in her basket in one berth and then went to sleep on the other. She slept until about 5 o'clock and then I fed her and we slept again until we reached Tientsin, an hour late.

Mr and Mrs Mould were there and in the car we were soon at their home. We had to have a hurried breakfast and then dash for the

Peiping train. There had been a very heavy fall of snow and the main roads were swept, but the surface was like glass. We had several attempts at skids, but nothing happened and we just got to the station in time for the Peiping Express. Again I was lucky and had plenty of room for myself. The journey passed quickly and we were in Peiping by 11.30. All the way the country was snow covered.

At Peiping I had asked Miss Cowie of the Missionary Home to send a boy, but no one appeared, and, as there was a snowstorm and it was bitterly cold, I managed to get a taxi on my own. I had Rosemary in her padded cape so she was all right, but I was rather helpless and had to hope for the best with regard to my luggage. However, all went well and I got to the Missionary Home. Miss Cowie was awfully upset when I arrived. She had mistaken my letter and she herself had intended to meet the Shanghai Express at 1.30. The Missionary Home is a comfy place. Lovely warm rooms. I had a bathroom with hot and cold running water all to myself. Such luxury! I wished I was staying longer!

Out here it is not really difficult travelling, especially with a babe, everyone is so kind. All the Chinese wanted to know all about Rosemary and were so thrilled when she smiled at them, as she does at all and sundry now. On the trains there are always "Car Boys" who are very willing to help in any way and they always put your luggage up and take it down and so on, which is such a help when you are alone with a babe.

And now comes the real news of the year. Don't be alarmed, but this morning we created a record I think for the BMS in China, by flying from Peiping to Taiyuan!![75] What do you think of that? Rosemary was very blasé about it all.

The journey by train takes nineteen hours and would not have been an easy one for me to do alone. Someone would have had to come to meet me and we added up all the expenses and found out that there was only about 10/- difference. But the difference in time amounted to seventeen hours! So we decided on it. I didn't mention it at Chouts'un as I thought I'd rather be sure of getting a seat and then announce it afterwards. As soon as I got to Peiping I rang up and booked the seat, the last available one for this morning's plane. I'd to fill in a long form and swear that Rosemary was under 20lbs (otherwise she would count as a passenger).

---

[75] This news must have come as a real surprise for the family at home. Passenger air travel was still very much in its infancy, and until the late 1930s it was only those going on business or the very wealthy who would normally have considered it. It was also thought to be more dangerous than other forms of travel. It was enterprising – and brave – of Gwyneth to undertake the journey by air, especially with such a young baby.

This morning I'd a taxi at 8 a.m. with Gunn and Newton, two of the BMS students at the language school, to escort me and help if necessary. The aerodrome is thirteen miles out from Peiping. On my arrival I had to sign another form and they saw to my bag. I just brought Rosemary's basket and enough things for one night and sent the rest by rail as you are only allowed 30lbs luggage by plane. Then promptly at 9.00 we were off! The boys were awfully envious.

Inside there were eight seats, four each side for passengers, and in addition was a pilot and an engineer (or whatever he's called), a wireless man and a car boy, the latter served excellent coffee en route. We had cellophane packets of cotton-wool handed out, to stuff in our ears, as some folk are worried by the engine noise. I'd already put it in baby's. By each seat was a packet of air-sickness remedy but I did not need to investigate it! The plane is German and we had a German pilot. But the others were Chinese. One girl passenger who felt faint and was sick, poor soul, was going on to Nanking, another five hours.

Well it felt just like a noisy car. We did not seem to be going quickly but as we took about an hour and fifty minutes to do over three hundred miles we can't have been crawling. All but the last few miles we were over mountains, marvellous ranges, all brown with snow-covered tops, like chocolate blanc-mange with cream over it! Wee villages dotted in some of the valleys looked like little spots. It really all looked rather like those relief models you see of hill country – rivers and all seemed so small. It was a perfect day, no clouds and we could see for miles. It was a lovely experience. My only regret is that Ronald was not there to share it. However, after a while the big plateau came in view and I could see what appeared to be a biggish place and concluded it was Taiyuan and in a few minutes we were circling round and landing. Just the tiniest bump, a run along the ground, the engines stopped – and there was Ronald waiting to welcome us.

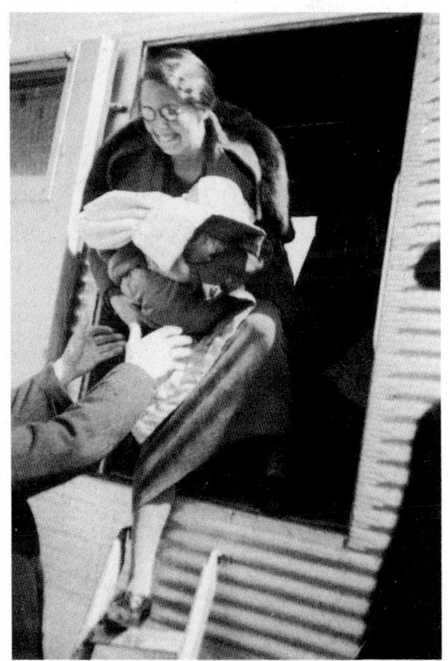

Gwyneth getting out of the plane at Taiyuan

Oh, it was exciting. Rosemary had her 10 a.m. feed up I don't know how many feet above earth and then slept until we landed, when she awakened to see her Daddy. It really was lovely and I thoroughly enjoyed it. I feel that I cannot realise that I have come so far in such a short time but when we go back by train I will realise it well enough!

It was such a business shutting up the house, all the woollies to be put away and so on and it took some planning getting packed for the journey with Rosemary, but I feel that it is well worth it. Many people who are out here thirty years only see their own Province and it makes it so difficult to understand the work of other people. And I don't feel really worried about Rosemary. You see, she isn't like a little toddler on the fidget all the time and poking her fingers into all the dirty corners on trains and there is no difficulty about her having to have special food. She really seems to have come quite unconcernedly and is sleeping peacefully enough now and looks just as lovely as you can imagine. Ronald saw a big change in her.

Ronald to his father and mother

Taiyuan
30th March 1937

You will see from Gwyneth's letter that she and Rosemary have arrived here in Taiyuan but unless you already have the letter she wrote to Cambridge, you won't know that she and Rosemary came from Peiping to Taiyuan by air! What do you think of that?!

I worked it out that the difference in cost between travelling by air and travelling by rail and going down to Shih Chia Chuang to meet her (which would have been necessary) was only about 10/-. And if Gwyneth came by air it would save two days of my (or someone else's) time and I didn't feel it was right to leave the hospital for two days to go to meet Gwyneth, nor to ask anyone else to go to meet her. Since it also saved her and Rosemary a night on the train and a change at Shih Chia Chuang in the middle of the night, I think you will both feel as I did that it was worth the extra 10/-.

Gwyneth enjoyed the trip very much indeed. The Eurasia planes are splendid modern three engined ones, with a German pilot who has flown over a million miles in the plane without a mishap. It was a glorious clear day when Gwyneth came and she had a splendid view of the mountains of Shansi on the way over. The plane was in ten minutes before the scheduled time. Mr Price and I were at the aerodrome to meet her and I can't tell you what a wonderful thrill it was, first to hear and then to see the plane in the distance flying over the snow capped mountains towards us. It was a wonderful thrill and it increased as the plane drew nearer so quickly that it only seemed a minute or two for the plane to cover the miles from the mountains to the plain of the aerodrome a few miles north of Taiyuan.

The aeroplane turned once before landing, to get into position for the next flight, and it landed so beautifully that there was no bump at all, but just a puff of dust from the wheels as they touched the ground and then she gently taxied to a standstill and we were able to run up and help my two treasures out! It was a lovely trip and I am glad Gwyneth has been able to do it and that Rosemary has done something her Daddy has never done!

Gwyneth to Ilkley

Taiyuan
6th April 1937

Just a few lines to tell you about our trip to Taichow and Sinchow this weekend. We have had a lovely time, though Ronald was worked jolly hard all the time. We left here on Friday morning at 11.30. Ronald had outpatients till 11.00 and I had Rosemary to bath and get ready and the packing to see to, so the morning flew. We had lunch at 11.00 and then packed into the Mission car and started off. There was Li, the nurse, and the driver in front, Ronald, Rosemary and I behind with our case, Rosemary's basket and a big box containing the drugs and medicines.

Our first stop was Sinchow, two and a half hours out. On the way there we went through some lovely country, beautiful mountains and valleys, but we missed the green. There were few trees and all the hills and earth were brown. This brown soft soil has cliff formations and in these are caves where many Chinese make their homes. They don't seem to have barrows here as we have in Shantung, mostly carts. Whereas men push barrows, here there are donkeys and mules to do the work. Until the railway was built all the travelling was done on mules and donkeys, on foot, cycle or cart. The latter are still used for mission work. They amble along slowly, but time does not matter in China. The carts have rounded tops, a bit like the old tradesmen's carts at home, and are very dirty. It is impossible to keep anything clean, the dust is thick everywhere. The roads are all just loose sort of earth that flies up every time there is a gust of wind and every now and then there are real dust storms, which are as dense as an English fog and much less pleasant.

At Sinchow, Mr Lower's gate-man met us and relieved us of some letters and parcels and then we went on again. The country was much the same, except that the earth changed to a sandy red tint. There were men at work in stone quarries and also building up the track for the railway. Trains are running nearly to Taichow and it looks a bit unsafe in parts, as they've not finished the track properly. We went over several rivers, the bridges just sort of rickety plank arrangements. We didn't feel too safe.

We got to Taichow about 5.30. Good old John Henderson Smith[76] had cycled out a little way to welcome us. It was good to see him. The walls of Taichow are not in very good condition, but all the same are fairly stout. At the gate, as at all these city gates, the police and soldiers stop you and ask who you are. But they did not keep us long and we were soon on our way up to the compound where Ernest Madge, John's colleague, welcomed us. They were alone, so did all the entertaining. There were just two houses there, both built in Chinese style. It is a pretty compound and has lovely views over to the mountains. John Smith was born in Taiyuan, but his parents took him back to Taichow at a few weeks and he was the first foreign baby most of the people had seen. So he has returned to his old home. Later when he gets married he will live in Sinchow.

On Saturday morning while I bathed and fed Rosemary, Ronald had the clinic. Oh, before that John took me up the Drum Tower, where an old blind man beats an enormous drum every day and night to tell the city the time. From the top we had a glorious view of the city and surrounding country. It is all very beautiful, but it seems like the edge of the beyond. Those early missionaries, who lived there in the days when it took at least a week in good weather to get to Taiyuan, were plucky folk, but of course there are still plenty living two or three weeks' journey from any other foreigners and medical aid. The streets are mostly wider than in Chouts'un and the shops are different. One of the industries is string-making and it is very interesting to see them doing it all by hand.

At 11 a.m. we packed into the car and were ready to go out to the chapel where Ronald had the clinic. He had to stop to see some more patients, so I sat in the car with baby. I wish you could have seen the crowd! The whole car was surrounded and faces were pressed closely

---

[76] John's parents, Rev and Mrs S Henderson Smith, had been pioneer missionaries in Shansi from 1907 to 1928. John had been a student at Rawdon Baptist College, Leeds, at the same time as Ronald.

into every available inch of the windows, front, sides and back! Evidently Rosemary and I were better than any museum. It was funny to see how they stared at us. Of course foreign babies are very rare there. John stood outside the car and the people were saying to each other, how clean the baby was. Of course theirs are dirty, but some of them couldn't afford soap and anyway if you saw the hovels they live in you would not be surprised they are not keen on washing. John took up the subject of Rosemary's cleanliness and gave a little talk on hygiene, at least told them that babies should all be bathed all over every day. But they didn't think that seemed at all the thing!

The work in Taichow and indeed in all the province is made a lot harder by the fact that there are still many people who remember the tragedies of the Boxer Rising. Some actually saw the Christians being cut up and burnt, others lost their relatives that way, and others of course helped in the butchery. So that there is always the memory of it all in people's minds and it makes them afraid to be Christians.

Ronald finished his clinic and we went to a biggish village called Kuo Hsien where we have a chapel and a house where Mr and Mrs Stonelake were staying for a few days. We have no permanent missionaries there, but they go for meetings at certain times of the year. We had lunch there and then Ronald went immediately to the clinic while I fed Rosemary and talked to Mrs Stonelake. Then we had tea about 3.15 as soon as Ronald was ready and off we started again.

We reached Sinchow at about 6 p.m. Mr Lower and Nellie (his daughter aged 19) and the two new men, Dawson and Jasper met us at the gates. We had to leave the car there and walk up, our bags coming in a cart. The men took Rosemary in turns. She had been very good all the way again and seems no worse for her journey. I have luckily managed to keep her feeds regular. On our arrival at the compound Mrs Lower met us and showed us straight to our room. I fed Rosemary at once while Ronald got things out and poured out the tea, which Mrs Lower had kindly sent to our room.

Next day, Sunday, we went to the Chinese Church in the city. The Shansi dialect is very different from Shantung and I didn't understand at all what was said. Ronald had to hurry away to go to Ting Hsiang for another clinic. He had a big lot of patients, didn't get back till supper time. We enjoyed being with Mr and Mrs Lower very much.

The mission compound is high up above the city and although it is a stiff climb it is worth it for the lovely views. The first missionaries lived down in the city. The houses had been started in the present position in 1900 but they were broken up by the Boxers. All Monday morning and afternoon, Ronald was kept hard at work with patients. I looked round the Girls' School and also walked out to the cemetery where they buried the remains of our BMS people killed by the Boxers. Sydney Ennals was one, you know[77]. On our way out in the afternoon we went to see the actual place where they were killed. They had been promised an escort to the coast and were taken to the East Gate. It is a double affair between two enormous walls about sixty feet high and the city gate was shut behind them and the gate to the country outside was shut in front and the soldiers just set on them. Going to this actual place made us realise more than ever before how ghastly it must have been to be trapped like that. The walls are high and thick all round and the gates quite smallish and of course well-guarded, so there was no possible way of escape. There are always soldiers at the gates now and they are quite friendly, but they profess to know nothing of the Boxer riots. I think they are ashamed of it all.

Tuesday 8 p.m: In the most wobbly train ever invented!

We left Taiyuan at 7 a.m. and had a rather cold journey down to Shih Chia Chuang. To our amazement we had snow yesterday! And the heat has been stopped on trains, but it was only our feet that were cold. It is a lovely trip. The railway winds in and out of mountains and you can often see the engine and first coaches going round a bend in front. No time to describe it properly now, but it was very beautiful. Rosemary slept all the way except at 10 a.m. and 2 p.m. when she asked for a meal. We two had Chinese food – quite a good meal, rice, a pile in a bowl and then four other dishes from which we helped ourselves with chopsticks. We got to Shih Chia Chung at 4.05 and just had nice time to change stations and get the Peiping train at 4.45.

---

[77] All eight BMS missionaries based in Sinchow were beaten to death on 9th August 1900. Rev Sydney Ennals, aged 27 when he was killed, had only arrived to take up missionary service in China a few months earlier. He was known to both May and John Johnson, having been a member of Burlington Chapel, Ipswich, May Johnson's home congregation, and having attended St Andrew's Street Chapel in Cambridge during 1890-2.

At Taiyuan at 7 a.m. we had five people up at the station to see us off. Wasn't it good of them?

Rosemary really is a perfect baby to take about as she seems perfectly content to sleep in her basket or lie and look around. She is no trouble. Oh, how I wish you could see her – she is just a chubby bundle of warmth and cuddliness! I love the way babies dribble and make rude noises so unconcernedly in public, don't you?! Everyone on the train looks at her – there are always lots of soldiers and police and they nearly all thrill over her and think she is so good. When the ticket collector comes, he usually has at least two police and two soldiers to support him! It is so funny. They are mostly very friendly.

I was telling Ronald this morning what a long journey we used to think it was to Ipswich[78] and what a long time we spent over packing and how we always had to take something to eat and something to read on the way and now we start off on a three day journey without turning a hair. Queer, isn't it? But you will find I have not really changed at all inside, so don't worry!

Home again! It is lovely to be here, all together again. The boys had made it all so nice and tidy and clean, and got the garden all dug and seeds sown, and our favourite puddings etc. for meals! They brought the pram to the station so Rosemary was able to go home comfortably. They were so bucked to see us back.

Your parcel was here and I am ever so thrilled with the contents – the remnants are very pretty and I look forward to making them up. Rosemary was very pleased with her rattle, though a bit scared at first. The first time she touched it and it made a noise she jumped a little but now she thinks she is a little bit of all right being able to make a noise with it. Will you please tell Dray how pleased we are?

Ronald to Ilkley and Cambridge

Chouts'un,
20th April 1937

You will see by the notepaper that we are safely back in Chouts'un again and, after Taiyuan, Chouts'un seems fairly calm and restful. It was an invaluable experience for me to have the responsibility of running the men's hospital there, but, as much as that opportunity, I valued the opportunity of meeting with the other members of our Mission staff, and of seeing how they do things and of hearing their views. It

---

[78] from Cambridge – about 50 miles!

gives you an entirely new view point and outlook, and I think it helps you to see things in what is much more their right proportion.

The Men's Hospital at Taiyuan is a little bigger than ours here at Chouts'un. In the seven weeks I saw over 3,400 outpatients, as compared with 2,400 during the corresponding period last year, and we took in 113 inpatients, as compared with 102 last year, so that you will guess I was quite relieved when Dr Bloom arrived to take over. I think the most difficult operation I had to do there was a bad case of appendicitis, gangrenous and perforated, in a young Japanese man. It was the worst I have had to do and, to add to my embarrassment, the patient's Japanese doctor, himself a surgeon, had flown over from Peiping that morning to see me do it! It took about two hours, but eventually it came out all right, and the boy did very well.

I wish you all could travel on the railway from Shih Chia Chuang up to Taiyuan. It is a lovely run, winding up and up through the Shansi mountains to a height of about seven or eight thousand feet before eventually dropping down again to the plateau in the centre of which lies Taiyuan.

We made some good new friends at Taiyuan, and at Sinchow and Taichow. Taichow and Sinchow are beautiful compounds – wish you all could pay them a visit.

Gwyneth to her mother

Chouts'un
1st May 1937

Fancy that, May morning gone and I never thought of it in time to bathe my face in the dew! I have only just realised the date, so I will have to go on being ugly for another year!

Your letter in reply to the aeroplane news just came. I didn't do it at all for the thrill, but because we had decided I should go to Taiyuan and thought it right to go the easiest and quickest way. You know I am like you, I really can't think of things I want for myself, so Ronald hasn't given me a birthday or Christmas present since we were married, not a big one. Therefore he gave me the trip to Taiyuan instead. I would much rather he did this than spend money on buying things I don't really want. The more I think about it, the less inclined I feel to buy a lot of trash for our house. Some folk have their homes full of vases and ornaments and Chinese nick nacks, but I can't be bothered with things like that. Out here most people have to evacuate on more than one occasion and the fewer possessions you have the better it must be. I am glad for all we brought out – wedding gifts and so on - but I don't want any more till they are all worn out or smashed!

We felt that Rosemary was not in the least likely to feel any effects from the trip and if you could see her now you would not worry. She is sunburnt and lovely, so chubby and happy, lies playing so contentedly with her fingers and smiles as brightly as can be if anyone goes and speaks to her. She has just discovered that there are two more fat pink things at the other end of her and stares at her toes for ages with great interest. I think the people here didn't disapprove of flying, but wished they had a chance to do it!

Oh, you don't wish any more than I do that you could see Rosemary in her pretty things – she looks so lovely in them all. I feel it is a waste that Ronald and I are her only admirers! She really 'pays' for dressing well, but I suppose nearly all babies do. We go crazy over her, she is so bonny. She is now really most interested in everyone and everything. Wu and Kao are thrilled with her and are sure she knows them, but I am not so sure! However, they are happy about it.

The Manger-Woods are going this week and have sold up nearly everything. Really we didn't want anything, but we felt we must buy something, so we bought two chairs with cane seats, low ones, which are nice for bathing baby and more comfy than dining room ones if we have to use extra for meetings or anything. We also got two bedside tables, very old, but they will do for us. And we got an old hammock – it may please Rosemary later on. I always remember our thrills over the hammock. Ronald couldn't resist some of the books, and got a good English-Chinese dictionary, Soothill's 'Analects of Confucius', two books about Chinese Proverbs, and 'Songs of Praise'. Miss Manger asked if I could do with any Lux flakes. How much do you think she has for sale? Three cases, each containing seventy two packets! It would last me till we retire. I declined graciously!

You will like the Manger-Woods if ever you meet them, but do be careful not to say anything that isn't absolutely gospel, as Miss Manger always thinks you mean everything and we get into all sorts of muddles over it! She is very outspoken and will probably ask how old you are and why you didn't have more children and so on, but she is very sweet and Miss W is great fun, full of funny yarns, especially about China.

Our roof is to be re-tiled next week and so we are going over to Logie's to sleep. It's a nuisance just now when I am so anxious to get on with Chinese. I can't settle easily to work elsewhere and I will have to pack away lot of upstairs things, which all takes time. You can't imagine the dust when they take the tiles off. They slide them down shafts and they drop into the earth and clouds of dust fly up and the workmen sing and talk hard all the time. They don't do it in bits, but have crowds of men and are all over the place. But our present tiles are in an awful condition, likely to slide right off if we have a strong wind. We are having bright red ones this time. I don't like them as much as grey with our grey bricks but they are apparently more satisfactory and also cheaper. The whole job will take our house repairs allowance for the next ten years so I don't know what will happen to repairs during that time.

I didn't realise you were keeping my letters. It will be amusing to see them. I quite forget now what my first impressions were – it is queer how soon you get used to things out here.

I have not yet thanked you for the pretty white ribbon. Oh such a joy, to have an English haberdashery counter send me selections at times! It's economical having no shops here. You don't buy things you don't need, but then that's not a failing of mine on the whole (or do you think it is?) All the same, I do often wish I could have a squint at shops at home. All the things you send are so welcome and the third vest has just come. She looks a dream in it, especially back view. You know how adorable babies' necks are, and her chubby dimpled elbows and her sweet little seat all go to make her look lovely!

Ronald to his father and mother

Chouts'un
2nd May 1937

Your last letters were dated April 14th and you had just heard of Gwyneth's aeroplane trip when you wrote them. I can guess how surprised you would feel.

I hope you won't blame Gwyneth for coming to Taiyuan. It wasn't that she couldn't bear to be patient for another three weeks without coming. I know she would have been quite prepared to do that if we had thought it right. The reasons why we decided that it was right for her to come were

1. That we felt it is important that we should have as wide and definite a knowledge of the work of our mission as possible. It is impossible to form an opinion of the relative importance of the various pieces of work without having actually seen them, and especially now that the question of the devolution of the Shantung work in favour of Shensi and Shansi is being reopened, I wanted Gwyneth to have as clear an

idea of it as I had, so that we should both be able to take an intelligent part in subsequent discussions. The Mission paid my travelling expenses, and something towards the extra cost of board while I was away but Gwyneth and I are paying all Gwyneth's expenses while she was away from home. As for the risks, they were of course the most important objection to Gwyneth's going but we felt that they were not really very great. Rosemary was able to sleep in her own little bed all the time, as the little corrie which Gwyneth had converted into a cot was just as easily reconverted into a corrie again for travelling.

2. The second reason why I specially wanted Gwyneth to be able to go to Taiyuan was that I wanted her to have the experience of living in a mission station other than Chouts'un. I can't explain very well in a letter but I had felt to benefit so much myself from being able to work with the Taiyuan community, that I felt I wanted Gwyneth to have the benefit of the experience as much as I had. You have some idea of the difficulties we have at Chouts'un, but I feel I can take a much broader view of them now than I could before we went away – and I am sure it was right that Gwyneth should have the same opportunity that I had had of forming this broader view.

Just one piece of news I know you will be pleased to hear. We are hoping to arrange with Pastor Yin, the minister of the Chinese Church on the street here, to have a Dedication Service for Rosemary on Sunday May 23rd. I am hoping this will reach you in time for you to be able to think specially of our little treasure on that day.

Gwyneth to Cambridge

Chouts'un
3rd June 1937

I am really more than angry, I am vexed! Today is Saturday and the mail due yesterday morning still hasn't come so I can't get on with answering your letter yet. I have done Chinese till 9.30 p.m. and now want a few minutes change before bed. We are both hard at it and of course don't feel at all well prepared. I feel they won't have the heart to fail me as I am taking it four months before it is due and have had a baby too! However, I am not relying on the kindness of the examiners' hearts. When this reaches you they will be nearly over and we go to Tsingtao on June 30th I think.

The Luke and Acts and essay are corrected in Shensi. The examiner there last year is reported to have said we absorbed Chinese like a sponge absorbs water!! I am glad he won't see my efforts this year (he is on furlough). The Classics, which I do in place of medicine, and the Readers and History are corrected in Shansi and the rest Mr Drake does. I'd like to do well for him, because he's always been so decent in helping us in every way. Dr Ingle does Ronald's medicine. We have eight hundred characters to write and two thousand to recognise and you will understand that that won't be easy.

Well, Rosemary seems able to bear the strain of all this very well and is in excellent spirits. I have tied Auntie Dray's rattle over the cot and in the mornings now we hear it hard at work. She adores it, knocks it to and fro and is awfully excited about it. Her cot is so arranged that we can see through the connecting door from our bed and watch her – it is priceless.

All our Shantung mishes were in Chouts'un for the Provincial Conference last week. It was lovely having Connie Allen here with Elizabeth. She and Rosemary look like being the only Shantung babies, unless any more couples come out, so we hope they'll be great friends. Elizabeth is very friendly and so cheery, and Rosemary was thrilled with her – just sat and gazed in wonder! Connie is awfully nice and Tom is too[79].

Now it is Sunday and still no home letters, my vexation is turning to pained grief! Rosemary is in her pram in the sun kicking as hard as she can. Her legs are lovely and brown. I daren't put her face in the sun, it is too hot and too bright for her eyes.

Gwyneth to Ilkley

Chouts'un
19th June 1937

We have got the bigger half of the exam over and so feel that at last we are nearing the end. It is an enormous relief. During the exam baby has been marvellous. We have written our papers in the dining room with Annie looking at us, and Rosemary has been in the pram outside the window, most of the time not making a sound, but occasionally just gurgling forth quite cheerfully. It has been a little awkward to feed her and myself in the time-table, but we arranged it all right in the end.

We shall not be sorry now when our holiday comes. We hope to leave here on the midnight train July 1st. We are taking Kao to Tsingtao

[79] Rev T W Allen and his wife, Connie had been in China since 1931. She was formerly C M Greening, daughter of A E Greening, a missionary with the BMS in China from 1897 until his retirement in 1936. Elizabeth was just six months older than Rosemary.

with us, so he has gone home for a few days to have his clothes repaired and so on, and Wu is managing alone. He has done very well. They are both good boys but it is heavy work for one. The fetching of water is the worst. The well is at the far end of the garden, and in this hot weather we use such a lot of water, and it is hard work carrying it. They never complain but we feel they must get tired. They get up very early, and do as much as they can before the heat. Chinese mostly expect to get up at sunrise, so they are used to it.

Ronald to his father and mother

Tsingtao
6th July 1937

We left Chouts'un on the midnight train, and got here about 9.30 a.m. on Friday morning. Tom and Connie Allen and Elizabeth came up to Chouts'un from Tsingchoufu to get on the train. (It passed through Tsingchou about 2 a.m. and if they hadn't come to Chouts'un they would have had to spend about five hours waiting in the station, as the town gates are closed about 10 p.m. and the station is outside the town.)

We have a very happy party down here. They are all extremely nice people and I am sure we couldn't have had a nicer company for a house party. I imagine that if the company is not congenial, such a party could be rather difficult sometimes. Miss Manger's house in which we are staying is very beautifully situated – it overlooks the sea and we only have two minutes' walk to a good bathing beach and we bathe two or three times a day. There are some lovely mountain peaks that we can see from our bedroom window, and some good mountain trips that we can go from here.

PART TWO

JAPANESE INVASION
July 1937 – January 1938

Tsingtao, with its temperate climate, delightful sandy beaches and pine covered parks, was a popular resort town. Its natural charms were complemented by the attractions of the town itself, its cobbled streets and unusual Germanic architecture. The Germans had seized the small fishing port in 1895, and over the next twenty years had constructed a fine modern city, complete with government offices, banks, hotels, a post office, concert hall, brewery and church, and an array of picturesque residential properties built in typical German style.

When Japan joined the western allies in declaring war on Germany in 1914, it saw its opportunity to take over Tsingtao, along with the German owned Shantung railway and other German concessions in the province. By 1937, Tsingtao had more than 14,000 Japanese residents, the biggest Japanese population in any Chinese city apart from Shanghai. The enormous cotton mills were Japanese owned, the streets were lined with Japanese shops and Japanese employees were prominent in businesses, banking and shipping firms.

On the night of 7th July, Ronald and Gwyneth were relaxing in their holiday home. Several hundred miles away, on the outskirts of Peiping, Japanese troops were conducting a night exercise near the railway junction at Lukouchiao, not far from the marble bridge made famous by Marco Polo. Claiming that one of their men had been killed or captured by Chinese soldiers, the Japanese party demanded entry to the nearby town to find those responsible and, when refused, surrounded and attacked it.

Many such incidents had occurred over the years when Japanese troops had been stationed around north China and it was by no means certain how this one might be contained or might escalate. The expansionist goals of the Japanese military were not always shared by the civilian government and tensions often arose between them. The General commanding the Japanese army was appointed directly by the Emperor and was independent of the Japanese Parliament and Prime Minister.

A provisional ceasefire was agreed locally. Elsewhere, however, incidents multiplied. Within days, it was rumoured that thousands of

Japanese troops were pouring into north China from Manchuria, Korea and Japan, supported by bomber squadrons and tanks.

Some days later, Chiang Kai-shek issued a statement to the Chinese people making clear his own stance towards the Japanese, 'To seek peace once war has begun would be to invite the subjugation of our nation and the annihilation of our race. ... If we allow one more inch of our territory to be lost then we would be committing an unpardonable offence against our race. Whether there is hope of peace between China and Japan depends on the Japanese army. ... We do not want war, but we may be forced to defend ourselves.'[80]

Ronald to his father and mother

Tsingtao
23rd July 1937

I hope you haven't been anxious on our account because of the political news of the North China situation that you will have been reading in the papers. Today the situation seems much more hopeful.

Chiang Kai-shek made an important speech two days ago when he stated that China was anxious for peace, but that she would not submit to any further encroachments on her territory. It remains to be seen to what extent Japan is prepared for war and is willing to support her militarist party in the demands they are making. It seems as though the Japanese militarists wish to treat the northern provinces of Hopei (with Peking) and Chatar in the same way as they treated Manchuria and Moukden, and that this situation has been 'arranged' with that object in view. I think the Chinese are now sufficiently united to resist such an attempt. Personally, I do not think that the Japs will dare to risk a first class war and will modify their demands and the situation will be settled peaceably. The next few days will clarify the situation considerably, I should think.

In the meantime things are very quiet and peaceful in Tsingtao. Dr Ingle and I were talking yesterday of what the effect would be on our mission work if a first class war broke out. He thinks that the women and children would be evacuated, probably to Shanghai, and possibly to England, if the war zone extended into Shantung and Shanghai. If a major war should ensue, I expect the Japs would take Tsingtao and advance inland along the Tsingtao-Tsinan (Kiao-Tsi) Railway. The

[80] See Farmer, R, *Shanghai Harvest*, pub. Museum Press, London 1945, pp14-15

Chinese would probably attempt to offer resistance at Weihsien, east of Chouts'un. In that case, Chouts'un would be pretty near the fighting line. Dr Ingle thinks that the medicals should remain at their hospitals, and I think so too. But I don't really think for a moment that a war of such dimensions is at all likely, and all the indications are at present that the trouble will be localised.

Meanwhile, we are enjoying a very happy and pleasant holiday here. The weather has been good and delightfully cool as compared with the interior. We have been bathing two or three times a day and one day had a splendid trip up Lao-ting, the highest mountain in the range near here, about 3,500 ft high and quite near the coast. There was a marvellous view from the top, sea and coast for miles round the Shantung coast, with lovely mountains and islands and clouds.

We saw the Coronation film[81] in Tsingtao last week! We did enjoy it - very like the pictures we had seen in the papers, but thrilling to see the movements.

Gwyneth to Cambridge (and Ilkley)

Tsingtao
2nd August 1937

You will have seen in the papers that there has been fighting at Tientsin and Peiping. It is not very near us, but as there is just a possibility of it spreading into Northern Shantung, we have been advised to stay here for a bit. The men, except those due here on holiday, are still inland, but all people with children have been evacuated.

We're lucky to have somewhere to stay, it would be awful in a hotel. There wasn't room where I was last month, but Mr and Mrs Phillips had taken the next house for this month and invited me and Connie Allen to stay with them till we are able to go inland again. So we have a big bedroom, and she and Elizabeth are one end and Rosemary and I the other. It is very jolly. We both feel happier than sharing with anyone without a baby and the children amuse each other, standing in their cots chattering away nineteen to the dozen.

Tom Allen returned to Tsingchou and Ronald to Chouts'un on Saturday. We miss them terribly and I was most frightfully disappointed not to go too. I had so looked forward to being at home and not swotting for the exam and had lots of jobs I was longing to do. I hate Ronald not having company in the house when he is in charge of the hospital, but I

[81] The coronation of King George VIth, May 12th 1937

could not go. If I had not had Rosemary I might have persuaded them to let me. It is awful for the Chinese. Our boys here are so troubled, poor lads, but are carrying on splendidly. I am so thankful Kao is here.

Don't be alarmed. This is one of the safest spots and the British Consul is constantly in touch with us. We are all registered and if any need arose we should be got out of the way - there are British ships in port.

Rosemary is making rapid progress, pulls herself up in the cot very easily now and works her way slowly round till her arms and legs give way and then just flops back, only to start up again. She is such a comfort and so bright. She still shows no teeth, though constantly rubs her gums.

I had hoped to write letters this month, but with only one sitting room, there is always a noise. I am managing a little knitting but otherwise nothing much. In addition to Mr and Mrs Phillips and their three children, there is a Mr Rowlands (LMS, wife in England), Mrs Payne (Tsinan BMS), Miss Bain (Shanghai BMS), Miss Bent (Peiping BMS) and Miss Evans (Shanghai LMS) and Connie and me. It is great fun being with Connie. I wish they weren't due for furlough so soon – they'll be away fifteen months.

These last three weeks have been very unsettling. So many rumours, and, although we have not believed it all, it has been rather upsetting. Having our plans altered again and again, we have felt it difficult to settle to letters. We keep hoping for more definite news.

Ronald to Ilkley and Cambridge

Chouts'un
4th August 1937

By the time this reaches you I expect you will have heard that Gwyneth and I have been separated again, she being still in Tsingtao with Rosemary, and I being back again in Chouts'un. We are all quite well and safe, and so are all our foreign friends, and so far as we can tell not likely to be in any immediate danger. The situation is a bad one, but very much worse indeed for our Chinese friends than it is for us, who, I think, are not likely to be affected at all, except for such things as the interference with our work, and temporary separations.

We hoped that the incident of the Marco Polo Bridge would be able to be regarded as the insignificant thing it was, and for a time it looked as though war would be avoided, but evidently the Chinese Government decided that the time has come for China to refuse to accept any further humiliation, and has been firm in its refusal to submit to any more encroachments on its sovereignty, with the result that, although formal war has not been declared, fighting on a large scale is going on at present in North China.

The situation began to affect us when it began to seem likely that the fighting would become generalised. We were of course in Tsingtao at the time, and the British Consul-General there, Mr Handley-Derry, after communications with General Han Fu-ch'u, the Governor of Shantung, advised all foreigners to leave stations in the interior and to evacuate to the coast.

The crisis came just about the time when we were due to return to Chouts'un. The decision was a difficult one, as I suppose it invariably is in similar circumstances. General Han had definitely said that he wanted all foreigners to leave the province at once. I suppose, in the event of fighting in Shantung, the presence of foreigners in the province would be an embarrassment to him. On the other hand, there did not seem to be any immediate likelihood of fighting in Shantung, and people were naturally not willing to give up their work and endure separations unnecessarily.

Eventually it was decided that Dr Ingle and Tom Allen and I should go back to our stations (Tsinan, Tsingchoufu and Chouts'un) and Gwyneth and I decided that it would be best for her and Rosemary to stay in Tsingtao. Mr and Mrs Phillips were planning in any case to stay in Tsingtao in August, Connie Allen is staying there in the same room as Gwyneth, and Dr and Mrs Flowers are there too.

The situation now is, so far as we here are able to tell, that the Japanese, after heavily bombing Tientsin, have occupied Tientsin and Peiping. Fighting is going on between Chinese and Japanese troops in the neighbourhood of Paotingfu, on the Peiping-Hankow railway line. Chinese central government troops are advancing northwards from Nanking to oppose the Jap troops. Jap aeroplanes have bombed Techow in Shantung, and have flown over Tsinan. The Japanese have evacuated most of their nationals from Tsinan and Shantung generally. There have been train-loads of them passing through Chouts'un on their way to Tsingtao, and a large number of Chinese too have left Tsinan for the safety of the smaller villages.

I had a letter from Dr Ingle this morning. He says that all their Chinese doctors there are under orders to take up Red Cross work in the event of an emergency, and it is very doubtful whether they can carry on the hospital work with only foreign staff. In an emergency, he expects that a few representative people (himself included) will stay, and he does not anticipate leaving unless the situation becomes frankly impossible. I think that it is very much less likely that Chouts'un will see any bombing or fighting, though some of the Chinese here are building themselves bomb-proof shelters.

I think Tsingtao is safe for foreigners. Our Consulate down there has made elaborate preparations for the protection of British subjects, and they have all had their instructions as to what to do in case of an emergency. All the signs, so far as we know them at present, seem to suggest that there will be no actual fighting in Shantung, and that the fighting will be confined to Hopei, round about Peiping, Tientsin and Paotingfu and that region.

Everybody here in Chouts'un is very calm. They are naturally anxious, but are keeping wonderfully calm in the circumstances. It is really amazing how restrained they are and what little anti-Japanese feeling there is. When we came back from Tsingtao the other day, we passed a train full of Japanese women and children and a few Japanese men, leaving the interior for the coast, but there was absolutely no demonstration against them, and no sign of hostile feeling, which I thought does the Chinese very great credit.

I am afraid that it may be some time before we hear from you again. The line south of Tientsin may not be open for some time, and I don't know how long it will take the postal authorities to find a way through with the mails. I understand that Dr Williamson was to cable home saying that all the members of our mission staff were well and safe, so perhaps you may have had some word of us from the Mission House.

On 29 July, during the occupation of Tientsin, the University in Tientsin, Nankai, had been heavily bombed. The following day Japanese artillery pounded the remains of the campus, and then set fire to the ruins. In Peiping, Tsing-hua University was systematically stripped by Japanese looters, and then its buildings converted for the use of the Japanese army, first as a barracks, then later as hospital, bar, brothel and stables. It appeared that the Japanese were taking revenge on the universities for their outspokenness against Japanese aggression.

Because the railway south of Tientsin and Peiping was blocked, many of those trying to escape from the fighting in the north travelled by sea to the Shantung ports of Chefoo and Tsingtao, flooding the province with refugees. At one point in August, the population of Tsinan mushroomed overnight from 300,000 to 600,000.

On 11 August, Chiang Kai-shek sent troops into Shanghai with the apparent intention of provoking Japan into war on a second front, where his own forces were concentrated and where the presence of a large foreign community would draw the attention of the Western powers. Three months of carnage and chaos followed. Bombing from the air, bombardment by shells from warships anchored in the river, artillery fire from city rooftops, hand to hand fighting in the surrounding villages together brought to Shanghai 'a panoply of almost indescribable destruction'[82]. Hundreds of thousands of Chinese sought refuge in the International Settlement, clogging the streets and sleeping wherever they could, in parks, factories, warehouses and office corridors.

Refugees pouring out of Chapei district, Shanghai
(photo courtesy of Imperial War Museum, London AP8146F)

Gwyneth to her mother

Tsingtao
12th August 1937

Still here, but still hopeful of getting home soon. The situation seems just about the same and likely to go on indefinitely, but after three weeks we have at last got some home mail through. There are still letters missing but it is said that lots have been destroyed, so we just hope ours are not among those. By the way, don't send anything out to us until things here are better, and tell the girls. If letters are going on being opened, it is a risk sending things.

I am so fed up being here. If it wasn't for Connie Allen it would be even worse. Since I last wrote all I have done has been look after Rosemary. I can't leave her alone in her pram at all – she is so energetic - and it is too hot to take her on the beach. It is so beastly being away

[82] *North China Herald*, 3 November 1937

from home and all our things are being ruined by mildew. However, we are lucky to have this house. It is really a nice house and marvellous position.

The news today is less hopeful – fighting in Shanghai now but we still hope for peace. I wish I had gone back with Ronald. I would have had at least these two weeks with him, but we had to act on seniors' advice and of course we were anxious not to involve Rosemary in any danger. Ronald says Chouts'un is as peaceful as ever, except that all the Chinese are very very anxious. It is really awful for them, they are so in the dark as to what is happening. I think they really carry on awfully bravely. I wish I could explain things to you, but it is not possible.

Oh, I do loathe being away! Sorry to sound so cross but we had looked forward to this month more than any. Logie and the two of us would have been on the compound and we had planned so much. I especially wanted to do things in the house. However, it is always the unexpected that happens in China and it might be a lot worse. The Chinese really are much worse off, poor souls.

Don't worry about us.

Gwyneth to Ronald's father and mother

Tsingtao
20th August 1937

I have just written a few lines to Will and Reg and am sending them to you with some snaps, which I have initialled. Do you mind forwarding them? We are awfully short of cash at the moment and even 25c stamps are precious! Don't be alarmed because we have money in the bank – it is just that for a few days we can't get it out. We are all in the same boat here and so we are economising till the bank starts to pay out, which it probably will do tomorrow. Meanwhile, we are keeping what cash we have in case of any emergency.

Things here are still about the same. We keep on hoping for something that will decide for us the problem of returning. Ronald and I are so anxious that I should go back as soon as possible. Logie is the only woman in Chouts'un and I should be company for her, even if not a great deal of help in hospital, but it still seems wisest to wait awhile and see if there is any trouble in the province. If I were alone it would be different.

Rosemary *(left)* with Elizabeth Allen

Connie Allen and I have got an old playpen and the babes have been in it this morning thrilled with themselves. I am longing to get home and have Rosemary's own made.

Gwyneth to Cambridge

Chouts'un
28th August 1937

Home again – isn't that nice? I arrived yesterday at 5.40 a.m. We decided that it was no use waiting indefinitely and so I planned to return Wednesday evening, but Tom Allen was travelling up on Thursday so I waited and came with him. Connie and Elizabeth are still in Tsingtao as they are expecting to start home for furlough on the first available boat. They are due to leave in October but owing to unsettled conditions, they have been advised to go now.

Will you please send this letter to Ilkley with half the snaps? I am sorry not to write separately again, but really these unsettled days make it so hard. We don't know how to settle to writing or what to say. We can't write about the political situation, though we don't know enough to say about it if we could. Lots of people have had letters destroyed or damaged. So far we seem to have received most of ours, later than usual.

Ronald seems well. It is good to be together again. Mr Harris is still here. He is a cheery sort and we are very happy to have him with us. Kao of course is overjoyed at being back. Many servants left because they were scared, and wanted to come back to their homes, but he stayed and so I am glad to bring him safely home. He is a good fellow and Wu seems to have done his best for R.

Ronald to Gwyneth's father and mother

Chouts'un
31st August 1937

At present the fighting is confined to Shanghai, and a few spots on the railway lines south of Tientsin and north of Peiping on the Suiyuan railway, and it looks as though Shantung is going to escape. Tsingtao is peaceful at present, and it really looks as though we are going to be able to carry on more or less normally.

We are affected in various ways. The hospital's main lines of communications for the supplies of drugs and dressings (to Shanghai and Tientsin) are temporarily broken and we only have a limited supply in hand, and it may be difficult to carry on if we are not able to get fresh supplies. Our two Chinese doctors have left us, one to join the army, and one to return to his home in the south. We shall have some difficulty in replacing our Chinese doctors at the moment, and in the meanwhile Flowers and I are carrying on.

Rosemary is a lovely little treasure.

Gwyneth to Ilkley and Cambridge

Chouts'un
11th September 1937

The whole staff, foreign and Chinese, is here now and things are more or less normal. Ronald is out most of the day now, but of course he comes over for odd minutes and for meals so I do just see something of him still!

I think the most important piece of news is that we now have no cause to shrink from displaying Rosemary, because we need no longer blushingly admit that at nine and a half months she is still toothless. Today I really have found one of her bottom ones right through, the other one and the two top ones look as if they will follow at any moment. I have only just discovered it, and apart from Ronald have not told anyone, so you are the first to hear!

In spite of this big piece of work on which she has been engaged this last day or two, Rosemary seems to have retained her very good spirits, walks round and round her cot laughing and talking to herself most of the day, and is taking quite kindly to the various alterations which we are making to her diet. I was very loth to wean her, because with the possibility of an evacuation the problem of feeding her might be a very difficult one, but we felt we ought not to delay any longer. So we now feed her up on goats' milk, groats, soup and such like things, which on the whole she finds not too bad, and I myself feel heaps better. If we do have to evacuate we shall just have to trust to being able to get milk wherever we go, but in case of emergencies, I have a big tin of Klim milk powder. You see except where there are foreigners it is almost impossible to get milk, as none of the Chinese take it. However, we hope the problem may not arise, and if it does we think we shall manage somehow.

Although we hope that there may be no need for us to leave here, we feel that in this troubled time it would be foolish not to make some preparations, so this week I have been busy thinking out the very minimum of things that I could manage with if it came to going away with just one case. You will guess that when I have thought of all the things I feel necessary for Rosemary in a north China winter, I find I could easily fill a trunk with her things alone. The case would have to include blankets, bed linen and pillow (I would manage without) also towels. I don't like to think of leaving any of her nice things behind, but we shall just have to do the best we can if the situation arises. As far as the other things are concerned I am just trying to get everything into decent order so that I know exactly where everything is, and can pack it all away quickly if it becomes necessary to go.

Please don't be alarmed by all this. We ourselves are not living in anything like the state of tension there was down at Tsingtao last month. Everything is so quiet and normal, and ordinary routine is going on just as usual, so that we really find it hard to realise the trouble going on in other parts of the country. We are only making these few preparations because in the circumstances it seems unwise not to have some plan in mind. I feel sure you will all understand.

Yesterday Kao was to have set off for home on the 9.50 train, but it was pouring with rain, so he waited and went on the 12.30. He has half an hour on the train and then about twelve miles of road. I am afraid with all this rain he had a very bad journey. I expect it would be too bad walking, and a rickshaw would be impossible. The only hope was a donkey, so I expect he hired one. Today is a festival so he was keen to get home for it, and he has not been since before his time in Tsingtao. Probably he is the only man in his village who has ever been so far and seen the sea, so he will be a man of importance.

Ronald to his father and mother

Chouts'un
12th September 1937

It is not easy to write and tell you much news. There is evidence that some of our letters are being opened and censored somewhere on their journey through China, so not much good can be done by trying to write much detailed news.

You will want to know how we ourselves are, and the answer is "Never better"! Gwyneth and Rosemary and I are all quite well and very happy and as contented as we can be in these troubled and unsettled circumstances.

The main fighting is going on in the region of Shanghai. The Japanese seem to be concentrating their efforts on blockade of the ports (with the exception of Tsingtao, which for some reason, perhaps the recent friendliness shown by Mayor Shen to the Japanese, is escaping the blockade), and on bombardments of ports on the South coast, Amoy, Foochow, Swatow and Canton. There is also fighting going on south of Tientsin on the Tientsin-Tsinan line (the Tsin-Pu line as it is called) and also on the Peiping - Kalgan line, where it is thought that the Japanese are hoping to force an entry into Shansi.

Today's paper says that the British Consul in Tientsin has advised the evacuation of British missionaries in Shansi. Several of them are still at places at the coast, having been unable to get back to their stations after their holiday. It may be that some of the others will evacuate to Shantung. Shantung is certainly very peaceful and quiet at present, and, so far as we can judge, looks as though it is going to remain so for some time.

Shantung's chief trouble at present is that the Yellow River has once again burst its banks, in the neighbourhood of our mission field quite near to Peichen, almost due north from Chouts'un, and is causing a great deal of distress. The flood waters are finding their way into the Hsiao Ching Ho, a small river which runs to the sea south of and parallel to the Huang Ho[83] without joining it, but the waters are only subsiding slowly on account of the unusually heavy August rains. The floods, in addition to the political situation, are making many of our people here very sad and depressed.[84]

---

[83] The Yellow River

[84] Flood victims were encamped along a seven mile stretch of the river, where BMS staff from Chouts'un were involved in relief work with them. Later, a refugee camp was established in Chouts'un itself.

Missionary work is not easy in these circumstances. All thoughts are of the political situation, and it is not easy for people to give much thought to other matters. In the hospital we have had the problem of whether to open the nursing school. Many government schools are not opening, and in the circumstances it becomes a serious responsibility to invite new girl students to travel often a considerable distance from their homes. Eventually we have decided to open the school and the term begins tomorrow and five new pupil nurses have already arrived.

The hospital is not over-busy at present. It is just the beginning of harvest-time, and all who can take a share in the work of harvesting do so, and haven't time to come and "kan bing", or 'have their diseases looked at', as they put it. And the unsettled state of the country makes them unwilling to spend more money than is necessary, especially on the women members of the family.

I am doing full-time hospital work now and am kept busy. Flowers has asked me to undertake the outpatients on Tuesdays, Thursday and Saturdays and I am responsible for inpatients admitted on those days. Flowers has also handed over the X-Ray work to me and at present I am doing my own developing of the negatives. Logie has asked me to give the course of lectures on genito-urinary surgery and it is rather heavy work[85] preparing the course for the first time. I am also giving an English lecture once a week, and conducting the men's ward evening service every week.

I told you, didn't I, that both our Chinese doctors had left us, Chang Jun-jen to join the Army Medical Corps and Meng, I think, because he was rather afraid to stay on. We got another Chinese doctor this week, a Dr Jen (pronounced Wren), a Moukden graduate of 1931, who has had post-graduate experience at Moukden, the Mackenzie Hospital Tientsin, and at the LMS[86] hospital at Tsangchow, so I think he will be very useful. He seems bright and energetic and I hope he will stay with us and do good work.

Glad you had the news of the China cable in the Baptist Times. Miss Thomas here thinks that if you send a request to the Mission House, they will inform you directly by post of the contents of any China cable re our health and safety. So perhaps it would be good to write them and ask them to put your name on the list of people to whom such information is sent.[87]

---

[85] Classes for nurses in training in Chouts'un were conducted in Chinese

[86] London Missionary Society

[87] Surprising that next of kin of serving missionaries had to *ask* to be put on the list!

I think I have been able to help to save a patient's life here this week. She came in in obstructed labour a week ago and needed a severe operation. She had been in labour some days and had been subjected to manipulations by not too clean hands before she came to us and her uterus was full of offensive pus, but with the help of a new drug that is at present being spoken of very highly[88], she is now making a very good recovery and is a very grateful patient.

Gwyneth to her mother

Chouts'un
25th September 1937

Mummy dear, yours of August 29 came this morning. Disgustingly slow, isn't it? And you didn't seem then to have received any letter of mine later than August 4. Several letters have been returned to the writers, torn in two, or otherwise damaged, so that there's a chance that some of ours may have got stopped that way during the trouble in Tientsin.

You will have heard long ago that I came back at the end of August, as soon as I had permission. I will be glad I came even if I have to go away again. Really those weeks in Tsingtao were hectic, we got nothing but rumours and were expecting to evacuate at any moment. Connie and I had no idea how we would manage without our husbands. We got on awfully well and had a lot of fun out of it really, but it was terribly upsetting. At one point we couldn't get a cent from the bank and all the tradesmen demanded cash, so we didn't know how to manage. All the troubles gradually righted themselves, but it was rather trying at the time.

Unfortunately when I came back, things were so bad that nearly all the shops were shut[89] and I had a job to get just the few things we really needed. We can't even get snaps printed, as they have run out of paper! So you will not have to expect any more of Rosemary for ages. I have taken several, but can't get them printed and we may not be able to buy any more films, I don't know.

---

[88] It is likely that Ronald was referring to one of the sulphonamide drugs. The first clinical trials using them to treat streptococcal puerperal infections had been undertaken in 1936, with dramatic results. See Colebrook, L P and Kenny, M 1936, *Treatment with Prontosil of Puerperal Infections*, Lancet, 2, 1319

[89] Most of the Japanese residents of Shantung, including those who operated shops and businesses in Tsingtao, were evacuated from the province during August and September. Many of the Chinese residents had also fled the town and hidden in the surrounding countryside in anticipation of the approach of the Japanese military.

All this trouble is very unsettling and I feel like sticking here whatever happens. If it weren't for Rosemary I would. I hate to think of leaving Ronald and it is no joke being separated at a time like this. If only home were nearer and I could come home it wouldn't be so bad.

Rosemary at present seems to have no needs, except mackintosh knickers. In emergencies they are an absolute necessity to save washing long trousers. Could you buy now as soon as possible and post at earliest? Two pairs of rubber knickers, size 2 I should think. Don't pay a lot for them – Woolworths is the sort – they all split quickly. Dray will say they are absolutely immoral, but tell her she doesn't know everything with snips and brass knobs.

I hope to hear about Ross on Wye in the next letter and about your meeting Auntie Nellie and Daisy. I want to hear all the latest about them both. I feel it very hard to write letters now because it seems mad not to comment on the situation and yet, apart from saying we are all well and happy, I can't say more. You get the news fairly accurately at home – wireless tells you it long before we know of it out here.

I am not keen on getting landed anywhere alone. I can't leave Rosemary a minute unless she is in a reliable cot. She is so full of noseyness, pokes her fingers into everything and pulls things on top of her in no time. She really is a sweet little thing. I know you would go crazy about her – we do! She is so bright and happy all day, just playing by herself. She claps her hands now and sits for ages just doing that and looking so thrilled every time she makes a good smack! She loves all my frocks with flowery patterns and tries to pick the flowers off me! Also grabs hold of buttons in a greedy manner and is an expert at snatching my specs off.

I don't think I ever mentioned our exam results, did I? Of course I was amazed at them, though I honestly felt I deserved all the marks I got[90]. I really did slog and so did Ronald. Very few wives bother to take the 2nd exam and some don't even take the first and I managed it in under the two years and had a baby and no amah.[91] So we feel we really have cause for a tiny little spot of pride, but we will get our fall no doubt. In fact I get it nearly every time I try to speak Chinese, but I do really like trying.

---

[90] Ronald's overall average for the 2nd Year language exam was 94.5% and Gwyneth's 89.8%, including both written and oral exams. Gwyneth scored particularly well in the paper on character writing and analysis.

[91] amah = nannie

Ronald to Ilkley and Cambridge

Chouts'un
Thursday 30th September 1937

We are all still in Chouts'un. Rosemary ten months old today, and celebrating by squeaking loudly for joy all day in her fine new playpen. Did Gwyneth tell you that we were getting a carpenter from one of the workshops on the street to make her a playpen? Gwyneth showed him a picture of one in one of her treasure-cot books, and he has produced a splendid copy, beautifully smooth and with rounded corners, floor boards raised from the ground out of the draughts – and Rosemary is delighted with it.

Our latest news is that the Japanese line at present is just to the south of Tsangchow[92]. The next important spot south of Tsangchow is Techow, which is just within the Shantung border. We have heard that in view of their approach to Shantung, the Japanese have made overtures to Han Fu-ch'u, the Governor of Shantung, offering him a post in an autonomous federation of the five northern provinces (Shantung, Shansi, Hopei, Chahar and Suiyuan), in return for his allowing them to come peaceably into the province and not putting up any resistance. Today's paper says that Han has declared that he is absolutely following the directions of the Nanking Government[93]. If he is sincere in that declaration, hopes of a peaceful settlement as far as Shantung is concerned are remote and we may expect the Japs to continue their advance down the Tsin-Pu line towards Tsinan.

We had a meeting of the Shantung Advisory Council at Chouts'un on Monday, and the council recommended that women and children should evacuate to Tsingtao in the event of there being generalised hostilities in the province. It is thought that Tsingtao is likely to be a safe place for as long as any other place in the province, because of the extensive Jap interests there, and there are British warships in the harbour there ready to take off British inhabitants in case Tsingtao itself should become unsafe. So if the Japs advance beyond Techow I think that Gwyneth and Rosemary and Mrs. Flowers and the other ladies from Chouts'un will go down to Tsingtao again. It is very fortunate that there are Miss Manger's two houses down there, isn't it?

---

[92] About 100 miles north of Chouts'un

[93] i.e will resist the Japanese overtures and take up arms against them if they advance into Shantung.

As for the rest of us, Flowers, Miss Logan and self, I understand that Mrs Ingle had an interview with CEW[94] at Furnival Street the other day, in which he said that he expected every BMS doctor or nurse would stand by their hospital, and he hoped that there would be no 'scuttling'! So that is where we get off!

It seems to be obviously the best policy to stand by and carry on with our ordinary work as long as we can. It may become difficult for us to do so if our nurses have to leave us, as they may have to do if the war becomes nearer. It would be a big responsibility for us to undertake to look after so many young girl nurses if there was a possibility of fighting and troop movements in the neighbourhood, and, if the nurses go, our work would necessarily be cut down very considerably, but the thing to do seems to stick here as long as we think we can be of any service to the neighbourhood.

It looks as though we have to look forward to a change in the local government of the province in the not very distant future – much the same sort of change that came over Moukden five years ago[95] – and it remains to be seen whether the change-over will take place peaceably or not. In any case it seems as though it is going to raise very big problems for the future of the BMS in China.

I am afraid all this is very pessimistic. It is certainly the worst that I have told you and it may turn out to be very much better than this after all.

Meanwhile, everything is very peaceful here in Chouts'un. If it were not for the news in the papers, and the interest that people show in the papers, it would be hard to guess that there was a war in progress. The nursing school here is going on with its classes, and the hospital work is going on as usual. We are running short of some drugs and aren't able to replace them because of the interrupted communications, but outwardly everything is calm and peaceful, and our Chinese colleagues are being wonderfully patient and forbearing and brave. We all pray that this war may be speedily brought to an end, and I know that that is your prayer too.

---

[94] Rev C E Wilson, member of BMS London staff responsible for affairs in China at that time.

[95] Referring to the possibility that Shantung might be taken over as a puppet state by the Japanese, as Manchuria was in 1931.

Ronald to Will

Chouts'un
4th October 1937

Although the posts have been irregular, letters from you have been coming with a regularity that makes me very ashamed. I have both letters from you for every week up to Tuesday 7th September. We do thank you for them, Will, even though you must think me ungrateful often. I know what it must mean to you to spend so much time regularly every week writing such long and newsy and interesting letters. Thank you for all the news cuttings too which are always interesting, especially the photos, like the recent ones of changes in City Square.

We have had a Japanese report in today's paper claiming that the Japs have forced their way through the Yen Men Kuan pass north of Taichow in Shansi and have actually occupied Taichow. Our missionaries who were in Taichow had all left for Taiyuan previously, but it is not a difficult task for the Japs to get from Taichow to Taiyuan and we are waiting anxiously for confirmation of this news and for news of our Shansi friends[96].

This afternoon, too, we have had our first glimpse of the Jap planes. Two came over at about 3 p.m. flying at a great height towards Tsinan following the Kiao-Tsi (Tsingtao-Tsinan) railway. They returned about an hour later and we are wondering whether they dropped any bombs in Tsinan or were just on the lookout. They have been flying over a good many parts of Shantung during the last few days, evidently looking out for troop movements, but not dropping many bombs. We had a buzzer in the town warning us of the arrival and we had a rehearsal of getting our women patients downstairs in case there should be any bombs.

We were very interested to hear of Geoffrey's going to school. We can guess how proud you are of him. Well done Yorks[97]! How did they get on in the Challenge match against Middlesex and against the rest of England? Tell Geoffrey we love to see his drawings and we think he does them very well indeed.

The enclosed is not a very big present for your birthday, Will, but I hope the stamps may include some you haven't already got.

---

[96] During the Japanese occupation of Shansi which followed, the local population, including many of the Chinese church members, suffered terribly at the hands of the occupying forces.
[97] Referring to the County cricket again.

Gwyneth to Ilkley and Cambridge

Chouts'un
16th October 1937

It really seems now as if we are going to the coast. It will need to be within the next two or three days, as it seems inevitable that Tsinan must become involved very soon. We all wish something might happen to prevent trouble but it is difficult to feel really hopeful. We try to carry on normally but you can't plan ahead at all and can't really undertake new work lest it should need to be dropped.

I am now fairly ready to go. Could pack and be off at a few hours notice. My only fear is that it may not be possible to take anything except small luggage and without the cot and pram Rosemary is going to be rather a problem. But we are not worrying. We feel sure things will clear and that we shall manage somehow if need arises.

We were very grateful to Kao for staying on in Tsingtao with me and Rosemary. It was such a help, and Wu did his bit here. I forget if I told you that the other Chouts'un boys all got scared and left Tsingtao, so we felt Kao did jolly well to stay on alone.

And now today he has shown again his faithfulness to us. Last weekend we decided to explain to the boys how we were placed and what our plans were. We felt it was up to us to let them know as clearly as possible, so we told them that if fighting came here, Rosemary and I would try to get away to Tsingtao if that were possible, and that Ronald intended to stay on while there was any work he could do here. Then we had decided that if Kao would come with me, it would not only save Ronald leaving to act as escort on the train, but would also save trying to get a local servant, who now are not only difficult to get, but if obtainable are often not trained and insist on exorbitant wages. Also Ronald would feel happier if he knew I had Kao there. There are so many problems out here that do not occur at home, in which a man servant is really a necessity and to have one we know is reliable would mean a terrific lot to me if I were away without Ronald.

So we decided to put it to Kao. We told him that if he came I would do my best to see that he came to no harm, but could guarantee nothing in the way of personal safety and that if there was fighting there I might be evacuated on a ship and he would be left, but if that happened I would see he had sufficient cash to get back here. We told him we should not think worse of him if he decided he would like to stay here and left him to think it over and today he has said he will come with me if I need to go. We feel very glad, although we still hope the necessity may not arise. I have written at length about this because I think you will be glad to hear and to understand the situation.

I am glad the last snaps got through safely. Rosemary seems to change every day and we long to snap her a hundred times a day. I am always wishing we had television so you could see her in her play pen – she plays so happily there in the sunshine. Oh, I do hope I don't need to take her away. At Tsingtao it is not suitable leaving her in the garden unattended at all, and that means I need to sit and watch her all the time, which would spoil her for playing by herself.

You all sound so busy starting on the winter session – I almost envy you being able to settle down to it. This atmosphere is so unsettling, we can only try and do our best as each day comes and we understand that our Chinese friends, whatever they do or say, always have the war in their minds. It is awfully hard for the nurses. Some are nearly through their training and now they may be unable to finish. Already several have gone home and others are talking of going to base hospitals[98] and so on. I don't see how we can try to keep them if they feel they want to get home. Some of them are very young and naturally their parents are anxious to have them with them.

I wonder if you will see anything of Tom and Connie Allen while they are home. I wish they were here. Apart from Elizabeth who is six months older than Rosemary, I have not seen any foreign baby at all since Rosemary was born and I do so wish I had another mother with whom to compare notes. Connie and I got on famously and, Elizabeth being so near in age to Rosemary, Connie hadn't forgotten what she was like at Rosemary's age.

Tom and Connie Allen with Elizabeth

Rosemary's little Chinese coat is made and it is so pretty, I wish you could see it. She is very pleased with the bright red and it is lovely and cosy for her. Today there is a bit of wind

[98] hospitals situated at the Chinese armies' front line.

and I begin to feel in need of my woollies and tonight we wished we had got a fire we could light. The midday sun is still hot, but the nights are very cold. I am getting a Chinese gown made for myself. The cotton wool lining is so light and cosy and really the only way of keeping warm in rooms that aren't well heated. I shall be so glad of it if we go to Tsingtao where there is no real heating arrangement. The hospital is warm, but men who work in the country all have to wear padded garments as there are usually no fires.

You ask about the tension when I was at Tsingtao, mother. Well, it really was rather trying, but Connie and I kept each other cheery and managed to see the funny side of things which helped considerably. There were some days when such startling developments were taking place elsewhere, when everyone, foreign and Chinese, came in with a new rumour or alarm and we all began to feel anything might happen. If we go again it may be worse, for the trouble is nearer home and we shall be really anxious about the safety of our loved ones.

Before I forget, if there is fighting here, and we go to Tsingtao I expect the BMS will get a cable and you will hear. If so, if you write to me the address will be again 14 Huang Hai Road, Iltis Huk, Tsingtao. It is still uncertain as to whether I go to 14 or 16, but as both are BMS houses either will find me. There are a number of complications which I would rather not explain in a letter and it is difficult deciding which house to go to.

Today, Sunday, we have lit a fire in the sitting room and it is such a comfort. I bathed and fed Rosemary by it tonight, her room seemed so chilly.

Ronald to Ilkley and Cambridge

Chouts'un
23rd October 1937

When I wrote last, the Japs were advancing southwards on from Techow towards Tsinan[99], and it seemed as though it would not be long before they had managed to cross the Yellow River, and reach Tsinan. Actually they reached a post about nineteen miles north of the Yellow River, and then, for some reason which at present remains a mystery, they either halted or turned back, and there seems to be a lull in the fighting. Whether it is because the troops have been called away to assist in the attack on Honan and Shansi, or whether it is only a temporary lull

[99] Techow to Tsinan = approximately 80 miles

and will be followed by renewed fighting, we don't know. Most of our people here are hoping that it means that Shantung is going to escape further molestation this time.

There was an anxious time here about a week ago, when it was thought that the Japs were about to occupy Tsinan. It has meant quite a lot to our staff here. Several of them come from long distances away, some from Tsinan itself and some from places further away to the south. If Tsinan had been occupied it would have meant that they would have found it very difficult to have got back to their homes, and so some of them have already left us so as to reach their homes before communications were cut, and these have included our Chinese doctor, who came to us so recently, and our dispenser, who came to us last July.

If the Jap advance is continued, I think it is almost certain that the majority of our nurses will leave us, some because they will want to get back to their homes, some because they will want to get to the south, so as to assist in government hospitals which are taking in the wounded in Nanking and other places. Today a letter has reached us from Nanking asking for volunteers from our graduate nurses and final year nursing students to go to Nanking, where the hospitals are all heavily over-worked, and it may be that three or four may feel that their place is in Nanking.

We are hoping that there may be no further advances in Shantung, and that the rest of our staff may feel able to stay here and help to carry on the work of the hospital, but in these circumstances, each one has to decide what he feels to be his own duty, and we cannot hinder anyone who feels that his duty is elsewhere. It is a matter of waiting from day to day. If it should happen that the majority of our staff should have to leave us, I think we should try to carry on with what help we could secure locally. It would be difficult to do satisfactory work, but it would be the best that could be done.

In the meantime, we still have twenty one of the nursing staff remaining. We have about fifty patients in hospital, and another six came in today from my outpatients. We are much better off than they are at Cheeloo where almost the whole of their Chinese nursing and medical staff have left them, and a good many of their foreign staff.

In the absence of our Chinese doctor, Flowers and I are carrying on ourselves. It makes quite a busy week for me. Operations on Tuesdays, Thursdays and Saturdays, and outpatients on those days too, writing up notes on the cases admitted on those days, surgery lecture on Mondays, ward service on Wednesdays, English lecture on Fridays, ward rounds and treatments and injections on those days too, and any x-rays that have to be taken. We do about five or six x-ray photographs each week, and I develop them myself. Results not quite so good as yet as Daddy produces with his camera, but I am improving!

No more news at present – except that Rosemary grows lovelier every day!

Ronald to his father and mother

Chouts'un
6th November 1937

I have longed very much this week to be able to talk things over with you and to be able to have your advice and judgment. I wish I could write about it, but with the present uncertainty of the post I don't think it would be right to do so – perhaps some day we will be able to tell you.

Our remaining graduate nurses have now left us, including Mr Ma, our most senior nurse, who had recently been appointed to the post of superintendent of our nursing school, the new government regulations requiring that the post should be occupied by a Chinese in government registered schools. He and others have gone in response to appeals from the government. The latest news from Shansi is not reassuring, and it seems as though Taiyuan may soon fall. There are still a number of our folk there, and I think it seems as though they are intending to stay in spite of the fighting.

We are not seeing any of the wounded here at Chouts'un as they are all being sent directly to base hospitals further south or further inland, but we are getting some of the flood refugees. I think your papers will have mentioned that the Yellow River again broke its banks this summer, and it is now pouring through a breach more than 1½ miles long, and has flooded countries with a total population of about 200,000 people, and has made about 80,000 people destitute. Plans are just being made for 500 of the destitute to be housed in our mission compounds at Peichen and at the west side of Chouts'un, where Mr Harris lives. They are hoping to provide some work for them, and also some classes, educational and evangelistic.

I am still getting quite a good deal of surgical experience. I operated on a woman for cancer of the breast this week, and she is doing very well so far, and on a man for gastric ulcer last week, and he is doing very well too.

On 8th November, Japanese troops entered the north gate of Taiyuan, and ordered the city to surrender. At midday, Japanese planes dropped notices warning all foreigners to evacuate before 7 o'clock the next day. Any who remained would be treated as combatants. The city fell on 9th November, the Chinese defendants fighting desperately to the last.

Meanwhile in Shanghai, the Japanese had kept up a fierce onslaught since August and the city fell three days after Taiyuan. Outside the International Settlement, all was in ruins and the streets were clogged with rotting corpses. In Shanghai itself, 50,000 Chinese were killed during the fighting and, by the end of 1937, the corpses of more than 101,000 others, who had died of disease, starvation or exposure, had been picked up off the streets. In the small towns and villages surrounding Shanghai, heavy and indiscriminate bombing of helpless civilians had caused widespread havoc and dismay.[100]

With Shanghai under their control, the Japanese turned north towards Nanking, where Chiang Kai-shek and his government were based. Advocating resistance, Chiang himself flew out of the danger zone, transferring the seat of government to Hankow. At the same time, the Japanese were beginning a fresh advance in North China. The first aerial attack on Tsinan occurred on 14th November. Although the city itself was spared, the aerodrome and other outlying military establishments were set on fire.

All over China, the population was on the move. Wherever they could, whole factories, hospitals and educational establishments moved to the remote west and north west, in conformity with the scorched earth policy of Chiang and his government. The universities and colleges established new campuses in the interior or in Hong Kong. One group of 257 students and 11 professors trekked over a thousand miles, mostly on foot, to their new campus in the west.[101]

Millions of ordinary people simply fled before the advancing armies, hauling what they could of their possessions, and dragging, wheeling or carrying the less able family members. H R Williamson describes the scenes on the railways, 'Trains, as long as they continued to run, were crowded to bursting point. The roofs of carriages were thick with people, bundles, carrying poles, barrows, even goats and sheep. The platforms and steps of the coaches were packed with passengers and baggage, some of the more venturesome perched precariously on the

[100] See Timperley, H J, *Japanese Terror in China*, Books for Libraries Press, 1938

[101] See Eastman, L et al, *The Nationalist Era in China 1927-49*, Cambridge 1991

buffers, hanging on at the sides by the window frames, or even suspending themselves underneath the carriages.'[102] *It is estimated that up to 90 million Chinese became refugees over the period of the whole war. In Shantung itself, between 30 and 70% of the total population were homeless at any one time.*

Ronald to Ilkley and Cambridge

Chouts'un
Sunday 14th November 1937

For many things I wish you all could be here in China today as I write this. I am writing at 3.00 p.m. on Sunday afternoon. The sky is a glorious deep blue without a cloud, the sun is shining bright and warm, quite warm enough to sit outside without overcoats, the leaves are glorious colours, and everything seems calm. The flies are flying lazily about in the garden, and from the study window as I look out I can see roses in bloom (perhaps you can equal that in Ilkley and Cambridge). Rosemary is upstairs on the outside veranda in her play pen, playing very happily with the tin of Johnson's baby powder that she loves so much, and chattering away saying all sorts of things that perhaps Elizabeth Allen could understand if she were here, but which we certainly can't, unless they mean "I am quite content and happy out here, thank you, Mummy".

It all makes it very difficult to believe that a war is being carried on so near at hand and affecting so many people in such a terrible way. As I began this letter we heard the "ching pao!", the warning buzzer from the electricity works to let us know that aeroplanes were close at hand. That was the second time we had heard them this morning. One sounded just as we were leaving church and we had to wait in the churchyard until the "all clear" buzzer sounded, as the orders are that people are not to move about in the streets while planes are in the offing. But we saw no sign of the planes either time. Evidently we were not to be favoured with a visit this time.

Our Chinese friends are very downcast at the recent news. The Japanese army seems to be successful on all fronts of this big battlefield. During this week both Shanghai and Taiyuan have fallen and once again, after a long period of inactivity, the Japs are advancing again along the Tsin-Pu line, and it seems as though Tsinan is endangered again.

---

[102] H R Williamson, *British Baptists in China*, Carey Kingsgate Press, 1957

Today's papers from Tientsin have just brought us the fullest reports we have so far received of the fall of Taiyuan. It affected us very deeply to think of this fine old city that we had seen so recently, being destroyed by shells and bombs, and its fine old gates being blown up to admit a conquering army. We understand that there are eight of our English Baptist missionaries still in Taiyuan. The paper says that they are all safe at present, so we are relieved about them, and hope that they will not have any further cause for anxiety now, at least so far as their personal safety is concerned.

Our papers during the last few days have had very sad stories to tell of the sufferings of the wounded in Shansi. Medical assistance is inadequate, and supplies almost non-existent, and the wounded have in many cases had to be left untended for several days while being transported to base hospitals, and have had to travel in open trucks, often standing up and without overcoats through the cold Shansi winter nights. The death-rate among the wounded who have been treated at the base hospitals has been high, 20-30%, a good many of the deaths being due to tetanus which could be prevented if supplies of anti-tetanus were available.

So far we have been in a kind of backwater as far as the war is concerned. But today there has been a change in the situation. We heard that the Japanese troops have left the Tsin-Pu railway line and are advancing southwards towards the Yellow River. On the east side they have reached as far as Wutingfu and there has been fighting there, and we took in our first wounded soldier today, a Chinese with a gunshot wound of the chest, who was shot in the fighting at Wutingfu.

We can only guess what the plans of the troops are now, and whether they will try to cross the Yellow River near Wuting, or whether they will now work westwards along the north bank of the river towards Tsinan. The next few days will show, and by the time this reaches you, you may know all that has happened.

So far as Gwyneth and Rosemary are concerned, it is a comfort to know that the houses in Tsingtao are still available if they should need to leave here. There are no signs that the Kiao-tsi railway is going to be interfered with, or that they would not be able to evacuate down to Tsingtao if need arose.

I know you will understand from what I have said what the feelings of our Chinese colleagues must be, and will remember them in your prayers. One of the things that has struck me most about their attitude all through the fighting has been their freedom from hatred and resentment, and I can't help admiring them very much for it. Their whole attitude seems to have been one of sorrow because their country has been forced into this war, and that men should resort to such means to secure their ends, but they seem to harbour scarcely any feelings of deep hatred or anger or resentment against their enemies.

The flood conditions in Northern Shantung are worse than I said in my last letter. Dr Williamson says that he thinks that this is the worst flood in the last fifty years and that about two million people are affected. Mr Harris is expecting the first crowd of refugees to arrive in Chouts'un during this week, and perhaps we may have some extra work in looking after the health of the members of the camp.

During the last two or three weeks we seem to have had a large number of patients admitted to hospital for treatment of injuries they have received in family quarrels! I can think of at least nine or ten whom we have taken in during the last two or three weeks – cut scalps, and nasty bites and broken legs. Perhaps the reason is that their anxiety about their country makes them a bit more short-tempered with their friends!

Gwyneth to Ilkley

Chouts'un
14th November 1937

Things here are developing so rapidly that we don't know what is happening but we guess it won't be many days before we hear of the fall of Tsinan, and after that? We are deciding to stay on at present, Rosemary and I. It is doubtful if Tsingtao would be safer and it makes complications if we divide the family. Our big anxiety is Rosemary's food. We could manage on local products, but if the goats are commandeered and communication cut, we may find it hard to get milk.

But we aren't over-worried. The nurses all plan to leave today, so they will have to rearrange in the hospital. I don't suppose I will do much, because of not being able to leave Rosemary.

Wu is probably having his family here for a few weeks as there is no man at his home and there are so many soldiers about now. Kao has his father and a brother at home and anyway his home is rather off the main roads and less likely to be in for trouble. Wu's people will all need to share his room, as there is no other and it is about the size of perhaps half the dining room at home! But they will not object, that is better than what many have.

There are thousands of war refugees now, as well as flood ones and the conditions are appalling. We feel almost ashamed of our comforts and yet I really do not believe that we could survive as the

Chinese. We could certainly do with less than we have got in some ways, but I am sure we would die of pneumonia if we lived in their conditions a couple of days.

Ronald to his father and mother

Chouts'un
29th November 1937

I am hoping that the post office authorities will be kind and that this letter will reach you in time to wish you, from us all, a very happy time this Christmas. We long more than ever to be with you this Christmas. The war here hasn't brought us any real hardships, but I know you will understand how much it would mean to us to be able to join with you round the fireside in an atmosphere free from anxiety and especially in the peaceful and happy atmosphere of our home at Christmastime.

Don't think from the above that we are feeling anxious here. We are not anxious, but it is difficult to feel really settled in the circumstances. Flowers was saying to me last night that he finds it very difficult to give his people at home a true idea of how we are being affected by the present circumstances and that is quite true. Each time we write there seems to be some big change in the circumstances, and sometimes it is difficult even to guess at what may be going to happen next.

During the last week we have had big changes in hospital. You will remember that all our graduate nurses had already left us to go to Nanking in response to government appeals. We were left with eighteen nurses, including six probationers. Last week an appeal came for ten of these remaining nurses to go to Nanking, and one day last week they all went, and on their going, three of the others went home too, so we were left with only five nurses, of whom four were probationers.

To make things much more difficult, our dispenser left us too, and now we no longer have Mr Ma our former dispenser to fall back on, so Dr Flowers (who had some dispensing experience before he qualified) had to do the dispensary work in addition to his other duties, and we had to call in such people as were willing to come to help in the wards. We hadn't any skilled help, and the responsible work like sterilising dressings, and taking charge of the theatre, and so, on meant a good deal of extra work for those in charge. I tried to take my share by being responsible for the dressings of patients in the wards. Most of our patients are surgical cases at present, and it was a good morning's work to get round and see that all the dressings were changed satisfactorily, and in the evening some of them had to be done again.

Miss Logan came in for a big proportion of the extra work. She had to supervise the work of the theatre and wards, and in addition had to take charge of the midwifery work, which has been quite heavy lately, as we have had an influx of people who have come to Chouts'un from places further north, in an attempt to find a peaceful place for the arrival of the baby.

To our surprise, two days ago our ten nurses who had left all returned. When they got to Nanking they found that in the meantime, as you will know, most of the government offices and hospitals had been transferred to Hankow and other places, and Nanking itself was in a state of confusion. Not being able to get transport up to Hankow, back they came to Chouts'un. But today four have set off for Hankow by rail, and the remainder, for the time at any rate, are staying on here. As things are so unsettled, we have had to give up our nursing school classes, and are keeping on our nurses not as pupils, but as assistants, until such time as we are able to open the school again. It may be that within a few days the nurses may want to be off again.

There is a temporary lull on the Tsin-Pu line, though Tsinan is coming in for some shelling from the north bank of the Yellow River. It may be that the Japs are at present concentrating on the attack on Nanking. and after that falls they may return to the attack on Tsinan. For the present, things are quieter here and, but for the absence of our dispenser, not excessively busy in hospital.

Gwyneth to Ilkley

Chouts'un
7th December 1937

There really is very little to report this end. The only exciting thing has been the arrival of home mail. We appreciate letters even more than usual now that we are so cut off. We are very impressed by Geoffrey's letters. He seems to be making such rapid strides. We were also very interested in reading all about his lovely bonfire and the fireworks. As for Margaret[103], we are awfully amused to hear how efficient she is in the house and would love to see her helping, I

[103]Three year old daughter of Reg and Phyllis

sympathise with her in her desire to take off the cloth without bothering about the crumbs, I have always thought that rather a bother!

I suppose when you get this the Christmas festivities will be over. We do long to hear all about them and shall be thinking of you all on the days, when we think you will be together. We already talk about Christmas 1941[104], and think we shall try to have two Christmases, one each in Ilkley and Cambridge. The other evening we were talking over supper of the things we would specially like to taste, such things as Father's fried fish and potatoes and Mother's apple pastie. We did not find thinking about them was quite up to tasting them!

We still have made no preparation for Christmas. We feel that with so much poverty, even worse than normal, and so much suffering, we cannot go in for anything very much in the way of extra food, even if we are able to get it. We hear that there are to be a few freight trains. We must try to get enough for a pudding, but we are not going to do much else. The foreigners have decided not to give each other any presents, the idea being to give the money we should have spent on it to refugees of war or flood. I think it is a good idea to give money like that, but I feel rather that we could buy tiny gifts off the street for each other and that would just help to give us the feeling of Christmas and still make a contribution to the refugee funds.

It will seem a strange Christmas, but I know we shall be happy as long as we are together, and it seems likely that we shall be. The policy of the mission seems to have changed and we do not seem likely to evacuate. For one thing it seems that no other place is any more likely to be safe than this. Also, the trains now are very few, very crowded, and take hours and hours, and you may quite possibly be told half way that the train is wanted for troops so you must turn out, and that might mean a long wait on a station, perhaps a couple of days.

I see very little of anyone these days except at our foreign services. Logie is very busy, and so are Su and Miss Thomas. I find plenty to do too, though I am not as busy as they are. I seem to spend a lot of time trying to prepare my ward service, and then it is rather disheartening when I get there and there is no one awake at all, except a baby who screams all the time I hold forth to a ward of sleeping patients! The men seem always to have some who are up and take an interest in things, but the women seem to get tired out and are nearly always asleep or at any rate have their eyes shut. At least I feel consoled by the fact that no one notices my mistakes.

---

[104] When Ronald and Gwyneth expected to be in England on furlough.

Today, December 8, Rosemary took two steps all alone! Great thrills of course, on her part as well as ours!

Gwyneth to Ronald's father and mother

Chouts'un
12th December 1937

Just a tiny wee note to go in with the typed ones, to say thank you very, very much for your very generous gift to us. We thought the things Dr King is bringing were for Christmas! Just now you certainly couldn't give us anything more useful. We don't want to add to our possessions here more than necessary and anyway mails are uncertain. It is lovely to feel we have got some money being saved at home too and also to have some to add to Rosemary's own account. We hope to save some of it towards her education, that will be an expensive item later on.

You will understand what a wonderful little joy and comfort she is to us in these troubled times, but I hope you don't get tired of me writing about her. We just feel she is such a lovely little girl, we know you would love her. We say again and again, 'oh, if only they could see her at home' and as you can't then we try to share her as much as we can in our letters. Especially during the days when we are being more than usually upset, Rosemary's bright ways cheer and comfort us and we long for her to grow up to be a bright, loving, generous girl.

Don't worry too much. We do find things difficult, but we are together and having each other and Rosemary is such a joy. You will understand.

Nanking was taken by Japanese troops on 13th December. Word of the fury of this assault, and the atrocities that took place in the six weeks that followed, spread quickly around China and, indeed, around the civilized world. The 'rape of Nanking' has become synonymous with wanton cruelty, rape and torture. On the first day, one Japanese division alone killed more than 24,000 prisoners of war and fleeing soldiers. The total death toll has been put at more than 300,000. [105]

In Shantung, Chiang Kai-shek had ordered the Mayor of Tsingtao to destroy all Japanese property in the city. The Mayor had procrastinated, reluctant to take an action that might later cause drastic

[105] See Chang, Iris, *The Rape of Nanking*, Penguin 1986 and Fenby, Jonathan, *Generalissimo*, The Free Press 2003, p306-7

retaliation on the part of the Japanese. On 20th December, at Chiang's insistence, the Japanese cotton mills in Tsingtao were blown up and destroyed. Japanese shops and businesses were looted, and all Chinese troops withdrawn from the city.

Meanwhile, General Han Fu-ch'u, Governor of Shantung, had escaped southwards, taking with him large sums of cash from the provincial treasury. Before making his escape, with his troops close on his heels, Han had blown up the railway bridge at Weihsien, and effectively immobilised the only remaining Chinese forces in the area.

Shantung province was now undefended.

Ronald to Ilkley and Cambridge

Chouts'un
22nd December 1937

I want to get off a note to you in the dinner-hour today if I can. The days just fly by and during the last two or three weeks we seem to have been specially busy. When Sunday came round I was hoping to be able to begin my letter in the afternoon, but at two o'clock a message came from the railway station asking if we could send along to attend to some soldiers who had been injured in an explosion not far away, and there was no time for letter-writing after that.

I went along to the station with two of our nurses, and found seven men lying in a covered railway truck. One had been killed by the force of the explosion, and of the others, two had limbs shattered, two had eyes and hands injured, and the others were not severely hurt. We dressed their wounds and brought the four most severely injured back to hospital, and spent the rest of the evening trying to clean them up. Poor things, it was a sad business. Two of them died in the night, and of the other two, one I am afraid will be quite blind and the other has one eye destroyed. Poor things. It is terrible, and dreadfully cold weather for all wounded and homeless.

We are all well and happy here, as happy as can be in the circumstances. The news of the fall of Nanking will be old to you by the time this reaches you. We are wondering now what course the hostilities will take from now on. We have had news today of the destruction of Japanese property in Tsingtao, which I am afraid can only do harm.

I am afraid Christmas will be a quiet one here this year. Our Chinese friends will not feel like celebrating very joyfully. There are now a lot of the Yellow River flood refugees (about 250) in Chouts'un, and the church here is doing its best to provide for them and to give them some little extra treat at Christmas, and for the very poor in Chouts'un itself too – not very easy when the church members themselves are only poor.

Gwyneth to Ilkley and Cambridge

Chouts'un
29th December 1937

Just a tiny note to let you know we are all well and safe. I don't know what you will have heard on the wireless about this part of the world, but anyway, the Japanese troops took over on Christmas night and we are all, all right. So don't worry. Rosemary is lovely. Has been such a comfort. She has had a cold in her nose these last two days, but it doesn't seem to have damped her spirits in any way, and she has been as cheerful as could be all the time. W and K have been bricks. You will understand if I don't write any more about it at present – I hope this gets through to you safely.

Dr King went through on December 23[106]. We didn't know till too late to see him (he was on about the last train but one, so he only just got back), but we got our parcels and opened them on Christmas Day. It was lovely having them. Ronald is delighted with his lovely warm sweater, Mother, and his aertex shirt from Cambridge. Rosemary will look absolutely adorable in the wee knitted frock from Ilkley. It is such a dainty pattern and so beautifully made. The other things from Cambridge were all very welcome – I will be writing later.

We think you probably know more about our other colleagues than we do. We are anxious for news of Drs Ingle and King and Dr Williamson and Mr Phillips, but we shall get it in time and we have all had wonderful protection. Everyone is safe and well, which is like a miracle. Mr Harris is just going to take this to the PO for me. It will go by runner if it goes at all as there are no trains now, but don't worry and please try to be patient about letters, because it will be slow going for some weeks.

I think later on, I will write a book of the experiences Rosemary had in her first thirteen months! Will you share this letter all round, please. We all three send lots of love, and thanks for all your loving thoughts and prayers.

---

[106] Passing through Chouts'un on return to Tsinan from furlough, and bringing with him parcels for Ronald and Gwyneth from friends and family in England.

Gwyneth to Cambridge and Ilkley

(letter, uncharacteristically, has no date or sending address but was from Chouts'un, about 3rd Janary1938, received in Ilkley 31st January)

For over a week there have been no trains at all. No contact with the outside world. We used to set our clocks by the station and hearing the trains go up and down was almost like company, but now the station is smashed up and goodness knows when it will be repaired. Nothing from Tsinan or Tsingtao, so we just hope all our friends are safe.

For months we had known that this province would eventually be drawn into the front line and had had several alarms, when we really felt something must happen but, actually, when it did happen we were not at all expecting it. We were just planning our Christmas, packing hospital patients' presents etc, and then on the day before, a lovely bright day, the aeroplanes suddenly roared up – no alarm this time – and, before we realised it almost, the bombs were dropping.

Rosemary, the boys and I were in our little cellar and perfectly safe. Rosemary was so excited, laughed and talked all the time so happily. I can't be too thankful that she is too young to understand. Wu and Kao took it in turns to hold her to relieve me. They were wonderfully brave and have been splendid all through. After about thirty minutes all was clear and we emerged into a house of broken glass, scarcely a window not smashed, but no further damage. The boys stuck paper up and it really works quite well and it is 'homely' to see brown paper windows with a HJ&N.[107] label on! Some of the windows have been 're-paned' now on the ground floor.

The Japanese entered the town at 7 p.m. on Christmas Day. We didn't know till the next morning though we heard firing during the night. For three days we had no electricity, the bombing had done for that, so we used oil lamps and candles. Luckily Wu had bought in a little extra meat and vegetables for Christmas, as we had planned to invite folk in, so it is lasting us over. It is difficult just now for him to go onto the street and buy. We hope it will be better in a few days.

[107] Harry Johnson & Nephew – the family stationer and bookshop in Cambridge, in which Gwyneth worked with her father before her marriage

Ronald to Ilkley and Cambridge

Chouts'un
4th January 1938

We are expecting a post office motor lorry to pass through here today on its way to Tsinan from Weihsien, and so there will be a chance for us to put a letter on it and get it to Tsinan, and so I hope through to you. The Tsinan GPO sent the lorry down two days ago, and it called here on its way to Weihsien, and brought us a nice big pile of very welcome letters. There are still quite a lot of missing ones, but we had letters from all of you. There are still no trains running on the Kiao-Tsi railway, all the engines and coaches having been transferred to the Tsin-Pu line before the Japanese take-over, and it is doubtful whether the Tsinan GPO will be able to continue sending and collecting mail by motor lorry in this way, so this may be our last chance of getting letters through for a long time.

After the fall of Nanking we had heard of the Japanese advance northwards towards Hsuchow, but north of the Yellow River there did not seem to be a great deal of activity. Tsinan had been shelled from batteries north of the River, but otherwise things were quiet. On the night of December 23rd when I went over to hospital to do my night round, we could hear away to the north west the sound of heavy guns firing. We have since heard that it was just at that time that the Japanese were crossing the river north east of Tsinan, and the firing that we heard must have been the sound of the engagements that took place as the Japs crossed and occupied the Chinese positions on the south bank of the river.

Next morning just as we had finished hospital prayers, and were scattering to our various jobs, the whole building was shaken by the concussion of bombs, which sounded to be fairly near us somewhere to the north. In a surprisingly short time, rumour had it that Chang-shan, about six miles north of us, had been bombed, and it did not seem many minutes before the injured were being brought in. One died from his injuries in the waiting room, two others needed immediate operation, one with an abdominal injury, and one with severe bleeding from a thigh wound, and several others had less severe injuries.

By about a quarter to twelve we were in the theatre starting on the abdominal, multiple injuries of the intestines, which needed a resection of a fair amount of bowel. We were just finishing this one, when we heard the zoom of planes overhead and we had a feeling that our turn had come. We had had a good many planes over Chouts'un, and there had been bombing of places not far away before, but so far we had escaped. This time Chouts'un was for it. As we changed our gloves for the next operation, we could see the planes from the theatre window, in two pairs flying over the town, and it gave you a horrible sickening feeling to see them power-diving almost vertically down on to the town to sweep the place with their machine guns, then rising again to circle round again and repeat the performance.

We got on with the next case, and while we were doing it we could hear the planes zooming down, it seemed directly on to us. The rat-tat-tat of the machine guns was so loud that we thought there must be an anti-aircraft gun just outside the wall, and inwardly we felt like cursing the silly fellow who was attracting so much undesirable attention to himself so near to us! But we found afterwards that the machine guns were on the planes, and not anti-aircraft. Two or three big bombs dropped near to us while we were in the theatre, and I couldn't help feeling a big sense of admiration for the little theatre nurse who stood by her theatre table the whole time, just under the big windows, and in danger of breaking glass, if of nothing worse.

Well, those four passed over, and after we had finished the man's leg we hurried off home to get some lunch. We expected to have a busy afternoon dealing with the casualties of the raid, but we got worse than we expected. As we went back to hospital after lunch we could hear the distant sound of planes and the dull thuds of bombs falling and guessed that it was Tsouping's turn. Some of the Chouts'un wounded were already waiting in the outpatient department when we got there, but we had hardly started to attend to them when we heard the roar of planes again, and in what seemed like no time a squadron of seven planes was over the town again.

It is difficult to remember clearly what happened in the next half hour or hour, and we have had a good deal of amusement in comparing (and contrasting!) different people's accounts of the same story. It wasn't very nice while it lasted. Some of the bombs sounded unpleasantly near and loud, and the windows of the outpatient department were blown in while we were there. The planes must have circled round many times. People who saw them from a distance say that there were seventeen of them over the town at once.

When at last, about 3.30 p.m. they finally disappeared, we went hurriedly round to see what damage had been done. Ten bombs had fallen on BMS property, seven within the walls of the hospital compound. One fell just outside the gate that leads from our garden into the hospital compound, about twenty yards from the cellar where Gwyneth and Rosemary and Wu and Kao and Su were.

All our houses had most of their windows smashed, several hundred panes altogether. Our house has three machine gun bullets through the roof, and the nurses' home has several too. But the wonder of it is that, with all these bombs falling within such a small space, not a single person on the compound, of patients or staff or work-people, received a single scratch or the slightest injury. It really was a miracle, and the deepest feeling we all had when it was all over was one of thankfulness.

It is difficult to tell exactly how many bombs fell on Chouts'un. Most people say about three hundred, and that is probably not very far from the truth. There are about a hundred holes that are known to us and there must be a good many more that we do not know about. Almost all fell in an area less than a square mile. This area contains the railway station and railway lines and the main road leading to the station, on which there were said to have been Chinese troops at the time, and the hospital is situated in the angle formed by the railway line and the road, with the station at the apex of the angle. The station was badly damaged, and several big holes were made in the lines.

The air raid caused panic in the town. Everybody feared that it would be repeated the next day, and all who could do so hurriedly left for neighbouring villages where they felt safe from bombardment. Our church pastor estimated that about 80% of the population left the town. All the patients in hospital who were able to leave hurriedly left that night. Illness or no illness, they felt that they would be better off further away. But there were still a number of patients in hospital who were too ill to move, or who couldn't leave because their relatives could not come for them, and in addition there were about a dozen injured in the raid who had just been brought in. The greatest difficulty was caused by the fact that almost all the hospital coolies left during the night, because they feared that the next day would certainly bring a repetition of the day's events.

Not a very peaceful Christmas eve, and not a very restful night! Christmas Day came, and of course all our plans for Christmas celebrations had to be given up. Somehow food was prepared for the patients, and their wounds were dressed. All the women patients had been brought downstairs, and were crowded together in the rooms at the east end of the hospital, and we had piled mattresses on the floor above as some sort of protection against bombs.

Planes came over during the day but not bombers, for which we were thankful. We had wondered whether it would have been better for Gwyneth and Rosemary to go over to the west side to Mr Harris's house during the day, but decided that it would be best for us to stay together.

So the day passed. Wu Shih-fu tried to get home to Tsouping during the day to see if his folk were all right, but he returned about 7 p.m. saying that he hadn't been able to get to Tsouping. Everywhere he had met soldiers retreating towards Chouts'un, and people saying that the Japanese were rapidly advancing. By the time he had got back to Chouts'un, people were saying that they were already within four or five miles of the north gate. At the time we took that to be an exaggeration, but it must have been not far from the truth.

That evening we had our Christmas dinner at the Flowers'. Gwyneth and I took it in turns to stay with Rosemary. I went first and had my dinner, and then came back and Gwyneth went. Although we didn't know it, at the time we were eating our Christmas meal the Japanese troops must have been entering the north gate of the town.

That night all the Chinese nurses slept in the hospital, and Logie slept with them, all sleeping on the corridor floor on their mattresses. Gwyneth and I slept at home, and not having slept very well the night before, were soon asleep. About midnight we were awakened by the noise of firing – machine guns, and what sounded like big guns. The machine guns sounded to be just outside our garden wall. We had no idea whose they were or in which direction they were firing. I guessed they were Chinese machine guns firing in the direction of the Jap field guns, but it turned out later that the machine guns were Japanese posted on the town wall and firing in the direction of the station, to prepare the way for their troops to reach and occupy the station.

In the night we didn't know this, and I felt I had better go over to the hospital to see that all was all right, and of course Gwyneth and Rosemary went over with me. All was well at hospital, and Gwyneth and Rosemary spent the rest of the night sharing one of the nurses' mattresses with Logie, and I slept on a couple of forms in the entry hall, with lots of offers of pillows and bedding and wadded quilts to keep me warm and comfortable.

Next morning - there had been no further shooting during the night – we woke thinking that there would be worse fighting to come, but as soon as we were up and about we learned that it was all over. Japanese soldiers had passed the hospital on their way to the station, and the fighting was over. We went to the gate and saw some of the khaki-clad Jap troops go past, and felt relieved to think that there would at least be no more bombing now.

Since then the Japanese have been in occupation.

.

PART THREE

IN OCCUPIED CHINA
February 1938 – December 1941

Before very long after the occupation of Chouts'un, the signs of conquest began to appear. The people were made to fly the Japanese flag and on the main street large posters appeared on the walls. The messages were all pro-Japanese and anti Central Government, with slogans like, 'Down with the Pro-Soviet Central Government' and 'Congratulations to the newly established Provisional Government'. Ruthless orders were issued to ensure obedience to the new régime: anyone tampering with the street decorations would be executed; if any Japanese soldier was injured, not only would the person who caused the injury be executed, but the whole street would be held responsible; on entering and leaving the city gates, all Chinese men would be required to take off their hats and all Chinese women must bow to the Japanese soldiers on guard.

Life in the town came to a standstill. Streets that normally teemed with life were empty. Shops remained closed and shuttered. Business ceased and factories closed. The fields and roads leading to the town became almost completely deserted, as any who could do so took refuge in the surrounding countryside. The villagers spent their nights in caves in the hills, returning to their homes in the daytime.

The mountainous areas, which the occupying army was unable to control, became the province of bandits and of guerrilla units, who were active harassing Japanese communication and supply lines. Explosions on the railway line became a frequent occurrence. In reprisal, the local garrison burned down the villages adjacent to the damaged section of the railway line. In the first months of 1938, more than 150 villages between Tsinan and Tsingtao were burned down by the Japanese, and the inhabitants shot or incinerated. Night after night, for miles around, the sky glowed an angry red.

The road past the hospital, normally crowded with passing people, was deserted in the daytime, and silent as the grave at night. A machine gun planted outside the main gate sprayed the fields to the north with gunfire. Low flying planes roared overhead, searching for any irregular troops or guerrillas, and for several days subjecting the compound to particular surveillance.

Ronald to his father and mother

Chouts'un
6th February 1938

The winter will soon be over now. The worst of the cold is past, and in six or seven weeks the spring will be here, and we shall be glad. Spring is the loveliest season in China, and next Autumn, and next I like summer, and winter least of all, though even in winter there is lovely bright sunshine and bright blue skies. It is only the extreme cold and the biting wind that make it uncomfortable.

It's not very easy to write much about our present circumstances, for reasons which you will understand. Most of our admissions these days are gunshot wounds, and, owing to the absence of the usual authority, there is a good deal of lawlessness abroad and we are seeing a good many of the casualties. It is another sad feature of this terrible war. Smallpox has broken out among the flood refugees at the west side of the town, and we have had five cases in hospital, two unfortunately in newborn infants, and both have died. We have vaccinated all the other refugees so I hope we will not get any more cases. We have about fifty patients in hospital at present. Cheeloo have about the same number of patients as we have here. The Tsingchoufu hospital staff are still at their posts and are carrying on as usual in the new conditions.

No food shortage here yet and we had in good supplies of coal fortunately, so I think what we have left will see us through the winter. And the goats, after being two days without their goatherd, who ran away after the bombing, are now producing milk well again, and Rosemary can have as much as she needs every day.

The war is making a big difference to the hospital income. Few people want to turn out to come to hospital unless absolutely necessary, and there is very little money in circulation, so that the hospital has been running at a loss for this month and is likely to for some time to come. We have already received $2,000 (about £120) from the Lord Mayor of London's Relief Fund, via the British Consul General in Tsingtao, to help us towards the expenses incurred in war relief work, and it is possible that we may still receive some more.

Wu and Kao were wonderfully good at Christmas time. They have been very faithful and loyal helpers.

I am so grateful to all our friends who are doing such splendid work for the Missionary parcel. I only wish I felt sure that the parcel will be able to be sent out to China in the present circumstances. Until just before Christmas, Tsingtao and Tientsin were the only ports open by

Ronald and Gwyneth's wedding, 30 May 1935
From left: William & Elizabeth Still, Dray, Ronald, Gwyneth, Polly, May Johnson, Karl Britton, John Johnson

Ronald and Gwyneth in the garden at Cambridge
15 August 1935, the day before they sailed for China

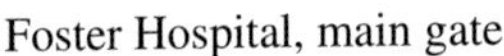

Foster Hospital, main gate

A patient arriving at hospital

Foster Hospital, outpatient department

Chouts'un foreign staff, Autumn 1935
Left to right: Dr Flowers, A (Su) Smurthwaite, A E Emmott, Nurse Logan, Michael & Ian Flowers, A Flowers, Ronald, Gwyneth, Nurse Wheal

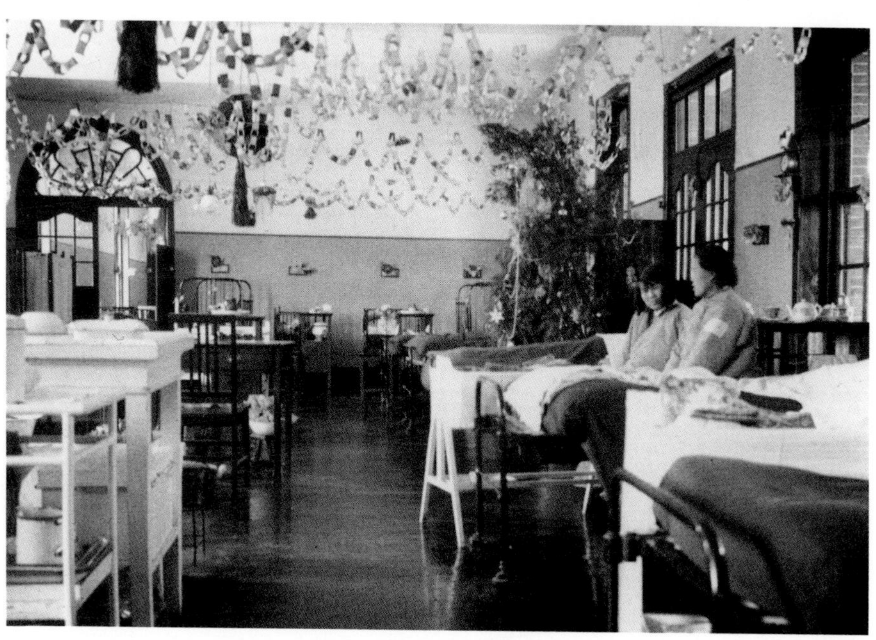

Women's ward, Christmas 1935

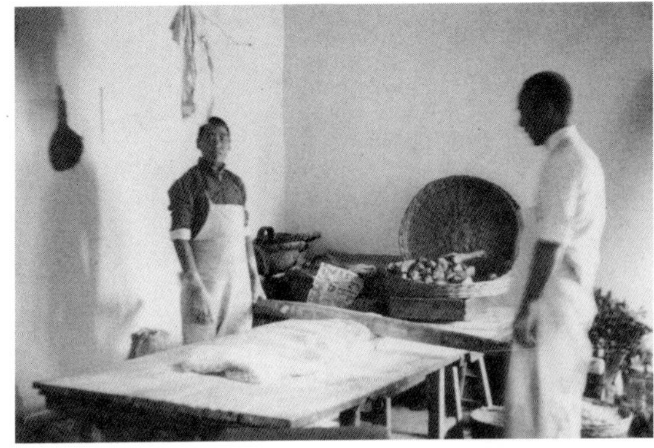
In the hospital kitchen

Carrying food to the wards

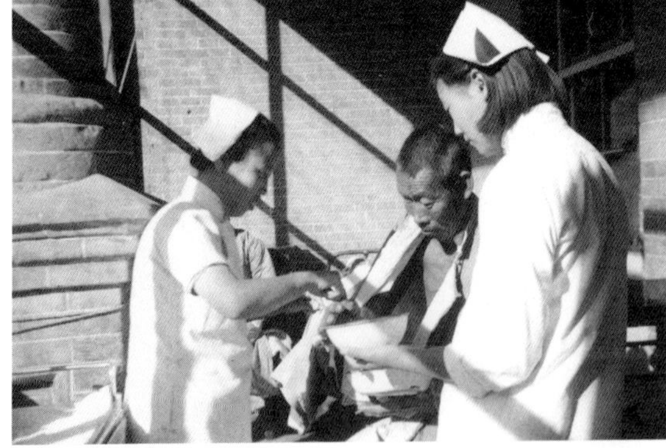
Nurses attending to a patient

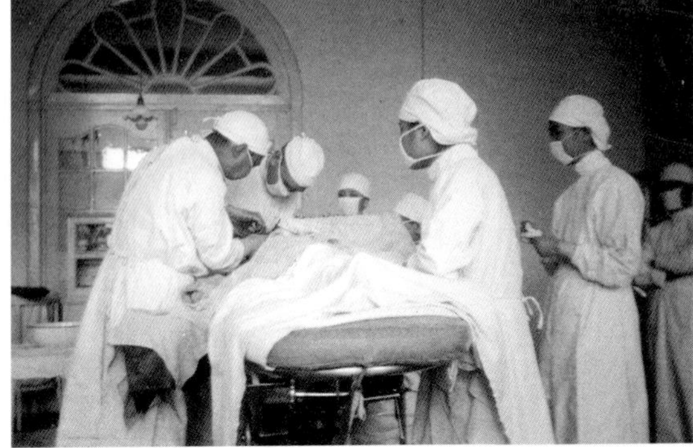
An operation in progress

Chinese nurses' residence

At work building the X-ray unit

Gwyneth with F W Price in Taiyuan, April 1937

Ronald with patients at Tsingchou leprosarium, 1939

Gwyneth & Rosemary, December 1937

Ronald, 1937

Dining room in Gwyneth & Ronald's Chouts'un home

Mr Harris being met at Chouts'un station on his return from furlough

Mr Harris & Rev Chang Szu-ching

Kindergarten children

Wu Shi Fu with his wife and children

Wu Shi Fu's mother

Wang Ta Sao

Street scene, Chouts'un

Bridge in central Chouts'un

West end of Chouts'un, mission compound to the right

Rosemary with Wu Shi Fu's children, 1937

Gwyneth and Carrie Scott with
Sheena, Rosemary, David and Tom
Tsingtao, 1938

Audrey on the beach
at Tsingtao, 1940

Refugee family, Chouts'un

Kao ta Ko at the well

Nurses' graduation, Foster Hospital, 1941

Japanese soldiers patrolling the railway line
(photo courtesy of Imperial War Museum, London PLP2952F)

Ronald & Gwyneth with Rosemary, Audrey & Catherine,
Shanghai, Autumn 1942

Lounge, Columbia Country Club, August 1942

Japanese sergeant in charge of guards at Columbia Country Club, 1944

Returning from the meal queue, late August 1945
(photo courtesy of John Ewing, pictured front left)

From left: Audrey, Rosemary, Catherine
Shanghai, September 1945

Children's party on board HMS Belfast, September 1945
Audrey and Catherine in the background, held aloft by two sailors
(photo courtesy of Imperial War Museum A30855)

which goods could reach us, and Flowers sent instructions for our annual indent of drugs and instruments and wants boxes to be sent to Tsingtao, our nearest port. Since those instructions were sent, there has been the Jap occupation and now the Tsingtao rail communication is broken and the Yellow River bridge (between Tientsin and Tsinan) is also cut so that it is going to be a long time before we are able to get supplies of any kind.

With these difficulties of transport, it seems unlikely that the BMS will want to send extra parcels out to us here, and may want to divert "Wants parcels" to other stations. If that is so, you can guess how disappointed we shall be, and I know you will be disappointed too. Still our loss will be someone else's gain and we shall rejoice and be grateful with them.

Sorry our chess has been interrupted, Father. I am afraid we must wait until more settled times to continue it. Now I must get this ready for post and hope that a mail will soon be leaving for Tsinan. Goodbye for a while. I wish we could be nearer to you but we feel close to you in spirit.

Gwyneth to her mother

Chouts'un
15th February 1938

Well yesterday's van brought us so much post that I have not yet finished reading even the letters properly! And as for the pile of daily papers, I doubt if I will ever wade through them. I will enclose a list (49 letters, 46 daily and other papers and 32 other items!) and ask you to let the girls and anyone else convenient know of their arrival. I will try to reply in time but you can guess that with such a crowd all at once it will take some work. It really is marvellous how things have eventually got here.

You didn't want us to be with you at Christmas more than we wanted to be with you. It was the worst day we have ever known. Oh yes, we would be very sorry indeed if all our efforts at study recently were wasted. We have been so very happy in all our work. Especially during the last two months I have often longed for Rosemary to be safely with you all, though I couldn't bear to part with her and she has been such a wonderful blessing. She is busy now 'posting' all her oddments through the pen bars and waiting for me to pick them up, so she can 'post' again! I should just hate to miss any of my time with her, especially as I know I must part with her when school days come, but where we will be then is far from certain. The uncertainty previously was nothing to what it is now.

By the way did I ever tell you that for several days after Christmas all our lights were cut? Fortunately, only two days before, Su had lent us a big oil lamp, saying she had two and felt we had better have one in case the electricity ever failed. So we managed with that in the dining room and candles elsewhere. Su has really helped us in lots of ways, she is a very generous sort of person.

Am glad you had such nice presents, wish I could see them all. How lovely of Daisy to ring up on Christmas Eve and Auntie and Max too! I have almost forgotten about telephones, we haven't one here now at all.

Our Christmas duck wasn't appreciated, I felt too sick to eat all day! I have made up since, though I think I should really enjoy a meal at home best now! Alas, Uncle Harry's tuck box hasn't come. I am afraid it will be too strong a temptation. Of course, no parcels at all have come for three months, so I suppose there is still hope.

Today Wu has gone off home. He had news some time back that his old mother was not so well and he feels it is his duty to go and see her. They cannot rely on letters getting through now, and he is the only son, so he feels his responsibility, especially as he has no father. Meanwhile his wife and family are still here and look like staying some time. They had to leave home on account of the trouble and will be here some weeks I expect. It is not really safe for them to return yet. We do not find the family at all noisy or in any way a bother. In fact I am glad to hear the children playing about the garden, it is a change to have some life! His two daughters are sixteen and nine. The boys are seven and about fifteen months. They are always so vague about their ages. Whenever they see us they stand and give us a very stiff little bow! I think as soon as our backs are turned they probably giggle, but that is a detail.

Rosemary is very keen on walking now, and has been able to go for several little walks in the garden. The paths being cobbled are rather rough and unsafe for her present efforts so we have to hold one hand. She struts along so proudly, beaming all over her little face, and if we meet anyone in the garden we have to stop while she talks to them. Wu's children are very interested in her, though the baby is a bit scared of foreigners, having seen few before now. I should not really like to say whether it is Rosemary who looks most proud or the one who is holding her hand, probably we are a good tie!

On Sunday we had an invite to eat Chinese food with a member of the hospital staff. I was very thrilled and the food really was fine, about twenty dishes all excellent. They do it so very tastily and I like it because it is nearly all savoury. We are still getting enough to eat, though not the usual variety.

Gwyneth to Cambridge and Ilkley

Chouts'un
19th February 1938

I expect I told you that when we had no window panes, I wore my Chinese gown all day, and found it such a blessing. Altogether we had forty four panes broken, and everyone else had similar numbers or more, and one of our small windows fell right in, and a lot of the frames are very loose and let in even more draught than usual. I do not know when all these small things will be seen to, but as the windows are all in again we are not very concerned. We shall probably never know how much damage was done to the beams and foundations, because the whole houses shook and seemed as if they were falling on us. The great wonder is that there was so little big damage and no lives lost. The more we think about it the more we wonder at it.

Perhaps with Father's help I will manage a book about Rosemary's first year one day, but I don't feel like it now and, unless you let me consult all the letters we have written, I am sure I will have forgotten heaps of things. All the same I would quite like to try one day.

We had a letter last mail from the Mission House congratulating us on our exam results, and informing us that in anticipation of a satisfactory probationary report being received from the field they were recognising us as full members of the mission, or words to that effect. Dr Chesterman who should normally have written the letter was away and it was Mr Wilson who had to do it. He said it 'gave him peculiar pleasure to write to congratulate us'. We could well understand that, remembering that his great argument against our coming out married was that we should never get the language!

Wu arrived back safely tonight to our relief. His mother is much better, though still has a cough but Wu thought that was because she was old, and did not seem worried. He had no real difficulties on his way there or back, but we can well believe that if you have no very urgent business home is the best place. We are glad he and Kao are both here now, we should hate them to be in trouble.

Food still lasting out. Ronald and I can manage on local products, but it is a bit harder for Rosemary. However, so far we have done quite well.

Wu Shih-jung, Kao Yun-Jen to Ronald and Gwyneth's parents
(sent in Chinese with translation as follows by Ronald)

Chouts'un

26th day of 2nd month of 27th Year of the Republic of China (27th February 1938)

Old Pastor and Old Mrs Still, and Old Mr and Mrs Johnson, dearly loved in the Lord,

We have heard, from your letters received on 22nd February, that your honourable place has just received the news of the unfortunate happenings at Chouts'un. At that time, those living on our unworthy compound received a special blessing from our Heavenly Father in being kept completely safe.

In today's letter, you specially thank us servants for helping Mrs Still and Rue-may[108] during the bombing of our unworthy compound. Truly we are unworthy of your thanks. There are two things that to this day we cannot forget, the first is that our Heavenly Father pointed us the way into the cellar in good time, and granted us the special blessing of His peace; the second is that we servants were only trying to fulfil our duty, and do not need any words of thanks.

We thank you too for your enquiries about our families. Your servant Shih-jung's home is about thirty five Chinese li (about twelve miles) from Chouts'un. Those at home fled during the fighting, and subsequently escaped to our compound here, and not very much damage was done at home. Your servant Yun-Jen's home is about sixty five Chinese li (about twenty two miles) from Chouts'un, in a place where there has been no fighting.

In our unworthy country at the present time, everywhere there is natural calamity, human misery, and the desolation and disorder of soldiers and horses. That our Heavenly Father should early have planted His servants Dr and Mrs Still here, that they should have come from far over the sea, not refusing bitter toil, that they should have cherished the resolution to help their age and to save men, that they should have come to our unworthy country and, relying on the power of our Heavenly

[108] Rosemary's Chinese name, She Rue-may, meaning 'as rare as plum blossom'

Father, healed not a few of our brothers and sisters in body as in soul, for this we ought to thank our Heavenly Father.

And further we would ask you both to pray for our unworthy country, to pray our heavenly Father to shorten the days of our troubles, and quickly to bring peace both to China and Japan.

We too pray our Heavenly Father that He will bless you both with good health. With our respectful regards, your servants, Wu Shih-jung, Kao Yun-Jen.

Ronald to Ilkley and Cambridge

Chouts'un
6th March 1938

I am writing this on Sunday evening, about 6 p.m. There is a March wind blowing, and by the feel of it it has come from Mongolia.

I am glad to know that our letters telling how we spent Christmas got through. There is some sort of letter censorship in existence – letters reach us that have obviously been tampered with – but it is reassuring to know that our letters are getting through and yours are reaching us. Did Gwyneth tell you, the parcel that Uncle Harry in Australia had told us he was sending, reached us last week, badly battered outside, but with all the contents complete and undamaged inside?

As far as our own personal health and safety and comforts are concerned, our position is not in any way different from that under the old regime. We are beginning to get short of a few foodstuffs. We haven't seen butter for a long time, though lard is available on the street as a substitute. We have finished the last of our baking powder (and almost simultaneously the hospital dispensary ran out of tartaric acid, so we can't make our own), so that rather cramps Wu's style in the kitchen! Meats are becoming limited in variety, and we are having to fall back on the eternal Chinese chicken, which I think must have something of the Phoenix in its ancestry, because whenever one is killed in China, another seems to spring up to take its place. I know you will think it is no hardship to 'have to fall back on chicken', and of course we agree with you, and are very grateful to China and its self-sacrificing chickens. Fish is hard to come by. None reaches us from the coast, but very occasionally there is river fish to be bought on the street. But the goats are doing well for Rosemary, and you should just see her little mouth open for scrambled eggs every morning at breakfast. We have still got coal and the worst of the winter is over and the warmer weather will soon be here, so we haven't anxieties on that score.

The hospital situation is rather more serious. Fortunately so far we are not short of any essential drug, and we have supplies of the most important ones like chloroform and ether and local and spinal anaesthetics sufficient for some months. One or two important ones such as iodine are running very low, but they can be substituted if necessary, though at some inconvenience. One shortage is in the kind of gauze used in making plaster of Paris bandages. We are completely out of this, and supplies cannot be obtained locally. This is a real problem. We are taking in a considerable number of fracture cases, and, in the absence of plaster of Paris splints, their period of hospitalisation is necessarily considerably lengthened, causing extra expense for the hospital, extra work for the staff and occupying beds that might otherwise be occupied by new patients.

The difficulties are caused partly by the fact that communications are so badly disrupted, making us unable to obtain such supplies as we normally obtain from the ports, Shanghai, Tientsin and Tsingtao, and partly by the fact that the annual indent of drugs which comes out to us each year from home, which usually reaches us about Christmas, this year has been unable to reach us. The drugs were first held up at Hong Kong, as at that time Tsingtao and Shanghai were not unloading cargoes. They can now be unloaded at Tsingtao if we get them sent there, and we shall have to find some means of getting them up here. The Tsingtao-Tsinan railway is now running a through train service, but entirely for military purposes, and civilian passengers and freight are not yet being accepted.

As far as the actual hospital work is concerned, we are rather busier than we usually are at this time of the year. After the Japanese occupation, patients from the outlying districts for several weeks were unwilling to be on the roads, and so didn't come to hospital. Since then, the unsettled conditions prevailing round about have resulted in a large number of casualties, and have more than made up for our lack of business in the period immediately following the occupation. The net result to the hospital has been that about four out of every five patients admitted to hospital is suffering from gunshot wounds. In January and February we did over eighty operations in the theatre, of which over sixty were for gunshot or bomb or shrapnel wounds.

One was a lad of about twenty one who was admitted to hospital a week last Thursday. He and his father had both been attacked by armed robbers in their home the night before, and both were shot. The father's wound was through the shoulder, just a flesh wound which is now almost healed. When I first saw the lad he was lying on the stretcher on which they had brought him to hospital. I asked where he had been shot and they said, through the head. I took his hat off (the little round Chinese hat with a little button on top) and found that inside it was quite a fair quantity of the lad's brains. When I looked at his head, there were two holes in the back of his head, brains and blood oozing from each. We took him in and operated on him next morning. We excised his wounds and exposed the hole in his skull, a big hole about 2½ inches by 1½. We cleaned up the edges of the fracture as well as we could, and removed bits of damaged brain, and stitched up his scalp, and drained the wound. It sounds unbelievable, but by last night the wound in his scalp was completely healed except for the corner where the drainage tube came out, and he was sitting up in bed helping himself to his own supper with his chopsticks!

Another lad of about twenty three came in on New Year's day. He had had three machine-gun bullets through him, one through his left lung, one through his left loin, just missing his abdomen, and one through his right knee just missing the joint. The first two missed killing him, and the third missed crippling him by about an inch. He was a wonderfully grateful patient, and said he felt that the hospital had brought him back to life. He bought a Bible while he was in hospital, and when he went out he was beginning to know something of Christianity. Poor lad, he got back to his home village, just in time to find the village burned, his mother and father killed, and he himself had a second miraculous escape from death. He came back to hospital himself to tell us the story, and to bring with him a friend who had been shot through the face.

Do you remember me telling you about those young fellows who were injured in an explosion and brought to hospital one Sunday before the occupation? Only one of them lived, and he is still in hospital. One of his eyes was completely destroyed by a piece of stone, and the eye had to be removed, and the other eye's vision is almost completely gone. He can just distinguish light from dark. All his friends and those responsible for him have now left the district, and he is alone here, almost completely blind. The other day I heard that in a neighbouring district there was an old blind evangelist who has been helping our mission for a long time, and who reads and writes Braille, so we asked this old man if he would come along and see if he could help this young fellow to learn Braille. At the time of the explosion his hands had been damaged too, and he had to have an operation to remove several big lumps of stone from the palm of his hand, but fortunately the sensitive part of his fingers has not been damaged. He has been at his Braille for about a month now and can now recognise the forty or fifty characters of the Chinese Braille alphabet. I am writing this week to Shanghai to get copies of as many of the Chinese books that are printed in Braille as I can, with some of the money that Ruth Collins has sent me, and also a Braille writing slate for him.

He now goes about the wards smiling and singing, and chatting cheerfully with the other patients, whereas before he just lay on his bed, and asked day after day whether he would be able to see with his remaining eye. The best part of it is that his old blind teacher is a fine old man of tremendous enthusiasm and sincerity. He took our hospital evening service this evening for us, reading the lesson from his Braille Bible, and speaking in a way that encouraged us all. Blind people in China easily become the most miserable and pitiful beggars. I still don't know what will happen to this young lad, but I hope that we may be able to help him to some useful piece of work.

The most anxious part of the situation for us and for everybody is the unsettled state of the countryside around Chouts'un and, so far as we can gather, in most of the occupied territory. The occupation has not been accepted with equanimity by the local populace, and in the absence of central government troops, and of the regular provincial troops, the responsibility for resistance has been undertaken by bodies of people who call themselves variously 'plain clothes troops' or 'moving striking troops', and who are carrying on a guerrilla warfare wherever they are able. They are not strong enough to attack the main body of the enemy troops, but confine themselves to attacking lines of communication and weakly garrisoned places.

In addition to these bodies, who may be taken to be genuinely fighting for their country, there are considerable numbers of other people abroad who are more self-seeking. These consist of, in a small part, disaffected troops who have taken to looting on their own account, and in part of the worse types of civilians, who see in the present unsettled conditions an opportunity for paying back old grudges or looting for themselves. The present conditions are in part responsible, as the disruption of normal business and commerce must have led to a great number of people who could in normal circumstances just earn a living being pushed below the poverty line. With all these people the great difficulty is to obtain supplies of guns and ammunition. They hide in the hills during the daytime, and come out to the surrounding villages at night to try to obtain guns and ammunition and food and money. The villagers have a hard time in trying to decide which are genuine guerrilla troops and which are armed robbers, and you can imagine what follows. While we ourselves within our compound walls are in no personal danger, the repeated sounds of gun shots by night, and of larger explosions, which are used by both the Japanese and the people in the villages to warn off unwelcome visitors, serve as a constant reminder of the unsettled state of the countryside.

The future years are going to be hard ones for everybody, and China will be in need of all the service and the best service that can be offered her. Gwyneth and I shall be happy if we can be of any service to the country we have learned to love, and I know you will be glad to do all you can too.

Japanese soldiers on the move
(photo courtesy of Imperial War Museum, London PLP129288)

Gwyneth to Ilkley

Chouts'un
13th March 1938

You will have heard by now of the arrival of Philip John Allen – it is lovely for Elizabeth to have a small brother. I am longing to hear all about him. I doubt if they will be able to come back[109], at least Connie and the children in the autumn. They won't unless there is a big change in conditions. It is not really fit for children at present.

I think that the nurses were all splendid at Christmas. They and Logie went on carrying the women patients downstairs, even when the

[109] Tom and Connie Allen were still in England on furlough.

bombs were dropping in the compound and the glass was falling. They are all such young girls but showed a fine spirit. One of them carried a child downstairs and then fainted. She came round in a few minutes and was up and wanting to help again at once. That evening Logie had a prayer meeting for the girl nurses and I went. It was a lovely service of thanksgiving for the protection we had all received. We must all the time remember that these Chinese friends of ours, in addition to the awful experience they themselves passed through, have great anxiety for their home folk. They are getting so little news and when letters come, they are brief. The people are afraid to write freely.

We have just had wireless news of the trouble between Germany and Austria, so we are wondering very much where Olive is, whether she will get back or not. Oh, what a lot of awful things seem to be happening everywhere.

The fact that I haven't mentioned Rosemary doesn't mean that we like her any less! She continues to be all joy to us. We went to tea with Logie yesterday and Su and Miss Thomas were there and Rosemary sat in her pram watching while we had tea and then afterwards walked round and round the room, talking and getting different people to take her hand.

We are all three well, but tired. I think it must just be the constant strain, though Ronald has a real reason for his tiredness. He and Dr Flowers are hard at it all day, and in addition there are all the many difficulties caused by the present situation.

Ronald to his father

Chouts'un
15th March 1938

I am hoping this will reach you in time for your birthday. It comes to bring you all loving wishes from us both and from Rosemary too. Gwyneth and I want to send you, for a little birthday present, the North China Herald for the next six months. It is the weekly edition of the North China Daily News, published in Shanghai, and I think it is one of the best and most reliable of the China English papers. You will be able to sample it during the next six months and afterwards if you would like it continued, we will have it sent on.

Things are very unsettled here again at present. The guerrilla troops in the neighbourhood made an attempt to retake the town here a week ago. There was a good deal of firing in the early hours of the morning last Thursday. We heard the bullets humming past our windows and one hit our roof, but we were safe and sound inside and in bed, and nobody was hurt. The attempt was unsuccessful, but it has led to a good deal of tightening up of local conditions. The city gates have been kept locked since the incident, and no one has been allowed to go in or come out. Flowers and I were allowed in to accompany two of our patients who were taken from the hospital for investigation, but since then Flowers has been refused admission to the city.

These conditions naturally mean a setback and a hindrance to the re-establishment of normal conditions. As a result we have not had many patients attending hospital during the last few days. Those from the town are not allowed to come out and those from country outlying districts are afraid to turn out, and we only get those from outside the town in the immediate neighbourhood. Even so, we are getting a few of the inevitable gunshot wounds almost daily.

Gwyneth to Ilkley

Chouts'un
6th May 1938

We are late with your letter again, but I have been thinking perhaps we could give you news of Alice's arrival[110]. Dr Flowers went down to Tsingtao on Wednesday to meet her. In these times it is not nice for anyone, but especially a woman, to travel alone unless absolutely necessary and as she will have her luggage too, it was not fair to expect her to come up alone. We do not of course know whether he reached there safely. He may have been delayed in which case Alice would wait for him.

Ronald and Logie are going to the station tonight in the hope of their arriving. Unfortunately that train varies in its time of arrival between 5 and 7 p.m. so it may mean a long wait. I wanted to be on the road, or at the gate with Rosemary, but we have decided in the circumstances it is better to get her to bed at the normal time, and then if the train is late I shall go to the gate.

There was a good bit of firing the other night. There is some every night, but this was extra loud and extra near. Rosemary slept peacefully through it and she made me feel I was wrong to feel nervous at all. She just slept trustfully on and I felt I ought to be able to do the same! I think she is like what I was like, as far as I can remember photos of myself, but she is sweeter than I could ever have been. I have just been up (10 p.m.) and seen to her and it is so lovely. She didn't wake

[110] Alice Wheal was en route to Chouts'un from England after her period of furlough.

properly and her little head sort of flopped about and she was all warm and cuddly and smelt so sweet. I feel I love her more every day.

I have heard from Tsingchou that Connie Allen's 'Wang Ta Sao', her amah, pronounced Wong da Sow – will be more than delighted to come and help me at Tsingtao. She is a queer little woman but very honest and a most sincere Christian and, as I don't intend to leave Rosemary to her much except when she is asleep, I think she will be O.K. I hope Rosemary likes her but she seems to like most folk. I only pay her about 10/6 a month and she provides her own food, so it is very cheap, though I feel I will loathe to leave Rosemary to her or anyone!

I am honestly counting the weeks and nearly days to our holiday. I think it is unwise when things are so uncertain and we may not get away, but I do so long for a change, though I still love this place. I think you understand. I feel a bit scared taking Rosemary on the journey. We may be lucky, as Annie was, and get through in twelve hours without mishap, but sometimes the train gets held up a few nights and then it will be a bit awkward!

Well, Ronald and Logie and some coolies had about two hours' wait at the station last night and we went to the gate several times on hearing trains, which turned out to be goods or coming the wrong way, and then finally at about 8.30 they returned from the station without Alice. They were not on the train, but an American who had come up from Tsingtao said he thought Alice had not yet reached Tsingtao. We have not heard of her actual arrival even in Shanghai as we cannot get telegrams through now, and we don't know how soon she could get a boat up from there, so it was rather an optimistic guess that she might get here yesterday. They had to go to the station on the chance, though it is a most unpleasant business these days in every way and I was relieved to see them back. Poor old Ronald must go trailing up every night until they come, and apart from the waste of time and tiringness of it, it really is not at all nice for him.

When you get this it won't seem so long to your holidays will it? I always thought at home that the last month went quickly, but it isn't going quickly here! There is still more than a month before we reckon to go, but we may go earlier than we intended.

Gwyneth to Ilkley and Cambridge

Chouts'un
12th May 1938

How little time seems to have gone since I last wrote and yet it is nearly a week, and still Alice is not here. We got a card from Dr Flowers on Sunday saying that she could not reach Tsingtao until the middle of this week, so he was not waiting for her, but coming back as soon as he could get a ticket. The trains are crowded as there is still only one passenger train each way a day. We aren't looking forward to the journey down when we go for our holiday. Ordinarily it is so easy. We travel through the night when it is comparatively cool, and we can sleep and there is no need to take any food, but this year it will be in the heat of the day, probably crowded We shall have to take food for about twenty four hours or more in case of a delay, which is not easy with a child, but we shall manage I am sure. It is certainly safer to travel by day, and I hope we get through before dark.

We have heard from Mrs Scott and she says there is the warmest welcome waiting for us whenever we go to the Pines and the sooner the better. We shall have the big room that I had with Connie Allen last August. It will revive some memories! It is a nice room with lots of windows overlooking the sea, and I think we shall be as comfortable in it as we could be anywhere away from home.

Yesterday we went to tea with Miss Thomas and Miss Jagger. It is a nice change, but fresh topics of conversation are hard to find. When we have speculated on when Alice is likely to come, and discussed the weather, and talked about when Mr Harris is coming back from the country or going out again, and mentioned how hard it is to buy meat, there is really nothing to say, unless anyone has had a very newsy home letter.

I am sorry this is so dull, but it is exceedingly hard to write in these days when you cannot write freely. I suppose you have heard the tale of the man who wrote home and said he could not say much as he knew all his letters were read, and when the letter arrived home, there was a note on the back, "you are wrong, they are not read"!

Tuesday 17th: At last good news, Alice arrived safely last night at 7.30. Mr Emmott escorted her and stayed the night next door. She has got all her goods through and seems very fit and well and pleased to be back. We just saw her for a few minutes last night and she has been round to see Rosemary this morning. She has not yet done her unpacking, but I will write again as soon as I can tell you what we think of all the things she has brought for us. It is so exciting to be getting things now, I am terribly thrilled.

For the Chinese living in Japanese occupied Shantung, the spring and summer months of 1938 were times of constant fear and deprivation. Though the main theatres of war were far away from Chouts'un, the sound of gunfire was frequent. Chinese 'guerrillas' or 'irregular troops' did what they could to disrupt Japanese transport and communication lines, mining roads and railway lines and sabotaging rolling stock. From time to time, pitched battles would break out between the 'irregular troops' and local Japanese garrisons. Casualties and reprisals followed.

As the year advanced, conscription to the Chinese army was made compulsory for all males between the ages of 18 and 45, except students and only sons. Since there was no effective system for getting soldiers' pay to their families, wives were condemned to poverty as long as their husbands were away. There was no government relief, or compensation for deaths or injuries or damage to property. The loss of a husband or father resulted in destitution.

The exodus of the wealthy and professional classes to Free China, and the closure of shops, schools and businesses, meant that those living in the towns had fewer opportunities than ever to earn an honest living. Indiscriminate looting by the occupying troops was commonplace. Everywhere they went the Japanese ransacked towns and villages for firewood. Doors, window frames, posts, rafters, tables, benches, wooden farm implements were carried away or yanked out of buildings and used for cooking and heating. One refugee woman told with tears in her eyes of her weaving loom, her only means of livelihood, being taken away for fuel.[111] *In the countryside, the guerrilla bands exacted heavy taxes in crops and cash, reducing many to starvation. Mr Harris described visiting a family in one village where the seven year old daughter worked day and night making hairnets, in order to be able to earn eightpence a month towards the family budget.*

In early June, Chiang Kai-shek ordered the military to break through the dykes on the Yellow River, changing its course and causing it to flow into the sea to the south rather than the north of the Shantung peninsula. The strategic objective was to halt the advancing Japanese army, but the consequences for the Chinese living in the area were devastating.

[111] Timperley, H J, *Japanese Terror in China*, Books for Libraries Press, 1938

Flood refugees arriving at a concentration point
(photo courtesy of Imperial War Museum, London MVI130ggB)

The flood waters, twenty miles wide in places, swept away thousands of villages and eleven large towns. Almost a million people lost their lives and four million were made homeless.

In the face of such hardship, the mission staff were all too aware of how little they could do to help. Members of the Chinese church were active in assisting with the children's refuge, led by Miss Thomas, in helping with the repair work on the Yellow River dykes, in operating soup kitchens in four centres and in running a large refugee camp on the Yellow River bank. They also contributed funds from their own modest resources to enable free treatment to be given to those in hospital who needed it most. But always there was a painful awareness that there were many more that they were unable to help.

Gwyneth to Ilkley and Cambridge

Chouts'un
18th May 1938

I think you will have heard before this of the very sad news from Shansi, of the wounding and supposed death of Dr Wyatt and Miss Glasby[112]. We still hope it may be proved to be wrong, rumours so easily spread in these days, but it seems likely to be true. I feel terribly sorry

[112] 'On 4th May 1938, in the course of a motor journey northwards to take supplies and reinforce the Madges at Tai-Chou, Dr Harry Wyatt, Miss Beulah Glasby and their Chinese chauffeur were killed near Kuohsien by Chinese guerillas, who mistook them for Japanese. Dr Wyatt was shot as he was helping the wounded Chinese chauffeur to safety. Rev and Mrs Vincent Jasper, who were with the party, were seized and bound, and only saved from execution by the last-minute intervention of an officer who recognized them.'
Williamson H R, *British Baptists in China,* Carey Kingsgate Press, 1957

for Mrs Wyatt. It would be hard for anyone, but with four small children, the oldest only nine, it is hard, and she herself is not well. She has had a terribly hard year, first there was all the worry of Dr Wyatt's typhus, and then almost as soon as he got over that the war broke out. They had gone to Chefoo for their holiday, and the return journey took them several weeks owing to the trouble, and then after they had just got settled back she had to evacuate with the younger children (the others are in Chefoo). Since then she has been travelling round from one place to another, as war conditions altered.

We hope that when this reaches you, there may be better news. You will get it as soon as we do if there is. We have had no details yet.

Gwyneth to Ilkley

Chouts'un
30th May 1938

We do not lack for rumours and alarms, but on the whole we have had a fairly quiet week.

Wu took his family home last week, the big girl carrying the baby (it is about ten miles). He arrived back yesterday. He feels quite relieved to get them safely there with his mother to keep an eye on them, and as he and his wife and four children had to sleep in a room about half the size of one of the Ilkley rooms, I am not surprised they found it rather trying. They shared one big bed too! We did suggest finding another room, but they preferred to be all together. It may have been all right in the cold weather, but it is getting too hot now for such close quarters I think. Kao will probably go home for a few days this week to see his folk and then he will be tied here till we get back in the middle of August.

Fancy we are in our fourth year of married life! How old I feel! I am afraid this year won't be more peaceful, but we can't tell. We have had some quiet nights lately which I have been thankful for. I just rejoice in a wet evening because it is much more hopeful[113]. It is pouring with rain now and I think the earth will get sufficiently soaked to guarantee a night's rest, but if the sun shines all the afternoon, I can't be sure! A lovely heavy downpour now. I suppose I ought not to feel so pleased but all these affairs are so hopeless. It is tragic how little they do and what big losses they involve.

[113] Guerrilla action against the Japanese was usually abandoned on wet nights.

Last night, instead of my usual sort of English conversation class with the nurses, they came to supper and then we had the gramophone, and played games. They stayed till after ten, which is very late for them, and seemed to enjoy themselves. The great thrill of the evening was when we played snakes and ladders, which Miss Thomas had lent me for the occasion!

We can now get no meat or chickens. The sellers are not allowed to bring chickens in from the country. Eggs too are becoming difficult to buy, but Wu is doing awfully well, and we are not going short of food. We were without potatoes for a couple of days, but yesterday we had a great treat, new ones. I *did* enjoy them, the old ones were getting horrid and the new ones with a little mint were grand! We have been lucky lately in having a few strawberries from our own garden every morning for breakfast, just enough for a plate each, they are very nice, and it is good to have some fresh fruit. Of course being greedy, I frequently sigh for cream to eat with them, but that is a detail.

Rosemary is as fit as ever. The last few warm days have made her feel rather hot, and she goes about saying ‘ot’. She prefers it without the ‘h’. Her little face is streaming with perspiration, she is so busy all the time, but she seems quite happy and not at all worried.

We feel very homesick for England sometimes these days, and would love a day in Bolton woods, or climbing Simon’s Seat! I just long for a real grassy field for Rosemary to play in, she would so love the grass. Everywhere here she has only brown earth to play on, and although she is very happy I can’t help wishing she could have a nice lawn!

Ronald to his father and mother

Chouts’un
13th July 1938

We had a very enjoyable fortnight in Tsingtao. There were just ourselves and Emmie Johnson, and Jim and Carrie Scott and their three children in the Pines when we were there. Jim Scott is on the Cheeloo staff as lecturer in Geology and Biology. They have been in Tsingtao since last Autumn, and he has been carrying on some of his experiments while he has been down there. And in addition he has given a lot of time to helping many people in various ways. He has an old second hand car which has paid for itself many times over in meeting people at the station and seeing to people’s luggage and so on. I don’t think there is anyone in our Shantung mission who hasn’t cause to be thankful to Jim for the time and trouble he has taken for them recently, and lots of people not of our mission too. Carrie has a very sweet disposition and Gwyneth and I like them both very much. They are both very forthright, and yet you never hear them speak unkindly of anyone. Jim was very good in helping me to learn to drive the car while I was there, and I became proficient enough to be trusted to drive into town and through the town without an escort, and without a big 'L' on the back either! You never know what accomplishment will be useful in China, and perhaps this one I may have reason to be thankful for.

So far we haven't had any too difficult problems to cope with in Flowers' absence. We have had about twenty five admissions this month so far, and about the same number of operations. Some of the admissions were very ill patients, including an old man of seventy who was burnt by his mosquito net catching fire from his oil-lamp. He was burned from head to foot, and died the same day. The old lady of seventy three who was admitted with a shrapnel wound of the knee died too. I advised amputation for her, but the relatives took her out, saying that they had been promised medical attention from our J.[114] friends, but they brought her back next day wanting amputation, but by then, partly as a result of the long and difficult journeys she had had, she was in too bad a condition to operate, and she too died that day. A third death we have had was a man who had tetanus. He was in convulsions when he arrived, and he died within two hours of admission.

My blind patient, Hui, is still in. I am hoping to be able to help him to go to a blind school soon, and we are making enquiries in Peiping for him. He read the lesson from his Braille bible at the ward service the other evening. I am wondering whether he would like to start a blind school himself, after having had some training in handicraft etc. He has the ability, and he would have the inclination too I think. He is hoping to be baptised this coming month. I found a blind school in Tsingtao when we were there. It is only a poor little struggling school, run by two fairly young blind teachers, but they both seemed splendid enthusiastic Christians and we admired the work they were doing. They used to be supported by Admiral Shen the Mayor of Tsingtao, but have had a struggle since he left.

I had seven operations on Saturday, and five yesterday, including a young lad of fourteen with a knee joint smashed to pieces by a shell wound. I felt sure he could not get a useful leg by conservative treatment and so advised amputation for him too, and I amputated through the thigh

[114] 'J' = Japanese

yesterday. It is decisions like this that I find most anxious when I am by myself, wondering whether it would be possible to save life, and at the same time conserve the limb.

All is very quiet round Chouts'un itself just now. We have only had our nightly fireworks on one occasion since I came back[115], but the patients we get are evidence that all is not quite so quiet in the surrounding districts.

Ronald to Ilkley

Chouts'un
7th August 1938

Dr Flowers got back from Tsingtao this morning, and so already I feel more free. It is a relief that my period of sole responsibility is over, although it hasn't really seemed a very difficult month, and it has been an experience that I know will be valuable. We have had forty eight inpatient admissions, about 550 outpatient visits, and sixty operations during the month.

With a good deal of anxiety, I attempted a hysterectomy yesterday morning. The patient was a woman who had had an 'issue of blood' for over a year, and now came to suffer more things at the hands of yet another physician! She was almost blanched when she arrived and her haemoglobin was only 10% instead of the usual 80 or 90%. Her husband gave her nearly a pint of his blood in a blood transfusion, which brought her haemoglobin up to 25% and we fed her on iron pills for a week which further increased it up to 30%, and yesterday she had her operation.

It was the most serious operation I have attempted so far, and you can guess how anxious I was about it. Miss Wheal and the Chinese nurses helped splendidly with all the preparations, and I used a special method of 'splanchnic' anaesthesia (to help to diminish the shock) which I had learned from Mr Hughes at Bradford. She really stood the operation wonderfully well, and was sitting up propped up in bed fanning herself last night. The operation took an hour and a half, but seemed to go quite satisfactorily. I hope very much she will do well.

I was all the more anxious about her, because the day before I did the operation, a patient died on whom I had operated for a similar condition. She was a widow of 40, who also had a large fibroid tumour

[115] From two weeks holiday in Tsingtao. Gwyneth and Rosemary stayed on there after Ronald returned to Chouts'un.

of the uterus, and because of the tumour, the uterus had turned itself inside out, and when she came to hospital the whole uterus and the tumour had been lying outside her body for two months. She had bacillary dysentery as well, and so we at first tried to cure her dysentery. After about a week, her dysentery seemed better, and she was very anxious to have her operation. It must have been an error of judgment to operate on her then. The operation at the time seemed technically to have been done satisfactorily, but about ten days later she collapsed rapidly and died. I think that her weak condition and anaemia together with the operation were too much for her heart, and she died of heart failure.

She was the sister of the president of the local branch of the Red Swastica Society[116], a wealthy and influential man, so that I have not helped my reputation. I felt I was doing the right thing at the time, but I think I allowed myself to be influenced too much by her wanting to have the operation done quickly. It often happens out here that, if you delay too long in preparation, the patient thinks that the doctor does not want to do the operation, and goes out without having it done. So that sometimes you have to use discretion in judging the patient's state of mind, as well as the indications of the actual disease.

Ronald to his father and mother

Chouts'un
5th September 1938

We start nursing school again next Monday. It's going to be hard with our short staff. Alice has given herself nine lectures a week in addition to all her other work. I have three, anatomy, ophthalmology and genito-urinary diseases, and the preparation for these and for ward services will keep me busy, I know.

I just want to tell you about the hysterectomy lady I told you about. She made a splendid recovery and went out of hospital just before I got back and was very pleased and grateful. She and her husband have presented me with a big framed Chinese kind of 'Scroll' which is now hung up in the hospital outpatient waiting hall. It has on it a quotation from the Chinese 'Classic of History': 'Tien kung jen tai'[117] – 'God entrusts his work to men'. I can't help feeling a little proud of this scroll, but I am more pleased that the lady got better and feels so much better and so grateful, and I am glad to have the lesson that the scroll teaches.

---

[116] A Buddhist version of the Red Cross. The use of the swastica as symbol was unrelated to its use in Nazi Germany.
[117] Pinyin = tian gong ren dai

Ronald seldom spoke about his personal beliefs, except when asked to do so or when leading prayers or public worship. As a student at Cambridge, he had spent many evenings with his fellow undergraduates reflecting on questions of politics, philosophy and religion and examining his childhood beliefs in the light of his maturity.

In the summer of 1928, at the end of his first year at university, he embarked with one close friend on a week long walk from Cambridge to Birmingham, during which the two young men undertook, as Ronald put it, ' a complete reconsideration of the story of Jesus, an earnest study of his character and teaching.'

At the end of the walk, Ronald recorded his conclusions: 'To me our walk has meant a wonderful revelation of God.... It has strengthened my belief that religion must be sought out not in the church primarily, but in Jesus in the gospels. Our walk has helped me to remember that life is primarily an action, that our characters will be determined by our relations with and our actions towards those around us.'

Later that same year, he wrote a seventeen page letter to his parents. 'This is an important letter', he wrote. 'In brief, I feel a call, and a very definite call, to be a medical missionary. Now I know that that simple statement will astound you. It almost astounds me as I write it.'

Explaining his most unexpected decision to his parents, Ronald went on, 'I believe, with all my powers of mind and soul, that the true way of life is that which Jesus lived and taught, namely the complete abnegation of self and of all selfish thoughts, motives, aims and acts, and the seeking to live the whole of life in accordance with the will of God.'

Ronald was convinced that the way he lived his life was the most important statement he could make about what he believed. It is no surprise, then, that he found the message of the scroll so pleasing.

Gwyneth to Ronald's father and mother

Chouts'un
28th September 1938

We await anxiously for European news these days, and keep hoping that all may be well. What an awful mess the world seems to be in.

I do hope you meet Tom Allen. He is such a splendid fellow, one of the very best. We wish we might at some time have the privilege of working with him and Connie – they are both so very nice. We are very

Margaret Logan

sorry about Connie not being able to come back. If it did not look like being such a long drawn out business it wouldn't be so bad, but it is difficult to see any satisfactory end for years, even if peace is declared. I hope you meet Logie, too. She is just the finest person, is always able to find time for anyone and is always so thoughtful and helpful. I feel I've lost an awful lot now she's gone. You felt you could go to her about anything and that she would never break your confidence.

Rosemary is as bonny and lively as ever. She is very keen on drinking tea at the moment, and spends hours with a tiny cream jar, pretending to drink and give her 'dodo' and 'bunny' a drink too! She amuses herself very happily.

Wu's elder girl has been in hospital with pneumonia. She seems better but we have been a bit anxious. He is so devoted to his children that we should be very sorry if anything happened to any of them, especially in hospital as the family have a rooted objection to foreign hospitals.

Well, the postman has just brought your letters of September 10, for which we are duly grateful. We knew you would share our gladness over our news[118], but it is good to hear from you and we are glad for all you write about it. I am and have been very well all the time.

Ronald to his father and mother

Chouts'un
16th October 1938

Gwyneth is just getting ready to go across to the Hospital evening service. Rosemary is fast asleep in her cot, hugging her bunny in one arm and her 'Do-Do' in the other, and it is my turn to stay in to look after her.

Yes, Miss Thomas is in charge of the children's refuge and they have about a hundred children living in the premises formerly occupied by Miss Smurthwaite's Ming Tao School. Miss Thomas invited the hospital staff to look round on Friday and we all went, Rosemary included. The premises have all been repaired and nicely painted since the bombing and look very well again. It was really a great satisfaction

[118] That Gwyneth and Ronald were expecting a second baby in December

to see the children so well behaved, and well-disciplined, and so obviously enjoying themselves in school and play, and especially satisfying when you think of the condition of their homes that have made such a refuge necessary for them. It is a good piece of work that Miss Thomas is doing, and, like everything she does, she is doing it well.

The children have a lot of minor ailments, and most of them have trachoma, so they swell our outpatient numbers to the extent of about twenty or thirty a day. They haven't had any serious illnesses as yet. I hope they can keep free through the winter. They were badly nourished when they arrived. We have received supplies of about 200lbs of Marmite through the Lord Mayor's Fund and this is proving a real blessing to all of the children, but especially to some who had symptoms of deficiency diseases when they arrived.

We shared your anxiety about the European situation. You will have gathered by now that we have a wireless set – brought it back from Tsingtao. Only cost between £5 and £6 second hand, but we can get London and Berlin direct and London relayed from Hong Kong and Delhi very clearly indeed, and it has been a great blessing, these last few days especially. We have felt to be closely in touch with you all and it is a great relief to know that there is, for the time at least, a more peaceful prospect. It is a strange situation, and full of inconsistencies, I think. I haven't any faith in the piling up of armaments. I find it hard in present circumstances to visualise a cause in which we should feel justified in using them, and they don't seem to act as a deterrent to the bullies of Europe or elsewhere. Our instrument here enables us to get news from Berlin direct so we were able to form a good idea of the type of propaganda that was being used.

I've just switched on to London to hear the beginning of the St Martin's service. They are just singing 'Soldiers of the Cross arise' and the subject of the address is to be 'The New Opportunity'. Wish we could all hear it together. Big Ben comes through splendidly and makes us homesick! Not the only thing that makes us homesick, but we are very happy here, and are glad to be able to have work here – and will be glad when the time comes when we can come back to you.

We have had quite a busy week in hospital. We had two gunshot wounds of the abdomen on Monday and Tuesday but both died – they had multiple intra-abdominal injuries. On Tuesday I had a man in who had been gored by a bull. He had a wound in his right lower abdomen with coils of intestine extruded. They had been covered by a chicken skin, the Chinese nearest approach to a sterile first aid dressing. I operated on him that afternoon, with Flowers' assistance and put back the bowel, which fortunately hadn't been injured, and repaired the abdominal wall, and I think he is going to recover. He's doing well so far.

Lectures still take a lot of my time in preparation, but I'm enjoying the work. Two more of our girl nurses came back today, some who left us when given the opportunity to do so before last Christmas. Wish we could see the prospect of a good Chinese doctor to help during Flowers' furlough.

Gwyneth to Ilkley and Cambridge

Chouts'un
24th October 1938

On Friday, instead of the usual devotional service at C.E. the girls were sewing garments to give to the children in the Refuge on the compound. They had a collection several weeks, and then when there was enough, bought cloth and cotton wool, and are making up the coats. I'm afraid I did not do very much, but I did a bit, and learnt a lot about how the Chinese make their padded garments which has always intrigued me, and I also learnt a little Chinese. The girls all sat around the room and I was able to move my place fairly frequently and speak to most of them, which I enjoyed. It is so much easier than speaking to a group of them at once. On Saturday we had another lot of the nurses in for supper. We hope to entertain them all in turn, but it is not always easy to fit it in with other things.

Rosemary is really very funny these days. We have told her to say 'sorry' to Kao when she spills anything on the floor, and so she seems to think she must always be saying it. The other day some workmen were repairing the roofs of the rooms at the back, and the ground was littered with bricks and tiles. She stared down at it solemnly for a few seconds and then very seriously said 'sorry Kao Ta Ko'! She evidently thinks he has to clear up any and every mess on the floor or ground.

I am finding it rather difficult when I take her out in the compound for walks just now. There is a Mrs Lu living here and her little girl is three months younger than Rosemary. Rosemary is always very pleased when she sees the little girl and runs up to her and chats with her and admires her brightly coloured trousers etc. We both feel we do not want Rosemary to grow up feeling she is superior to the Chinese children on the compound, but on the other hand we know this child has had dysentery badly recently and is still not properly well, and we naturally don't want to run any risks with Rosemary, especially just now.

The wee girl always has dirty fingers and insists on putting them into Rosemary's mouth, and also her mother is always offering Rosemary little bits of fruit or other eatables which are absolutely filthy, and it is most awkward to refuse. They think you are stuck up or something, but we both feel we can't let Rosemary eat such things. Hundreds of small children die of tummy troubles every summer. We often hear of families with one child, where five or six or more have died in infancy from tummy trouble of one sort or another. It was just after she had been playing with this child that Rosemary had her tummy upset before, so it makes us more careful.

Wu's little boy is really a sweet little chap. He and Rosemary get on well together, though I don't leave them to play alone. I always watch them. Wu's big girl is out of hospital now and much better, but not as fit as she ought to be to be doing the jobs she does, looking after the smaller children. It was no use trying to get them to let her stay in any longer. We are relieved she has recovered, as we were a bit anxious about her at one time.

The lack of home mail is a never ending topic of conversation, because even when there is a batch of it in, there is always one of us who has not got all he or she expected! You see, last week Mother's did not come, nor the cardigan, so I keep on hoping, and other people also miss things and so we go on, never completely satisfied. Awful, isn't it, when we have so much? Mr Harris of course always counts the days to the one when we may expect home letters, now that his wife is at home. He is a real home bird, and must miss his family terribly, though he never complains.

Gwyneth to her mother

Chouts'un
13th November 1938

Rosemary really is all joy, she's so lovely now. The weather being cooler, her cheeks are so beautifully rosy and she looks so bonny. She wears a pretty little blue silk padded short coat (just over her seat) and woolly trousers. The coat is one Wu's daughter made and gave her, we presume in gratitude for the fact that we paid her hospital expenses when she had pneumonia. She looks such a gem in it, with her fair fluffy hair, rosy cheeks and bright eyes and this bright blue silky coat. Of course when I take her for walks around I nearly burst with pride. She knows several useful Chinese phrases and usually brings them out nicely, which thrills the various coolies and so on.

I suppose I have told her to be careful when she is near the well. It's kept covered, but even so I want her to grow up with the idea of avoiding wells, as several aren't covered. This afternoon Ronald was showing her the pictures in his Bible and came to Jesus sitting by the well - she immediately recognised it as a well and said 'Hsiao Hsin Jesus' (be careful, Jesus).

Wang Ta Sao arrived here at midday on Wednesday. She had come from Tsingchou by train all right, but to get there she had a journey of thirty li (ten miles) and owing to the fact that there was a visit to that district from a certain party, no one would risk taking her in a rickshaw, nor hire out a donkey to her. So the poor little thing walked all the way, carrying all her luggage - not much because they don't have changes of winter garments like we do, but she had all her bedding, so it must have been pretty hard going. She just hoisted it all over her back, but she must have been terribly tired on arrival. All the way she could hear fireworks of various sorts so it was an unpleasant journey I am afraid. How she managed I don't know, but she is a faithful little woman to come under such conditions.

Kao has been home for a few days. The district where he lives has been experiencing similar troubles to those we had last Christmas and he was naturally very anxious. Fortunately his home escaped by about a mile and his folk are all safe. His mother has trachoma and he has brought her back for treatment, so now we have Kao and his Ma, Wu and wife and four children and Wang Ta Sao, all in three tiny rooms! So far all sounds peaceful but we feel it is rather a crowd and we wonder if there will be any ructions!

Gwyneth to her mother

Tsinan
29th November 1938

Well, we reached Tsinan in safety, without any real trouble. Alice, Emmie and Miss Thomas all came to say goodbye but only stayed a few minutes. We got onto the station fairly easily and had about half an hour to wait. When the train came, the crowd was awful and I got wedged between those pushing to get off and those pushing to get on and at one point quite thought I would land on the line. However, at last I got on the train. Ronald was ahead with Rosemary. The carriages were 3rd class, like when we went to Tsingtao, very crowded and very dirty, but the journey went quickly. We were only three hours and there was no unpleasantness, apart from the stuffiness. Rosemary was thrilled with everything and behaved beautifully.

We got to Tsinan at 3.10 p.m. and it was nearly 4.00 by the time we had been able to get our trunk and cot from the van. It depends a good deal on who is on duty, but they now insist on it all being checked before handing it over. At about 4.00 we got into rickshaws, the trunk and cot on the first, Wang Ta Sao and her bedding next, then me and Rosemary and then Ronald and the case. It was a sunny afternoon so we didn't feel cold and I took a rug too. We thought we would be out here in good time for 4.30 tea, but we were held up outside the city gate for an hour in a jam of barrows and carts and rickshaws. If it had been colder it would have been horrid, but we were very amused watching the people and seeing how calmly they took it.

At last we were able to move and gradually got to the gate. By accident I didn't realise I had got to the sentry and was bellowed at fiercely so I had to get out. You're supposed to get down and walk past the sentry and I couldn't do it very quickly with Rosemary and the rug, and before Ronald had time to help, the man yelled again and brought his bayonet unpleasantly near my face! However, I eventually got out and walked a couple of yards and then got in again. It really was funny to see him so angry, because I'd no intention of disobeying, but just hadn't been able to get out quicker. After that we raced along and thought we would soon be here, but again were held up. Certain streets were closed and we had to wait about and then do the trip by roundabout ways. So it was after 5.30 when we arrived.

Mrs Ingle, not knowing what was happening, had concluded we were too late to get into the city and probably wouldn't arrive till next day. However, we were welcomed and as soon as we had got Rosemary's night things out and the cot up we left her to have her supper with Wang Ta Sao and had our tea.

The nursery is a big room with a big veranda and is very sunny and nice, much nicer than our own really. There is a big stove in it and it is very cosy. Mrs Ingle has borrowed a sweet little chair from the Phillips with an animal on the back, which thrills Rosemary and she sits on that for her meals.

Ronald left at 7 a.m. yesterday. He will come up again just before Christmas and hope to be here until after the event. It will be such a help if he is. I will feel so much happier leaving Rosemary if he is here for a day or two, but it may be awkward to get away.

Both Lawrence and Nan[119] are extremely kind and thoughtful and yet there isn't any fuss. It is so nice too to be in a 'wider' atmosphere. It seems almost unavoidable that you get narrow and that little things upset folk in a small community as at Chouts'un, but here it is a far more normal life. There aren't anything like as many people here as normally, but it is quite different and much less full of rumours and alarms. Every time we go through the gate we have to write our names, ages etc down for the benefit of the powers that be, which is amusing, but otherwise there is no trouble. We have to bow to the sentry if he is about too.

Gwyneth to her mother

Tsinan
2nd December 1938

Well, it's this month now and probably you will have the cable before you get this. I am very excited, though shall be thankful to get it over, of course. Dr Gell[120] has seen me and seems to think all is well. I still feel fit. Poor old Kay seems set on a nephew and I feel sure it's a niece! I don't know why.

Ronald said in his letter yesterday that the Wu family have another daughter, a big bonny girl of eight lbs! I am afraid ours will look an awful squit beside it. Kao has a son of twelve and two girls about nine and four, but they live with his people and I have only seen the boy, quite a nice wee lad, very much like his father I imagine. Wu's home is in a much less peaceful area, that is why they have been with us more.

Since being here, I have done nothing much but read and eat and sleep and take Rosemary for a walk. Mr Phillips very kindly lent us his pram, so I push her to the campus and back and then she can run about and play as much as she likes there.

At the gate, there are Japanese soldiers and Chinese police on duty. Rosemary is a great help, every time I take her through, the policeman and sentries are so busy looking at her and talking to her that they forget to snap at me. She can answer the Chinese ones quite nicely, which thrills them, but of course the Japanese ones are quite hopeless for us both. She usually smiles at them which is the main thing and they sometimes understand if she says 'Good morning' in English. She looks so sweet in her blue suit.

---

[119] Dr and Mrs Ingle

[120] Dr Gell was the obstetrician who was to officiate at Gwyneth's next delivery. Dr King had moved from Cheeloo to an appointment as Professor of Obstetrics and Gynaecology in the University of Hong Kong.

Ronald to his father and mother

Chouts'un
6th December 1938

I hope by the time this reaches you that you will already have received word by cable bringing you our good news. Rosemary has been such a joy to us all the time, that we can hardly believe that another little child can bring as much joy, but we are looking forward to it gladly. Gwyneth writes very happily from Tsinan, and I am glad that she is there.

Thank you again for your generous gift of the Lancet. I get a very great deal of help from it, and shall get more help as time goes on, I know. I have now got twenty three volumes of journals (BMJ, Lancets and Chinese Medical Journals and a British Journal of Surgery) and I have made an index of them all under analysed headings – general surgery, abdominal surgery etc. - so that I can turn up articles on any particular subject at a few moments' notice.

Hospital is still busy. We have about sixty patients in at present, and now that we cannot use the verandas in the coldest weather, we only have about sixty five available beds. We haven't had so many wounded the last fortnight. Two weeks ago we had visits from the military authorities who said they had been informed that we were shielding guerrillas in our premises and they looked round the place. Nothing else happened, but we think that the visit may result in wounded people being afraid to attend for treatment. The result has been that we have had more people with civilian complaints recently. We have had two cases of cancer of the breast in, both of them with histories of over three years. I did one and Flowers the other.

The other interesting things I have done lately are mostly unmentionable in circular letters! So I will tell you in this one! One a man who fell astride an iron bar in the pit about thirteen years ago, and his ruptured urethra has been followed by a bad stricture. I did an operation on him that Lawrence Ingle told me about when I was up in Tsinan and it has proved very successful, and the patient is very pleased. Another man with a horrible advanced cancer of the penis, which needed complete amputation. He has done well too and is pleased with himself and me. The boy who was gored by the bull has done well and is just about ready to leave hospital.

It was good of Eddie to take you to the Sanatorium, Father. One of my headings in my index is tuberculosis. It is such a terrible scourge in China, more commonplace than leprosy, but more devastating, I think, in its results. If times were more settled, I would like us to be able to attempt something on a larger scale to help the poor sufferers. Did I tell you about the artificial Pneumothorax apparatus that I rigged up for the treatment of pulmonary TB? And about our nurse, Mr Ts'ai, who started spitting up blood just after the bombing last Christmas? We have been treating him by this apparatus, and he has made a splendid recovery, and we hope that it has been the means of saving his life.

The wireless is a great boon, and we are very thankful for it. Why, we heard that Cambridge had won the rugger match, the day after it had happened!

Ronald to his father and mother

Tsinan
23rd December 1938

You will have had our news for nearly three weeks now, I think, but I know you will be longing for details. Audrey arrived about 9.05 a.m. today and seems to be just as lovely as her big sister was. She has fair hair, too, and blue eyes, and cries ever so nicely and opens her eyes and yawns and has five toes on each little foot. And apart from that I know very little about her yet, because I have only seen her for a few minutes, but she seems a lovely little darling, and Gwyneth came through splendidly and seems very well and fit and happy. I won't write any more this time but will send this with love, lots of love, from us all four.

Gwyneth, Rosemary, Audrey and Ronald.

Ronald to his father and mother

Chouts'un
30th December 1938

I stayed in Tsinan until Monday morning, and got back to Chouts'un at 11 a.m. on Monday. I was able to slip into hospital to see Gwyneth very often, and by Christmas day she was able to sit up in bed and enjoy opening our Christmas parcels together.

Rosemary really was good all the time I was there. She plays so happily with whoever will play with her. Once or twice she asked for her mummy, but when I told her that she had gone to hospital, she seemed to think that that was all right. I expect she knew that it was the place her Daddy often went to, and must have thought that Mummy and Daddy were changing places for a change! Then on Christmas morning I took her to hospital to see Gwyneth and Baby Audrey. She hardly knew what to make of her Mummy sitting up in bed, but she sat on the edge of the bed, and looked so sweet and lovely in the little blue winter coat and leggings that Gwyneth made for her. Then I took her along to the room where Audrey was in her cot, and lifted her up to look. She could soon say 'Baby Audey' and 'Audey seepy' and kept wanting to go back and look at her again, saying 'See Audey'.

Our Christmas celebrations at hospital were different from last year's. We were able to decorate the wards and have a fine big Christmas tree in the women's ward, and Father Christmas arrived on Christmas day and distributed gifts to all the patients and coolies. Mr Phillips has been down here spending Christmas with Flowers, and Mr Harris has been staying over this side too, so they had company. The nurses had a party on Wednesday, when we provided the eatables and they played some games, like sticking on the donkey's tail, and having blindfold fights, armed with a rolled up newspaper. They all seemed to enjoy themselves very much.

Gwyneth to Ilkley (and Cambridge)

Home
25th January 1939

Well, Ronald managed to get up to Tsinan on Thursday evening and they got me out of hospital on Friday morning. Having been sent back once, I scarcely dared believe I was really out, but it was good to be at the Ingles', and to see Rosemary again. Four weeks was a long time to go without seeing her, but Mrs Ingle was afraid it would upset her and she'd been so good that she didn't want to risk it.

Ronald decided to bring us back on Monday. We felt we'd troubled the Ingles long enough so, at crack of dawn on Monday, or to be exact 5 a.m., I fed Audrey and then Ronald got up and got Rosemary onto his bed while he packed her cot. Wang ta Sao dressed her and gave her her brekker, while I had mine and saw to Audrey's dressing for her first real venture out of doors. We had a taxi at Tsinan. The big luggage, including a big fireguard for the nursery which Mrs Ingle gave us, went on ahead, and Mr Payne very kindly took his man and saw it onto the train for us, so that Ronald could be with me. We got on without trouble – it was rather cold, but I don't think we took any harm. We were here on time and got through without difficulty. Wu and Kao and Miss Thomas and Miss Jagger were up at the furthest point allowed without special permits and Alice was at the hospital gate, so we had a good welcome.

Oh, it's so nice to be home, though I am sure it was right to go to Tsinan, and the time there before December 23 was really a big help. I so enjoyed the freer atmosphere and meeting more people.

Rosemary is now no longer the 'little girl' – she's the big one and Audrey is Er Ku Niang[121], 2nd girl. Our two little cots look so sweet side by side and the wee treasures inside look even sweeter!

Ronald to Ilkley and Cambridge

Chouts'un
12th February 1939

The chief event of importance that has happened here recently has been our Shantung BMS foreign Conference, which was held last weekend in Chouts'un. It was quite a treat for us to have so many foreigners all gathered together in Chouts'un, sixteen including Rosemary and Audrey, Mr and Mrs Pailing from Tsinan and Mr Payne and Mr Drake; and Mrs Smith and Mr and Mrs Emmott from Tsingchoufu, in addition to the Chouts'un folk. We had Mr Drake and Mr Harris staying with us and very much enjoyed their company.

From the medical point of view the most important business was appointing Mr Pailing to take Flowers' place as Hospital Superintendent here while Flowers is on furlough. We also invited Dr Margaret Jenkins (who is at present at the language school) to come and live here during Flowers' furlough before she proceeds to Shensi, and we confirmed the invitation to Nurse Jagger to come here after her term at the language school.

I'm very pleased at the prospect of the Pailings coming here, and I think it's right that he should be asked to take over the Superintendency. He is of course much my senior, and I'm sure that we shall be able to divide the work very satisfactorily with him as superintendent. I shall be able to take charge of the clinical side of the work, which should give me plenty to do, and he'll be able to superintend the administrative side, besides being a big help in the dispensary, and being able to help in the nursing school by giving the materia medica lectures. Mrs Pailing will be a big help too. Gwyneth and I are looking forward to spending a very happy year with them.

We had hoped to be able to secure the services of a good Chinese doctor. We had begun negotiations with an old Cheeloo graduate, who has been at Weihsien for several years, but we have just heard from him

[121] Pinyin = er gu niang

that he is unable to come. Disappointing, but perhaps we shall be able to get hold of someone else before long.

It's certainly going to be a strenuous year with Flowers away. I haven't any misapprehensions about that, but at the same time I am not unduly anxious about it. I've no doubt that there will be lots of occasions when I should be grateful for the advice and help and experience of a senior colleague, but if they are not available I will do the best I can by myself, and the patients will have to put up with it! I'm hoping very much that I shall be able to keep well all the time. If I can, then I'm not afraid that the actual work will be too heavy. Anyway I'll do my best, and shall have to leave undone what can't be managed.

One thing has impressed me this last week. A few days ago we took in a Chinese soldier who, while acting as a J guard, was shot by Chinese guerrillas. He had a bullet through both his lungs, and was very seriously ill when he arrived. He's been operated on twice and we got the bullet out, and I'm hoping that he's now on the way to recovery. I've been impressed with the kindly treatment that he's received at the hands of all our nurses and coolies since he might easily be regarded as a traitor to their country. I think it's truly 'Love in Action'.

Gwyneth to Cambridge

Chouts'un
26th February 1939

This week has been upset with Wu getting sick. As Alice was in Tsingchou till Tuesday afternoon, her cook did our meals till then and Wang ta Sao and I did the clearing up and so on. We were quite alone Tuesday night and till supper on Wednesday. I know that doesn't seem anything to people at home without servants, but without running water and with four stoves to see to it's quite heavy. Dr Flowers' boy drew the water for us, but Wang ta Sao did all the stoves, the first time she'd ever tackled these sort of stoves! Got up at 5 a.m. to do them.

On Tuesday, we decided we must send for Kao[122]. He'd intended to return Saturday but Ronald said Wu wouldn't be better for some days and we felt we'd have to have a man. So we sent, and Kao returned Wednesday evening – cheerful and quite willing to do all the cooking and so on.

On Thursday, we persuaded Wu to go into hospital. There's no-one here to look after him, and his two children worried him in the room.

[122] He had gone home for Spring Festival

Wang Ta Sao has really been marvellous, so willing and tackling all sorts of heavy jobs and ones she'd never done before. And now in addition she's looking after Wu's children when they're not in school. She is really a splendid little woman and we feel we couldn't have had a better amah. Wu has pneumonia. It's rotten for him, but Ronald isn't specially anxious about him.

Gwyneth to Cambridge

Chouts'un
5th March 1939

The Drs Chou

A Dr Chou from Tsingchou, and his wife also a doctor (name pronounced Joe) are to be transferred here for Dr Flowers' furlough. We hope he can relieve Ronald of some of the routine work, and she is a very attractive person and bright and we think she'll be quite a help. Though she's had very little experience, if she's bright and willing that's a big thing.

Wu is better and more or less doing his job now, though I think Kao is still doing the shopping. It's such a relief having two boys who work so well together. They very seldom have the least sign of disagreement and we never get complaints about one from the other and they share the work very well. I think it's partly because Wu is so good-natured, he doesn't mind giving in. I think Kao would like a better job and although we'd hate to lose him, we feel he deserves a cook's job. He's quite capable of it and he is thirty five or thirty six now and doubtless feels he should be promoted. However, he's happy here, I'm sure, and would only leave if he heard of anything in the way of promotion.

Tom Allen says Connie is just waiting for him to say 'come' and she will shake the dust of England off her feet and come immediately. As the Mission is advising women with children to stay at home, they decided it wisest for him to come alone and see for himself, and then decide whether to send for them. It is far from ideal out here, but the news we get now indicates that it is not by any means peaceful[123] in Europe. I think the folk who are planning to go home by Siberia are beginning to wonder if they'll manage it all right.

On Thursday evening we had three more nurses in for supper. The three we had were all easy to talk to, and of course as we have more language we feel a little easier with them. Two of the girls went to their homes in south Shantung as the war drew near to us, and they were telling us how they were obliged to leave their homes with their families and go into the country, when the fighting started. They both live in the same street, and it was practically all wiped out by bombs, and they lost more than half their belongings. We were amazed at the calm way they told us about it, and the quiet way they came back here and started nursing as soon as they were able to get here. They were in a small party, the first civilians to travel by train up to Hsuchou. They came in military trucks as far as that, but then the trains were running with ordinary coaches, so that it was all right from there. The Chinese seem able to suffer so much without letting it get on top of them. They go on quite calmly, whereas we should have all sorts of nervous breakdowns.

The infants are both well. Audrey now begins to take a definite interest in life, and it won't be long before she starts kicking her blankets off. She has a good try now, but so far she can't manage it. Rosemary goes off quite happily with any of our nurses and they're thrilled to bits. She takes their hands and goes into their garden and never bothers a bit about me. There's one old woman living on the compound. She's old and deaf but whenever she meets me she shouts out to ask if the baby is all right and if I've enough milk for it, and whether Rosemary still has my milk! Her shouting always attracts a small crowd and as she's deaf she never hears my reply and so a coolie or someone yells to her that I've plenty of milk thank you!!

Ronald to Ilkley and Cambridge

Chouts'un
26th March 1939

During this last week I have paid a visit to Poshan and Tsingchoufu. Poshan is the terminus of a little branch railway line that runs southwards into the hills from Changtien, an important junction two

[123] Referring probably to the German annexation of Czechoslovakia.

stations to the east of Chouts'un. Regular train services are now running on these lines, and all the journeys were made without untoward events. Almost every village that we passed on the two hour journey showed evidences of the ravages of war – the ruins and roofless shells of houses destroyed by fire, - but in most of them repair works had begun, and patches of new yellow straw-thatched roofs stood out among the rest.

Poshan nestles in a hollow among the surrounding hills. Unlike most Chinese towns and villages, its streets do not run quite so regularly east and west and north and south on account of the hilly ground, and it's not quite so easy to remember at once whether you are facing north or east. It has at least three distinct town walls, and, on our way up to the church premises, we threaded our way in and out the gates of these walls in a way that was confusing for a newcomer. A stream, a good-sized stream, of clear water tinged rust-coloured with iron, runs down from the hills through the town, and at the side of the stream is a market place on which stand the temporary straw matting shelters of stall holders who sell the hardware products of the Poshan furnaces.

Mr Harris had arranged for me to be met at the station, and when I got there, there was Deacon Han to meet me. He is a man of fifty six (I guessed his age right in the inevitable age guessing competition that took place in one of the shops that he took me to. My age was variously guessed at twenty five and thirty five![124]) and he was formerly a deacon of our Tsingchou church, and owned a watch and clock shop there. He took me up to the compound which belongs to the mission and which is a residential compound, at present occupied by the pastor, Pastor Su, and about thirty or forty men, women and children, many of whom are refugees. Some of them are the parents of children who are at present in Miss Thomas' children's refuge here in Chouts'un. The compound itself is a rectangular courtyard of buildings, single-storeyed, and in the middle of the yard is a big mound of earth which serves to cover the dugout which was prepared at a time when shells were flying dangerously near the compound not so very long ago.

As soon as I got there a meal was prepared in Pastor Su's room, a Chinese meal of steamed-bread, savoury scrambled eggs, and a kind of soup with meat balls and other Chinese delicacies in it, to which the three of us and another deacon named Chang sat down. One of the things that impressed me most in my visit was the wonderful spirit of patience and cheerfulness and kindness of the Chinese whom I met. They have all been through extremely hard and trying times. Pastor Su has lost his only

[124] Ronald was 30 years old at this time

son during the past year in the war, Deacon Han has been forced to leave his home, and Deacon Chang's little eleven year old grandson had only a few days before been carried off by bandits and held to ransom for $1,000 (£40). And yet you did not hear a single hard or bitter word, and only met with very kind and thoughtful hospitality.

After dinner, Han took me to show me the various places of interest – the Church, a good-sized brick and stone building which would hold about two hundred and fifty, and behind it a two–storey building now being used as a day-school for about two hundred pupils of elementary school age, run by the church with six voluntary teachers. Then up one of the hills to a little Buddhist temple on the top, from which a good view of the town could be obtained, the town itself dirty with coal dust, and a haze of smoke covering that part where the furnaces of the glass-workers' homes are just beginning to be busy again after being idle for a long time, and the surrounding hills green with the early spring wheat, and pine woods. Down again, and over to the west suburb where most of the glass work is done.

Our Hospital medicine bottles are made here, and Han took me along to the place where they are made, the entrance just like any tiny Chinese compound in a tiny back street. Inside, a good-sized shed with about ten or twelve furnaces hard at work, and about thirty or forty glass-blowers looking like elves, stripped to the waist, and the molten glass at the end of their long blow-pipes shining like little fairy lamps. Some of them are just young lads of twelve or thirteen, but they told me that they could blow about 7,000 tiny eye-drop medicine bottles in a day. Several families co-operate together to do the various branches of the trade, blowing polishing, painting etc. One of the interesting things I saw was a very clever workman, painting on the inside of a bottle with the aid of a long brush, slightly curved at its tip, inserted through the neck of the bottle.

By the time we had finished looking round, it was almost dark, and we made our way back to the mission yard. By that time Mr Harris had arrived from Chouts'un on his bicycle, and I was glad to see him. Supper was waiting for us. It was much the same as the midday meal, the remnants of the scrambled eggs heated up again, and some grain gruel. After supper, the folk who lived on the compound began to assemble in the pastor's room for a weeknight meeting, about twenty five or thirty of them, men, women and children. They are a very nice friendly, kindly people, and I enjoyed the meeting, and the time we spent in conversation afterwards. They get little reliable news, and they were glad to meet someone who had heard recent wireless news.

To bed, in a room with Mr Harris. Lots of things I could tell you about that if there were time! A hard board bed, softened and warmed by wadded quilts, wrapped up like the crust of a sausage roll, with me inside like the sausage! I was up earlier than I'd been for a long time, just in time for a breakfast of steamed bread and a big bowl of bean-curd milk, a visit to the school again where the children were just beginning their classes, and the rickshaw ride to the station to catch the train back to Changtien. Packed like sardines – it was one of those carriages in three tiers like the one we went to Tsingtao on last year, and I was up on the top layer, with no room to straighten up my back. My chief regret was that I couldn't look out of the window to see the scenery. At Changtien a wait of about an hour for the train to Tsingchou.

Mr Emmott met me at Tsingchou, and I renewed my memories of the town as we rode through in rickshaws. At New Year time, Chinese families usually paste strips of red paper on the lintels and door-posts of their houses with good luck texts. This year the Tsingchou people had all been compelled to paste up patriotic slogans such as "Don't alter the old family customs" (i.e. stick to the old Confucian morality – one of the present Jap slogans), and "Put into practice Sino-Jap co-operation" etc. Tsingchou has big city walls – the gateway must be thirty feet high and the walls about thirty or forty feet thick.

Our mission premises are to the south of the town, inside the south gate. Since the new regime, the south gate has been permanently closed, and to get to the leper hospital, which lies in the hills about a mile to the south of the south gate, you now have to go out of the east gate, and wind back again outside the wall to the south, quite a longish extra journey.

No time to tell the whole story, but I was glad to see our friends the Emmotts and Mrs Smith and especially Tom Allen just back from furlough. He took morning prayers at the school while I was there and kept all the two hundred-odd children wide-eyed with interest while he spoke. Dr Ching and Dr Chou very kindly and generous in their hospitality, a meal with them and a visit to the Leper Hospital in the morning. The place does Dr Ching very great credit – twenty five lepers there just now, about twelve of them free.

Tsingchoufu, about fifty miles east of Chouts'un, was the first inland station established by the BMS in China when the pioneer missionary, Timothy Richards, moved there in 1875 from the coastal town of Chefoo. Richards chose it for the new headquarters of the mission because of its longstanding importance as a religious and administrative centre. A training school for teachers and preachers was opened in 1887 which subsequently formed the basis of the theological faculty of the Shantung Christian University in Tsinan. The importance of Tsingchoufu declined after 1904 when the railway from Tsingtao to Tsinan was opened, enabling travellers to cross the province from the East without stopping at Tsingchoufu.

Medical work was started there by the BMS in 1885, when Dr James R Watson and his wife Dr Agnes R Watson opened a small dispensary. A fully equipped hospital was later established in Tsingchoufu under their leadership. Dr Ching took charge as medical superintendent in 1927 and remained in overall charge of the hospital until the late 1940s, with occasional back-up from the Chouts'un doctors. A separate facility for lepers had been added in early 1936.

Ronald to Ilkley and Cambridge

Chouts'un
14th May 1939

It's now six weeks since Flowers handed over the medical responsibilities of the hospital, and since he left the place has been exceptionally busy in all the departments. Last month there were over two thousand outpatient attendances, and we had an average of eighty three inpatients in hospital every day, with eighty six as a maximum on some days. All these figures are records for the hospital.

And the patients who are coming to hospital now mainly come for civilian complaints, and gunshot wounds are becoming much less common, though we still see a number of patients who come in for treatment of injuries received some time ago. One little lad, hardly in his teens, had had a bayonet right through his chest from front to back a month ago. It must have missed his heart by the merest fraction of an inch, and it's a miracle that he is still alive. His chest was full of pus when he arrived here, and he had an operation yesterday to let some of it out.

With all these folk to look after our days seem very full, and often tiring as well. Now that the weather is warmer we are having our morning prayers at 7 a.m. so we are up soon after 6.30 and we're usually ready for bed after I have done my evening round after the London news broadcast which begins at 9.15 p.m., or the Chungking[125] broadcast at 10 p.m.

Dr Chou is being a tremendous standby. We all like him more the more we see of him. He seems extremely steady and reliable, is very pleasant to work with, and has a very sound knowledge of medicine. It's a tremendous help, too, having the Pailings here. Bill is doing the whole of the administrative side of the work – accounts, buying-in, looking after property - and you can guess what a big relief that is to me. Besides, he and Muriel are taking a very keen interest in the evangelistic work of the hospital, for which they are both very well fitted by training and experience.

I think you'll be interested to hear about some of the cases we've been treating and some of the operations we've been doing lately. I'll tell you first about my disappointments, and then something about the ones I'm more pleased about. We've had three deaths following operations in the last six weeks. Two of them were following gunshot wounds of the abdomen, and as both were nearly twenty four hours old when they arrived, the odds were heavily against them from the start.

The other death I am very disappointed about. He was a man of about fifty five whose leg I had amputated two years ago for gangrene of the foot. The gangrene was due to a disease of his blood vessels, and he came along this time because he was beginning to get gangrene in his other foot. I attempted an operation on the sympathetic nerves in his abdomen hoping to stop the progress of the gangrene and leave him with a leg to get about on, and although the operation seemed technically satisfactory, he was evidently not strong enough to stand it and his heart gave out and he died. Without the operation he was doomed to be a cripple for the rest of his life, but I was very upset at the result.

We've had quite a number of other patients whose treatment has given a good deal of satisfaction. The operation that I am most pleased about is one I did on a woman patient aged about forty four who presented herself with a cancer of the breast and with a large abdominal swelling as well. The tumour in the breast was an advance one and not a suitable case for operative treatment. The Professor of Surgery at Glasgow has described in the Lancet two such cases, in which the removal of the patient's ovaries and spleen has been followed by a disappearance of the malignant growth. This woman's abdominal tumour was an ovarian tumour, which itself might have been malignant, and it seemed specially unwise to attempt to remove the cancer of the

[125] Headquarters of Chiang Kai-shek's government – see below

breast if she was going to die anyway from a malignant ovary. On the other hand, if the ovarian tumour had to be removed, it seemed justifiable at the same time to remove the other ovary and the spleen, in the hopes that the tumour of the breast might regress, as in the Glasgow cases. We explained the position to the patient and her relatives, and, to cut a long story short, she had the operation about three weeks ago and has done splendidly. The operation took two hours and I was jolly glad when it was over, and more glad than ever when the days went past and I knew she was going to be all right. We shall follow her with very great interest to see whether there are any real hopes of this operation proving a cure for malignant disease.

One other patient that I'm very pleased about, a woman who came in ten days ago. It was as difficult a labour case as I ever want to come up against, and I didn't expect that she would recover, but she too has done splendidly, and I think she is going to get better now. I think her life has been saved here and I'm very pleased about it.

There's our 2 o'clock gong just sounding and time for outpatients. Tom Allen is coming to tea this afternoon and perhaps he and Pailing and Dr Chou and I will be able to get a game of tennis after tea. Tom has been staying with Mr Harris for a few days while paying a visit to the churches in this district.

By the beginning of 1939, Chiang Kai-shek's government had removed inland to Chungking, high on the cliffs in the gorges of the Yangtze river. Meanwhile, the Japanese had come to realise that, despite their capture of the major Chinese cities in the north and east, it was unlikely that they would be able to achieve a decisive victory over the country as a whole. They decided, therefore, to consolidate their control of the areas already captured, while at the same time attempting to wear down the Chinese by continued indiscriminate bombing raids elsewhere. Chungking was a primary target: it was bombed two hundred and sixty eight times between 1939 and 1941, with heavy casualties.

In early June, one of the Chinese puppet officials appointed by the Japanese was assassinated in the British concession in Tientsin. When the British refused to hand over the suspected assassins, the Japanese military instituted a blockade of the British concession and ordered body searches of everyone going in and out. The British Government, faced with the possibility of a war in Europe, wanted to avoid conflict with the Japanese at all costs and failed to challenge this encroachment on its Treaty rights in the concession.

This encouraged a general stiffening of the Japanese attitude towards the British in China, and in particular towards missionaries who they suspected of collaborating with the guerrilla forces. Japanese inspired Anti-British demonstrations were staged in all the areas where missionaries were deployed, and there was widespread intimidation of Chinese Christians. Threats of reprisals were used to try to force Chinese servants to walk out on British employers.

Gwyneth to Ilkley

Chouts'un
17th June 1939

We're just hearing about the situation in Tientsin, wondering how it may affect us. It's not too cheerful at the moment – no doubt you will be hearing it too.

Ronald hopes to write, but he really never has a minute except when he's just too tired for anything. They're still very busy and having a good many emergency operations. A little boy in the Refuge had appendicitis on Friday. They aren't supposed to operate without parents' permission but it would take at least two days to get word to his home. Ronald felt if he waited the lad might get peritonitis and yet to operate was a responsibility. Miss Thomas left it to Ronald and he decided to operate. It went well and the lad seems to be going on all right – his father has just arrived this morning. Ronald feels sure he did right, the appendix was in a bad condition, but if it hadn't gone well we might have had a very awkward time.

Mr Harris left here on Tuesday[126] and we are quite anxious as to how he'll fare in Tientsin. He has to go into the Concession to arrange about his passport - I do so hope he gets through safely. He has had no holiday for two years to save up for this and has prepared everything here so as to leave an absolute minimum for us to do in his absence, and of course he's so thrilled at the thought of seeing his wife.

I thought Rosemary was good and contented but Audrey is just as good. She never cries for her feed in the morning, she goes to bed after her 6 p.m. feed and I never hear a sound. When I go in about 5.30, I find her lying wide awake waving her arms and legs about so happily – always gives me such a lovely little smile. She can take her bath

[126] On his way back to England

leisurely in these hot days and I love to feast my eyes on her firm little body and dimpled limbs.

I'm making a kimono for Alice. It's her material but she's not time to make it before she goes to Tsingtao. It's being done in the Japanese style, which takes a bit more time, but I think it'll look quite nice. I'm trying to make up my last cotton remnant for myself into a sleeveless frock, for very hot days at the sea, with a short sleeved coatee to wear here. Rosemary and Audrey are both fairly well off for frocks now, but I'll probably need to make them new ones next year, so shall be glad not to have any of my own to bother with.

Ronald thinks you (Father) are remarkably quiet about the Yorks and Lancs cricket and reminds you that we get the scores here so you can't hush it up![127]

Gwyneth to Ilkley

Chouts'un
24th June 1939

Tremendous joy today, there is a steady rain. We had a few drops two days ago and then it cleared up and we were all so disappointed. Yesterday was hot and sunny again, so it was a surprise to hear rain in the night and this morning there's a lovely fall. The earth has been terribly dry. This should be a help, and although it's very late, there is just a hope that some of the crops may be saved. The Chinese are full of thankfulness. Our garden has huge pools so it's not easy to get out, but no one expects to go far when it's raining here.

Although it seems unkind, I feel glad that some of the outpatients will be frightened away by the rain because Ronald is so terribly tired. But he just keeps on without complaining. The heat has been very trying this week. Even at home I've felt plenty warm enough, and the children both have a little prickly heat. Audrey has such fat little arms and the creases get so hot, and her wee neck is all prickly heat too, but neither she nor Rosemary seems the least concerned by it.

There's a Chinese hymn, very popular,

There's only one true God, the Heavenly Father.

He gives me food, he gives me clothes, and always pities me.

(That's a very bad translation.) Anyway, Rosemary knows the words in Chinese, and the other day when she was chatting with the carpenter, she

---

[127] WKS, born in Liverpool, was a keen Lancashire supporter, while the rest of the family supported Yorkshire – evidently Yorkshire were doing well that summer.

started off 'there's only one true God' and then said 'shih Yin Shih Fu' ('that's the painter'!), the painter being a pal of hers. Of course this caused a good deal of amusement!

The Pailings had us in to supper one evening when they first came and we had quite a nice meal. While we were eating it, Mrs Pailing was saying what she thought of the Flowers' boy who is doing her cooking. She seemed to think he was quite good and able to make anything she suggested. The next morning I was talking with Wu and he tactfully asked me if we had had a nice pie the night before. When I said 'yes', he admitted that not only had the boy been to him for help in making it but actually we had lent him the meat to put into it! I told the Pailings and they appreciated the joke as much as we did! Once or twice when we are invited out to Chinese meals we find our own crockery on the table, 'borrowed' for the occasion, though our boys seem better than most - we are usually informed beforehand that it is wanted.

You really seem to think I have an awful lot of birthdays! (not that I object, as long as you don't add on a year each time!). I'm sure you've already given me a present and now you tell me you've bought that length of silk. It sounds most attractive and it's lovely of you to get it. I think Logie is sure to be willing to bring it.

I'm thinking of sending Wang Ta Sao to Tsingchou on Monday for a few days. She may not be able to get home, but she has friends in Tsingchou and can hear all her home news. She *won't* take time off. Even when there really isn't a thing to do, she still feels she ought to be upstairs listening in case the children wake or something, so I really feel it's the only way to give her a change. If she returns to Connie in the autumn I'll have to make new arrangements. Meanwhile we're very thankful for Wang Ta Sao's faithful service just when we seemed to need her most.

I hope you won't be alarmed by any news you may hear. We'll do what we think is best in any circumstances and we don't want you to worry.

Gwyneth to Ilkley and Cambridge

Chouts'un
2nd July 1939

It is still very hot, and in spite of a fairly heavy shower of rain one day, everywhere still seems parched. Three of four showers in nine months is absolutely inadequate for the needs of the farmers, and indeed for our own garden. The boys water it so carefully every evening, and we have been having vegetables from it, but we have had to give up most of the flowers. There is not enough water to spare, and anyway we decided in our first year that as long as the boys did their best we would not worry them to water the flowers. It's such heavy work drawing the water and carrying it in the terrific heat.

I have had anxious moments at Prayers in Hospital this week, fearing that Ronald or I, or both of us, might burst with pride at any moment. Rosemary has come with us every day but one when she slept late, and she has been just as good as gold, and so terribly pleased with it! She and I have sat at the back so that we could slip out if necessary, but the novelty of it has over-awed her, and she has sat absolutely still and quiet, though the first day, she did say in a whisper as Wu came in, 'Hullo Wu Shih Fu'.

Wang Ta Sao went off on Monday, and left for her home on Tuesday. She intended to walk, she refused our offer of rickshaw fare, as she said if she rode she might be taken for a wealthy person and have difficulties on the way. We expect her back on Friday, I do hope she has no troubles. In some ways it has been nice to be without her, I love having the children on my own, and it is not at all difficult, except that I cannot get out without them - not that I ever want to, but it is expected of me sometimes.

The other evening I had a scare, I found the first scorpion we have ever seen in the house, just under our bed-side table, very close to my slippers. It was most fortunate that I happened to be up just then and see it. I quickly 'did' for it, a horrible big fat creature. I didn't enjoy killing it at all, but I daren't wait lest I should lose sight of it. Now I am wondering if the rest of its relations are going to turn up. The boys were not exactly comforting when they cleared up the remains the next day. Kao said that if it had stung one of us, we should have had agonising pain for at least eight hours as it was such a big thing. Wu went even further and said that it would certainly have killed Audrey if it had got at her. Maybe they were both right, but I did not really thank them for the information.

We feel a little more hopeful about things here at the moment, but the European situation sounds pretty poor and that is bound to have a good deal of influence on things here too.

On 16th July, Anti-British pickets in Taiyuan surrounded the Baptist church during the evening service and arrested some 200 Chinese men, women and children. They were detained for three days while the local Anti-British Committee threatened to execute them unless the missionaries evacuated the town. Sixteen, including hospital staff, nurses, and evangelists, were taken to the Japanese military headquarters and charged with collaborating with the guerrillas. All were bound and beaten, and some tortured to extract information. One evangelist suffered several months' imprisonment and ill treatment, before eventually being killed. When it became clear to the missionaries that it would be in the best interests of Chinese Christians if they withdrew, they left Shansi province to take up work elsewhere in China.

Gwyneth to her mother

Chouts'un
23rd July 1939

I'm really finding it hard to know how to write in these days. Since last Monday there has been one thing after another which I'd better not write of in detail, but it has caused us to change our mind almost daily as to the possibility of fulfilling our plans for next week.[128] The situation is really difficult and serious and we simply cannot tell what a day may bring. I know that the political situation your way isn't rosy, but you are among your own folk and there's no unpleasantness in that way. Please don't say much about all this. Fortunately the infants are still flourishing and Ronald, although tired, is quite cheery.

Your letter came yesterday. So glad that your holiday was all so nice and that you got home safely. I'm afraid I'll just want to go out to shows or something all the time when I first get home, after being so shut in here! It's not bad in the compound, but we do long to get away sometimes. You can never be sure, apart from anything else, that they won't suddenly have curfew and stop all use of roads. That happened here on Saturday. Kao got back as far as the road that runs past the hospital, but wasn't allowed to cross to our gate for about two hours! He was as near as the Winships' house to No. 8[129], but couldn't cross! And there's never any warning, so I loathe leaving the children.

I heard what marvellous kippers you sent from Yarmouth, I think you might have remembered us too!

My younger daughter is just seven months, and quite a bonny specimen. She still can't get her teeth through, rubs and rubs her gums in

---

[128] To go to Tsingtao for a summer break.
[129] 8 de Freville Ave, Cambridge

desperation when she's tired. I'm first going to try her on groats, just a taste before her feed. I don't intend to wean her till September but want to give her a little extra to help us both.

Monday Well, I tried groats and she's expressed in no uncertain terms her utter contempt for such horrid stuff. And when I tried tomato juice this morning she thought that even more revolting, so I'm afraid she's not going to be so easy as her big sister.

Rosemary is upstairs shouting to herself, 'Please Jesus, come and have some tea with me' !!

I've got things more or less straight now for going away. At least I've got all the sewing done, except a few buttons and so on, but I'll have time this week I expect. If Ronald can't come, and he must be guided by events, I intend to go two days early and get on the train with the Phillips. I'm still not quite sure if that'll be the thing to do but at the moment that's how we feel.

Gwyneth to Ilkley and Cambridge

Chouts'un
30th July 1939

Well the blow has fallen, the staff have five days in which to clear out, and it looks as if they will have no choice but to go. We still hope that even with all of them gone it will be possible for some of the foreigners to stay on. Otherwise with no-one here the place will certainly be lost to us.

It seems best that I should take the children away if possible, as there will certainly be difficulty in getting fresh food, and our stores will not last long. The fewer here the longer they will last. Ronald does not think I ought to go alone in present circumstances with the children at their present ages, so he hopes to be able to escort us to the coast and then try to get back. Farther than this we cannot plan at all. If Ronald gets back here he will probably be unable to keep in touch with us. If there is no ban on luggage, I hope to take some warm things with me, in case we do not get back before the cooler weather comes. But we hope very much that it will blow over and we shall be able to return.

Do not be anxious about us. Apart from our very natural disappointments over the whole thing, which you will understand even though I cannot give more details, we are not upset. There does not seem to be any danger, and we only just wish that we need not separate, but it seems wise to get the children away. Although the other place may not be much better, the community is bigger and there are British ships there.

I think that is all I can write about it now. You will understand that I have lots of things to think about, and do. I will try to write again from Tsingtao as soon after I arrive as it can be managed.

Gwyneth to Ilkley and Cambridge

Tsingtao
3rd August 1939

I'll just tell you that we've arrived safely in Tsingtao. After a great deal of talking we eventually decided that Su and I should travel together, Miss Thomas waiting to keep Alice company and to see how things go. Our whole outlook changed a dozen times a day as fresh events occurred. Ronald felt he couldn't leave for a few days. He's waiting to see which way things develop.

Having prepared well ahead for our holiday, I have had a hectic last two days re-packing, leaving out Ronald's things and packing some other things in case we can't get back for a time. Of course, although a lock can easily be broken, I wanted to lock away things as much as possible, and I managed to clear everything out of drawers, more or less. We still hope the place will not be looted, though if everyone leaves, it's a very small hope. It was a hectic rush, terrible heat, and people calling all the time. I've scarcely seen Ronald since the news arrived in the middle of tea on Sunday.

We were all packed in excellent time on Wednesday and Ronald went off to take the big stuff. With my trunks, Su's and one for Miss Thomas, one for Alice, and with the cot and pram there was a big pile, but he was there in plenty of time. However, when we got there with our small stuff, they still hadn't finished 'examining' them. I'd no chance to speak to him and hear why, but I've a good idea the extra delay was not accidental.

We just managed to get on the train with our small stuff and they said there was no time to check the big luggage so we went off leaving them on the platform. We had real trouble in getting help to get our small things on. I was fairly useless with two infants, but Su did her best and we managed to get on necessities for a night, and a basket for Audrey to sleep in. It's awkward having no cot or pram, but it's a detail really.

I can't give details, but Ronald really has had some unpleasantnesses. Our cases, the smaller ones were opened – everything displayed to the crowd – this was all on the road! – thermos flask opened, every little thing picked up and then all left for us to re-pack, in the glaring sun. As we'd had a job to squeeze things in at first, you can guess what it would be after they'd been tumbled about. Su was very kind and helpful. Ronald couldn't help as he was tied up with the big things, and Kao was not with us, for obvious reasons. However, it's really local. Once we moved out we had a pleasant easy journey.

We went first class, partly for space and partly to be able to take more luggage, but as it was left behind anyway we missed out in that line. However, we were most fortunate in getting a coupé with a young soldier. He was polite and friendly but not too talkative, and Mrs Smith was able to join us at Tsingchou and there was still room for Audrey's basket. We met with courtesy from everyone. Of course children melt the hardest hearts, and I believe if I'd been there with them, Ronald might have been treated better! Audrey slept almost all the way, and when she didn't she just looked around with interest. Rosemary was good and really enjoyed everything. We were most grateful for the drinks we'd taken, as it was warmish, but not too bad. The time flew and we were quite surprised to find ourselves here so soon.

Edward Phillips met us and managed everything, which was a big relief. We had no bothers, no examination or trouble and were soon in a car and up here. The children were in bed and asleep in no time and seem none the worse for their journey. After a welcome meal I came to bed, but didn't drop asleep as soon as the babies. However, it was good to have the breezes and hear the sea splashing below, and we've enjoyed a bathe this morning. Our costumes haven't come but Rosemary's pants did for her and I was able to borrow.

My only anxiety is for Ronald. I wish I felt he would be able to get a holiday soon. I think he'll probably be obliged to come before long. Kao and Wang ta Sao arrived safely. We had nothing to do with them – felt it better[130]. It was good of them to come. We really have so much to be thankful for. Our three helpers have been splendid and there seems a complete absence of ill-will on the part of the people. We meet with nothing but friendliness from all, except one variety.

Tsingtao is a lovely spot. The trees are so green and the hills and mountains in the distance all purple, and the sea the most glorious bright blue and oh, so delightfully warm.

PS Trunks arrived by goods train, all safe. Keys still not come, but expect they'll be here soon. A letter from Ronald says all patients and nearly all servants gone. Wu was staying till the last minute. Alice,

---

[130] Not wanting to draw attention to the fact that Kao and Wang Ta Sao were working for British employers.

Miss Thomas and perhaps Mrs Pailing coming down today. Ronald and Mr Pailing staying on for the time being.

Ronald to his father and mother

Chouts'un
5th August 1939

You will no doubt have had news of the closing of the hospital, from the cable that Drake has sent home advising Miss Logan to delay sailing, and you will be anxiously waiting for further news.

Before we had any disturbance here, we had already had news that Baptist missionaries had had to evacuate Kaifeng, in Honan, and Taian in Shantung, so we were not unprepared for what might occur at any time here. Since events have occurred here we have had news of the evacuation of Taiyuan and of other mission hospitals elsewhere. It seems as though in all the procedure has been similar.

The first indication we had of any change was last Sunday afternoon, when our business manager came to us and told us that he had been warned by a person in an influential position, that all our employees were shortly to receive orders from the head of the local (Chinese) government, to leave our service at five days' notice. If they did not, armed troops were to be placed at the hospital gate, no one would be allowed in or out, no foodstuffs would be allowed to enter the compound, and the staff would 'lose their freedom'.

On hearing this we called a meeting of the senior hospital staff and talked the matter over. A factor at the meeting which carried great weight with the staff, and which has since caused me a good deal of anxiety, was the attitude adopted by the business manager, who seemed quite to have made up his mind that we had no option but to comply with this order when it arrived. And he had already given full weight to his opinion by beginning to move his belongings from the hospital compound before even he had told us of the report that they had heard. Naturally, this opinion and this example carried a good deal of weight with the rest of the staff, especially the junior members.

The result of our meeting was that we decided that Billy and I and Mr Hsia, our evangelist, would go to interview the chief local magistrate, ie the 'Mayor' of the local Chinese government that has been set up by, and which is entirely answerable to, the local Japanese military government. He agreed to see us, though we were not allowed inside the town gate, by special orders, until we said where we were going and permission had been obtained by telephone for us to enter. The Mayor received us with the greatest courtesy, but told us that he was afraid that it would be necessary to insist that all our staff should leave us by today or be subject to the above threats. We asked him whether he had orders from above to act in this way. This he neither admitted nor denied but the impression our Chinese colleagues got was that, even if he had no direct orders from above, he had no option but to act in this way, lest the anti-British demonstrations occurring in his district should fall short by comparison with those in other districts.

We told him that we had a number of seriously ill patients in hospital and that it would not be an easy matter to arrange for their satisfactory disposal in five days. In response to this, he said that he would send on a representative to find out the number of such patients, and their condition, and would himself make arrangements for their transfer to other hospitals in the town. With this arrangement, we could not but comply. We also asked him if he would take steps to ensure the protection of the British community here, and also of our property, especially indicating the necessity of having a minimum staff of servants, such as gateman and cook. In reply to this he undertook to consult 'those above' and to give us an answer later, and with this we had to leave.

Later in the same day the Mayor presented to Billy an official, but only oral, message to the effect that the whole of our Chinese staff must leave within six days, on pain of the penalties mentioned above, and he had been unable to obtain permission from the higher authorities for Britishers even to obtain passes to go in and out of the town walls. In view of the extreme likelihood that our staff would leave us by the end of the week, we considered it necessary at once to begin to empty the hospital, lest we should find ourselves suddenly faced with the emergency of having to care for sixty or seventy ill people without nurses, cooks or work-people of any sort.

So there began a steady exodus, and by Thursday evening all the patients had gone. Many were able to walk home, and the relatives of many were able to come and take their friends home. Only six presented any difficulty, and three of these we were able to arrange to be taken into the small hospital of an old Cheeloo graduate who used to be a house-surgeon here, and the other three were taken into the home of one of our work-people until the following morning, when their relatives arrived from a long distance away to take them home[131]. You can imagine how

[131] Elsewhere, Ronald elaborated, 'All our patients had escorts to places where they could be cared for. Little Chou Ch'un, our youngest, who had been in hospital for two years, and had a cheerful smile for us all nearly every day, perforce had to leave us. Our old sewing woman took her into her little home for a night before her relatives came and took her home, splint and all. So our staff left

upset we all felt at the sight of our patients having to leave the hospital in these conditions.

By this time too our staff were beginning to leave us. They all stayed on very faithfully until the patients could be satisfactorily arranged for, but in the meantime they were all making their own plans for leaving before the date fixed for the imposing of the guard. Alice Wheal had returned from her holiday in Tsingtao on the Monday evening and of course was grievously disappointed and shocked at the turn events had taken. The whole of her luggage had been unceremoniously turned out on the station platform when she arrived back in Chouts'un. By Thursday we had said goodbye to all our nurses. Most of them too have gone to their homes, some are staying near at hand.

On Wednesday our Chinese doctor and his wife and our dispenser left us, on the same train as Gwyneth. Gwyneth took four trunks with her and, in view of Alice's experience on Monday evening, I was at the station in good time in order to try to get the luggage through, but a policy of deliberate delays successfully prevented me from getting the luggage on the train. Fortunately, Gwyneth had planned for this emergency and had with her a suitcase of necessities which she was able to take on the train, so that I do not think she would have any serious difficulties at Tsingtao.

On Thursday, the absence of the Chinese doctor and dispenser and the pressure of innumerable jobs to be done, and the absence of all assistants, made us very regretfully decide that we would have to close the outpatient doors and decline to receive patients, so that from Thursday evening, the hospital has been officially closed. It is a physical impossibility to cope with the number of patients who would turn up here for attention if you have not a single assistant, and there seemed nothing for it but to close the gates.

It is some consolation to us in a situation that has not very many brighter aspects to feel that the hospital is not being closed through any dissatisfaction on the part of the Chinese with the work that is being done. The outpatient attendance figures for the months April, May, June and July have each been the highest recorded in the whole history of the hospital, and the average daily census of inpatients during the present year (88.8% occupancy of the available beds) is also the highest figure ever recorded in the hospital's history. But it is very sad to think that the work has to be stopped just when it is seeming to meet so big a need.

---

us, but not before they had fulfilled their duties to their patients, and as they left each came to ask leave and to say goodbye. Sad goodbyes! not knowing when or in what circumstances we should meet again.' RJS, *Foster Hospital Annual Report, Year ended December 31st 1939*

Sunday We have still had no further communication with the authorities, either C or J, and no attempt has been made to picket the hospital gate. We take this as a sign of unwillingness to accept responsibility for the property, and are consequently 'staying put' ourselves, until we get some further indication of the official attitude. A very reassuring feature of the situation is the very friendly and sympathetic attitude of the great majority of the local Chinese. Everywhere we get expressions of sympathy, and disappointment that the work has had to be discontinued, and testimonials as to the high regard which is held of the work of the hospital by all kinds of people.

We are well and happy and being splendidly cared for by the faithful W[132]. Gwyneth too writes happily from Tsingtao. Our situation here seems to depend on the attitude of the local J authorities. If they are bent on getting us out, they will no doubt find some way of doing it, but we feel that until we come up against some obviously impossible situation we must stay here to protect the property. Once we leave, I'm afraid that it would not be long before the whole place was ransacked.

Japanese anti-British poster
(photo courtesy of Imperial War Museum, London HU53640)

[132] Knowing that letters were subject to scrutiny by the Japanese censor, Ronald was probably being deliberately cryptic here about Wu's involvement. In his annual report, however, he was more expansive: 'One cook' (Wu) 'remained after the appointed day. "I don't think they'll do much", he said. "They might beat me." (They had killed people in Honan.) "If they do, I might not be able to come back, but I'll wait and see. Anyway, this is my job, and I must do it." Some of us think that but for his faithfulness, the hospital might not have been open again today.' RJS, *Foster Hospital Annual Report, Year ended December 31st 1939*

Ronald to his father and mother

Chouts'un
28th August 1939

What an unhappy world it is! We had news last night that the Cabinet was just meeting to discuss a reply to Hitler's message brought by Henderson to London, and it seems as though the issue of war or peace hangs on this reply, and on Hitler's reaction on receipt of it.

We are troubled for you and for Will and Reg and Florence and Phyllis. Your position seems so much more serious than ours. The whole issue seems to rest with Hitler, and we can only go on praying that he may be influenced to throw his weight on to the side of peace. It seems incredible that any man should be willing to throw the whole world into such a terrible catastrophe as a present-day war would be. We go on praying and hoping that you may be still at peace by the time this reaches you. We are thankful to have the wireless news, which keeps us very well informed with the latest developments, and with the views that are being expressed in England and Germany as well as China. It may be that if war breaks out our communications will not be so easy and letters may take a long time to get through.

Since I wrote last we have had no disturbances of any sort here, and the situation has been peaceful in every way. So much so that Mrs Pailing is planning to come back today and we are going to the station this afternoon hoping to meet her.

After the workpeople had all left the compound, we had no further interference from the authorities. They came daily to find out how many people were living on the compound, but apart from that took no notice of us and they raised no objections to our having Wu and Chia helping us, nor did they object when Mr Pailing's table-boy returned a week ago to help out. We are now not allowed inside the town gates, and when we attempted to go in to see the J authorities, we were held up at the gate. When we told our mission, we were directed first to the Chinese authorities, and when we got to the office we were told that 'The Mayor had just been called away on urgent business' and we have not since been able to see him.

I have been seeing patients at Outpatients all the time since we closed, so as to make it easier to reopen later if we were able, but there have been only four or five daily. I do not think that we can attempt to reopen unless we get official permission to do so. It would only render us liable to further interference and trouble and might endanger our workpeople. Since we closed here we have heard during the last few days that the Tsingchoufu hospital has also had to close. We have had no details yet, but we imagine that it is all part of the Anti-B movement there and that the situation is similar to ours.

Most of our workpeople are poor people and it will cause them great distress if they have to be unemployed for any length of time. We paid them an extra month's wages when they left, but we shan't be able to do anything more for them if we cannot reopen. Those of them who are lads and young men are already being pestered to join up with the puppet Chinese troops in the district, and being out of work they are in a very awkward position.

And it is not only our work-people who suffer. Outside the hospital in the road that runs past the gate there are several inns and lodging houses who depend for their livelihood almost entirely on the custom given to them by patients and patients' relatives and those who carry patients from far distances, and these inns have been empty for the whole of the past month – and rickshaw pullers too who derive most of their fares from the hospital are also out of work.

The other hospitals and dispensaries are feeling it too. In the past they have been in habit of referring all their more serious cases to us, knowing that we would not refuse to take any of them in, but now they are unable to do so. Our closing down has brought us a good many unsolicited testimonials, showing that the hospital really fills a big need in the life of the local community, and a good many people, non-Christians, are using their influence to try to get the place reopened.

There has been some criticism to the effect that we closed in too much of a hurry, and that if we had held on nothing would have come of the authorities' threats. But in that we were entirely in the hands of our Chinese staff. The threats were levelled at them, and we couldn't put any strong pressure to bear on them to brace out those threats. The experience of other places, too, seems to show that it wouldn't have been possible for us to keep open long. All our Shansi people have had to come out, though they held on as long as possible, and the Tsingchoufu hospital where the staff is entirely Chinese has had to close too.

So for the last three weeks Billy Pailing and I have been 'gatekeepers in the house of the Lord' – and a very quiet job it has been! I've been very thankful indeed of the opportunity of getting some medical reading done. There was a great deal that I was needing to do and that I hadn't been able to do for the last five months, when I've hardly had time to open a book at all, so this has been a splendid opportunity for me.

Gwyneth to Ilkey and Cambridge

Tsingtao
1st September 1939

It really is difficult to get a quiet moment here. The house has been very full and the only time when I'm not busy with the children is after supper and then everyone is playing games or talking so it's not so easy to concentrate. However, Ronald has written to Ilkley and I scribbled a line to Cambridge so you'll know we're all well.

We are all still anxious about affairs in your part of the world, but feel that each day of peace, brings greater hope for permanent peace. You must be having a ghastly time.

These last two days we're enjoying a typhoon. The wind is terrific and the rain pretty heavy and the sea is as rough as can be. Every room in the house has had the rain in at one place or another. I've had to move Audrey's cot from one spot to another as the leaks appeared! Lots of trees are down and huts smashed to bits, and no boats could leave the harbour. Fortunately, one family moved out just before this started so we've been able to use their room as a playroom, and the children have been very good. We've just been out to see the damage. Parts of the main road are smashed to bits and big beach houses wiped away, stone steps in smithereens and so on.

We are experiencing no difficulties here, can buy freely (I mean without interference!) at the shops. Of course it's mostly one nation's goods, but we can't help that. Tradesmen call twice daily for vegetables, grocery and meat orders. Milk is delivered early morning and afternoon. We have a great deal of bother getting permits to leave the town, filling in endless forms, but I'm not worried about that at present.

Enid Phillips is hoping to take Rosemary[133] to Chefoo and leave her at school on Sunday, but the boat will probably be delayed by typhoon. Then as soon as she gets back they all return to Tsinan. I shall miss them terribly, they are a delightful family.

There haven't been any good films, except 'Wuthering Heights' which we enjoyed very much. I have enjoyed the Sunday Services very much. The Hall is full and it has been such a treat to join in the singing. Rosemary has behaved pretty well, the first time she has been to a big service in a Church. The only comment she made at all loudly was 'Mummy, so tight, my trousers!' She had rather tight elastics, but I didn't really think she need have commented just then!

---

[133] Rosemary Phillips, oldest of Edward and Enid's three children.

Mrs Pailing returned to Chouts'un on Wednesday and we've heard that she had a very easy journey and no trouble on arrival. The railway-station there is usually the worst part, they seem to have a specially unpleasant crowd there. It is encouraging to know her return received no disapproval from the powers that be. I feel more hopeful of going myself, though if the hospital doesn't open, we can't go on doing nothing.

The rail to the north and south of Tientsin is flooded and they are having to use little boats to carry people and goods across, so that mails are being somewhat delayed.

Ronald to his father and mother

Chouts'un
3rd September 1939

The news from home is so bad[134] that it makes me wonder whether and when this will ever reach you. The last news we had was last night's wireless news of the demands sent to Hitler by the British Government that German troops be withdrawn from Poland, and that failing a satisfactory reply the British and French ambassadors had instructions to ask for their passports. Before long we shall be listening in again and shall know, I think, whether war has actually been declared or not. What a terrible calamity it is. It is just unmixed sorrow and misery for countless thousands and millions of people, isn't it?

I'm so sorry that you two dear ones have to go through all this terrible anxiety again. You had enough with the last war. And I'm so anxious and concerned for Will and Florence and Reg and Phyllis. I don't know how they will be affected or how their feelings will guide them[135]. I know they'll do what is right in everything. We're thinking of you and of them all the time and praying for you all.

There are now three of us Britishers here, the two Pailings and I. The Vice-Consul has been up to Tsinan during this week trying to get some assurances from the J authorities which would enable us to reopen hospital work here. He had several conversations with both the civil and military authorities, but the results weren't encouraging. It was made clear that the British were an obstruction to Japanese ideals in Asia and

[134] On 1st September Germany invaded Poland. Children were being evacuated from London, and the armed forces were being mobilised for war.

[135] Referring to Will and Reg's pacifist ideals and the possibility that they would want to register as conscientious objectors.

that for the next ten to twelve years, during which they are completing their programme, we might expect to have a pretty thin time.

Meanwhile, here in Chouts'un our old gateman had been again threatened by a J authority and the postmen who bring our letters had also been threatened "with death" if they came into our compound again. Since the hospital wards closed at the beginning of August, I had tried to keep the outpatients going by seeing any patients who would come, but after these renewed threats we felt it best to close the gates altogether.

Soon after I had written the above we got the news of the declaration of war from London. We had been expecting it. Mr Drake came down here on Saturday to tell us the news of the Consul's visit and to talk things over with us. He is a man on whose confidence Gwyneth and I feel able to rely completely, and on his judgement too, so it was good to be able to talk to him. I had wondered whether I should be right to leave the Pailings here alone if I went down to Tsingtao to talk things over with Gwyneth. Drake reassured me about that so I am now deciding to go down tomorrow.

I shall have to decide where I think my duty lies, here or in Europe. Of course there's a big pull to come back to England. The need for doctors must be very big, and if Gwyneth and I decide that it's right for me to come back I'll get in touch with the BMS as soon as possible and find out what their attitude is. I expect we shall probably be receiving instructions from them by cable before long.

Of course I shall have to make arrangements for Gwyneth and the children. I don't know yet what the best arrangements will be, but I'll try to do the very best that is possible for them. I hope to see the Consul while I'm in Tsingtao and I'm hoping that he will be able to give me some helpful information about ways and means of transport, if these should be necessary.

Ronald to his father and mother

as from Chouts'un
20th September 1939

I'm writing from Tsingtao, where Gwyneth and Rosemary and Audrey and Wang Ta-Sao and Kao Ta-ko and I are now by ourselves at Miss Manger's house, the Cedars. Our fellow guests all left us today, so now, except for Miss Smurthwaite, who has accepted a temporary appointment as kindergarten mistress at the St Giles' school for British children in Tsingtao, we are the only English Baptists here.

We were hoping to go back to Chouts'un tomorrow, but yesterday we had a letter from the Pailings advising us to stay here a little longer, until they have had time to see what sort of a reaction there is to the return of Alice and Miss Thomas. If after proper consideration it still seems unwise for Gwyneth and the children to go back to Chouts'un, we have arranged for them to go to live temporarily in Tsinan, first at the Phillips' and later on perhaps by themselves (with Kao and Wang Ta Sao) in one of the BMS houses. We have talked this over with Mr Drake, and he approves entirely. It seems better that they should be in Tsinan than in Tsingtao, if Chouts'un is impossible.

I am hoping to go back to Chouts'un as soon as possible, and we will see what can be done about reopening the hospital. Unless our presence is likely to prove an embarrassment or even a danger to our Chinese friends, I don't think there will be any reason why we all should not be able to go on living as usual in Chouts'un. My big hope is that we shall be able to reopen.

You'll be wanting to know what decision I have arrived at myself following the war declaration at home. After talking things over with Gwyneth down here, I decided that, if it seemed as though there were an immediate and urgent need of medical help at home or in the army, and if that need seemed greater than that which my position as sole BMS doctor in Shantung placed upon me, then it would be my duty to offer my services.

I was not sure at that time what the exact state of need of the medical services at home would be, and so I asked the Consul-General here in Tsingtao. He told me that there was no immediate need for medicals at home, and that the Government was not at present proposing to recall people from China, and he gave it as his advice that those who had jobs out here should for the present stick to them. This view coincided with that of the British Ambassador who made similar remarks in a broadcast speech. The consul gave me registration forms which are being issued to British subjects out here, asking for information about qualifications, age, family responsibilities etc, and asked me to fill it in and return it to him, but expressed his opinion that it would be some time before the services of people out here would be called upon.

In view of these statements, it did not seem to me that the need at home was sufficiently great or urgent to justify my asking the BMS for permission to offer for immediate national service, and it seemed clear that for the time being at any rate my duty is to stick by the Chouts'un hospital, and the BMS work in Shantung. If at a later date the needs at home should change, I take it that the Government will get in touch with me through the Consul. So I have filled in the registration form and handed it to the Consul here.

One question asked whether I was willing to apply for immediate national service, and to this I felt bound to reply that the answer was dependent on my being able to make satisfactory arrangements for my wife and family, and for handing over my present job. Subject to these conditions, I said that I was willing to apply for either army or civilian surgical service.

After I had made these decisions I wrote to Pailing and Drake and have had replies from them in which they say that they are glad and relieved that I have felt able to take this line. I have heard that Flowers and Ingle[136] have both offered their services through the BMA[137] for national service. I don't know at the moment what work they have taken on, but I imagine that it will be for the duration, and that in the meantime I shall be the sole BMS medical in Shantung.

If the hospital can be re-opened, we shall be able to carry on as usual, but if we can get no permission to reopen, we shall have to make some plan for the protection of the property. I am willing to stay on here for two or three months, exploring the possibility of reopening and looking after the property, but if at the end of that time it still seems that we shall not be permitted to reopen, I do not feel that I want to stay on for a longer time not doing any medical work, but only acting as gatekeeper for the property. I have written to Drake about this, and the suggestion has come from him that if work seems definitely impossible in Chouts'un, I should go to Cheeloo and do temporary work there.

Gwyneth to Cambridge

Home again
28th September 1939

You'll probably be surprised to see we're back. I'm surprised myself! Long may we be allowed to remain. We had a very hectic last few days. In addition to packing our belongings, we had the responsibility of closing the house for the winter months. Not a very big job, but there are all the curtains to wash and everything has to be checked over and so on.

We were up early on Tuesday and got a car to the station in good time. Tom Allen very kindly came to see us off. We were most grateful,

---

[136] Both Dr Flowers & Dr Ingle were on furlough in England when war was declared on Germany.
[137] British Medical Association

because Ronald is busy with the luggage and I carry Audrey and poor wee Rosemary has to walk, and it's horrible if there are big crowds as there usually are, so Tom carried her onto the train. It was a big help. Before the war, we never had trouble getting porters, but they're terribly scarce now.

On our arrival, no-one met us. We expected Wu but our letter was delayed, so he didn't know we were coming. Ronald was able to manage though our luggage was a trial. There were four cabin trunks, a cot, a camp bed, a pram, two large suit cases, one medium suit case, one big corrie (basket for Audrey to sleep in), one rucsac, two baskets fruit, one microscope, two wicker chairs (tiny ones for the children which cost about 9d each!!), my handbag and the children – quite a crowd! We waited till the things were all assembled and then I sat down and Ronald went through the examining business. It's said to be worse in Chouts'un than any other station. They went through our two big cases in detail, and the microscope, and I thought we'd be there till doomsday, but he suddenly said we could go.

Nearly all the soldiers had gathered round and were very interested in Rosemary and Audrey, and I think it was because of them that we got off so lightly. Kao, on seeing that Wu hadn't turned up, came back and offered to help, and Rosemary ran up and got hold of his hand and chattered to him in Chinese and that impressed everyone. And Audrey just smiled all round and when the soldiers tickled her chin she didn't cry, but just smiled back. We got a rickshaw for me and the children and Ronald walked beside, and Kao managed carts for the baggage. When we got here Wu was overwhelmed with delight at seeing us all again, though very upset that he'd no fire alight. However, Miss Thomas's boys soon made us tea and we had supper with the Pailings.

Yesterday was wet, so I was rather depressed over nappies which had accumulated, but today has been sunny, so all is well again! Wang Ta Sao got off at Tsingchou – she wanted to get winter clothes and to see her people. She's coming on next week. I'd have been glad of her help while unpacking, but Ronald has helped and we've managed all right.

The place seems very strange with no Chinese. At least there are two gatemen, one at each gate, and our own house-boys, but otherwise it's all dead. It's not a bit nice. I don't mind much, but it's dull for Rosemary to have no one to go and see. She loved playing with the nurses and of course I miss their admiration. It seems a waste to have two such lovely children and no-one but us to appreciate them!

Ronald to Ilkley

Chouts'un
29th September 1939

They did allow us to travel back by rail from Tsingtao this year[138], but oh, the red tape! In order to travel on the Kiao-Tsi railway at the present time, the passenger has to provide himself with a military pass OK'd by the Jap consulate, a certificate of recent immunisation against cholera, also stamped by the Jap consulate, and, worst of all, a certificate of faecal examination (as a protection against cholera) which is only valid for five days! You can imagine what a game it was complying with all these regulations, dashing about trying to find the right office to get all these certificates, and having to do the business all over again when we found that our first specimens had been sent to the wrong place! The regulation about the certificates only being valid for five days only came into force just as we were coming away. We all but got turned back at the station barrier because our certificates were thought to be out of date, but eventually we got through and had a safe and easy journey home.

Looking back on our holiday, it seems as though at least half the time was spent in trying to get back home again, and in visits to the dentist and the consul, and in getting certificates for other people and giving them anti-cholera injections etc. Even so we had a very enjoyable holiday, as enjoyable as we could have with the knowledge of what was going on at home in England, and of the difficulty of carrying on our job in Chouts'un. We enjoyed very much having on opportunity of being with the Phillipses, and later on with Tom Allen, and the weather was glorious most of the time. Gwyneth says she has never felt better in her life, and I feel thoroughly rested after the busy time we had before the hospital was closed.

Ronald had taken the opportunity of being in Tsingtao to meet with the Consul to discuss the situation regarding the Chouts'un hospital, and he reported on this in a letter to BMS headquarters in London: 'The Consul had been informed that the Japanese military attitude was that our hospital was known to be 'assisting the guerrillas' and that as long as this continued we must expect to have trouble. The Consul replied

[138] The previous year, because the East-West railway line was out of use, they had had to travel home from Tsingtao by sea around the north coast of Shantung and then by train from Tientsin.

that he regarded this as a grave allegation, and asked for substantiation or withdrawal, but he received no reply to this request. Although of course we treat any wounded who present themselves, there is no truth at all in the allegation that we take sides in the political struggle, and we co-operate in whatever ways we can with the Japanese authorities in their investigations and examinations.'[139]

The closure of the hospital, coinciding as it did with a period of enormous uncertainty on the home front, culminating in the declaration of war on Germany on September 3rd, raised all sorts of questions in the minds of mission staff in China and London.

Running costs in both the Chouts'un and Tsingchou hospitals had risen dramatically during 1939. Meanwhile, income had fallen, due to a combination of the war in Europe, the Japanese war, and bad harvests, insect plagues, floods, drought and banditry in China. In Chouts'un, over the whole year, income from Chinese sources amounted to only 50% of the total income, whereas in pre-war years it was around 85%. Free treatment, amounting to a total of approximately 3000 days, was given to one hundred and nineteen patients. At the Leprasorium in Tsingchou, only three of the fifty outpatients and fifteen inpatients had been able to meet their own expenses. For both hospitals, grants from the Lord Mayor of London's China Fund had made a significant contribution to their ability to remain solvent.

In the light of this and of financial constraints at home, it was inevitable that the possibility of permanent closure of the Chouts'un hospital should be considered at mission headquarters in London. Bill Pailing who, as hospital superintendent, had charge of the hospital finances, wrote in early September to suggest that, if permission to reopen was obtained from the authorities, it might be best not to attempt to reopen the inpatient wards but to concentrate instead on maintaining the outpatient facility.

Ronald, in his own letter to the Mission House reviewing the options from the medical point of view, argued for the retention of the inpatient wards. He felt the most important needs which the hospital fulfilled in the community were for surgery, good nursing and midwifery, all of which required the provision of inpatient facilities. 'Difficulties do exist,' wrote Ronald, 'but I do not accept the implication that the Foster Hospital is, because of its present financial state, a suitable early victim if a policy of retrenchment from home becomes necessary.'

---

[139] Letter from Ronald to Dr C C Chesterman at the Baptist Mission House, London, 28th September 1939.

He concluded his letter, 'Meanwhile it is my view that we should make our present inactivity as masterly as possible, and take whatever steps seem possible and desirable in an intricate political situation towards the speedy reopening of the whole hospital work.'

Gwyneth to her mother

Chouts'un
15th October 1939

Mummy dear, our last letters are still August 27, so it's five weeks since I had one from you. But although no letters have come, our 'Jagger' parcels[140] have. Ronald brought them back with him from Tsinan. It was a marvellous treat I can tell you!

Everything is in perfect condition although they've been in Tientsin during a blockade, a flood and so on. You always pack so carefully. Teddy is lovely and Rosemary and Audrey are both delighted with him. I really am thrilled with everything and I love the photos of you, Mummy. They're very good and it's fine to see you looking so bonny. Why didn't Daddy have his done too?

The voile, which was a surprise, is a pretty colour and just what I needed. Very many thanks for it. The cretonne is useful and the organdie for the children I'm longing to make up. I hope you'll see them wearing them one day. Will you please pass on to Dray, till I've time to write to her, my grateful thanks for the very pretty jersey?

Wang Ta Sao got back as planned. She's a faithful little soul, and, although I'd still prefer to be able to do without help, I'm thankful to have her. She's company when I'm alone and it's so good for the infants to have close contact with Chinese. Rosemary chatters so freely in Chinese now and Audrey will go to anyone without a murmur. We were over at the West Side last week to see the Pastor. He was out, but his wife was in and Audrey went to her at once and played with her face and was quite happy, which thrilled her, and Rosemary talked to her in Chinese, which impressed her favourably and also filled in the gaps for us! While other people have no definite work and talk about being dull and lonely, I'm as happy as can be all day with the children (and Ronald when he's here!)

---

[140] Parcels from England, brought out to them by Amy Jagger. There had been numerous delays and mishaps between the time the goods were handed over to Miss Jagger in England and their safe arrival in Chouts'un.

We are still much as before, no work going on except clearing up, and Ronald is doing a lot of study. We've been able to walk a little way through the field opposite several afternoons. A road of sorts has been made, on which it is just possible to push the pram, so we push Audrey and Rosemary runs along beside, both of them thrilled to bits by everything they see, and we of course thrilled to bits by them both!

We feel so out of touch with everyone at the moment. Miss Thomas is the only one who has had mail written after the declaration of war.

Gwyneth to her mother

Chouts'un
22nd October 1939

Well, three letters from you have arrived in the last two days, so I feel somewhat more cheery! Where do the Pearsons come from and which school are they in? Are you expected to use the cellar or have other arrangements been made? I'm longing to know so many things and about so many people. How much do you get from your 'boarders' and do they pay or does the Government? How is Daddy being affected at the shop? Not too well I'm afraid. What about your maid? Is she still about to help you? I do hope so. What about Ipswich, is Auntie Nellie able to carry on?

I do miss not only letters, but also papers, especially the women's ones. Just before we left in August I had good clear out and sold all my old mags except those I specially wanted. It seemed unlikely that we'd return and anyway I thought I'd be getting plenty of new ones. Now I'm getting none! I'm reading my old 'My Mags', though that doesn't help me to plan new clothes for the kids. Not that they really need any new ones, but I love to think about the ones they'll need soon. If we don't think well ahead, when the time comes it's impossible to get the material, pattern etc in time. I'm already thinking about coats for next winter! What do most children of four and two wear in winter at home in the way of coats, hats and leggings? Since I came to China four years ago, I've never seen any girl of that age, except Chinese, in winter and I find it quite hard to picture them at all.

Gwyneth to Ilkley

Chouts'un
9th November 1939

The situation here has seemed brighter this week and we feel fairly hopeful that we shall be able to re-open before so very long. Of course we've had spasms of optimism before, but there really does seem to be a change of policy. Miss Thomas is starting her refuge next week and although that is a different thing and much more likely to appeal to the authorities, we feel it is the beginning of better things for us all. It will be grand to have the children there, the place has seemed so deserted. We've scarcely spoken to a soul, except the four other foreigners and our own servants for all the time we've been back, so that it has seemed very quiet. It's awful to go through the compound and see everywhere shut up and no one about and to feel that there are so many whom we could be helping.

For various reasons prices of food, clothes and coal have gone up tremendously and will be quite beyond thousands of the country people. The 'refuge' on the street has now got eighty children. They go in the morning for their first meal, about 9 a.m., and have lessons and play till their second meal at 2 p.m., and then go home. Most people go onto two meals a day for economy in winter. Various influential people were asked to choose twenty children each to attend, but most of them declared it was impossible to choose twenty, there were hundreds equally destitute. The little we can do seems so very little.

Gwyneth to her mother

Chouts'un
18th November 1939

Audrey has an enormous appetite. Rosemary eats well too, but is too energetic to be very fat. How she keeps going all day I don't know. She is running about and talking all day long, but the minute her head touches the pillow at night she is asleep, and she usually doesn't move again till 7 a.m. when she calls out to us 'God's light has come now, I look at my book now. That be nice?' She has a book by her bed and looks at it as soon as it's light enough. I do wish you could see the two of them in the bath. It's only a small one, about the size of the one we had at home. They sit one each end and splash and jump about together, terribly thrilled and excited about it all!

Tom Allen came along yesterday and Rosemary chummed up to him at once. He bathed her and gave her her supper, too, which of course pleased her enormously. Tom is very worried – he doesn't know if Connie and the children are sailing or not. All the uncertainty is so very worrying and it's hard on Connie with two small infants. I think, in view of the war conditions at home, that it's best for wives and children to come out. I'm very glad that we have been able to stick together. If I'd followed the advice of some folk I'd have gone home in September 1937, and there I'd be for goodness knows how long.

Tom and Ronald have been singing. Tom has a very nice voice and it's been good to hear them. I've been so glad for Ronald to have a man of his own age to talk things over with – they get on very well together. On Sunday the two of them went for a long walk to the top of a hill to the south of the railway. I've never been, but they say it's a lovely walk and a fine view from the top of the hill.

Gwyneth to Cambridge

Chouts'un
26th November 1939

It's turned terribly cold, a wind like an icy blast. We have decided not to try to economise on stoves. We think in about five years' time Rosemary will be at school and we can economise for ourselves then, but we want a cosy house for them while they're small, so we'll probably have a stove in the dining room too. Coal is awfully expensive and scarce, but I think we can get sufficient if we pay for it and we're careful in other ways.

I can't bear to think of Rosemary being in school in so short a time. She's already lived nearly half the time she'll have at home. I can't possibly teach her myself after eight I'm afraid, though I'm wondering if I could do it up to eleven, if Kay helped. If the Allens could be here, I think Connie and I between us might manage our united families. She is trained as a teacher and loves it, which I don't, though I can do all the practical stuff which she dislikes. But I don't really see much hope of their being near enough.

I've been busy this week knitting caps for the Wu and Kao children for Christmas, and finishing the knitted duck I'm making for Audrey. He's really a very stout fellow and I think she'll approve of him. I've machined six mattress covers for hospital and am doing another three. They take quite a time and it's a cold job now too. I've also spent a couple of days over with Ronald stocktaking drugs and making inventories of hospital goods. This is a grand chance for him and Alice to do such jobs that ordinarily they just haven't time to do. I'm so scared of making mistakes that I'm terribly slow at it.

As the months of closure continued, grass had begun to grow in the silent compound. Pigeons began to nest boldly wherever they liked. But behind the scenes, Ronald and the other mission staff had been determined to make the most of this period of enforced inactivity. Ronald took the opportunity to devour his growing collection of medical journals and update himself on developments in medicine and surgery, to make an inventory of drugs and hospital equipment, and to pursue his studies in Chinese language and history. Alice Wheal and Muriel Pailing brought a bright new look to the wards by scrubbing and polishing the floors and repainting the furniture. Gwyneth put her sewing skills to use repairing and remaking bedding and bed linen.

The hospital in Tsingchou had been allowed to reopen during October, without any unpleasant repercussions, and in early November they had their first indication that the general situation was changing for the better, when the senior Japanese military officer for the district paid them a friendly call. Despite Ronald's continuing attempts to obtain some assurances from the authorities that they might be allowed to reopen soon, it was not until December 6th and 7th that these initiatives bore fruit, and Ronald was able to report to the BMS at home that 'the Anti-British movement seems to have died out in this district, and, unless there should be some change in the general political situation, we do not expect we shall be subjected to any further interference'.

Soon a cheerful red poster appeared on the hospital gates announcing that on December 12th the outpatient department would be open again, and that on January 1st they would take patients into the wards. Nine patients attended for treatment on December 12th, including Li with a badly crushed leg, and young Ts'ao with a bullet through his abdomen, who was tended as he lay in the crowded inn across the road from the hospital.

Gwyneth to Ilkley

Chouts'un
17th December 1939

I was helping Alice yesterday to unpack the Leeds and Wakefield Wants Boxes, to which Reg and Phyllis contributed. They were lovely boxes, the most sensible things inside and all in perfect condition. We felt that every single thing had been worked with real thought and care, the same as we always feel with the Ilkley ones, as you know. Alice will be writing her thank-yous, but I know you'll be interested to hear.

At a Relief Committee yesterday an appeal from one district only in our own area said there were 200,000 people actually living on the verge of starvation. The cost of living has almost doubled and people are really living at the very limit. The courage of the Chinese people is amazing. The hardships and privations they endure are beyond our imagination.

The outpatient department has gone on without interference. Only a few attendances each day, but we don't expect, or want, a crowd at first. It is better to open gradually and of course it takes time for the news to spread. Even then, some people will be waiting to see if all goes well before venturing to come near us. The few coolies and orderlies and the two girl nurses who have already returned, all seem happy to be back at work again and, when there are no outpatients to attend to, are busy preparing for January 1.

Ronald is busy with correspondence, interviewing staff, arranging for buying in stores. He has had to take on a new business manager. This is slightly more difficult than keeping on the old, but it has been done in full co-operation with the other members of the Mission and with the Chinese Church leaders. The new man is a capable and faithful worker who has served the mission for years in a very satisfactory way, so we hope that all will go well. It has been a difficult question, but we feel the right thing has been done.

We did enjoy Mr Drake's eight day visit. He was out at meetings all day but he was in every evening and he is splendid company. We had Emmott here with him five days and Tom Allen was here four days too, so we've had quite a gay time.

We have had Pastor Chang[141], the Shantung Baptist Union Secretary, in for lunch on several occasions and we want to have various other Chinese in before Christmas if we can.

Miss Smurthwaite arrived back safely yesterday. It's good to have her with us, she's a great person. She seems to have had a very happy term in Tsingtao and I'm certain she has done a lot for the pupils, who need a missionary quite as much as the Chinese!

We hear that Connie Allen is on her way, so I'm afraid we'll be losing Wang Ta Sao. It's not easy to find good helpers and we feel we must have a woman at present. We've all grown to love Wang Ta Sao. She's such a devoted and humble little woman, a very real Christian, and we shall miss her very much. She adores Audrey and feels she's almost *her* baby, because she's known her from the start! Wu's daughter couldn't come and help now, as she's married, but I'm enquiring about a woman Wang Ta Sao recommends and if she sounds good, shall ask her to come up for a month's trial. I don't like to get her all this way just for an interview. Travelling is such a fag, they have to take socks off to be searched and it's rotten in this cold weather. Ronald has had his pockets all turned out and his shirt pulled out and trousers rolled up, but nothing worse.

Wang ta Sao with Audrey

[141] Pastor Chang Szu-ching was for many years an inspirational leader of the church in Shantung. In the 1920s he was the leading light in establishing the church and school in Poshan. In 1933 he was appointed General Secretary of the Baptist Union and Superintendent of all Baptist work in Shantung. His sacrificial support of mission staff, and his energy and faithfulness in keeping in personal touch with isolated groups of Christians throughout the long years of the Japanese war were outstanding. During this period he also reorganised the Mission school at Pei-chen and at the same time took responsibility for a government school at Changtien.

Gwyneth to her mother

Chouts'un
31st December 1939

I'm feeling heart-broken at losing little old Wang Ta Sao. I know it had to be, but I just feel I'm losing one of my best friends. She has begged me to write and ask Connie to let her stay here, but Connie would be so disappointed if she wasn't there to help her when she arrived. I just can't write and tell Connie she doesn't want to leave here, so I must let her go. And she, poor wee soul, can't see why I don't write. She even suggested I should write and tell Connie that she wasn't any good now, she was getting old and her eyes were bad, so that Connie should reply that she didn't want such a crock!

In the meantime I've got a woman from the village, also Wang Ta Sao. She's 37, her husband is away and her two children both died at eight months. She's never been away from her own village, where she'd made hair nets and lace. She hasn't ever been on a train, or upstairs, nor seen electric light. Unfortunately, she has bound feet and isn't as nippy as desirable. I don't care if she's quick or slow really as long as she has a good nature.

It's January 1st now and the wards opened this morning. They've six patients come in already, so it's encouraging, isn't it? We feel sure that unless we get interference from the same old source, the place will go ahead – there are plenty wanting to come. Our nurses and coolies have practically all returned. It's grand to have them all about again. Ronald is going to be terribly busy, but he never worries unduly and really can take responsibility more easily than many. Fortunately he has managed to buy two hundred bags of flour. We'd been having an anxious time about it, as not only has the price gone up but it has been very difficult to buy more than a bag or two. These two hundred will last a couple or more months.

Su is taking handwork in the Refuge, but when she goes back to Tsingtao on January 19 I'm hoping they'll suggest I do it. I'd quite like the job, if I've someone to leave with the children. I'd like to feel I was able to do something!

We both felt horribly 'down' at Christmas in some ways. We seemed so cut off with nothing at all in the way of home mail, but now that your letters and a few others have trickled along, we feel quite different. We knew you'd all have written, but it was awful not having any mail. If you don't get our letters, they're only one missing but if our foreign mail fails, it means we get none at all.

Gwyneth to Cambridge

Chouts'un
4th January 1940

Wang Ta Sao went this morning. It was terrible parting with her. She just sat and nursed Audrey for about ten minutes before she went, just gazing at her and murmuring every now and again 'Er Ku Niang, Hsiao er ku niang', '2nd girl, little 2nd girl'. She really found it frightfully hard leaving her. I don't see much hope of her ever coming back, but you never know in this life. It's not that she's so efficient, she's not as quick as my new woman in most ways, but it's her very fine lovable character that makes you so anxious to keep her.

Rosemary is very keen on stories now, but she has her own version of several. When the three bears came home and found the porridge was eaten, they said 'never mind, our Kao Ta Ko will get us some more'! If I venture to tell the true version, I'm very severely ticked off!

Ronald is pleased with this week's progress. Forty one admissions is good, isn't it? He's been busy with annual accounts and reports for here and Tsingchou. I can't help a lot, but I can check the accounts. I did up our own accounts the other day and got us only $500 out, so we've done rather well, haven't we? Unfortunately it was on the wrong side. Maybe a second effort will improve matters!

Our Shantung Conference is January 20-24 in Tsinan, and Mr Drake has invited us as a family to stay with him. It's very tempting in spite of the difficulties and I think we'll probably try to go. With such a small staff it's not easy, but Ronald is to be Chairman and will have to go if possible, and I should quite like to go. It'll be pretty cold, but we can wrap the children up in Chinese padded capes in the rickshaws and trains are well-heated again now, so they'll be all right.

I suppose you realise we're due home *next* year, but don't count too much on it lest the war should continue that long, and in that case we couldn't come. I've already planned (more or less) what the children will wear and so on! Ronald and I won't have much choice by then!

Early in 1940, the British community in Chouts'un found its number swelled by missionaries unable to return to Shansi following the evacuation of that province caused by the anti-British movement of the previous summer.

Amongst these were John and Georgie Lewis, a young couple married the previous June. John was a doctor and Georgie a nurse. Since Mr and Mrs Pailing had returned to Tsinan in December, the Lewises were able to occupy the Flowers' house on the hospital compound. Other Shansi 'exiles' were Vincent and Ceridwen Jasper, another newly married couple, who moved at the end of February into Mr Harris' house at the West side of Chouts'un. Amy Jagger, another nurse, also arrived in Chouts'un at this time.

The influx of these younger missionaries, and various others who came and went during the early months of 1940, made a big difference to life for the foreign community in Chouts'un, and Ronald and Gwyneth shared many happy times with them, both in the context of work and in social gatherings. Meanwhile, Connie Allen's return from furlough to Tsingchou, with four year old Elizabeth and two year old Philip, raised the prospect of meetings between the two families. By March, Gwyneth was already planning a visit to stay with Connie in Tsingchou.

Dr Flowers and Dr Ingle both stayed on in England for war work following their periods of furlough, and Ronald found himself senior BMS doctor in Shantung. This meant he was often called away from Chouts'un, to Tsinan for meetings with mission or medical personnel, or to the hospital in Tsingchou to consult with Dr Ching, the medical superintendent in charge there.

Gwyneth had taken over the handwork classes in the children's refuge from Su Smurthwaite and was enjoying this. Her letters show her as busy as ever with knitting and sewing projects. One, written in early March, is typical: 'The enclosed wool is what I'm using to make the infants' spring coats and trousers. The red and white check material you sent last year I am hoping to make for the autumn into two frocks. I've cut out the covers for two easy chairs, a chesterfield and a long sort of settee business, and have tacked up one chair as a try-out and it looks quite nice. Then I've lengths for two cotton frocks each for Rosemary and Audrey and a voile for myself to make up.'

Ronald to his father

Chouts'un
7th April 1940

We've now been open more than three months, and things have gone pretty much as they used to before the Anti British movement last July. There have not been any interruptions or disturbances of any kind, for which we are very thankful. We've had one or two officials round to investigate once or twice, but nothing out of the ordinary, and the attitude has always been courteous and friendly. The first three months of the year have been very similar to the first three months of other years. The hospital was very slack, as far as numbers of patients were concerned, in the middle of February, about the time of the Chinese new year, but since then we have gradually become busier, and now we have about seventy five patients in hospital and are seeing about forty or fifty outpatients each day, and I expect that from now until wheat harvest, about the middle of May, we shall get busier still.

So far as we can tell there is absolutely no Anti British feeling here in Chouts'un at present, and from the official point of view we seem to be treated on a level with the other Chinese hospitals in the town. A circular notice has just come round today, with long lists of instructions relating to medical institutions, doctors, and dentists, and this has been sent to us in common with other medical and dental practitioners in the town, and it can be taken as a sign of official recognition. Since the hospital reopened we have been fortunate in being able to be of some assistance to two officials of fairly high standing who have been in hospital as inpatients and this has been a help to us in various ways.

You will know from the papers of the very serious famine conditions which exist all over this part of China. Flour has become almost impossible to buy, and the hospital (which uses about a hundred to a hundred and fifty bags per month) was facing quite a difficult problem when our stocks fell to less than a month's supply. But just when things were becoming critical, we got a message from the local Chinese authorities telling us that the responsible Japanese official was in the town, and that if we called on him, we might be able to get hold of some flour. So we didn't wait to be told twice, but went along and were welcomed courteously and given a permit to buy two hundred bags, which should keep us going till nearly the wheat harvest. It is good to feel that the official attitude both J and C is at least not hostile.

Since I took over[142] from Mr Pailing last December, finance has been the biggest problem. The question as to whether we were justified, from the financial point of view, in reopening the hospital was almost as big a one as whether we should get official permission to reopen. Mr Pailing was doubtful about the advisability of reopening the inpatient wards, but we went into the matter, and eventually decided to take the plunge if and when we should be given the chance. We had in hand

[142] As hospital superintendent

some $5,000-$8,000 of relief funds, which we had received during the year but had not had the opportunity to spend, and I reckoned we should be justified in using a part of these funds during the first three months, when I expected we should have to run at a serious loss, until it became known that the hospital had reopened, and until confidence had been re-established. But it seems that I took a too pessimistic view, because we have actually been self-supporting during the first three months of this year.

We are still running on drugs that were bought before prices soared the way they have, and when next we buy we shall have to buy at prices which are 300% or 400% higher than last time. We have already received another $7,000 from the International Famine Relief Commission's relief funds, and with this and our balance from last year's relief funds, and our allocation from home, I think we shall be able to see our way through the year.

Certainly the times are exceptional. It is the combination of war conditions with the effects of the Yellow River flood of a year ago, and the drought and insect plagues and typhoon which followed it, that has caused a famine the people say is the worst in living memory. Mr Payne has just come back from Peichen, on the north bank of the Yellow River, and he says the conditions there for miles and miles, and affecting hundreds of thousands of people, are heart-rending! He says in a letter to the Relief Commission "In hundreds of villages not more than 3% of the families have any grain. This means that 97% need relief, otherwise they must leave home to beg, or subsist on what they can pick up. The bark of trees and dried leaves are eaten. Peanut shells and straw chopped up finely help to make up the diet of others. People are dying of hunger. Families are separated never to be re-united. Men are going to Manchuria in large numbers, hiring themselves out to Japanese Labour contractors for their food alone.

"Parents are selling their children, or giving them away to whoever will promise to feed the little ones. In one family there were three little girls. Friends were invited to choose any one of them and the youngest was taken by a family some distance away. After two weeks she was brought back to die because of her emaciated condition. Suicides are common. A widow with three children, finding it impossible to feed them, or travel far enough to beg food, threw all of them into the Yellow River and then drowned herself. Another family had a blind grandfather of eighty years. They sold everything worth selling and converted the money into millet, and left it with the old man.

There was only enough for two or three weeks. Then the whole family went off begging and have not been heard of since."

These are the conditions which prevail over a large part of the area which the hospital serves. We have reckoned in hospital that the cost of living is now more than three times what it was a year ago, and four times what it was before the war. Prices of all hospital supplies have gone up proportionately, and are still rising, so that were it not for the Relief Funds that we have so far been able to obtain we should be in a very anxious position, and that position may arise whenever Relief Funds are unobtainable.

Gwyneth to Ilkley and Cambridge

Chouts'un
17th April 1940

We had a good journey to Tsingchou last Wednesday, with no trouble. Tom and Elizabeth met us and we were soon in rickshaws on our way out to the Compound where we received a royal welcome from Connie, Philip and our old Wang Ta Sao. Rosemary was not in the least shy and chattered away at once to Elizabeth and Philip. Connie and I seemed to be talking most of the time I was there, but there are still lots of things we did not find time to say! It is nearly three years since I saw her.

Ronald was busy seeing Hospital people most of the time, so I saw very little of him, and he returned to Chouts'un next day, leaving us behind. We really had a lovely time, the first two days were very hot and the children played happily in the garden all the time. Their garden is much nicer than ours for children, and they have a lawn of sorts which was quite an attraction. We took the children one day to the Chinese children in the Kindergarten which of course was a great thrill for all concerned. I don't know who did the most staring!

On Sunday we took them to the service in the big church, and they were really quite good. The main interest was the little bags brought round into which they put a ten cent note! Rosemary was most intrigued and wanted to know where they got the bags from, and of course when Tom, who happened to be leading the Service, came down from the pulpit to receive the bags, there was great excitement and I was questioned loudly as to why they were giving him all their money. At our hospital services we have no collection, so Rosemary has no idea of it, and incidentally very little idea of money at all, as she never does shopping, and very seldom sees money used at all.

In the afternoon I went with Connie to a monthly meeting of the women workers. It was a splendid meeting, about seventy women there of all ages and all types, some very poor, others quite well-to-do. Connie had been asked to speak that day, so I was very glad to be there, she speaks well and so easily.

On Monday she took me to Prayers at the school, so that I could see all the children assembled together. We then looked around the various buildings and also went to another compound some little way away, occupied by Chinese workers. We called on all the various wives, and had a little chat with them. Connie is an ideal one to go with, she knows just what to say and how to say it, and is obviously really interested in all the people and they all think no end of her and Tom. So many of them have known her since she was tiny, and still think of her as the 'second girl'! None of the people were expecting us, yet there were flowers in pots and vases, and everything looked well cared for. How they managed it I don't know, they have so little money, so many children and practically no help at all.

Our old Wang Ta Sao had the time of her life, was obviously delighted to see the infants again. They both seemed as pleased to be with her, and she spent most of the time looking after them, I wasn't allowed to do much!

Rosemary is beginning to get hold of the idea of England a bit, though what she really pictures I can't imagine. She begins to realise now that she isn't Chinese, which annoys her extremely. She says very emphatically, in Chinese to Wang ta Sao, 'I ***am*** a Chinese. You look, my hair is as black as yours and I've tiny feet like yours'. She's always trying to walk in Audrey's shoes to be like the Chinese women!

Gwyneth to Ilkley

Chouts'un
25th May 1940

Just an extra wee note to tell you what we think is very exciting news, and we hope you'll agree. We are hoping that we may be giving Will a new niece or nephew for his birthday this year[143] – of course we shall expect him to share it with everyone else! Hope you'll all send bright suggestions for names, though we can't promise to choose them all!

---

[143] A third baby expected around October 28th, Will's birthday

We're very distressed by news from your part of the world and are constantly thinking of you all.[144]

Gwyneth to Cambridge

Chouts'un
24th June 1940

We can't imagine what things may be like with you when you receive this. It is an anxious time even out here and you must be having ghastly days or rather nights.

I don't really think you can be more keen to see the children than I am to show them off! Audrey gets lovelier. Her hair is now golden and wee curls all over her head – very attractive - and she's really quite bright, though still unable to say much. Rosemary's great interest at the moment is in amputations. She's seen patients about with one missing limb and now asks endless questions about it and is very keen on finding out what scissors Daddy uses etc. I'm beginning to fear I'll find Audrey with a toe half hacked off or something! They play together very well most of the time but when it's fearfully hot they get a bit displeased with each other.

Gwyneth and Ronald with Audrey *(left)* and Rosemary

We heard the next day of visitors who left an unpleasant trail[145] in your area, so we await further news anxiously. Wu Shih Fu asked me today if you and Daddy couldn't come here as he thought it would be safer for you. I appreciate his kind thought and wished in many ways you could follow his suggestion. Wouldn't it be marvellous? If only 'here' were slightly less unsettled! Wu really is amazing, always good-tempered and cheerful and whatever he's doing is always

---

[144] News of the war in Europe was grim. Germany invaded first Denmark and Norway, then the Netherlands, Belgium and France. By early June, allied troops had been evacuated from Dunkirk; on June 10th, Italy declared war on France and Britain; on June 22nd, France surrendered. The RAF bombed industrial centres in Germany and German planes had begun their onslaught on airfields and dockyards in Britain.

[145] A bombing raid in East Anglia.

apparently delighted to stop and do anything else I suggest. In the middle of cooking, making jam or whatever it is, if unexpected guests arrive, he's always pleased to give a hand in preparing for them. He's splendid with the children, never too busy to play with them or carry them upstairs if they're tired, and yet his work never seems to suffer. I can't remember once when he's failed to turn out a good meal.

We've had strawberries up from the coast and made about 20lbs of jam and this week hope to make apricot jam and bottle apricots. I took a basket of them to the Refuge the other day – the children were as pleased as could be. There were only four each, but they were quite big and juicy and their ordinary menu includes no fruit.

Ronald to his father and mother

Tsingtao
12th August 1940

Just now we are getting the news of increasing severity of the air raids at home. It makes us very sad indeed to think that you have to go through these terrible experiences for the second time in your lives, this time more terrible than last. These anxious times are not good for high blood pressures, are they, Mother?

These seven months since the beginning of the year have been the busiest and in many ways the hardest that I have ever had, and I was thankful when the end of last month came and John Lewis came back from his holiday so that I could get away and join Gwyneth here in Tsingtao.

We shall be going back to Chouts'un on about the 31st of the month and it will be good to get back to work again and to join John and Georgie Lewis and Alice and "Jagger". I've been thankful in a great many ways for John's company and help these last seven months, and Shansi's inability to reopen has proved a blessing to us in Chouts'un. I have a great admiration for John in every way. He's capable at his work, and is a perfect gentleman and a good friend and it is a privilege to be able to work with him.

The hospital has been just as busy as ever since we re-opened, busier than usual in some departments. We had eighty operations last month and over sixty x-ray examinations.[146] The authorities have all

[146] 1940, Foster Hospital's silver jubilee year, was one of the busiest in its history. Despite the obstacles to travel, the hospital dealt with almost 16,000 outpatient attendances during the year, and provided around 24,000 days of inpatient care. A total of 684 operations were performed, a very large number of them for gunshot wounds.

been friendly and we have had no disturbances, apart from a large number of red-tape enquiries which seem to be inevitable under this regime. So we have a great deal to be thankful for.

Gwyneth to Cambridge

Chouts'un
15th September 1940

This must have been a terrible week for you all[147]. I've been thinking specially of poor old Dray [148]. What a ghastly time she must have had, unless she's been moved out again. The little we had isn't anything compared with what you're getting. We're just listening to the news. I feel I don't want to listen and yet I like to know all I can about it. I usually listen at 7.30 p.m. but go to bed before the 9 p.m. bulletin most nights, and if there's new news Ronald can pass it on.

Rosemary asked the other day while we were having dinner whether you had Chinese food. I said 'no'. She asked why and I told her you didn't know how to make it, so she said why didn't your cook make it for you? I told her you hadn't a cook, so she replied that she'd like to help you cook and make Chinese food. About ten minutes later, after she'd evidently thought it all out she remarked, 'Granny could do the part where I would burn my fingers, couldn't she?'! You see, we always tell her to be careful and not touch Wu Shih Fu's stove lest she should burn her fingers – so I hope you won't object to doing that part of it when she helps! This week both Kao and Wu have had a few days off, so Rosemary and Audrey have both been busy 'helping'. You'd love to see them rushing about with the mop and brush. They're both so terribly thrilled with themselves and Audrey follows round after Rosemary with such enthusiasm, and as fast as her stout little body can go!

It seems funny to me how folk seem to imagine we're pining for a son. We don't feel we could wish for anything more satisfying than our daughters! and anyway, I never felt to miss anything by having no brothers. I suppose in some ways it's nice to have a mixed family, but out here they have to separate so soon, whereas if they're all boys or all girls they can stick together throughout school days.

Nursing School re-opens this week. Ronald has four new lectures to prepare for each week. It's really too much with all his other jobs but

---

[147] On 7th September a huge daylight raid on the East End of London left 430 dead, over 1,600 seriously injured and thousands homeless.

[148] Dray was still at University College Hospital. On 11th September 'hits' had been reported on several London hospitals

Alice wants it and he feels he must try. How he'll fit it in, I can't think. New lectures are bad enough to do in English but to do them in Chinese, at the rate of four a week, really is pretty thick, and of course Staff and Ward Services and English Services go on all the time. I'm supposed to be leading the English one next week – feel I ought to do it and then it'll be over till after Christmas.

Oh, I've had a note from the London Censor asking to whom he shall return the clydella as he can't forward it. Isn't it cracked? There's nothing it could possibly be accused of conveying to the enemy. Anyway, I'm afraid you'll be getting it back. Maybe I'll get it some day, in time to make the next infant a garment!

Gwyneth to Ilkley

Chouts'un
22nd September 1940

Exactly five years since we landed in Shanghai! – that was a Sunday too. We're celebrating by me leading the English Service and Ronald the Chinese one in Hospital! See what good mishes we've become!

What a lot has happened during this period, both to us personally and to the world in general. Everything seemed so peaceful then, though of course we did see Italian troopships on their way to Abyssinia, on our journey. I suppose that was the beginning of this world upheaval. Anyway, we're thankful for five happy years, for they have been happy ones for us personally, and none of the various difficulties and disturbances has been able to take that happiness from us.

We've just heard that last night was the fifteenth which Londoners had had to spend in shelters. What a ghastly time they and many others are having. We just feel we can't imagine it at all. We've received cable news of the damage to the Mission House, though no details, but we were relieved there were no casualties. We've been disturbed several times lately by the same sort of noises that broke our nights so often two years ago, but it is nothing compared with then, or with what you're having. Tonight we heard that one of the few London Hospitals not previously hit was damaged last night, no casualties. Every time I hear of hospitals I think of Dray.

The BMS has recently altered our allowance rate. Instead of getting exchange rates each month we're at a fixed rate now. We can manage on it so far, but we don't feel that people at home realise that whereas we're getting far more dollars to the pound than we did, yet prices have soared in proportion and, in many ways, in advance. Don't think we're complaining, because we feel we ***want*** to do our bit towards helping the Mission in these difficult days. And don't think we're anxious – we're not, because we can manage to have enough of everything. Probably in lots of ways we're far better off than you are.

Gwyneth to Cambridge

Foster Hospital (properly in it this time!)
(around 2nd November 1940)

I hope the cable which went from Tsinan on October 31 reached you safely and announced clearly that Catherine had put in her appearance on Sunday October 27. I can't think of any name it can possibly be mistaken for, but Post Office officials are very bright and may have announced the arrival of someone else by mistake[149].

She was 7¼lbs and arrived on a lovely bright mild autumn morning. I've not discovered any flaws in her. Her hair is quite plentiful, far more than either Rosemary or Audrey had, a medium-light brown; her eyes, big and dark blue. She's really a very pretty little creature, and of course very intelligent. At any rate she has the sense to tuck into the nourishing food supply which awaits her. I myself am feeling fine and eating like an elephant. Georgie, who is a nurse, is very kindly ordering all my food so Ronald hasn't the bother. Wu cooks it and Kao trots over with it. For a few days I had three meals and five snacks (tea, orangeade etc) a day, so he had plenty of exercise!

As the first of our foreigners to be in for some years I'm being made a great fuss of and the baby gets a lot of petting from the nurses. The Chinese girls have been awfully good. They're so very quiet and gentle and of course only the best has been good enough for the wife of the Acting Superintendent of the Hospital! Alice has been with me a lot and taken no end of trouble getting the room ready and taking care of me since, and Jags has bathed Catherine most days. They've given me a room at the end of the Hospital which is almost unoccupied, so it's fairly quiet. And the weather is so mild that I've been able to have verandah doors wide open all the time and it's been lovely to see the sun, and, since I've felt like it, to keep an eye on people as they go about the compound!

---

[149] The cable announcing Audrey's arrival had spelt her name 'Andrey', so that for almost a month they were unsure as to whether she was a boy, Andrew, or a girl, Audrey.

I'm so thankful I've been able to stay here this time. It's a great relief to think I'm only a few yards from home – the railway journey was such a blight on previous occasions. Both children are with Wang Ta Sao but Georgie has been in a lot and I'm not in the least anxious about them.

They are perfectly adorable when they come in. The first time they were both very thrilled, but Audrey very serious. Baby didn't open her eyes at all the first time, so when they got back, and Wang Ta Sao asked Audrey what she was like, Audrey didn't say anything but just screwed up her eyes in a very good imitation of the infant! They come for a few minutes now after tea each day and are adorable. They bring something for Catherine each time, usually a treasured plaything of their own, once a Chinese and an English chessman! Once Audrey came armed with an enormous Chinese vegetable just like a marrow. Needless to say Catherine enjoyed it raw for supper! They are really awfully excited and Rosemary is full of plans for helping to look after her when we get her home.

Gwyneth to Ilkley

Chouts'un
19th November 1940

Catherine and I came home on 16th. Although we were excellently cared for in hospital it is a joy to be home. The children are so very thrilled and delighted at having a baby. Audrey walks around saying to herself "my dear baby", and at bath-times it's quite hectic trying to prevent their enthusiastic efforts to help from causing any damage. Baby is really very good. She never makes a sound all day but has been rather more noisy once or twice at night, but I think she's settling down now. The first few days at home are always a bit difficult.

We've had letters from you all and it's been such a relief to know you were all well and cheery. We are so glad Uncle Hu[150] had been able to visit you. We can just imagine him. He's a great person and most entertaining. Don't believe too many of the things he said about us, I guess he made up a lot of them. What he wouldn't tell you is all the fine things he himself has done. He's one of the most humble people I've ever met. We still hope he'll come back. The Chinese are always enquiring about his return.

[150] Mr Harris, in England on furlough

Gwyneth to Cambridge

Chouts'un
26th November 1940

It's marvellous that with all the disturbances your end and ours, and on the seas, I am able to tell you that all Mummy's letters up to September 30 have arrived safely. You can guess how bucked we were, and of course especially so since September had been such a bad month at home. We just scrape every letter for its last spot of news, and any paper that trickles through is read from cover to cover. The wireless helps in one way and yet makes us more than ever anxious for letters. I hope you don't believe all you hear of us. We've all been turned out umpteen times according to reports and yet we're still here, thank goodness.

Wu asked me recently how old you were (that's quite polite here!). I said, 'oh, about 60'. He was amazed to hear that Father could walk and cycle actively and that Mother could cook and so on. So when you come here, you know you'll be expected to sit back and have people wait on you hand and foot. Wu would do it gladly. He'd do anything to help anyone and do it cheerfully, too. How I wish you could come. It's so awful to think you've not seen even one of our attractive babies.

You'll be glad to know that this time at home has just set me on tremendously and I now feel fine. Catherine is getting on splendidly, gained 6oz last week and is behaving better at nights. The other two are still very thrilled and sweet with her and altogether we're very happy to be all at home again.

Kao had his third girl yesterday, arrived about 9 p.m. in hospital. His wife has been here several weeks and suddenly decided the time had arrived. Ronald sent a stretcher for her, as she's been ill, and she just got there in time, but only just. So now we all have three girls, but Wu has two sons and Kao one son too. Of course people on knowing we'd another daughter all said, 'oh well, plenty of time, the next will be a boy'.

We never got Uncle Harry's last parcel. A great blow, because we appreciate them so much. Very few old friends write, in fact it's months since I heard from anyone except family, and Phil. She really is awfully good and I so seldom find time to reply. Pris writes fairly regularly, but I don't think I've heard from anyone else this year. I'm not going to write any letters once I get home! I shall talk non-stop, so be prepared!

Rosemary is a joke. Every Monday I do the accounts with Wu, and she gets a little notebook, too, and a pencil and very carefully goes thro' all the things she can think of, saying (in Chinese of course), '3lbs of apples – how much? What was the price of 2lbs of beef?' and so on. Wu Shih Fu always very seriously tells her some sum and she 'writes' it down in her little book.

Gwyneth to Cambridge

Chouts'un
7th January 1941

You say we won't need to send the children to Boarding School for many years yet, but most children go at six or seven and Rosemary is already four. I can't teach her properly at home, especially with two small ones about too, though I know that folk have done it.

For her birthday we gave Audrey a wee rubber doll in a tiny wicker cradle. She was thrilled to bits, kept saying "mine baby – mine san ku niang" (third girl). It was clothed, but had no bedding so the first afternoon she was playing with it and I found she'd taken off her own socks and folded one very neatly and put it in the cradle under the doll's head for a pillow and the other was very carefully put on top and tucked in to act as a blanket! She's awfully devoted to her dolls and they all have their feeds in the same way that Catherine has hers!!

Now we're really at 1941 I just begin to realise how much I want to come home and see you all. I've never dared to think of it before, but I'd certainly love it well enough now if it were safer travelling and more peaceful. A boat journey at present would be a nightmare with three children as young as ours. I shouldn't be allowed into England with children. Ronald would go to England and I'd be left in Canada in some missionary home. What fun!

Arrangements for schooling for their children had always created dilemmas for missionaries. In 1880, the China Inland Mission set up a boarding school for the children of missionaries in Chefoo, with separate sections for boys and girls and a preparatory section for children aged 5 to 10 years. In the first half of the 20th century, many Baptist missionaries sent their children there for their early schooling and then transferred them for their final school years to one of the boarding schools in England which catered specially for the children of missionaries, Walthamstow Hall in Kent for girls, and Eltham College in London for boys.

Long separations from their children were one of the hardest things for missionaries to cope with. Early in 1902, the China Sub-Committee of the BMS considered a particularly poignant plea from one of their missionaries about to return to his mission station in Tsingchou after a period settling his children at schools in England. He wrote, "The practice in Presbyterian Missions in China is to allow all missionaries who have children between the ages of six and eighteen, to come home for a short furlough at the end of four and a half years on the field. The granting of such an arrangement on the part of our Committee would be an unspeakable boon for us.

"I do not think anyone has ever heard me, or ever will hear me, speak of anything in the way of hardship in the lot of a missionary. The honour of being an ambassador of Jesus Christ, the privilege of helping to lay the foundation of his great church in China, the joy of training men to be leaders, pastors to their own countrymen, are all so great that I am more thankful than ever before that this great honour has been given to us. But God has given us these children, and they help us much in China, bringing us nearer the Chinese, and the Chinese nearer us. It is not for our sakes but for their sakes that we plead that we may be allowed to see them once again before they grow into manhood and womanhood.

"Our children are intensely loyal to the Chinese, and still speak of Tsingchoufu as 'home'. They speak of us returning as 'going home', and it is home, for our life is there. They loved the Chinese and were much loved and lovingly treated by them. In the dark time of the trouble[151] *they would not hear the Chinese spoken against. They are loyally willing to give us up, but it seems a terrible long time – eight long years – before they see us again.*

"My boy, eleven years of age, a manly little fellow, opened his heart the other night to his mother. I think any father who saw him, as shaken with sobs he clung to his mother and told how he had begun to count the days til we go and had begun to count the time til we come back, would feel that, if it be at all possible that we should see him and his sister in four or five years' time, it should be so.

"I could tell sad stories of parents who have come home after many years to find their children strangers, and alas have gone back with saddened hearts ... leaving them strangers still." [152]

In this case, because this family had had only two furloughs during more than twenty five years' service, permission was granted for

---

[151] The Boxer rising

[152] BMS China Sub-Committee Minutes, 20.1.1902, Angus Library, Oxford

them to take an additional half furlough (six months) at the end of four and a half years' further service. By the 1930s, the standard time between furloughs was seven, not eight years.

Gwyneth to Ilkey

Chouts'un
26th January 1941

Rosemary and Audrey when they're playing together almost invariably use each other's Chinese names. Rosemary is Ju Mei and Audrey Ju Lan, but they just say Mei and Lan. We think of calling Catherine Ju Li (Rue Lee), then the three will be:

Hsi Ju Mei	Rare as the plum blossom
Hsi Ju Lan	Rare as the orchid
Hsi Ju Li[153]	Rare as white jasmine

The hospital woman evangelist suggested Ju Li and most people seem to like it. She's getting on well and gaining weight more quickly. She's taking a great interest in everything and turns her head around with her big blue eyes looking here and there, as though she took it all in.

Tomorrow is the old Chinese New Year, which all the folk celebrate. Wu Shih Fu has gone home for it and Kao will go for a few days later on, and Wang Ta Sao too when the children are well. They eat special food and sit up talking all night, and everyone who can possibly manage it goes home for 'Kuo Nien'[154]. I'm glad Wu has gone home – he deserves it and he does so love to be with his children. Kao is fond of children, but not quite the same as Wu. We have been in this house five years (last Monday) and had both boys all the time. I can't be too thankful for them. We've had endless occasions to be grateful to them both. They've not just been good servants, but real loyal friends to us.

I'm making a bed-jacket for Georgie, and am busy on a pram suit for her infant. I've also been knitting for Connie's new baby and am now starting a sleeping bag for Catherine. As I couldn't get wool I liked, I've undone a coat of mine and washed the wool and it looks quite nice.

PS: Rosemary is going to teach you all Chinese. She's afraid if she doesn't you'll never know what Audrey is talking about!

---

[153] Pinyin = Xi Ru Mei, Xi Ru Lan and Xi Ru Li
[154] Pinyin = guo nian

Gwyneth to Ilkley

Chouts'un
4th March 1941

I hope you won't be worried by alarms and rumours of missionaries evacuating. Of course we all realise the possibility, but we hope there'll be no need. If we do, you may be sure we shall make the best arrangements possible in whatever circumstances we find ourselves. It usually seems that husbands accompany their wives, but as Ronald is the senior man here it won't be so easy. If Ronald and John both decided they must escort their families it would mean no one left here in the hope of carrying on, and that wouldn't be very good. If we separate, most likely Tom and Connie will too, and we hope to stick together – Connie and I.

An American friend of mine has recently very kindly sent me her home address and her husband's. She thinks it may be that we'll need a home in USA temporarily and tells us to wire either address and a welcome will await us. It's awfully good of her, isn't it? We feel more hopeful about the situation, but the Americans are all very worked up. They always get far more alarmed than the majority of Britishers.

We are receiving very friendly treatment locally and having no trouble, though Ronald has to waste an awful amount of time in 'official' visits. The powers that be make almost daily visits, which are long affairs besides being very tiring. There are always problems of one sort or another in connection with staffing arrangements, and of course finances are very complicated. As I think I mentioned before, our money is paid into Shanghai. We now lose 26% on everything we have transferred to Tsingtao, where we need our account for almost all our expenses. It's awful to feel so much goes on exchange, not only for our personal spending (that's bad enough) but a Relief Fund gift of money is equally reduced.

The nursing school term has started again, so Ronald has lectures too. I do wish he could see more of the children. Catherine is getting on nicely – tries to lift her head off the pillow, so I suppose before long she'll be trying to sit up. She's so sweet and has such bright little eyes.

While discussing possible evacuations on one hand, on the other we and the Allens are paying a deposit on a house in Peitaiho for the season! If we don't make plans there's so little chance of fixing it later, and we feel it's wise to take a holiday if we can. Ronald will take me and Connie and families up and stay July and Tom will come for August and take us all home. At least that's the idea now. It's a pity Ronald and

Tom won't be together, but their holidays have to fit in with other people's and that seems the way this year.

Gwyneth to Cambridge

Chouts'un
27th March 1941

The main item in this bulletin is the arrival on March 26 of Margaret Jane Allen, 8 lbs. We're all very thankful for her safe arrival. I've not yet seen her, but I hear she's very bonny and Connie is doing well. My only regret about her arrival is that it won't be long now before Connie has to go home[155], and it's been such fun having her here. Georgie and baby are fine, so we're all very bucked. We think of having a Dedication Service for all three babies, but I'll write about it later.

We are sending Connie's meals over to Hospital. The boys are ever so glad to do it, even though it means quite a bit of extra work. Kao has to go over six or seven times a day with a tray and the room is upstairs, so it's quite a bother, but they both seem very pleased that we're doing it. I don't know anyone, foreigner or Chinese, who wouldn't be glad to do anything they could for Connie.

I've just heard that Enid Phillips is coming here for four or five days with Rosemary and Roger. I'm so thrilled, it will be such fun to have them. They're all so very nice and our children just adore Rosemary and Roger. They've not been here before, though Enid has been for a flying visit when our Rosemary was three months old. Enid said she will look after Catherine, except at meals, and her two children will take our two off my hands so that I can have a real holiday.

Connie and I went thro' all our old snaps the other day. She's so interested in you all, and we had a grand time.

If we were given permission by the BMS, would you want us to travel home under present conditions? The tales we hear from friends who have come out recently make us very reluctant to think of taking three babies on the sea now. Of course we have been asked to postpone our furlough for one year, so that unless that order is cancelled there is no question of our coming.

---

[155] Connie had come to Chouts'un for the delivery of her baby at Foster Hospital.

Gwyneth to Cambridge and Ilkley

Chouts'un
13th April 1941

Last Monday, Enid Phillips, Rosemary, Roger and Nigel all arrived at 10 a.m., so we were busy on Saturday getting ready. It has been such fun having them and we've all enjoyed their visit. They are three grand children and Rosemary and Audrey have had a lovely time with them. Enid is a charming person and I was so glad to have her here. We have just seen them off back to Tsinan.

By the way, Mummy, have you the address of your brothers? Is Uncle George the one in America? I don't really think for one minute that I'd ever be near them, but I was thinking the other day that if I evacuate to Australia or Canada near any of our relations it would be fun to see them. Has Daddy the address of the Uncle in Sydney? If I went to Australia, I'd certainly choose Melbourne, cos I'd love to see Uncle H. But it's possible I might get dumped in Sydney and I was wondering about Pa's brother there. I can't even remember his name, but I know he has a daughter Mavis.

Gwyneth to Cambridge

Chouts'un
13th May 1941

Last Friday morning a young girl, about eighteen or nineteen, died in hospital. She's the daughter of the Head of our School in Tsingchou and was a beautiful creature and well-educated. She had very rapid progressive TB and was only ill a few months. I know there are plenty of sad things now, but we all felt this very much. We attended a memorial service for her, and it was very touching. Her parents were marvellously brave and self-controlled. The father is such a fine man and makes no complaints. He just went out of his way to express his gratitude for what was done for his daughter. Several of our pastors' and teachers' children have TB. It's much more common even than a few years back, due, I suppose, to the appalling conditions. What with wars, floods, locusts and droughts the people have had and still are having a terrible time.

By the way, do the BBC send messages abroad to civilians? Every so often we hear private messages (I mean from a family!) for various soldiers in the Far East and we also hear Americans sending messages to their friends out here so I wondered if the BBC offered the same facilities.

Gwyneth to Cambridge and Ilkley

Chouts'un
25th May 1941

Last weekend I went and developed a breast abscess and one day had a nice little temp of 104.5°. It was boiling hot weather to begin with, so you can tell how hot I felt. However, Ronald was able to give me some medicine which soon cooled me down and we think the abscess may subside without being opened. I feel quite all right, only my left arm is bandaged up and I find one arm, even though it's my right one, hardly sufficient for most jobs.

Fortunately Georgie is next door and has been awfully kind coming in to bath Catherine, to give me hot poultices, baths etc. I'm most grateful to her and so thankful she's here. I had five nights with scarcely any sleep so that I was glad when I slept all through last night and consequently feel very different today. Rosemary and Audrey have been awfully good all week and Wang Ta Sao has done splendidly, helping with Catherine too.

Unless we get a heavy downfall very soon the harvest will be ruined. The first crops have already died, but there is some hope for the second if rain comes soon. Even we living here can't really imagine conditions in some areas not far away, so it must be almost impossible for you.

Gwyneth to Cambridge and Ilkley

Chouts'un
25th June 1941

Well, I'm still in bed! – the sixth week. I've missed these last two weeks writing because the first I was running a high temperature, and on the second Tuesday I had another operation. The wound seems to be clearing up now – I hope finally, so that I don't need to return to Hospital again! I can only write a few lines again this week as I'm still in hospital and not supposed to use my left arm at all, and without it the paper keeps wobbling!

Wang ta Sao with Catherine

I'm having to wean Catherine. I don't think it'll do her any harm, only in the hot weather it's always safer to be able to feed her myself and for the journey much easier. I shan't be able to travel on July 2nd [156] of course, so we've postponed it to 15th anyway and I hope to be OK by then. Ronald will come back to relieve John for his holiday in August and then take a second fortnight in September we hope.

Wang Ta Sao is doing well with the children. She's had them all three almost entirely on her own. Ronald is scarcely ever at home and no-one else has been to help, except Su the last day or two since her school shut has helped at bath time. You can guess how I long to get back to them.

The temperature of the ward on this floor yesterday afternoon was 102°! And this room couldn't have been much less, so you can imagine how cool I'm feeling swathed in cotton wool and bandages!!

Since the onset of war in Europe, Japan had been feeling her way with the major world powers, the United States, Great Britain, Germany and Russia. She was anxious not to forego useful alliances, but was attracted by the rich natural resources of South East Asia and encouraged in her expansionist ambitions by the powerful militarist factions within the government. Hitler's attack on Russia on June 21st provided her with the opportunity to seize Indo-China. By early August it was apparent that Thailand was also threatened. As the British became concerned for the security of Singapore, the United States assured Britain of its support should its interests in the Far East come under attack. The general tension increased, and it seemed that war between Britain and Japan was inevitable.

[156] To Peitaiho for their planned holiday with Connie Allen and family.

In China itself, the war with Japan had reached something of a stalemate. The battle lines had remained largely unaltered since 1939, and the balance of power between the two sides was more or less unchanged. The provinces in the north east, including Manchuria, remained in Japanese hands, as well as Hainan Island in the south, while 'Free China', the vast mainland areas to the south and west, continued to hold out, despite repeated onslaughts. On August 12th the Times reported 'Four days of bombing in Chungking', when four hundred Japanese aircraft dropped more than three thousand bombs on the beleaguered Chinese war-time capital.

In Free China, mission hospitals and schools were flooded with refugees from the occupied zones and staff were kept busy with relief work, while evangelistic and teaching work continued alongside. At all times, they were harassed by frequent air attacks by the Japanese, and hampered by difficulties obtaining essential supplies.

In the occupied areas, most missionaries wanted to stay on as long as they could to provide help and support to the local people. As war loomed between Japan and Britain, however, their position became increasingly untenable. By the end of August, a partial evacuation of women and children was underway, and staff at the Mission House in London were exploring alternatives for those not being evacuated.

Gwyneth to Cambridge

Chouts'un
12th August 1941

At the beginning of July the authorities announced that special permits were needed by foreigners wishing to travel, so Ronald filled in the necessary forms, four each for himself and me, and four photos. (Mine with the family was taken the first day I got out of bed, so you can imagine how bright I look in it!) Anyway the passes didn't arrive until so late that we couldn't have left for our Peitaiho holiday until quite late in July, but it has all worked out for the best.

As it happened, on my second day home I shot another temperature (103°) and, after another week in bed, went back to Hospital for two more incisions, on different days. Altogether I had five visits to the theatre. I had three weeks there, coming out on August 6th and now I'm beginning to get about and feel heaps better. I have to have daily dressings, but I'm feeling much stronger. Connie too was unable to get permits so she could not have gone either. Eventually she was allowed to come as far as Chouts'un and she's still here.

Our Advisory Committee has decided to advise all women and children and a number of couples to leave for a safer spot. In fact everyone is advised to go, except Ronald in Chouts'un and Pan[157], Drake and Edward Phillips in Tsinan. I can't believe I'm to leave and go off, probably to Canada, USA or Australia, especially without Ronald. I've felt too wobbly - in bed three months nearly. Things are all muddles and I've forgotten where to look for them. However, I've managed to do a little with Wang Ta Sao's help. Ronald is far too busy, in fact I scarcely see him. He took a couple of weeks' holiday here in Chouts'un, but as I was in hospital it was not much fun, and the second week he seemed to be at committee meetings most of the time!

From my point of view I don't want to go for weeks (I don't want to go at all) because at present I can't do much for the children. It's all I can do to get myself around. I think I'll soon be back to normal again now, but I'll need to be on top of my form to manage all three children by myself. Catherine has made rapid strides lately, stands up in her cot making all sorts of nice noises and laughs and plays with Rosemary and Audrey. She is very firm and plump, very much like the other two were.

Gwyneth to Cambridge

Tsingtao
29th August 1941

Well, we came down on Wednesday. Quite a good journey, plenty of room. Very hot, of course, but for August not too bad. All our luggage had to be examined but I got it all safely away. Two locks were broken on the journey, but otherwise all safe.

I'm sharing a house with the Lewises and Connie and family. The bedrooms are rather small and I've not one shelf or cupboard in my room, only three pegs, so I'm not finding it easy to keep tidy! We're waiting here for passages to Shanghai and from there hope to get off for the States, but bookings are very scarce and we don't feel too hopeful. I think a cable will go to the Mission House to tell when we sail and where. If you hear we've gone to Australia write c/o Uncle Harry, as I'll certainly get into touch with him. And if it's USA or Canada write c/o Dr A E Armstrong, United Church of Canada, 299 Queen St E, Toronto, Ontario, Canada and mark "to await arrival".

---

[157] Chinese name for Henry Payne

I'll try to send a cable to tell of our safe arrival, if it is possible. We'll only send one, so please pass on information. We hope to settle in Toronto, so send along any names of friends there! We've been promised by the United Church of Canada that they'll find accommodation for our arrival, which will be a help.

Since arriving here I've had one letter from Ronald, and he seemed all right. I hated leaving him as you'll know, but we both feel that it's the right thing. He is very happy with all the Chinese there and so I hope he'll not feel too lonely. Kao will look after him at present. Wu is cooking for us here and I think of taking him to Shanghai, as Ronald won't be with me. He'll be such a help in all the roping and unroping of boxes, and also, when I have to go to the various offices for permits, I shall know the children will be all right with him and he'll help me with washing etc. Of course if it should be that we have only a few days I wouldn't consider it, but if we're to be several weeks then it would be worth the extra. You see, in any place I lived I shouldn't be able to have the children to meals with me, and I should have to leave them alone if I'd no help, and that wouldn't be wise in a strange place.

All these plans may come to nothing, but I think I may as well tell you what we think of doing! We hear that we may have to wait here a month for passages even to Shanghai, so things are fairly slow.

It's lovely here. Cool breezes are so welcome after the heat in Chouts'un. The children are all getting so nice and brown and are enjoying the fun of being with Elizabeth and Philip and of paddling and playing on the rocks. I feel heaps better, and although I'm still not quite healed up, I am able to get about normally. Goodness, three months' sickness does make me appreciate good health more than ever!

Your last letters (June 14 and 21) arrived the day before I came away and I was bucked. They'd been properly censored at home and then obviously pulled open out here and very clumsily stuck down again. I can't imagine they'd get much fun out of them, can you?!

Fancy old Kay being a Fire Warden! Do you have to send someone from each house or what? I should just wither with fright I'm certain. The last few weeks there's been a lot of firing around. The very last night before we came away it was terrific and we could hear shells going through the trees by our house and the big field gun was only a few yards from our house. The noise was awful and every time the nearest gun went I jumped! We just couldn't get to sleep. We are between the city wall and the station and you never know which way the firing may be. Upstairs didn't seem too safe to me, but we couldn't get the children down and anyway Ronald wasn't at all worried. It is a blessing to have a husband who keeps calm and sensible in all emergencies – you get enough excitements and annoyances to upset almost anyone!

Audrey is feeling the 'break up' of the family far more than Rosemary. Rosemary thinks it's all right, she knows that in other years Ronald has come on after us, but Audrey suddenly realises that Daddy and Kao haven't come and she's really quite upset. She keeps saying "Daddy is coming now, Daddy getting nearer now". I wish he were.

Gwyneth to Ilkley

Tsingtao
4th September 1941

It is horrible feeling it might be years before I see Ronald again. If he waits till the war is over, it may be two or three years I suppose, and if he gets turned out earlier it will still mean separation, because he'll have to take his furlough alone in England and I'll have to stay wherever I go now. But we hope that in some way it will work out so that we can be all together again soon.

It was a very hard decision to make but we still feel it's right. We want the children to be in a more settled atmosphere, and we don't feel it's right to risk internment for them, if we can avoid it. We feel that Ronald can best fulfil his duties to the Mission if I take the children away. Having them inland now is a big strain and responsibility, not only because of the tense situation between countries but also because of local conditions, though those alone would not have been a sufficient reason for such a big step. Ronald has tremendous responsibility in his job and now he's the only man permanently there, heaps of extra problems fall on him. Accounts, staff, goats, laundry, kitchen, repairs, building and all the many interviews with officials all take up such a terrific amount of time and energy. If he feels free of family responsibilities, and the anxiety of wondering if we ought or ought not to get the children away, it will make his task much easier I hope.

I got out with five large trunks, two suitcases, three carriers, one camp bed, one child's cot, one pram, one sewing machine and one basket of food for journey, so I didn't do badly, not to mention a handbag containing travel passes, passport, cholera certificates etc. With all this luggage, and the children, I felt I needed to keep on checking up numbers! You'll think it's a lot of luggage, but I've had to bring bedding, pillows, table linen, towels and as much as possible in the way of clothes. I hope eventually to find a house where I can settle in Toronto (or Melbourne) and shall not be able to afford all new linen, blankets and so on.

We're waiting here hoping to get news of berths in a steamer for the States. Failing that we'll plan for Australia. There are no direct sailings for Canada now, so we'll need to go to San Francisco and cross to Vancouver. We may be leaving here on the 15th for Shanghai and I don't know how long we'll wait there. We think there's a chance of a sailing during October, but we have to obtain special USA transit visas and this means a delay. I say 'we' – our party at present planning to go to Shanghai is John and Georgie Lewis and baby, Connie Allen and three children, Connie and Barrie Light, Miss Thomas and myself. In Shanghai we'll probably break up, but Miss Thomas will probably travel with me. I can't manage entirely on my own with two such babes. Connie Allen and I hope to make a home together later on.

Gwyneth to Cambridge and Ilkley

Tsingtao
23rd September 1941

The most important news is that I didn't sail to Shanghai on the boat I mentioned. I can't go into all the reasons and details in a letter, but Ronald wired me to postpone the sailing, which I did and, as far as we can, we have decided that it's best for me not to go now.

There are so many uncertainties whichever way we choose and at the moment it seems best that I should stay. Lack of escort was a big factor. We had expected to travel in company with one or two married couples, but they've all made other plans and it meant going just with Miss Thomas, who would go solely for my benefit, and we're not keen to take someone who would not otherwise be going. Just the examining of luggage alone needs a man – every trunk has to be gone through and I just couldn't open up boxes, keep an eye on the contents, and then repack them while I had the children with me. Anyway, I'm staying on here for a while and John Lewis has decided to return to Chouts'un so I hope Ronald will be able to get out for a little holiday with us.

September 28: Well, if I wait long enough there's always a change of plan. John and Georgie have decided now not to return to Chouts'un. We're awfully sorry, as he's such a pleasant colleague and Georgie and I get on so well. However, they've reluctantly decided that they must go to Canada. I hope he'll go up and relieve Ronald for his much-needed holiday, but that's not fixed yet.

At last my wounds are all healed. The last one lost its elastoplast yesterday so I'm hoping to get a few bathes before the sea gets too cold. If John lets Ronald get his holiday, we'll stay a couple of weeks and return together. If not, I'll probably go back in about a week.

Alas, all our Chouts'un goats got a pneumonia plague and died, so we'll need to live on tinned milk if we go back. Catherine is the only problem, but we can take a big supply back, I think. Later, when the frost has come, Ronald hopes to buy more goats. It's an awful loss, as they're hard to buy and are about $100 each.

Audrey is looking so brown and well and is enjoying the sea very much. Catherine too is very fit. She has such a lovely bonny little face and fat arms and legs. She says goodbye in Chinese now and 'bye bye' and 'Dada' and can walk holding on to chairs or table legs. When we watched the eclipse on the 20th (or 21st, I forget the date) the children were very interested and next day Rosemary asked me to tell Daddy that she'd seen the clips on the sun. Her great expression now is 'who cares?' – taken from Nigel of course.

Gwyneth to Cambridge

Tsingtao
29th September 1941

It's 7 a.m. and I've a few minutes before I must get up. How I wish you could see Audrey in the pretty flowery nightie you made, with her little chubby sunburnt arms, pouring out tea for herself. Since we've been here, she has slept with me and always pours out the remainder of milk and tea for herself! She talks incessantly now and is most amusing. She keeps saying "I do want mine Daddy and mine Kao ta Ko". Her great idea is sweets and she's always asking to go in a rickshaw. When I say where does she want to go, it's always 'to the shops to buy some tweeties'. She loves to help herself to the sugar and frequently makes a mistake and puts the sugar spoon, heavily laden of course, right into her mouth. Oh dear, I'll have to train her before she visits you or all your ration will disappear at one fell swoop, but I don't think you'd have the heart to be really cross. She looks so very pleased as she says in Chinese 'Lan ch'ih t'ang' (Lan is eating sugar) and goes on spooning it out.

John Lewis has gone to Chouts'un today, so Ronald may come tomorrow for a couple of weeks' holiday. Then we hope to go home together. Permits are a little easier to get now, but it's awful the number of photos we've handed in to the authorities this year alone on travel permits. As I thought I was going to Canada I brought out our extra linen and blankets, and I may possibly leave them here. I'll have to go through and see what can be spared.

Fancy, we've already been in China more than six years! We've three children who can all travel free on the railway. I feel it's quite an accomplishment! This is the last time though, as five is the age for half fares.

Gwyneth to Ilkley

Chouts'un
20th October 1941

We hear that several boats carrying mail from China to England have been lost, so we wonder if any of our letters to you are missing. All yours up to August 6 seem to be here now. We've been so grateful for them all and read them with such pleasure and interest. It's so good to feel we can keep up a little with home affairs, though we feel we shall be very out of date in many ways. You'll have to keep an eye on us when we're in company and see that we don't make too many mistakes!

It looks as if I may have to start teaching Rosemary before long. I'd hoped she would be able to start at a kindergarten at home this autumn but I think five and a half or six is early enough. It seems silly to try to teach them too soon, and she's so happy playing with Audrey and Catherine and she learns so much all day. She and Audrey can tell the type of goods on sale on the road at the side of our garden, just by hearing a bell or a gong, or whatever peculiar sound is used to announce the arrival of a seller of oil, bread, or cloth. Each street vendor has his own 'musical' method of announcing his arrival and the children have learnt them all from the boys. They're both very keen on Chinese food, and in fact everything Chinese. They like nothing better than to wear their Chinese clothes. We are just getting a padded gown made for Rosemary – it's likely to be difficult to buy coal later, so we want her to have a cosy garment ready.

Gwyneth to Cambridge

Chouts'un
27th October 1941

Last Thursday John and Georgie came back. The Mission wasn't willing for John to go to Canada at this stage and he and Georgie are unwilling to separate, so they have both come back. We only hope that they will have no cause to regret their decision. We hear that Tom Allen has gone to Shanghai to see Connie and the children again. They are probably sailing for Hong Kong and Australia on November 12. I do wish Tom could have gone with Connie, but he's the only senior man in Tsingchou and can't be spared.

Life here becomes more and more complicated in some ways. Firms can't supply us with goods and that of course will greatly effect the work, unless some arrangement can be made. Prices are still rising but we can still manage quite well without going short of any necessities, and we hope we shan't need any big clothing bills.

Tomorrow the Hospital Service is to be 8.30am instead of 7 a.m. It will be nice to stay in bed a bit longer, though I'm afraid I'll wake just the same, or anyway I'll be wakened by a little voice saying 'Mummy, Lan wakened up now. Shall me come and have mine tea?' They always wake so bright and cheery, and so anxious to get up. Even on the coldest days Audrey climbs out of bed and patters about with her little bare feet and seems quite happy about it.

We have three more girls taking their final nursing exam in December and so Ronald is busy giving extra lectures, which they've missed earlier owing to various hindrances. This is the last class of girls to graduate of the ones whose course has been interrupted by the beginning of the Sino-Japanese war, and also by the Anti-B movement. The class of seven, which should take their finals next year, all started when we re-opened after the Anti-B business, and so far they have had no interruptions in their studies. This year we've nine new students, a record number for recent years. They seem a nice crowd and very keen on their work.

Gwyneth to Kay

Chouts'un

30th October 1941

Now that American sailings are once more being interrupted on the Pacific, and the British were long ago stopped, goodness knows how or when we'll get further direct news of you. Does Mother get occasional news from the Mission House? Every now and again a cable is sent about our health and whereabouts, and I'd like to feel M and D at least get this general cabled news. The Ilkley people get it, so that they ought to too.

I'm noting Connie Conkling's address, it might be a great help. Of course, I thought I should be going through the States, and still may be, but it's jolly difficult to get in. I may give Phil Smart's aunt's name as a 'guarantor' if I ever apply for a transit visa. At critical times it seems necessary to get a permanent resident to guarantee you're OK. I wonder if she or Connie C would recognise my married name?

Do tell me what you do when you're 'up' on fire-watching. Oh, we do feel so terribly out of everything. Half the things we read in papers we can't fully understand these days!

Rosemary will not sing a line and everyone seems to expect her to sing terrifically long things. Elizabeth Allen sings hymns galore and it makes Rosemary shut up completely, poor lass. She's very quick at picking up most things and knows all her letters just through asking them when we look at books. I've not made any effort to teach her to read or write yet, though she makes letters occasionally when she's 'drawing'. Do you think that is sufficient till she's six? Or ought I to try to do more now she's nearly five? I've no books here and don't know how to get them now. She's very quick and good at Chinese and has a fairly large vocabulary in English too.

The other day she was looking at a book and came across a coloured view of a river, fields, with a church in the distance. She asked me where it was, so I said somewhere in England. She then asked me who was the person sitting by the river. I didn't look very carefully but said I didn't know. She then said, 'Mummy, I think it's Grandpa, wouldn't that be lovely if it was?' I then discovered that it was a fisherman[158]. She has an excellent memory and never seems to forget things like that.

Catherine celebrated her birthday, at least she marked the occasion, by cutting four more teeth, and walking two steps alone. She has four top teeth and still only one below. She has stood alone for some time, but only just decided to take the plunge and walk two steps before flopping heavily to the floor. Birthdays being much to the fore at the moment, I asked Audrey how old she is. She said, 'I'm isn't old'. Did I tell you that Rosemary hopes our next baby will be a boy so he can help Kao ta Ko?!

Today's paper gives a fresh warning to British women and children to evacuate. How to decide on the right course is more than I can say. I hate to keep the family here to face all sorts of dangers and hardships, but at the same time I hate to take them off to equally unknown possibilities. Travel by sea now is so bad and it's so difficult to get onto boats. Hanging about in Shanghai is no joke with three babes, nor would a shipwreck be! Not one of them could dress herself or get to

---

[158] Gwyneth's father, John Johnson, was a keen freshwater fisherman.

the life-boat alone in an emergency and I don't feel that any escort other than Ronald would be satisfactory in these days, and he is tied to his job.

Please don't think I'm really not contented with my lot, but I do like a little grouse occasionally, you know! And the decision to evacuate or not is really a most difficult one for us all. The younger the family the harder it is, too. However, we wouldn't have our family any different so we must face the difficult decisions, and we just hope we've done the right thing. It's just for the children that I can't help being a bit anxious.

Take care of yourself, and M and D, and be a good girl till I come home to take you all in hand.

Gwyneth to Ilkley

Chouts'un
3rd November 1941

Well, we hear that the Jaspers have left Shanghai for Rangoon on their way to Yunnan, and the Elders have gone to Hong Kong from where they will fly to Chungking on their way to Sian. And Connie Allen and family are coming back to Tsingchou. This has not yet been officially confirmed but they are certainly trying to get passes to return. I suppose they find it impossible to get away. It is really exceedingly difficult. No one who is British is allowed into Canada or USA now, so Australia is about the only possibility and boats are so few and far between.

We feel that there has been a certain amount of 'bungling' over this whole business and there is a lot of dissatisfaction about it. We hope very much that there will be no unhappy results. People have all felt they would just have to do the best they could independently and it has been very difficult. I am not referring to the 'Home' authorities, as they have done what they could in the way of guidance, but naturally they can't have the final decision in days when communications are so uncertain and the situation changes so rapidly from day to day. Unlikely though it appears, we still hope all may be well.

Ronald continues busy, much of his time being occupied with things other than his medical duties. Efforts to get permits to buy coal, flour etc for the hospital take a tremendous amount of time. They are going to get a couple of pigs to eat the 'rubbish' that the goats used to enjoy, so pig-keeping will be another of his accomplishments. We all hope to get good pork before long! Prices don't improve. Sugar four years ago was $1.90 per bag, and now it's $11.50. Flour is up from $3.50

to $16.50 and of course although the Shanghai dollar is about four times what it was, ours (the Shantung one) is only double, so buying isn't easy.

The Mission has, at last, doubled the allocation for work out here. It was paid in dollars, regardless of exchange rates, so that salaries to pastors and other Mission paid workers couldn't be increased and they hadn't had enough for food, much less clothes and fuel. It's better now, but even so, no pastor can live and educate a family on just his salary – they nearly all have to keep land to supplement it. They live so simply normally, that it seems awful if we can't pay enough to cover living costs for them, when we live in such comparative luxury. Now we are having to live very carefully, but even so we're far better off than the majority of Chinese and probably than many people at home. You folk probably know, though, that you will get a share of what's going, whereas we never know when our supplies may be cut off entirely.

Since I started this, we've had fresh warnings from the Consul about the advisability of getting away now, but the Mission isn't able to release any of the young husbands with families. The Mission authorities think there's no need to make any move: the resolutions passed earlier all seem to have been cancelled and regarded as 'alarmist'. Actually, we think they came too late as there are no British or American boats now. It's only the children that we feel anxious about.

Don't worry about us, because we have been very fortunate so far, and we haven't any of the difficulties and dangers that you have, and we feel sure that we shall be guided and kept safe whatever happens.

Gwyneth to Ilkley

Chouts'un
13th November 1941

We've actually had rain! I can't remember it raining since about the beginning of June and everywhere is bare and brown and dry and the farmers were almost in despair. Everything is so terribly expensive already, that if they had a bad harvest it would be tragic for everyone. It only rained three days and not much, but it's a help, and the air is better.

Rosemary has just asked if you eat persimmons in Ilkley and after thinking over my reply she said 'well, will you send this big pip in your letter and tell Granny to put it in the earth and then she'll have a tree with persimmons on it'. We decided after all that we'd bring the persimmon stones with us when we come, so keep a nice patch of garden free for them.

Did I tell you that after all Connie Allen and children are going to Canada? They had cancelled their passages to Australia and applied for permits to return, but then received the new warning from the Embassy and so decided to go and found suddenly that they were able to obtain permission to enter Canada. They sail from Manila for the States early in December. Since writing that I've seen Georgie, who says it's still uncertain, as there seems no way of getting to Manila from Shanghai. People talk of getting mothers and children away to safety, but no one seems to be able to do much to help them to get away. I expect Connie will get a boat, but she's been trying to leave China for four months.

I think I told you our head Chinese nurse is getting married on December 1 – she leaves here on Sunday. We have always liked her very much. She and Miss Chao, our other senior, came at the same time as we did, so we feel to know them well. They both came in for supper last night. They're nice, friendly girls and we know them well enough to be able to talk without a terrific effort. We want to have all the others in when we can.

Gwyneth to Ilkley

Chouts'un
30th November 1941

Rosemary's birthday - and now she's getting old enough to understand, we have to have proper celebrations or we hear about it!

The day before yesterday we had letters from you and Will of August 13, 20, 27 and September 16. A great joy of course. We were very interested in all you told us about Reg and Phyllis and family – we long to hear about the children. Will tells us bits about Geoffrey and we find it so hard to realise he's so grown up.

I forget if I told you a few weeks ago that our Chinese doctor in Tsingchoufu has felt for some time that he could not carry on much longer without foreign help. We're willing to go if others think it best, but now does not seem a good time to make a move. However, Ronald felt it should be considered and so went down to Tsingchou, on Rosemary's birthday.

Tom doesn't seem in favour of our going so I don't think we're likely to. I'm afraid Ronald will just have to go down more frequently, and I do so hate it. However, it may help the Chinese doctor and he's been a very loyal worker and we do want to do our best to help him. He's carried a heavy load of responsibility very patiently.

I think Rosemary has had a happy time. She had her presents at breakfast and was very pleased with them – a knitted suit and a golliwog (both home made) a book to colour, a bottle of perfume from Georgie (a great thrill for Rosemary!), some wicker doll's chairs from Alice and Jags, hankies from Su. To help make up for her disappointment at Ronald going away, she had two of her favourite Chinese nurses in for a Chinese lunch. They were very sweet and played with her and Audrey so nicely.

I'm sorry to tell you that Kao is in Hospital. He had seemed poorly for several days, and yesterday Ronald decided it was typhoid and sent him to Hospital. There's a terrific lot about the town and five cases in Hospital already. Fortunately, it is a mild form and so we hope Kao will very soon be quite recovered. In his six years with us, he hasn't before been off sick, unless perhaps for a day.

Food is getting more and more of a problem. It's so hard to buy even if you can afford the ridiculous prices. But although things are so difficult, another week has gone and we've not gone short of any essentials and we are very thankful for all our very many blessings.

We hear that Connie Allen eventually sailed for Manila without anyone she knew. Connie makes friends very easily, but even so, she must be having a very hard time. Elizabeth and Phillip have both been unwell.

PART FOUR

BOUND TOGETHER
December 1941 – August 1945

Except as otherwise indicated, the entries which follow were written by Gwyneth, who intended them for all the family at home in England. War conditions prevented this long continuous letter from ever being posted.

Gwyneth – to the families in Cambridge and Ilkley

Chouts'un,
7th December 1941

Well, yet another week over. We're thankful for each one that we're left in peace. There's really no news. No letters, even local ones seem to have stopped coming. An occasional paper several days old and a Reuters bulletin is all we ever see.

Today, was Ronald's Sunday 'on', which usually only means an odd outpatient or two, but today he's had a rather busy time and has still quite a bad cold, so I'd hoped he'd have a rest. He was in the Hospital as usual till 10.30 and then was called at 12.00, and was busy seeing to four wounded men till 1.45. He came home for lunch and went back at 2.15 to operate on them and didn't get home till 6 p.m. At 8.00 we went to the hospital service, and I hurried home at 9.00, expecting him to follow at once as he usually does – and now at 10.15, there's still no sign of him.

I think I'll go over if he doesn't come soon, and see what he's doing. I don't like to go to bed not knowing at all how long he'll be. If he's got another emergency operation, I'll just have to go to bed, but he usually sends or comes over to tell me if he has an operation. The children are all quiet.

Well, I've just been over and got a glimpse of Ronald in the men's ward. He seemed to be doing something to one of the fellows who came in today. He was too ill to be operated on, but Ronald hoped he might be able to do him on Tuesday. I do hope he'll get in soon, because it's 10.40 and I know he has yet to prepare for the service at 8.30 a.m. to-morrow!

19th December 1941

So much has happened since I left off in the middle of that letter that I think I must start a new sheet, but must write small now. Who knows how long our stock of paper will last?

Ronald eventually came in at about 11 p.m. that Sunday and after preparing for Hospital prayers, was up to bed by midnight. We slept soundly and were up as usual next day. Ronald went over to Prayers at 8.30 and I sat with the children while they finished breakfast, and then was just getting a big wash ready, when Ronald hurried in and told me to get Wang ta Sao to look after the family, as I was wanted over at the Lewises at once.

I was rather annoyed, as I wanted to get my washing done and out early, but I followed him over, and on the way he told me that the head of the Military Police wanted to talk to all the foreigners. We guessed by that that war might have broken out. On the wireless the night before, the only item that had seemed important in the Far East was the fact that Japanese boats had been seen going up towards the Bay of [159].

We all arrived in Georgie's and when all were settled - the Head of the Police and the Consul and an interpreter were all there too – they told us that owing to the relations between our two countries being very strained, they were obliged to limit our activities. The gist of his remarks was that we were to stay in the compound, and that we were to make inventories of all our personal belongings and of Mission furniture and equipment. He was very polite and almost apologetic for the inconvenience he was causing, and so far all the officials who have dealt with us have been like that.

I came home and did my washing, and while hanging things on the upstairs verandah I noticed that the place had police and soldiers posted at intervals all round. They were, however, all withdrawn when the Head of the Police left the Compound. As soon as the amah had finished her washing and her breakfast and was able to look after the children, I set about making lists of everything we possessed.

I didn't see Ronald again until we were half through our lunch when he appeared with the Japanese Corporal in charge of affairs on our compound, the interpreter, and three or four soldiers. They looked all over the house, but were very polite and made no bother. They talked to the children, but unfortunately we none of us understand Japanese. They none of them know any English, or at least only a few words I think.

---

[159] Word obscured here.

A big Alsatian accompanied the soldiers, that time and again the next day, but he was well-trained. On this first visit they apologised and then said they must take away our wireless. Of course we were sorry to see it go, but we knew it would be taken in such circumstances and were glad we'd had so much use out of it these three and a quarter years. After they had all trooped off to inspect the other house, Rosemary and Audrey both started to weep because the wireless had gone, but Rosemary tried to look on the bright side and said she was really rather glad because it used to keep her awake at night!

That evening we asked John and Georgie in after supper, and we'd just settled down to a game, when the Japanese Corporal, and the Korean interpreter came and stayed till after 10.00. They were quite friendly and asked all sorts of questions about England, where our homes were and so on, but not in any official way, just because they were interested to find out about our country. They smoked umpteen cigarettes and drank Chinese tea. They asked how Ronald and I met, and also told me that at my age a Japanese woman would have at least six children, the eldest being sixteen or seventeen!

I forgot to tell you that we'd sent along ½lb of foreign tea, a tin of chocolate biscuits and a tin of pineapple, for the soldiers – all such precious stores, for we're not likely to be able to buy any more 'foreign' goods till after the war.

The next morning they sent along before 7 a.m. for Ronald, some queries they wanted answered. He has been spokesman for us in everything, all the worry and responsibility has rested on him. That day at lunch he brought the crowd of soldiers round again. This time they listed all mission furniture etc. That evening Ronald was working in hospital till midnight making his inventories, and I was as late at home finishing off our three lists: (a) mission furniture in our house, (b) our own property too heavy or not suitable for moving (c) personal goods which we should take away if we moved. These all had to be typed in triplicate and took quite a time. Already they've asked several times how many bicycles, typewriters and sewing machines we foreigners possess.

Since then, I personally have seen very little of the soldiers. The corporal and five or six Japanese soldiers are living in the hospital classroom and just walk about keeping an eye on things. The hospital gate has Chinese police on sentry duty all day, and at night, after dark, Chinese soldiers under the Japanese are on duty and patrol the compound.

The first day outpatients were not allowed, but inpatients have stayed on. Now, however, we've been told we can admit outpatients, but it will take time for people to start coming and they're a bit scared of the sentries. The first ten days the Nursing School classes and Ming Tao Bible School classes were allowed to carry on, but they have been ordered to stop now. Hospital prayers and services have been as usual since the third day. That Monday, when Ronald was leading prayers, he was called out in the middle to see the Head of the Military Police and the Consul, so he asked our evangelist to carry on. When he told the Japanese that he was in the middle of prayers they said he was to finish them first, and then they'd do their business! So back he went and managed to finish the service. How he did it I don't know!

We've been told we may go out three miles but not be away for more than twenty four hours at a time. Ronald has been out several times to go to the Japanese headquarters, but each time with a guard to 'protect' him lest he should be kidnapped by the 8th route army[160]. The people in the city asked him and John if they'd like to listen in to 'our' wireless, so they went on Monday evening, but I don't think they'll venture again. They had Japanese and Chinese guards, all of whom carefully loaded rifles and revolvers before starting out, and at the city gate there were great goings-on before they were allowed in. It was good to hear San Francisco and Hong Kong and to put clocks right by Big Ben. We've now altered our clocks to coincide with Japanese time, but, to enable the hospital staff to get up in what daylight there is, we have pushed everything an hour later, breakfast 9.00, lunch 1.30, tea 5.00, supper 8.00 and so on. I find it a bit muddling but it's a minor inconvenience.

Our cooks have been allowed to go on the street. They're searched of course, but otherwise they carry on as usual. Now that we presume banks are shut, money is a problem. Ronald was afraid to keep too much in hand lest it should be confiscated, but now it hasn't been, we wish he'd had more. We've reckoned each child as a half - there are our three and Robin Lewis - and have worked out an equal share for every foreigner, and we're all trying to make it last as long as we can, as we've no idea when we'll get more.

No news except the Japanese paper, printed in Chinese of course, comes to us. No bulletins or letters. We get bits of news through the Chinese and hear that Tom Allen has been taken to Changtien[161], don't know why at all. We keep wondering about Connie and the three children. They would be either on the high seas or just landed at Manila

[160] The 8th Route Army, together with the 4th Army, were the two main Communist forces engaged in the war against Japan. In North China, having infiltrated behind Japanese lines, they co-ordinated much of the guerrilla activity against the occupying forces.
[161] Headquarters of the Japanese military police.

when war broke out. As Manila is being bombed, it would be foul and she'd be very short of cash. She had no one to escort her at all.

It's strange to think that when we next get news the war may be over! We long to know how you all are.

December 25th 1941

I'm afraid you'll have been anxious about us this Christmas, but we've had a very quiet happy day at home. I'm so very thankful the children haven't been disappointed. I was very much afraid they might spend today in very different circumstances, but we have been allowed to have our Christmas in our own home. We've thought a tremendous amount about all of you and wished more than ever that we could communicate with you.

All the week I've been getting ready the few things we planned for today – nothing much of course, but we've tried to give little gifts to everyone here. Yesterday, Audrey was so sleepy that I left Wang ta Sao to bath her at 4.30 and put her to bed, while Rosemary and I pushed the pram round and delivered our small presents! She was very thrilled to take things herself, and I took her in to see the decorated wards which was quite an excitement for her. She hung up her sock and Audrey's before going to bed and went off to sleep very happily. Her prayers were 'God, please let Father Christmas find a way to fill our stockings and please let the war be over soon so we can go to England and do tell our Grannies and Grandpas that we love them. And if you can let it snow for Christmas we shall think it's nice. Amen.'

We managed to find a few oddments to fill the socks, apple, pencil, book, home-made toy etc. Alice and Jags also very kindly sent Rosemary and Audrey a sock each full of lovely little gifts. Each contained, orange, scarf, toy-book, bib, doll's cap, sweets and one or two other things. I also decorated the little toy Christmas tree which Annie Flowers left behind, and then eventually retired to bed. Oh, I forgot to tell you that we went to the women's ward, Ronald showed four films and I 'helped' in carol-singing. He is in the men's ward to-night.

This morning Rosemary and Audrey were in our room and on our bed before it was light, opening their socks. They were so surprised and pleased to find two each and were so very excited at each new parcel. I'm afraid we rather left Catherine in the cold! – didn't even let her come and do her share of the opening of parcels after brekker! We were amazed to see what a pile we had, a record for an interned family I should think! Even one Christmas card! I wonder if we'll ever get back to the good old days when we'd piles of mail from home and even parcels and magazines?

Miss Chao made the children three very cute aprons, exactly alike except for the size – hope you'll see them one day. Rosemary had a 'work' box from Georgie, little pieces of material, cottons, needles and scissors. She's loved it and has been so busy sewing. Su made her and Audrey wee beds with bedding complete and two wee Dutch dolls. These have been a source of great pleasure all day. Miss Thomas gave them each a wee purse with a note inside and Rosemary was very disappointed when I told her it wouldn't be any use to spend in England. She and Audrey both talk of saving things to use when in England!

We had everyone in for tea at 3.30 – we saved Audrey's birthday cake and had that on the table. After tea, when Robin and Catherine had joined us, we put the lights out and lit the candles on the tree and Ronald put the gramophone on, and then later, just before folk went home, we had Christmas carols.

This morning before we were up the Japanese sent along for various details of our wireless. As they themselves are using it, I don't know why they suddenly want to know what make it is, what wave lengths and so on, but no doubt they've some good reason.

Today there's a little snow on the ground, so God is only one day late in His reply to Rosemary's prayer.

28th December 1941

We heard yesterday of the fall of Hong Kong. A blow of course, but we'd been prepared for it.

The Head of the Military came along with his interpreter again yesterday – said he'd like to have a look at our house. He went into all the rooms and we wondered if he was mentally arranging his own things in them! He was very pleasant and seemed quite interested in the children, and took photos of all three. I hope we get copies some day. We drank tea and had biscuits and apples (these apples had been given to Catherine for a Christmas gift, so it was a bit hard on her!). The soldiers on the compound still behave well and seem to be disciplined strictly – they're no bother. The big main gates are allowed open today and we hope that patients will soon brave the sentry. One patient was admitted today, but there are only five in the women's ward.

I wonder when we'll taste butter again, or cheese, raisins, currants, oh, and lots of other things. We're out of tomatoes now and daren't buy oranges – they're so expensive – so Catherine is missing some vitamins, but I hope she'll be all right. We've absolutely no idea how soon we'll get further cash, and so feel we must be careful.

It's bitterly cold, terrific frosts at night and freezing cold days, in spite of the sun. I'm so thankful I had the padded gowns and trousers made for the children this winter. They're so cosy in them and we couldn't afford to have them done now. I want padded trousers for myself, for getting up on cold nights, but can't buy the material and cotton-wool now. Not a cent can be spared for clothes at the moment!

I do hope we don't get moved in this cold weather. Even if we stay on here, I don't know how we'll get coal once our present supply is done, but we're not worrying about the future. We can only go a day at a time.

2nd January 1942

Ronald has had to send a lot of the staff home for 'holidays' to wait till they're recalled. It's impossible to pay wages when there's no money coming in. We hear Cheeloo Hospital had to send its staff away with chits promising wages if and when more money was available. So far, we've paid up all wages. Wu and Kao have been very good and not made a murmur at the cut we've had to make in their wage. In fact they offered to take less, before we approached them, and Wu is being very 'cooperative' in economising, though he finds it particularly hard to cut down Ronald's rations! It goes very much against his wishes. We can't be thankful enough for their loyal service to us. In all these difficult circumstances they've turned up trumps every time.

We keep thinking of you and wondering if you've any news at all of us. The BMS will know we're all here I expect, but may not know that we are actually in our own place. When shall we get further news of you?

7th January 1942

I'd a terrific shock yesterday. After four weeks of this isolation I suddenly received a parcel! The missing blue dress for Rosemary from Polly! How thrilling it was to open a parcel, though there was little opening to be done - it had obviously been examined on more than a few occasions. But, marvellous to relate, although the paper was worn almost to shreds and a big hole had been made by someone collecting stamps, the contents were all there, even to the little roll of silk thread and the six buttons. It's a lovely blue wool material and will be just right for

Rosemary for the Spring. It fits well, so before making up I've cut a paper pattern from it – I've no patterns big enough now for Rosemary.

Now of course I'm wondering if I dare hope for the other things Polly promised. They're so extra precious now when we haven't money and anyway can't buy wool materials. How I wish I'd a few of the old clothes I've passed on from time to time. Though I can't wear them, they'd cut up for small skirts.

We've had to cut down on coal again, we've no idea when we'll be able to get more. The weather is really very cold now, and today a biting north wind doesn't help, but it's warm in the sun if you can find a sheltered spot. We've still not reached the coldest time, so we may need to burn more later.

Today the big gates have been shut, an 'accident' having taken place on the road just outside. That's the second time it's happened in the last two or three weeks, on our doorstep so to speak. Also today the trains are all delayed from the East – a break on the line.

We keep thinking of Connie Allen in Manila, which according to reports 'fell' on January 2nd or 3rd. Philip isn't strong and the climate there would be bad for his asthma.

15th January 1942

On Sunday night there was yet another alarm and the guards here prepared a way of escape for themselves in case of need!

On Monday Ronald was asked to send along to the station to vaccinate all people getting on trains here. There are five passenger trains each way daily, but three of these are after dark, so it's a case of sending for seven trains. Luckily we're near the station so it's not much bother. Dr Chou has been and two of the orderlies. Ronald and John were prepared to go but it seems unnecessary. It's still bitterly cold and the station is very open and exposed. We've also been requested to prepare a part of the Ming Tao School for use as an isolation ward. They intend to send all infectious cases to us, it seems. Well, we're used to them, and it looks as if we're not to be turned out at once, which is good.

Flour and oil are unobtainable here now, but Ronald went to call on the Tui Chang[162] yesterday and he was quite pleasant and promised to see if he could make arrangements for us to get some. We can't afford to buy much, but flour is a good standby and we must have it if possible.

---

[162] Pinyin = dui zhang, ie local head of the military

It is likely that Dr Gell will be down to officiate at Georgie's event[163] next month, and if she comes she's staying with us. It'll be fun to have her, only I wonder how I can manage. No doubt she'll expect reduced rations and she's a most understanding person, no one could be easier. Georgie's mother is coming too, I think, if they get the necessary permits.

We're still trying to get goats, but they're hard to find and of course the price is a snag. I still have enough tinned milk for the children for about three months, but I don't want to use it all. I'd be glad to have goats' milk for Catherine, it's better for her I'm sure.

We have news of an allowance through the Japanese Consul in Tsinan, but at present it's only news and nothing concrete. If only we're allowed to stay on here I'm sure we can manage, even on a small allowance. The sum mentioned tentatively would enable us to manage at present cost of living, but this is rising all the time so there wouldn't be any margin. But we are lucky to have been so well treated so far – we couldn't have had less trouble. Ronald is the only one who has direct dealings with the authorities.

We've been asked to carry lights if we go out at night, so the guards will know we're not guerrillas! This is of course in the compound, we don't go further afield, except when Ronald is summoned by the Tui Chang.

Rosemary now goes to Su for weekly 'painting' lessons! She is terribly thrilled with it. The other day Dr Chou's little nephew came over to play with them. He's nearly four, and as tall as Rosemary but not very robust. They had quite a good time together. I want them to play with him sometimes, or they'll be so unused to other children. Rosemary does wonder what it'll be like on the boat, will the other children come and meet her when she goes up the ladder? Poor lamb, she really does long to play with other children.

22° frost the other night. Our bedroom is like an ice-house. The wind just blows in the north window and, with three outside walls and the fourth against places without a fire, it gets no chance to warm. We hope another month will see us to the end of the coldest weather. East winds on the Common at home are warm compared with the north winds here. We've still had no heavy fall of snow and scarcely any rain for months. Everything is terribly dry and if we don't get snow soon the crops will spoil.

---

[163] Arrival of Georgie's baby

Well, to-night the guards have all been taken off! Ronald has signed an undertaking not to carry on in an unseemly manner, and so he's left in charge. Of course, we're still under supervision from the city. We hear that in other places foreigners have not been as well treated as we have. We have certainly been most fortunate so far.

20th January 1942

Six years today since we moved into this house! Six very eventful, very interesting and very happy years, as far as we personally are concerned, but some of the worst as far as the world in general is concerned.

We all expected Dr Gell and Mrs Menzies[164] today and Ronald and John were at the station to meet them. Georgie and I and the children were at the Gate, but they didn't turn up. There are lots of guesses as to the reason and we hope for news soon. Maybe they'll come to-morrow. We'd lit a fire in the bedroom and kept it going all day in case our guest arrived. It seems a waste, but it's a treat to go in after our cold one!

23rd January 1942

'David' Gell and Mrs Menzies came on Wednesday 21st. Their passes were a day late in arriving, but they had a very easy journey and no bother. We were very glad to see them and to get news of the outside world. They not only told us all the Tsinan news, but also lots of other news we'd not heard about Manila, which makes us more than ever anxious about Connie. All our friends in Tsinan are well. In some ways they've not had such a good time as we have, but they're likely to be better off for money and they've stocks of coal, and are able to buy flour and things cheaper and more easily than we can here. We heard through them of a terrible train smash on the other line.

I had the two missing socks from Polly on Wednesday! The others came nearly three months ago and I'd given up hope of completing the two pairs. I'm very thrilled to have them.

1st February 1942

On Monday 26th Georgie sprang a surprise on us and Margaret Anne was born at about 2.30pm! Great rejoicings of course. Both

[164] Georgie Lewis' mother

Georgie and Anne seem to be making excellent progress. We're all glad it's safely over.

Dr Gell talks of returning to Tsinan on Friday this next week. She is anxious to get back, as she has responsibilities there, though the Hospital closed on January 15th. We hear that PUMC is closed too. We now have thirty inpatients and about thirty outpatients daily, which is not much below the average for this time of year.

On Wednesday evening we had five Chinese in for supper. It was all decided at the last minute, so we had Chinese food and it was very good. We have it for lunch three times a week now.

We've still no news of further cash supplies and although what we had was equally divided on the 8th December, some people are nearly out. We still have enough for another month, with care. We are having to think of more ways of cutting down. I wish I could persuade Audrey to eat porridge, I expect she'll go back to it one day. We're going to drink hot water instead of tea, except at special occasions, as soon as Dr Gell goes, and we're already using half millet for our bread. It's good, but not so pleasant. However, as it's full of vitamins and cheaper than white flour we don't object to it! There is only one main topic for conversation now, and it's how we can make our allowance last a little longer.

What to do when the stock of drugs is exhausted is yet another problem.

Oh, we've sold the Hospital pigs and got three goats. They won't be supplying us with milk for another five or six weeks, but it's something to know they're here. I'm so thankful I got the case of milk from Tsingtao just before war broke out. It will last another six weeks, I think.

10th February 1942

We had a Japanese gentleman and the interpreter and the Tui Chang looking over our house, and they took all our cameras. I'm so sorry I'll not be able to take any more snaps of the children, Catherine especially. The film was already exposed except for one. All snaps of the infants. What a waste.

We're down to about $70 now (£2.10.0), except for what is put by for wages, and that won't last very long for a family of five. We're going to have hospital kitchen supper for a while. Because they cater for so many they can supply it more cheaply than we can do it ourselves.

We shall eat just 'mo-mo'[165] and I suppose a couple of vegetable dishes. It will be simple, but quite all right and will help us out for a time. All foreign houses are doing alike. It will mean that some servants may be dismissed but we hope to keep ours as long as we can. There's plenty to do and it's hard on them to be turned off in these days. No one can take on new servants so they'd be hard hit.

We hear that we can send letters and cables home via the Red Cross in Geneva. Unfortunately, it's only at a high cost and at present we don't feel we can afford it, especially as we know that a second cable has gone to the BMS saying we're all well and in our own homes. I do hope Dr Williamson sends you this news as well as Ilkley.

20th February 1942

We're still enjoying our Chinese food and especially the New Year extras we had on Sunday. As it was Chinese New Year, Rosemary and Audrey dressed in their best red silk p'ao tze[166] and put flowers in their hair, and we went to greet various Chinese friends on the compound. The children were both frightfully thrilled and at lunch got through a big pile of jiao tze[167] (sort of pork dumplings – very tasty – the dish that every Chinese in the North has for New Year).

We've heard from the Tsingtao Bank, or rather from its liquidators, and we're all being allowed to draw out something. Our share is only $264 but Miss Thomas and Su both have more and have generously suggested that all is pooled and shared proportionately, so that's what we're doing. Our share comes to $700. It'll last us a couple of months with care. What a blessing Ronald and I have both been brought up in homes where economy has been taught! We've no extravagant tastes – at least we have, but we know how to do without satisfying them!

We've just heard of the fall of Singapore, the street is lined with flags etc. Ronald has been trying to get a pass to go to Tsinan and talk things over with people there and try to find out about finances too, but no luck so far.

Rosemary and Audrey were discussing God and Jesus over a meal today and Rosemary explained to Audrey that probably God and Jesus took turns at doing night duty, the same as the nurses do, as she

165 a form of steamed bread, popular in North China
166 Pinyin = paozi, i.e long padded jackets
167 Pinyin = jiaozi

said one of them always takes care of us at night! She then told Audrey that she thought God made Jesus die, so that He could go to heaven and help to make babies, as there were so many to be made every day!

I wonder if you'll eventually be able to get news to us via Geneva. I'm just longing to hear all about you all. Your last letters were written in September.

6th March 1942

On Monday afternoon Ronald and I walked over to the West side. We had to go outside the walls and it's a long walk there and back, especially as I've not walked since Tsingtao, but it was grand. I did enjoy it. The afternoon was a lovely bright one and the air was so fresh, and the country looked so peaceful. There are very few people living in the compound at the West now. We collected up some things Pan wanted, and looked over some new property acquired since I was over there and then came back, the Gate boy 'sending' us half a mile or so. The Chinese are great at that, always 'sung'[168] friends. No end of new pill boxes erected since I was out – I've not been over there since May 15.

Well, we've suddenly received loans from the Japanese government! Single ladies $200 each, and families $500. We with five mouths only get $100 more than the two single ladies together, but we'll manage all right and it's a great help to have a little in hand. With care, and with no unexpected big expenses, we'll manage several months I think. We've had several small trees and bushes dug up from the centre patch in our garden and are hoping to be able to grow more cabbages, carrots or tomatoes in the space. It's a blessing tomatoes grow so easily here. We shan't do much though if there's no rain, and so far there's no sign of it. The earth is absolutely dry.

On Tuesday morning the town gates were suddenly shut and weren't properly opened till Friday, and Miss Thomas's cook had gone shopping and wasn't able to get out again. If he'd had his identity card he might have wangled it as they did allow a few people through, but he'd forgotten it, so there he had to stay for three days. Wu shih Fu, fortunately, set out about an hour later and couldn't get into the town. If he'd been earlier, he'd have been caught too. What a life!

One great excitement on Thursday night was the arrival of twins – goats! They're really very sweet – we go to see them about twice a

[168] Pinyin = song, i.e send, see off, accompany

day! We hope soon to have fresh milk, at any rate for Catherine. Robin and she should have first place I think. Internment suits Catherine – she's gained 2½lbs in these last two months. I'm so glad she's putting on now. She went so thin when she was ill in the autumn and had quite a bit to make up.

13th March 1942

We had one pint of goat's milk yesterday, a great event! Catherine drank it all as if she'd had it every day of her life. Whatever we give her, she opens her little mouth wide and seems to enjoy it! She now climbs onto the small chairs and stands up and crows with delight, while Wang ta Sao and I look on in fear and trembling!

Now that we've a little more cash, we've raised our servants' wages again. I don't see how they could manage on what they've had these two months. We hear that Mr Black can draw out our savings in Shanghai, but one third or more is 'blocked'. We shall have to say cheerio to it I'm afraid!

Wang ta Sao plans to go home on Monday. She deserves her holiday and if we have no excitements I can manage all right.

24th March 1942

Well, Wang ta Sao went on Monday as planned and we had plenty of excitements of one sort and another after all! She went off after breakfast Monday morning and on Monday all was very quiet and peaceful.

Monday evening Ronald was going over an operation he was to do on Tuesday. It was one he'd not done often, and which had a good chance of success. The woman had been waiting and receiving treatment in preparation for several days. He was quite glad to be doing it and he explained it all carefully to me that night.

Next day before morning prayers were over, a lorry of empty packing cases, and about 30 officers and soldiers arrived. The patient was lying ready on the operating table and the nurses were all prepared, instruments sterilised and so on. Ronald was scrubbing up in the next room when the soldiers marched in, swept the instruments off the side-table and removed all the equipment. Instruments, cupboards, operating table, wash-basins, cloths, everything was taken. Then in the afternoon, they returned and took the drugs. Ronald and John were busy trying to check up, but it was quite impossible with soldiers all over the place.

Having cleared us out, they said that we were to clear the patients out and take no more, so that was that. In the afternoon a crowd of officers were in our house waiting about, drinking tea, smoking and playing the piano! As on previous occasions there was no rudeness or unpleasantness, they were all polite, but of course orders are orders.

From then till now seems to be a long string of visitors. On each day there have been lots of girl nurses coming in to see us. We've managed to have all the girls in for a meal. They were not busy and seemed glad to come in, play with the children and so on. It's got worse and worse. They were more and more depressed, until today they all went off in tears. Almost as loud as at a Chinese funeral!

Ronald has been just as busy as he could be, getting patients out, clearing up, checking drugs, settling wages and so on for coolies, deciding all manner of things, and also keeping in touch with the powers that be. He doesn't seem to have had a minute to himself all the week.

On Friday evening there was a sort of farewell feast for the nurses. Ronald and I both went. Su came to listen for the children (how I've missed Wang ta Sao!). We had lovely food and I enjoyed it all, as I always do! On Saturday Ronald was at the coolies' feed and then joined me at the last CE which went on till 10.00 or later. Then on Sunday, we all went to the evening service in hospital. I wonder how soon there'll be another there.

We were up at 6.00 on Monday to see some of the girls off and saw off various others during the day. On Tuesday we saw the last lot off at the gate and then a Tsinan pastor was here for morning tea and Dr Ching from Tsingchou suddenly turned up for lunch and stayed with us till Thursday. He's a very nice guest and the children like him very much. On Wednesday afternoon we invited eight guests, all Chinese and Japanese men, for supper at 5 p.m.

Wang ta Sao turned up safely on Friday as promised, and brought with her some Tsingchou 'chien ping'[169] and apples for the children.

5th April 1942

There's been talk of repatriation for some weeks and now we're told we may get a boat this month from Shanghai. It's very much in the air, but it seems certain that we've to move from here, so we've loads to do. We're to be shipped to Portuguese South Africa, Lorenzo

[169] a crisp kind of bread, made of millet or corn

Marques[170]! Nothing like seeing the world, but it seems that the boat has small accommodation and it's quite possible we'll be left behind. I don't fancy Shanghai, especially in summer.

We've been told that anything left behind must be regarded as a 'gift to the military', so I'm afraid we'll lose a lot of our nice things, but we've had a good deal of use out of most of them. On Friday the Military removed the X-ray machine and ultra-violet, so all the most valuable things from the hospital are now cleared right out.

Last week Dr and Mrs Chou moved into the town and their little nephew gave his rabbit to Rosemary. The children are thrilled with him, he's pure white and really very cute. I'm so glad for them to have him. Kao has made him a nice little underground house and a bricked in 'playground'.

The boys have worked frightfully hard in the garden this spring and it's lovely now, all the blossom so fresh and beautiful. How I hate the idea of leaving it all! We've been so very happy here. I loathe leaving the house and the garden, but the idea of leaving the servants is much worse. They've been such bricks all the time. I'm afraid they'll not have too good a time, but I think Wu and Kao will manage. It'll be worse for the woman. She has no one of her own and life in her village doesn't bear thinking about. Old Wang ta Sao is having to grind millet to earn a living and that's very hard work. Our servants have seemed so much a part of the family, especially since we've had the children. They love them and the boys have been so good to them.

26th April 1942

After I wrote the last, I got a girl in to help sew and she rushed through lots of jobs, finished off and helped with new. Though she hasn't done it all as I'd have liked, it's been a big help and I hope her mistakes won't be too glaringly obvious. We've made several frocks for Rosemary and Audrey, all out of old ones of mine, of course. No money to buy new material. If we'd been staying on here, I'd not have made anything new, but travelling they'll need more and I don't know if I'll have my machine with me later on, though I plan to take it if I'm allowed.

I've made white hats for Rosemary and Audrey too, (out of a pair of Ronald's summer trousers!) lined with red (an old overall cut up!). And then, thinking that it'll be hot if we travel, and that washing and

[170] Now Maputo, Mozambique

ironing will be a bother, I've made them each several sunsuits. Of course I'd no pattern, so I've made them up and they look quite passable I think, and will be comfy for hot days. Catherine looks sweet in hers – it shows off her fat and her dimples so nicely! These suits are all made of old dresses, aprons or curtains. Oh, and shirts!

On about April 12, we heard that the boats were delayed a month, so we slacked off somewhat. We also heard that we'd be allowed to take less than a quarter of the luggage originally suggested, so I've been gradually repacking trunks 1, 2, 3 etc. in order of importance, so that we shall know just which are the most important if we're limited to one each. It's fairly certain that everything we don't take will be a dead loss so we want to take all we possibly can. Our guest room is full of trunks and boxes. Ronald's books and papers nearly fill a trunk, even if he only takes the most vital ones.

We have had lots of Chinese visitors and, though we've been glad to see them all, it's taken a lot of time. Ronald has had lots to do in connection with the hospital. After the instruments were taken, some Japanese pastors hoped to get permission for the Chinese to take over the hospital. Well, there were several meetings here and in Tsinan, and it really seemed fairly hopeful. However, in spite of tremendous efforts, it was decided that the local government is to take it over. Last Saturday they all came along and had a good look round again and they told Ronald that they would take over officially on the 24th. We'd no idea what that meant but it turned out to be quite peaceful. They came along in the morning and demanded the unlocking of all doors and then the keys were handed over and Ronald now has no further responsibility for the hospital.

It's awfully queer to be here, and know that it's not 'our' hospital. At present it's not in use, but our own gateman has left and there are a couple of police in the gatehouse and the gate is kept locked and we have to be 'let out'. The police walk around with their guns as if they expect trouble at any minute! Quite fearsome.

The Ku Wen[171] Adviser to the local government tells us that he and other officials plan to live in our houses and that they want everything we don't take. You can imagine our feelings. We're hoping they won't turn us out until such time as we can go to Shanghai for the boat, but it still seems very doubtful if this repatriation scheme will really come to anything. Then we've no idea as to what may happen, except

[171] Pinyin = gu wen i.e adviser or consultant, most probably, in this context, Japanese. Most foreign properties were taken over by Japanese at this time.

that we don't expect to be left here. I've had nearly everything washed and packed, but the weather, which was hot, turned cold and I had to fish out winter clothes again. Our three servants have worked so hard helping us in every way possible.

One night at 9 p.m. soldiers came to the gate and said Ronald was to go back to the city with them. No one ever goes out after dark now and the city gates were shut at 6.00, so I wasn't too happy, fearing he'd not be let out again, and we both wondered what on earth they could want him for at that late hour. They said their senior only wanted to speak one sentence and then Ronald could return. When Tom was taken away, he was given the same message, so we couldn't help wondering what it was all about! However, he went off and I walked up and down the compound, unable to settle to anything. Eventually an hour later he returned and said he'd been sent for by a government doctor who wanted to know the treatment for gonorrhoea. Why on earth he had to choose that particular time we couldn't imagine, but it was certainly a relief to have Ronald safely home.

Yesterday, we went to a Chinese meal in the city, with a Mr and Mrs Cheng. His mother was Bible woman here for years and they're very nice people. His brother was with the Chinese Ambassador in London at one time, and is now at Canberra. We both wish very much that we were free to have more contacts with people in the city. Perhaps some day it will be possible.

9th May 1942

We hear that a boat is to leave on June 15, but as it's taking consular and such folk there isn't likely to be room for poor 'up-country' missionaries. We've filled in seven forms each about repatriation, so in time I think the authorities should begin to know who and what we are.

Did I tell you that Wu and Kao and Wang ta Sao invited all the foreigners to Chinese food as a farewell gift some weeks ago? It was when they thought we'd be likely to go any day. It was very nice of them, and they had the food brought in from the city – quite expensive.

On Wednesday the Hsin Min Hui, the New People's Movement, moved into the old Chinese nurses' home, which is just behind our house. All its windows overlook our back windows. At present, they use it just as offices and go out at night, but later on they will want people living on the premises. They're fairly noisy and spend a lot of time walking about our gardens, and picking our flowers. They're mostly Chinese with Japanese supervisors I think.

We are now allowed to draw on mission balances to help to pay our personal expenses and the Tsinan folk have worked out what they consider a fair monthly sum for everyone. We get $170 a head and $60 for each child – children over eight get more. We can just about manage on that, in spite of rise in living expenses, but this money will be exhausted in three or four months' time, so we don't know what will happen then, if we're still here.

We still get no outside news except what is printed in the local Japanese-owned Chinese papers. Ronald and John go through that and pick out occasional pieces of news that seem of interest. We gather the general trend of events from it, but as for detail we're absolutely cut off. We get letters from Mr Payne, all business ones, chiefly about property, cash and repatriation. Apart from that we have no letters. Can you imagine life without papers, magazines, wireless, letters or visitors? and almost confined to our own gardens? Ronald goes into the city two or three times a week on business of one sort or another, but I very seldom have occasion to go and we cannot get into the fields now.

Our gardens are looking lovely. We've the best roses we've ever had, plenty of them and finer ones than in other years. Our radishes, tomatoes, potatoes etc. are all coming on. I wonder who'll eat them? Maybe we shall after all! For the last five years we've seemed on the edge of a precipice all the time, and haven't yet toppled over, so maybe we'll stay on here longer than we think after all.

11th May 1942

A letter from Tsinan today says that probably the first British 'evacuee' ship will take twenty of the seventy two British in Tsinan district, and our Mission will probably have twelve of those berths. Our station committee met to discuss this and our names were put at the head of the list, but of course the final choice rests with the Japanese and Swiss Consular bodies in Shanghai. We're not panting to get on the first boat. In many ways we'd prefer not to go, but it seems wise to go if we're given the chance. We have offered to get all five of us into three berths, so it will be fun and games in the hot weather if we go like that! It's supposed now to be an Italian boat. There's nothing like trying out all nationalities is there?! – but it seems very much in the air still.

Last night there were visitors[172] in the building behind us, but we didn't know anything about it at the time.

[172] ie looters

18th May 1942

We heard last Tuesday that the Tsinan British Residents' Association had chosen us to go among the first twenty, but we still have no definite news as to date of sailing. British and Americans from all other small stations around have already been called into Tsinan, so we can't think it will be long before we're given the word to go, especially as we were told on Friday to start selling our goods.

Friday, Saturday, Sunday, Monday and today, there has been a constant stream of Japanese and Chinese coming to look at our things. We were quite powerless to prevent Sunday business – all the big officials came then and it was the busiest day of all. We put almost all our saleable goods into the sitting room, as the piano and the three piece suite were there, and we've tried hard to keep people more or less to that room, but they've been all over the place, picking up this and that and wanting to buy all sorts of things we'd never want to sell. Gramophones, sewing machines, carpets, blankets and easy chairs seem about the most popular items. We could have sold all our blankets a dozen times, but we hope still to be able to take them. It'll be a blight if, when we reach the boat, they restrict luggage to such an extent that we have to leave them behind.

We've now sold everything we intended to (and quite a bit more), except kitchen utensils, enamel jugs, pails, and these are still in constant use. The piano has gone. It was hard to see that moved off, especially as it won't be really appreciated. Eight policemen came to fetch it, and I regretted the fact that they hadn't had a spittoon provided. Really they are filthy! Although it's been so hectic and in some ways very sad, yet there have been many amusing things. John told one man who offered him $8 for what he'd asked $20 that he'd rather burn it than sell it for $8!

Of course, none of the things have fetched anything like the price we'll need to replace them, but that can't be helped. We're lucky to have sold things at all under present conditions and if we're allowed to take the money away we'll be very fortunate. We've no idea when we'll have a settled home of our own again. It's so sad to see this one all being 'broken up'.

There have been big meetings on the compound these last few days and the people have taken the opportunity of looking round thoroughly and, if they can get in, they walk in and 'do' the place, as many rooms as they can. If they can't get in, they stand outside and peer through the windows and watch the funny foreigners, eating or passing the time in other ways!

29th May 1942

Endless rumours as to when we're to go, and where. May 25, 26, 31, June 1, have all been mentioned by local officials as the date for our departure, but we're still here so far. We hear that whoever goes on the first boat from Shanghai will leave Tsinan by train on the 10th or 12th and travel 3rd class. It's very poor, wooden seats, no fans and very crowded, but if we foreigners are all in one compartment it shouldn't be so bad, though the nights will be a bit hard on benches! The Shanghai date is still June 16 and destination Lorenzo Marques, as far as we know, but we get no direct news and so are very much in the dark. We're still hazy as to cash but no doubt it will all work out all right in the end.

We've got a twenty five word message form to send you, but are waiting to hear if we're chosen for the first boat – the messages are to go via the International Red Cross.

On Monday, Ronald and I went over to the west side and chose out a few of Mr Harris' best things and are hoping to take them home for him. We're going over again tomorrow to have lunch with some Chinese friends there.

It's difficult to settle to much and to know whether to finish off our remaining stocks of food or to eke them out still and perhaps have to leave some behind. We've finished all the more urgent sewing now. I'm afraid you'll all shun me when I appear in the same coat I wore to leave in, in 1935! I'll just have to retire from the world till I can get something smarter! I've not a hat that I can wear at all, so it's not going to be easy.

7th June 1942

On the 30th we heard a rumour that the boat was again postponed and on Sunday we had official news that the date for sailing is now July 16! Having 'settled down' (if one can do any such thing in present circumstances!) to being here another month or so, we've just received orders to clear out of our house before the 20th! Ronald and John were called to the government offices and told that we were using houses that were needed by the officials. They first suggested that we all go to Tsinan, but Ronald and John resisted that and eventually were promised the Lewis' (Flowers') house and Miss Thomas and Su's – the nurses to turn out of their bungalow and us out of our house before the 20th. We'll have to go in with Su and Miss Thomas, the nurses with John and Georgie.

Tonight we received an enquiry through the Swiss Red Cross Consul on behalf of the Red Cross. We guess you sent it asking our whereabouts (later think it was HRW[173]). It was a thrill to get this request. It seemed as if we were really in touch with home again, though there was no indication as to who had sent the inquiry.

We seem to have been treated with more consideration than folk elsewhere and the request that we move out was all done in a polite way and we've been given two weeks' notice, which is very decent. Considering our position we couldn't have been treated more considerately I imagine, though of course this is the first time I've experienced such a situation! And let's hope the last.

10th June 1942

We hear unofficially that the British boat is now postponed till August. I doubt very much if it ever gets away at all and goodness knows where we'll spend the next year or so. It seems fairly certain that before long the remaining British are to be concentrated somewhere in a big place, Shanghai, or Tientsin.

The night before last there was an 'accident' about a mile from here and a passenger train was derailed. We could see all the mess from our verandah and the clearing up process. They were at it all day. Some of the victims were treated at hospital. The accident occurred about 1.45 a.m. and the first trains ran past at 7 p.m. that evening, so they got it mended fairly rapidly. Funnily enough, a few days ago, I'd dreamed that a passenger train was derailed at night at the end of our garden. I wasn't so very far out.

Later**:** Today there have been about five hundred Japanese and Chinese soldiers in the hospital garden, with horses. They marched in at about 11 a.m. and made themselves at home, using our pails, basins, etc., washing themselves and their clothes in our garden! They tried to use our soap, but only got away with a little. Considering we left several hundred packets of Sunlight in the hospital, we thought they might have used that!

They had great blisters on their feet and seemed scarcely to know how to drag themselves around. They all cleared off again at 7 p.m. We'd wondered if they were going to stay the night. The worst of it was that they used so much water, and all our wells are nearly dry, the little water in them is all muddy. We've not had rain for weeks and there's a

---

[173] H R Williamson, then working in BMS headquarters, London

terrific south wind, the temperature yesterday was 101° in the shade. Kao said that when he drew water for them, they were quite polite and thanked him, so it wasn't too bad.

We had our first batch of potatoes from the garden the other day. If they'd been things that appeared above the earth, I doubt if we'd have had any. Everything disappears so rapidly now. The magpies are great offenders, but not the only ones to blame! Our strawberries have all been removed by 'birds' and so have our peaches. May they have nasty pains!

Catherine has made rapid strides with her talking the last few weeks and now says almost anything, though she won't try her own English name. We say to her:

Catherine, say Wang ta Sao - Wang ta Sao
Catherine, say Wu Shih fu - Wu Fu
Catherine, say Kao ta Ko - Kao ta to
Catherine, say Rosemary - Rercemay
Catherine, say Audrey - Orday
Catherine, say Catherine - Lee Lee

She always insists on Lee Lee, which is what Wang ta Sao calls her.

15th June 1942

Well, the latest news now is that negotiations between Japan and Great Britain have fallen through and no repatriation scheme is possible[174]! So all our plans and hopes in that direction fall through! We'd never counted on it, but of course we were hoping it might be possible.

We're preparing to move into Su and Miss Thomas's house. Their house is slightly bigger than ours, but it won't be easy to move all our stuff into three rooms after having a whole house, and we want to move as much as ever we can, because we don't know how long we may be there. Earlier on when we had been told we were to leave almost at once, we gave away a lot of old clothes we couldn't have taken. Now we wish we'd kept some of the things!

We hope that we can clear out the things that we 'sold' earlier on. I forgot to tell you that nearly everything was returned! The things were all taken away as sold, except a few that we particularly asked to keep till we left. All the things sold to private individuals were paid for, but none of the officials have paid yet. About a fortnight after the 'sale' they

---

174 It was at this time that the Japanese fleet suffered its first major defeat at the hands of the Americans, in the Battle of Midway Island. It never won another major battle in the Pacific.

started sending stuff back and the government adviser came and told us that everything was to be fetched back, so that the Chang Tien military (who are senior to the folk here) could have their pick first! It's been an awful muddle, we've had to return cash, and some people haven't been willing to return their goods. Anyway, we hope to get rid of them this time, otherwise I don't see how we can squeeze into our new 'flat'.

23rd June 1942

We got all our coal, trunks and a lot of other stuff moved over on Wednesday but the military didn't come and take away our stuff for sale, so we didn't move our beds, but stayed on hoping for their arrival soon. The children had a busy day carrying things over. They did it in the Chinese style, a pole on their shoulders and the baskets slung over the pole. Fortunately, the day was the only cool, sunless one we've had lately. Since then it's been just as sticky as ever.

On Saturday, the boys got the kitchen stove over before breakfast and we had the meal in our new home. Ronald and the boys had a hard day, carrying things over. I stayed here most of the time trying to get straight. We got all the most important furniture over, and the children and I slept here but, as there was a room full of stuff for sale, Ronald slept there.

On Sunday afternoon, they came and took away all our personal belongings that we wanted to sell, a big clearance. This time it was all quite business-like, except that no money was handed over! After that all went, Ronald decided to sleep over here, so we had a busy time clearing out all the remaining things of value. It's not safe to leave an unoccupied house these days. We were wise to bring out the things as we did. This morning when we went over for a final clear-up we found that someone had been in during the night. There were foot-prints, window unlocked, key removed and various obvious signs. Fortunately, we'd left behind nothing we wanted.

The children are very happy in our new home and in fact we are all quite comfortable. I'm afraid Margaret[175] and Su get the worst of it, I can't keep the children quiet all the time. Now we've got straight we're very pleased with the new abode. Of course there are drawbacks, but nothing very serious. We're very lucky to be in such comfortable quarters in these days.

[175] Miss Thomas

Yesterday old Wang ta Sao, who used to help me, turned up here. She has been with a Chinese family in Tsingchou and recently in Tsinan. It's terribly hard work and this last week she was scratched or bitten by a cat and still had to carry on looking after the children. By Friday her foot was so painful that she felt she couldn't carry on, so she left and stopped off here on her way home. She is staying to rest here for a few days, till the swelling goes down. It's quite a bad infection and she must rest to get it right. Poor old soul, she keeps saying 'if only Connie hadn't gone'. At present it does look as if we're better off here, but who is really better off won't be known till after the war.

In view of the uncertainty of the next few months, we've made apricot jam and bottled apricots too. The later fruit crops may or may not be good, so we felt we'd be wise to lay in while we'd the chance. If we go in a hurry we can always have a grand time eating piles of jam with everything!

9th July 1942

There are still rumours of a British Repatriation ship leaving end of July or early August. Funny if we sailed August 16th! We've had no official information here, so don't really know what'll happen. We're planning so that if we go we shall be ready, and if we don't we shan't be too disappointed. Travel by sea is no game in these days.

On Sunday, folk moved into our old house and guards were on at night again. Georgie seems to find her new neighbours slightly more noisy than the old, but otherwise we know little about them.

Ronald has again approached the officials about the cash for our goods which they took off and again they said, oh, wait a while, you'll have the cash when you go. It is about £300 altogether, for we have all sold things, so it's worth getting.

The heat has been terrific, 105° in the shade, 94° at night. Yesterday we had a storm which cleared the air and we hope will have helped the crops, but more rain is needed. In old Wang ta Sao's village, they have to walk to a well seven miles away, for every drop of water! And it's mostly the women who do it – can you imagine what that's like in this heat? We feel to need baths all day long, but our wells are getting dry too, so we're having to take care.

The Americans got off eventually on the 29th and apparently received every consideration and were very well treated. Everything was well planned and families had a cabin to themselves and so on.

For my birthday I had several presents and at Rosemary's bidding, Wu produced a cake with icing! We still have a little cocoa left and it was quite good. In the evening Ronald and I went on the street and bought a few small things we'd like to have if we go home soon.

15th July 1942

Yesterday another surprise: news from Tsinan that if there is an English boat all of us can go - all our Mission, Tsinan, Tsingchou and here. The officials here called Ronald and John along and said we're to go on the 23rd! Only another week, but of course that will probably be altered again.

They tell us to take only forty kilos luggage per head. That would allow us two trunks as a family! Ronald said if he couldn't take more than that he wouldn't go! But he was told that he must go. However, on hearing that the Americans had been allowed six large trunks each, in addition to hand luggage, they said they'd enquire again! So we hope for something better.

We were sending Kao to Tsinan to enquire about restrictions there, but a bridge has been broken up the line and there's been no train to Tsinan for about thirty hours. He'll go on the first there is, and come back tomorrow, I expect. We shall try to insist on taking as much as Tsinan folk.

The conditions here are getting worse. It's terribly hard to buy flour, even though we now have cash.

25th July 1942

Still in Chouts'un! Kao came back with the news that, as there was still no settled date for sailing, the Tsinan folk didn't want us up there yet and we're still hanging on waiting for a date.

Our heavy baggage was all examined on Monday. We're hoping now to take ten trunks and I've packed most of them four or five times now! We got through our 'examination' all right, though the Tui Chang and Consul were at it over two hours! and did things fairly thoroughly. We had to re-pack two trunks entirely, but we'd no snags or unpleasantness – it was all accompanied by tea, cigarettes etc. In the afternoon they went to Lewis' and the nurses, but the Tui Chang sent an interpreter and two soldiers as his representatives and they took every single thing out, the whole room was chaos. It took a couple of days to re-pack. We hear that the Swiss Consul says five heavy pieces baggage per adult is not excess and two pieces hand luggage, so we can keep in all right.

Ronald has received the cash for goods 'sold', or rather 80% of it which is all the military decided to give us.

Yesterday and today, for the first time for over a year, we've had heavy rain. There are over four hundred refugees living in the Ming Tao School today. Their homes were all washed away, just between our compound and the town wall. At the other side of the town there are a lot of houses destroyed, too, I hear. In Tsinan and locally there have been many deaths, old people and children drowned before they could get away. The houses are mostly mud and washed away in no time in a heavy downpour.

31st July 1942

The latest is that we may have to be in Shanghai by August 8th and that will mean leaving here on August 4th. We're busy with cholera jabs, and vaccinations. Dr Gault, the only American left in Tsinan, has very kindly offered hospitality to our family for our two days stay in Tsinan. She has a huge house and it will be very nice for us. She is hoping to stay on and work in a Chinese Hospital in Tsinan. We were worried by the thought of a Hotel (Japanese) in the hot weather – children get dysentery so easily out here. They should be much better at Dr Gault's.

2nd August 1942

Date of leaving still uncertain, but probably the 8th from here. We've rushed to get ready for the 4th and now feel at a loose end – we now merely 're-dirty' things already washed and ironed! However, it does seem as certain as possible that we are to go, which is a relief to us now. We should like rather more than four days in Shanghai as we have several bits of business to do there, but it will probably work out that we have enough time, and it's sure to be unpleasantly hot and mosquito-ish.

We see that the first Japanese party left home from Liverpool[176]– wonder if we'll land there. We are thrilled at the thought of getting home, but still don't count on it too much. We've really done all we can, and had almost cleared out of food, so we'll have a job to last I'm afraid.

---

[176] Repatriation of British and American civilians in China was being undertaken on an exchange basis with Japanese aliens resident in the UK.

Fortunately, owing to sale of goods, we're not so terribly hard-up now – and aren't always wondering how to stretch the dollars.

Writing much later, in 1946, Ronald added a note on their experience of these last days in Chouts'un. 'At the time of our departure, we were virtually the prisoners of the Japanese, and no Chinese could display any friendliness towards us without risking the severe penalties that awaited those who 'collaborated with the enemy'. None the less, in spite of this, during our remaining days in Chouts'un, we received many touching expressions of friendship and affection from our former colleagues and friends on the staff of the hospital and from members of the church. They belong to the richest treasures of our memory.'[177]

Ronald to his father and mother

Shanghai
16th August 1942

I'm writing this letter from the Columbia Country Club in Shanghai and am sending it to you by the kindness of Dr H Jocelyn Smyly who expects to leave here tomorrow on the repatriation boat for England via Lorenzo Marques.

Until we arrived in Shanghai on August 12th we, and the rest of the party of 77 from Tsinan and district, expected that we too were to have places on this boat. On our arrival here we found that the final decisions as to who should travel had not yet been made and that for some reason or other there were many others who had prior claims to ourselves, and out of the seventy seven from our district only seven will be travelling

Columbia Country Club

[177] *Through Toil and Tribulation*, Carey Press, London 1947, p109

on this boat. But their going gives us an opportunity of sending you the first letter we have been able to write for a long time.

We have had no news, of course, by letters since December 8th and our latest news from you was about the middle of September 1941, nearly a year ago. We are longing to know how you have been faring during these intervening months.

We left Chouts'un on August 8th and went to Tsinan where we spent two nights on the Cheeloo campus before leaving (on the night of August 10th) for Shanghai. We reached Shanghai at about 3 a.m. on the 12th and are now quartered in the Country Club. There must be about three hundred or more Britishers here at present in the Club rooms. Gwyneth and the children have a private room with private bathroom, which however she has to share with other single ladies who sleep on the corridor outside and there are two others who share the room with her, a largish room with very satisfactory arrangements. I sleep with about thirty other men in a large bowling alley. Camp beds – quite comfortable and satisfactory[178].

About our prospects of getting home, it is suggested that there will be additional repatriation boats in the next six weeks or two to three months. If there are, it is not certain that we shall secure places on one of them. Our family has been voted by the Tsinan District British Missionary community committee for places among the first twenty of their seventy members still remaining, but it seems there are still large numbers of Shanghailanders and others in other categories who may get preferential treatment. We shall endeavour to bring our claims for preference to the notice of those concerned and shall hope that they will be admitted. It seems hard to have got so far on the journey homewards to be held up at this stage. No doubt doctors will be needed at home, but perhaps the British Government is reluctant to expend five berths on the boat in order to bring home one doctor!!

However, when we decided to stay here, we little expected that there would be opportunities for return home once the war started. If we get the chance, we shall be home as soon as the boat will carry us! If not, we shall endeavour to make ourselves useful here in Shanghai, and there are books (and medical books) available, and we shall try to put the time

---

[178] Knowing that this was likely to be the only news his parents would have of them for a long time, Ronald is careful to emphasize all that was positive and reassuring. Typically, in describing the beds as 'quite comfortable and satisfactory', Ronald omitted to mention that all the furniture in the bowling alley, including beds, was straddled across the bowling lanes, with consequent discomfort and inconvenience!

to good use. But we are hoping that there will be places for us on the next boat.

It was a great disappointment to us to have to close the hospital after managing to keep going for three months after the war started, but the closing of the hospital was part of a nation-wide policy and as such was beyond our control. On the morning of March 17th a patient with pyloric stenosis was waiting on the operating table, duly prepared for operation, and the instruments laid out ready to begin the operation. But it was not to be. That morning the instruments were taken away, and that operation, which we hoped would prove life-saving, had to be abandoned. Our X-ray and ultra-violet apparatus were also confiscated. We have detailed lists, in Japanese and English, of things that have been 'borrowed', and we have full inventories of the hospital property and furniture. That seems to be the most we can do towards securing restitution in due course.

In the Tsingchou hospital our own staff are still carrying on with a Japanese nominal superintendent, Dr Ching still acting as Assistant Superintendent with responsibility for most decisions. The management is now in the hands of the local municipal government, which accepts responsibility for finances. Dr Ching and Dr Chao and their colleagues are much to be congratulated on their faithful adherence to duty in difficult circumstances. I hope they may be able to weather whatever storms may still be ahead and carry their work through until times are peaceful again. The Leper Hospital is still functioning, with support from local contributions. Funds are short at present and it is not yet clear whether the local government intends to take complete responsibility or not.

Gwyneth has not written separately by this boat, so you will pass this on to Cambridge, we know. It was a great disappointment not to be on this boat and on our way back to you after all seemed set for our going. Rosemary, Audrey and Catherine are all lovely. Rosemary and Audrey are always talking about England and their Grannies and Grandpas, and Uncles and Aunties and cousins. Catherine just says single words or double ones like 'train – puff-puff' and 'mummy gone' – she is the loveliest little mischief. We long for you to see them all soon. And we long to see you all soon.

God keep you all safe and well and in peace at heart.

Gwyneth – Continuation of the letter intended for Cambridge and Ilkley but never posted

Shanghai
10th September 1942

Of course we're still in Shanghai, and unfortunately 'let down' not by the Japanese, but by the Shanghai British residents, who pushed their own folk in ahead of us. It's all been very unfair we think, as we had been cleared out of our own homes and the Shanghai people had their homes and all the conveniences thereof. We, about three hundred Britishers from Peking, Tientsin, Tsingtao, Tsinan and Hankow districts are stranded here, and have no real expectations of getting away.

We had a hectic time at home the last few days, but got off without mishap on the 8th. The officials were polite and helpful to the end. The government adviser (Japanese) gave our children $20 (15/-) and ditto to Robin and Anne Lewis. It was horrid leaving our home and all the things we'd brought out, but we were thankful to get away together in safety. It was hard saying goodbye to the boys and woman, and I feel so homesick for them now. They were so good to us and it seemed like leaving half the family behind.

We had a hot, but easy journey to Tsinan escorted by a local Japanese Consul. The Tsingchou folk were on the train, it was fun to meet them again. In Tsinan the officials took those of us with families to the Cheeloo campus. The single folk went to a hotel where they had a rather poor time. We were warmly welcomed by Tsinan friends and had the use of three lovely rooms in Dr Gault's house, so airy and comfy after what we'd been having our last few weeks at home. Mr and Mrs Will Rowlands were there and acting as hostess and host and made us so happy and comfy. All the other folk were busy selling up their homes.

The next day, we were promised rickshaws would come up to the end of the Campus, but at the last moment, they were stopped so we had to walk and carry most of our hand luggage and children. It was terrifically hot even though it was 8 p.m. We had about ten minutes walk to the rickshaws and then rode to the station. There we had about an hour and a half's wait. Our luggage was displayed the length of the platform (there were 77 in our party from Tsinan district) and it was all gone through very thoroughly. We had three big and four smallish pieces of baggage, a handbag, two small baskets and three children, all needing help up and down steps.

It was 10 p.m. when the train eventually arrived. We travelled 3rd class, just long seats to lie on. We were lucky in getting three between us in the end, though it was a terrific scrum and the heat was pretty awful and the dirt and dust ghastly. Of course, the children were all tired, but it was midnight before they were all off to sleep and I went along for a drink (we'd only taken milk for the children) and the restaurant car was closed! Mrs Dart saved my life with a sip of her tea! Never again will I travel without a sip of tea.

After that I felt better able to face life! Rosemary and Audrey slept one each end of one bed and Catherine with me. She kept waking and trying to push me out of the way. Altogether it was not one of my best nights, but I've learnt to sleep through most things now so I didn't feel bad when daylight came.

Some of our party had food poisoning on the train and when we reached Nanking our coach was cut off and held back – the Japanese thought it might be cholera. We had visions of staying there for days. However, suddenly at 6 p.m. they said we must get out and walk to the boat to cross the river (the ferry for the train is broken). We had quarter of an hour's walk and no help with the luggage. I don't know how we ever got there, especially as we had to hurry. I dragged a huge suitcase and carried Catherine and dragged Rosemary! Ronald carried two cases and half carried Audrey who was getting very tired and we both had oddments and one or two childless friends lent a hand half way, so we got there in the end. The three poison cases had to be carried by our own party and their luggage, so it made extra burdens all round.

The boat was crowded, but I got a seat with Catherine on my knee and the other two children were scattered with bits of luggage among friends. After we crossed the Yangtze, we got into buses and were driven to the railway station. Again our luggage was a nuisance. We began to think we'd have to drop some by the wayside, but we managed to cling on to it all.

We waited about an hour on Nanking Station with no place to sit, except on our battered cases. Shortage of drinks was the worst. Neither I nor the children like 'fizzy' drinks and it was hard to get anything else. In the end we filled a thermos with tea and made it last ages, by taking tiny sips. When the train came it was very crowded. However, we were again lucky and were on the spot as an extra coach was added and so got seats, but only enough for sitting up. Of course by then the children were all about dropping with sleep, but all determined not to give in. We managed to get them all off for a bit, but they had to lie all huddled up, so they didn't sleep at all well.

The train reached Shanghai at 12.15 a.m. and we were kept waiting on the station, without seats again, until 2.15 a.m. The children were all wide awake by then and full of energy. We didn't know how to stand up, but they wanted to dash around and talk to everyone! All the time we had to keep eyes glued to our little pile of baggage. At last at 2.15 buses came and we were brought up here. Again it was very crowded, but we got seats and Ronald and Rosemary and Audrey were one end and I was the other with Catherine. Rosemary and Audrey impressed all the adults by their brightness. A lot of Peking people were in the bus and a lady said to me only a day or two ago she'd never forget sitting opposite them in the bus that night. Everyone was half asleep, tired out and rather short-tempered, and Rosemary and Audrey were as cheerful as if they'd had their usual night's rest.

On our arrival at the Club we all queued up to be checked in *twice*, and then were given a sheet and pillow-case and towel each. It was an awful blow to discover Ronald couldn't come upstairs with me - it was such a drag with the children. However, the thought that we were really on the way home cheered us up, and I comforted myself that it was just for four days, and even though the ship would be crowded, it would be for a short time. The bath was a great joy. We were all absolutely black, so the children had to be bathed even at that hour. Some kind lady brought me in a cup of tea (I'll not easily forget these gifts of tea!) and at about 3.45 I got to bed, a camp bed with no mattress. It was cool and quiet and I was asleep at once.

We had to be down to queue for brekker at 8.30 – it was a frightful rush – and at that meal, we heard people saying that the Tsinan group had been knocked off the passenger list. We thought it just another rumour, but alas, it turned out to be no rumour. We'd been promised that every one of the seventy seven from our district would be given places, and our names were numbers 8, 9, 10, 11, and 12 on the preference list. The Tsinan list was followed 1 to 7 - and there it stopped at our names.

It was really hard not to be disappointed, and Rosemary and Audrey are always saying why can't we go to England to see their grannies and grandpas. It's not easy to explain to them. There's been a lot of really 'dirty work' in one way and another, but we'll talk about it later. We don't see any hope now of getting away till after the war, though every now and again rumours crop up and people's hopes rise again.

Getting onto the train at one point I carried Audrey and Catherine! – quite an effort.

From the day when it had first been opened to foreigners in 1842, Shanghai had been a magnet for speculators and traders, diplomats, businessmen and missionaries. The substantial British community was a mixture, including employees of multinational companies, like Imperial Chemical Industries or British American Tobacco, and employees of Chinese companies and of the Chinese Customs House. Others worked for the British run Shanghai Municipal Council (SMC) and the Shanghai Municipal Police. Some were posted to Shanghai for only a matter of months and others had been settled for two or three generations, had made their permanent homes there and considered themselves 'Shanghailanders'. Within the International Settlement they were subject to British Consular law. They managed their homes and conducted their lively social lives according to British traditions and British interests.

The British, with around 8,500 residents, were not the only sizable foreign community in Shanghai. The 1930 census showed there were almost as many Russians (7,366), many of them refugees from the Revolution of 1917. European Jews, fleeing from the pograms of 1900 and from Nazi Germany in the 1930s, had also settled in Shanghai in large numbers. By 1939, there were representatives of almost every European country, as well as Americans, Indians, Filipinos and Koreans. The largest single group by far was Japanese, many of whom had lived there since the end of the 19th century.

During 1941, when war had already raged in China for more than four years, the foreign residents living within the 'concession' areas[179] *had been able to continue their ordinary lives with very little disruption. Thousands of Chinese had crowded into the International Settlement for protection during the intense fighting and subsequent fall of the city to the Japanese in 1937, but the lifestyle of the foreign community had not changed significantly. The outbreak of war in Europe had likewise only effected superficial changes. The British regiments which had been stationed in Shanghai departed for active duty in Europe, and were no longer able to provide the usual Tuesday evening entertainment at Jessfield Park, with their full dress parades and marching bands. And some of the women now met to knit socks for servicemen or to raise funds for 'the war effort', and perhaps discreetly dropped German friends from their social circle.*

---

[179] The Treaty of Nanking had established the principle of extra-territoriality by which certain areas within China had been conceded to the control of foreign powers, and were not deemed to be under Chinese law or Chinese control. They operated under their own administration, had their own police force and were governed by their own legislation. The International Settlement and the French Concession in Shanghai were two such areas.

But when Japan declared war on Britain and America much more fundamental changes were set in motion. The residents of the foreign community awoke on the morning of December 8th 1941 to find that the Japanese military had crossed the bridges over the Soochow Creek, had taken over the banks, stationed troops along the Bund and set up check points at road junctions within the International Settlement.

For a while, British and American citizens were allowed to remain in their homes, and businesses were advised to continue normally. Very soon, however, lists were drawn up of those wishing to be repatriated. Many were at first reluctant to go: those with businesses felt that they had to stay to keep an eye on their property; others were afraid that they might be jeopardising their jobs in future if they applied to go. By the summer though, when Ronald and Gwyneth and the other 'outporters' from the north arrived in Shanghai, the trickle of those wishing to leave had become a flood – and the supply of ships for repatriation had dried up.

Shanghai
28th November 1942

We were overjoyed a few weeks back to receive Red Cross letters from Cambridge and Ilkley and know you were all well, and on Monday we could hardly believe our eyes on seeing a letter from Dray, written July 17! We were most thrilled because it means that you have now found out you can write 'Prisoners of War' post and we feel hopeful of getting more. I'm so hungry for letters from you all.

We're still in the Club in spite of rumours to the contrary and constant alarms. When about six hundred British men were rounded up in Shanghai a few weeks ago, people got very scared, but no one has been taken from the Club, and we are just living on and carrying on from day to day. We really are very fortunate in many ways. It's a relief not to have the responsibilities that we'd had in Chouts'un, and we have no catering or servant problems. But we do miss home life and sharing a room with another family is far from ideal. There is absolutely no place we can call our own or where we have any privacy or quiet. The first few weeks were a nightmare, but we have now settled into a routine and the children feel more at home.

At first we had all three children at meals and had to queue up and then carry our own trays and their three, and at the same time try to keep them with us. For weeks Catherine wouldn't leave my arms, so I had to carry her and a tray and keep an eye on Rosemary and Audrey. We had meals on a verandah, very pleasant except for millions of flies. So what with trying to keep flies off all the food and push spoonfuls down the children, I hardly had a thing to eat myself.

When we'd been here about three weeks they inaugurated baby meals for children of two or under, half an hour before the other meals, so Catherine was fed then and had to play around while we had our meal. The food is good but not very varied, and often not attractive, and Rosemary and Audrey found it hard to manage. They just sat and gazed around the whole time and I found meal times were a great trial. At last we persuaded the management to put Audrey onto baby food too and she's regaining the weight she lost earlier on. And having cleared those two up, we find it easier to deal with Rosemary and her food. She too is now making up her lost weight. Catherine has just gone ahead all the time and taken everything in her stride. She's still very plump and rosy and absolutely bursting with energy. I do long for you to see them all. They've all kept well, except for one or two minor upsets.

The Club is a pleasant spot in summer, but becoming very draughty now. Fortunately Shanghai winters are usually short. There is a big 'lounge' which we use all the time. I only go in after the children are in bed and sit and knit (or fall asleep!). One corner of that has been curtained off and houses about twenty ladies. Then the dining room and card room both house about thirty women each. The bowling alley has about seventy men in it, and also some of our baggage. The billiard room has now been converted into a dining room, and the bar is also a dormitory for men. Most children over eight or nine sleep in the big dormitories, boys with their fathers and girls with mothers.

The bowling alley in use as a dormitory

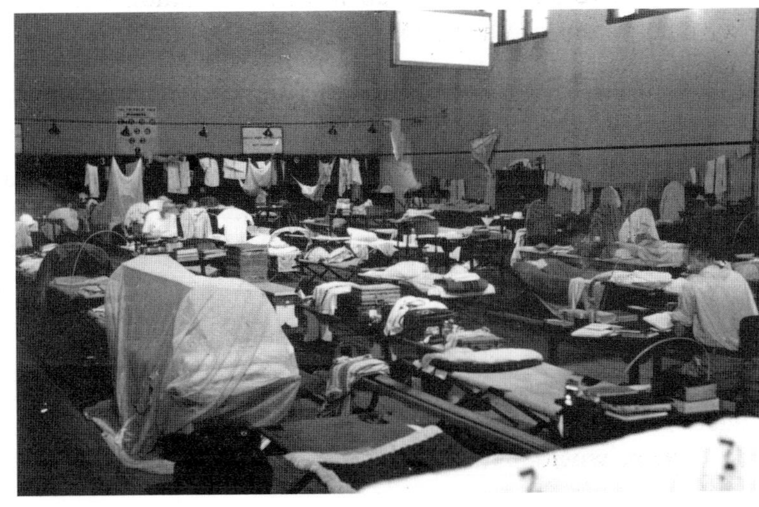

Upstairs there is one long corridor with about a dozen bedrooms leading off – each room has its own bathroom. There are fifteen ladies sleeping along the corridor and twenty three mothers and their forty three small children mostly under six, in the bedrooms. It's an awful crush, but we're better off than the folk downstairs. They haven't more than a foot between their beds and no cupboards at all. In my room I have the children all along one wall, about ten inches between each bed, one tiny table, one chair, three shelves in a small cupboard, a little hanging space and a line in the bathroom. Otherwise our things have to be on our beds or in cases under them, and with Catherine around it's not safe to have things at bed level. She has the grandest time if I take her into the big rooms, because she can reach and does reach everything she sees!. Mrs Russell and Martin (seventeen months) occupy the other half of the room, and three other people come from the corridor to use the bathroom. We're lucky in having hot water, so we can get our washing done easily and hang it on the verandah upstairs to dry.

The upstairs is up two flights, and that means a drag with three such small infants and when they first arrived they felt so overcome by all the newness, and strange people that they wouldn't be left. It's better now and Audrey and Rosemary feel quite at home. Catherine still dislikes to be left much, but she's happy with most of the people now and will stay with someone if I have to run up for anything.

When it became clear that there would be no boat, we looked around for a kindergarten and found one nearby (ten minutes walk) where Audrey as well as Rosemary could attend. About a dozen other children go from the Club and they are very happy there and Rosemary is learning very quickly. Audrey is very quiet about what she does and always says she does 'nothing' but at least she's happy and out of mischief and my life is much easier! The school is run by an English lady and is attended by Europeans only. The big majority are English, with a few Dutch and Norwegians.

We had to leave both our cot and pram up in Chouts'un and when the children started school we felt more than ever in need of a pram. Audrey seemed too small to walk both ways and even Rosemary needed a lift occasionally, and of course with no pram I couldn't get out shopping because I couldn't leave Catherine and yet she couldn't walk far enough.

We looked around for second hand prams and eventually found one which we bought. It's far bigger than any I've ever seen – it must have been made for the quads. It's a Marmet and has double hoods and is really marvellous for our family. We push them all to school in it and

bring Catherine back again, and if we want to go to the Park off we go without needing rickshaws. Everyone laughs at its size, but parents all seem glad if we give their children rides in it!

Then I found camp beds might do for adults but not for Catherine. She could get out so easily and came downstairs in her nightie and bare feet on more than one occasion. Also we had no mattresses and it was impossible to keep her warm, so about a month ago we bought a cot! It's an iron one, enamelled cream. We had a coconut fibre mattress made, so that we can now tuck her in cosily, and know that however hard she tries, she can't escape. It's a great relief to us to be able to buy both cot and pram. We are not particularly short of cash now as we're not paying our board at the moment, but of course we don't want to spend unnecessarily.

We've had to replace a few clothes and buy a few for the children, but prices are ghastly and woollen materials, wool and leather goods are almost impossible. Ronald has gone into corduroys! Lumber jacket and trousers. It is almost a club uniform, heaps of the men are wearing it to save their one and only cloth suit. We've also bought the children lumber jackets and trousers for wearing in the garden, to save their precious woollies. We've a lovely garden and playing field so the children can be out of doors whenever the weather allows.

10th January 1943

I'm afraid I'm missing quite a lot out, I never get a quiet moment. Even now, in addition to the baying of conversation of a couple of hundred people, there are about fifty singing hymns, so excuse mistakes.

We're still in the Club and all well. We changed our bedroom a few weeks ago and now share a rather smaller room with Mrs Russell, but it has the advantage of having a door onto the verandah, so Catherine can sleep out there every afternoon. Also we have a small radiator, so the place isn't too cold. There's no heating at night, and we have the door onto the verandah wide open, but we don't feel too cold.

We had some bad weeks when the nights were cool or cold and we had no mattresses. We couldn't sleep for cold and we personally haven't too many blankets anyway. However, eventually after much pushing, the British Red Cross supplied mattresses and quilts for all who needed them. So now we're all quite cosy. Catherine has her own mattress and plenty of cot blankets, Rosemary and Audrey have their beds close together, so that they can share blankets.

I told you they were all well and so they are, but I fear Rosemary has chicken-pox! There have been several cases here and tonight she has several suspicious spots. I do hope it isn't because the others will be sure to get it. They have to go to an isolation hospital too which is rather hard. Rosemary wants to go, because some of her pals are there, but I think Audrey and Catherine would loathe it. Audrey is a very 'homey' bird and hates to have any member of the family missing, and I'm sure she'd loathe to be the missing one herself. And Catherine calls for 'Mummy' all the time there is any difficulty. She's a very energetic, decided young lady and she would let the nurses and doctors know what she thought of them! She does her best to boss the others and now she is talking more, she ticks everyone off when she feels like it. When Martin throws toys out of his cot, she dashes up and shakes her head at him and says 'No, Marty, no, naughty Marty'. She has been slow with talking, but is coming on now and talks fairly clearly. At present she's a very vivacious child. She has lovely round rosy cheeks and bright eyes.

When we first came here, we were absolutely free to go out and about as we liked. Then on October 15th an order was issued that forbade British and Americans to go to places of amusement, bars, night clubs, and so on. Fortunately cafés without orchestras were not closed to us, so we are still able to have a coffee occasionally. Shortly after that, another regulation appeared – all British and Americans over twelve had to wear red arm bands. I'm now labelled B2576 wherever I go. Americans have A. It doesn't seem to make any difference to us when we go out. We have certainly been well treated so far. Internment rumours are ever with us, but it's no use worrying.

On November 1st or thereabouts about six hundred British and American men were taken off and are confined in a barracks. It's bad luck on the wives of the married ones. Married life here is not exactly as we'd like it. We never have any time alone – anywhere – but at least we see each other and occasionally get a few minutes to talk. Oh I'll never have time to make up all the lost time.

Social life in the Club is well organised now – all sorts of games, tournaments, singing, bridge, chess, dancing etc. We don't join in much, though Ronald is chess champion! Rosemary enjoys Brownies and games of various sorts with all the others.

Ronald *(right)* with fellow chess players

Although the big majority of us are missionaries, there are school teachers, BAT[180], ICI[181], APC[182] representatives, cotton mill and insurance people, accountants, reporters, ships captains, engineers, mechanics, customs officers, bank managers and clerks etc. With very few exceptions, everyone mixes amicably and there are few difficulties in that way. In the bedrooms and dormitories there are plenty of minor disagreements, about opening and shutting windows, lights out and so on, but nothing very serious. People coming in after 'lights out' invariably kick the bars at the end of the other camp beds and cause no little annoyance to the occupants!

27th January 1943

Well, my fears about Rosemary were unfounded. She didn't develop chicken-pox then, but Catherine has come out today with about three spots. And someone else has scarlet fever in the next bedroom! Also we hear we're to be put into a concentration camp in a few weeks time. Certainly life is far from dull for mothers in these days. We hear that all the British and Americans in Shanghai are to be put into big camps, a thousand in each of seven. We also hear, and hope it's true, that families are to be in the same camp. But all these are rumours. All we know is that four hundred men have already been called for assembly.

---

[180] British American Tobacco
[181] Imperial Chemical Industries
[182] Asiatic Petroleum Company

We understand we're to be allowed two trunks and one bed each as luggage and children one trunk, so that we'll not need to leave everything behind, but the thought of packing in these days is ghastly. Our trunks are all in such an awful muddle. Did I mention that for about six or more weeks we had to live with only our hand luggage, which was packed to last for four days! Thank goodness I learnt years ago always to leave out a woolly garment per head, so we managed, but it meant very frequent washing. We fear that any move must be for the worse, as conditions here, in spite of all the inconveniences, are bearable and we have plenty of hot water, and big grounds.

We keep hoping for Red Cross messages or letters, but no more have arrived. We do so long for news of you. The last letter I had from Mother was written about seventeen months ago – it's such an awful age.

We can get no margarine now, so the babies are given pork fat on their bread. The rest of us get no margarine and no substitute at all. In the Civil Assembly Centre[183] we get two bowls of rice per day and you know how I dislike rice!

7th February 1943

Rumours are not lacking. Already twelve hundred single men and grass widowers have been ordered into a Civil Assembly Centre, as well as four hundred odd people, families in the SMC employ. We hear two families are to share a room with a curtain down the centre!! There is also fresh talk of repatriation, but there seems to be absolutely no foundation for such a hope, and anyway, after our treatment last time we should not expect to get away if there should be another boat.

Ronald has done quite a bit of study here, but there is never a minute when the place is quiet and he gets many interruptions on his time. Did I tell you too that he is going every afternoon to a Chinese Hospital and taking care of the surgical cases there?

The other day there was a scare that the downtown go-down[184] would not be open to us after February 2nd so Ronald and I felt we should go and do some repacking. We got a young girl who'd had chicken pox to look after the children and had a morning at it. It was a miserably cold wet day and the place was horrible and damp. I loathed it, but we managed to repack one whole trunk of things that we think we shan't need till after the war. Of course we doubt very much if we'll ever see it

---

[183] The official name for the prospective internment camps.
[184] Warehouse

again anyway, but we can but try. We now have six trunks up here, all a muddle of clothes, books etc. I simply must go through them and see just what is in each, in case we have a hurried packing.

There are quite a number of Yorkshire people here, but I've not found a soul from Cambridge or anywhere near.

Ronald and Gwyneth and those others temporarily housed in the Columbia Country Club were technically the guests of the Japanese government who had arranged for them to be brought to Shanghai, but it was the Shanghai British Residents Association (BRA) who organised their food and accommodation. After the worries about money and supplies experienced in Shantung, they were grateful for the fine efforts of the BRA, and enjoyed the comparative ease with which they were able to move around Shanghai.

By the beginning of 1943 it was evident that this state of affairs would not continue. The call-up to internment had begun, and with it instructions from the Japanese as to what prospective internees might take with them into the camps. Within the tight allowance of permitted baggage, they were required to provide their own beds, bedding and tableware (including 'a vacuum bottle, napkins and tablecloths'), and were also encouraged to bring not only clothing and provisions but books and 'goods for sport and amusement'[185]*. Those who had been forced earlier to sell their possessions and leave their homes in the north had to start equipping themselves again from scratch. Here again the BRA was able to help out by organising sales of beds, mosquito nets, enamel plates and mugs, stools, buckets, wooden clogs and other basic commodities.*

Meanwhile, something else had happened which would change for all time the position of the British in China. On 11th January 1943, the British and Chinese governments signed a new agreement abolishing the extra territorial rights which, since 1842, had governed the residence of British subjects in China. The missionary societies had never been happy with the inequalities to which the original treaty clauses had given rise, and, since 1925, the Conference of British Missionary Societies had been campaigning publicly for the abolition of extra-territoriality. The China Sub-Committee of the BMS recorded the new arrangements at their meeting of 12th January 1943 with 'deep thankfulness', describing it as an 'answer to continual prayers' and expressing to the British and

[185] Notice issued to prospective internees by the Consul General for Japan, March 1943

Chinese governments 'their appreciation and gratitude for this timely and hopeful readjustment of relationships with the Chinese people.'[186]

The 1943 agreement by the two governments also signalled, however, the inevitable demise of the SMC and the Shanghai Municipal Police, which provided not only the organisational framework for the lives of the majority of British residents in Shanghai, but was, for many, their source of income and employment.

Gwyneth to Olive in Buenos Aires

Columbia Country Club
301 Great Western Road, Shanghai
23rd March 1943

I can scarcely believe my eyes – a letter from you at long last! Yours of September 9th 1942 has been forwarded from Chouts'un. It's only the second that has got through since December '41. I'd one from Dray in October. There was very little real news in it, but it was great to know that all were well.

I hope you'll have heard by now from some source or another, what has happened to us since December 8th '41. Life down here has been far more free than in the North, and we have had enjoyments of sorts – all details later. The big snag has been complete lack of family life. It's terribly hard to train the children in a place like this, everything has to be said and done in public. After living in a small compound, life here was not easy - there were about two hundred and eighty most of the time. The children were all rather scared in such a big crowd. However, we've settled down fairly well.

Ronald was working in a Chinese hospital for some months but is now helping to deal with people desiring medical exemption from Civil Assembly Centres. In January they started collecting people into these 'camps' and now there are very few of us left free. We expect to be in by the middle of next month and after that I shall be unable to write again, but I think you might write addressing it to Ronald, full name and nationality, c/o International Red Cross, Shanghai. If you should hear of repatriation to your part of the world, I think it would be well to write to us c/o British Consul at that particular spot. If possible, please let me know your cable address next letter, one never knows in these days when it might be needed.

---

[186] BMS China Sub-Committee minutes, Volume 11, 12.1.43, Angus Library, Oxford

We've been able to buy in stores of sorts and are spending all we have. We feel that if this isn't the rainy day, there never will be one. After the war, we'll have to start at scratch, but if we come out with our lives and health, what else matters. The children really are bonny, I'm so thankful that they start 'camp' life fit. Conditions haven't been too bad, but our beds are only six inches apart, so you can guess that cat swinging has been out of the question.

Please buy up any bargains in the clothes line. We don't look too refugee-ish yet, but if we have to last long, it won't be too jolly. Of course we've lost everything, except clothes and a few extras. I feel to understand better now how these people must feel leaving an estate that has been in the family for years!

Rosemary said to me the other day, 'Mummy, don't ever talk to me about Wu and Kao and Wang Ta Sao, or about my Grannies, it does make me feel too sad.' Audrey is a quaint little creature. Rosemary told her the other day that she'd die if she did something or other, and so she said, 'I don't care if I do. Mummy can just ask God for another little baby, and He'll send me back again!'

There have been some very nice families with us and jolly children, too, but we're all separating now. The Phillips have just left us, much to our regret. Our mission is now very broken up. Members of it are already in five different camps and there will be at least two more holding some of our people. It looks as if the Scotts and ourselves may be the only ones in our camp, with possibly Miss Smurthwaite who may get in as a kindergarten teacher.

After all those abscesses I took a bit of time to pick up, but I've been very well since. Ronald and I both weigh exactly what we weighed when we landed in China! The children have each gained 10lbs since January '42, so they've done well so far.

Food was an awful problem at home, not only on account of finance, but because we just couldn't obtain it even with cash. Here it is far better, and almost anything can be bought at a price. We try to supplement the children's meals with peanut butter, honey or jam, but shortly it will be impossible to do this.

I do want more news from home, so please write quickly. We think often of everyone at home and long for the time when we'll see you all. Life in a community like this is not without its humourous side – we'll have some funny tales to tell. No doubt you'll have one or two stories too.

PS Can only send one snap, taken October 1942. If it reaches you, please let Mother see it. The children had all been racing round the garden in the wind so excuse untidiness! They're all wearing their overalls, but it's a natural snap. I'm wearing the dress made of material Mother sent me in 1939. You'll observe that the 'girls' have grown pigtails while I have had my hair off! I simply couldn't cope with a bun in these conditions. The children have had theirs off since the snaps were taken. Audrey's is really very pretty – it waves quite nicely and is a nice golden colour. Catherine still looks more like a boy. Rosemary says you're a 'lucky bean' to live where there's no war!

April 19th Posting now – expect to enter 'Civil Assembly' in two days' time.

Gwyneth - Continuation of letter intended for Cambridge and Ilkley but never posted

15th June 1943

We're all safe and well after eight weeks in internment camp. Before the chicken pox was really over, people from the Club began to be called up in bunches, but we were fairly near the end. At the end of February Ronald was asked to help at the BRA as medical officer and that meant full time out. He left at 8 a.m. and was never back before 8 p.m. By then life was so disorganised in the Shanghai British community that there was no school and the children were with me all the time. We had to repack everything and bring in lots of things for 'camp'. I had all of this to do myself and I pushed the pram with the three children all over the place shopping. Shopping was exceedingly difficult. The sort of stuff we needed was partly rationed, at least we could buy only one tin of this and one of that at a shop, so I had to dodge from one shop to another. Our funds were limited, so of course we had to concentrate on essentials, bean milk preparations, jams, tomato juice, honey, soap.

We were 'called up' for the American Camp[187] on March 22nd. About two hundred British with small children were sent there and we hear now it's terribly overcrowded, so we're glad that in the end the BRA wouldn't spare Ronald to go as early as that. Then we had another call for Ash Camp[188], for April 20th, and were all packed and ready to go when, two days before the Assembly date, news came that we and three other families and a few single people were to stay on and form the nucleus of a new camp here! In some ways it was a relief not to have to move, but in other ways we were not so pleased. However, there is no

[187] Later known as Chapei Camp, on Chungsan Road, occupying the premises of the former Great China University.

[188] Ash Camp, 65 Great Western Road, a former British Army barracks

choice in these matters and we settled down for goodness knows how long.

It's strange living here under these conditions after having been here for eight months under such different ones. On the whole we're quite happy and are reasonably well fed and have no real complaints, except lack of privacy. There are twenty four people in our room (later thirty) – five men, six women, five boys and eight girls! Can't you imagine the fun it is at bed time trying to get the children to sleep? However, it's surprising what we get used to and now we feel almost as if we'd not know what to do with the space if we had a house to ourselves.

We're sleeping and living in the Bar! Yes, a proper Club Bar, with a long counter one side and in our cubicle down one side we have the snack bar counter! I never expected to become a permanent inhabitant of a place like that[189]. Not a patch on the bedrooms we shared upstairs before, but anyway Ronald is with us now which makes up for a lot.

We have running water near by but toilets are a short distance, and I have to walk past all the main public places, main entrance, and Commandants' offices to get there. We're lucky in having a double door on to a little lawn where the children can play and where we hang all our washing. We have some tiny cupboards, but trunks are our standby. We've twenty three by eleven feet, and it's fairly convenient.

We had to buy new beds, mattresses, enamel ware, basins, cups, saucers, plates and so on, zinc pail and bath for children. You'd laugh if you saw our junk, but we'll cast off or wear out most of it before we see you I guess. With the toilets so far off, the children and I do our washing in the cubicle, so we have bathroom, bedroom, dining room, all in one – very handy of course.

One of the main snags is mosquitoes. There are thousands in our room every night and they're the greediest imaginable. We're chewed to bits. Even with nets, which fortunately I brought down from Chouts'un, we get chewed. Ronald and I are using Miss Kelsey's net and are jolly thankful we have it.

You'd probably be surprised if you could see our children – they all look so well now. Catherine is especially bonny, so fat and podgy and full of energy all day long. Her hair has taken to curling, little fluffy curls all over her head, quite smart and the envy of many who spend hours making their hair curl!

---

[189] Ronald and Gwyneth were lifelong teetotallers, as were both their parents.

I think I'll give you a rough programme for one day. Each day is slightly different from the others, but there's very little to remind us what day it is and the time flies for those of us who are busy.

We usually get up soon after 7.00. It's not much good being up earlier because we only disturb others if we get up before that, and anyway lately Ronald has been so late at night that we've slept late. I get up and tidy around and get the children dressed and then at 7.45 go down to queue for breakfast. I have to take the tray and plates and mugs, so it's heavy to hold while I wait.

We have a plate of cracked wheat porridge each and a cup of tea, and at brekker we collect a loaf of bread each, our day's ration. They're small loaves and the five we get just does us comfortably. The children get eggs each day, but we pay for them ourselves. We are also able to buy good fresh milk so far, better than any we've had since we came to China and the children love it. I do hope we can continue to buy it, that depends largely on funds. The children usually come in the breakfast queue with me and carry back the bread for me, otherwise I need to make two journeys. Then we feed and I make the beds and do the washing up. We have taps in the bar, so we can wash our dishes nearby, luckier than most folk.

At 9 a.m. there is roll-call. Everyone attended originally, but now only those over twelve. We line up and are counted, that's all. Then I get the children ready for lessons if there are any, but now they're stopped as there is no room for them to meet in.

Every day I wash. That takes till about 10.30, with sweeping and dusting as well. Then I give the children a drink and Ronald one too if I can catch him. Catherine is with me most of the time or running in and out of other children's cubicles. Rosemary and Audrey were both attending lessons, but at present I have to keep an eye on them all, all the time, to see they don't get into mischief or trouble.

We've so far been able to buy oddments like honey and peanut butter in the canteen. That means queuing for about half an hour. Then that's the morning almost gone, what with a few other odd jobs. At midday I queue for our milk and then go back and get the tray and queue for children's tiffin. As soon as they're through I rush off and queue for our own meal and then we eat that and clear away and wash up.

At 1.45 we queue again for boiling water. We can only drink boiled water, and queue for thermos filling twice daily. 2.00 - 3.00 is supposed to be quiet. I usually spend the time trying to keep the children quiet – they sit on their beds and play with bricks, chessmen, books and so on.

At 3.00, I start to tidy up ready for tea and then dash off to queue again for tea. We get a ladle each. We have our brown bread for tea, with whatever spread we have. Sometimes for economy I keep one egg from the morning and mix it with a little lard or tomato paste for the sandwiches. Other days it's peanut butter or jam. Fortunately I've always liked bread and as long as I've 'spread' for it, don't mind how much I have. After tea and clearing up, I sweep the room again and get ready for the children's bath, take in my washing, put it away and do other odd jobs.

Then if I'm lucky I get half an hour out in the garden with the children. I bath them at 5.15. Recently the carpenters have altered the old sink in the bar and made it possible for a children's bath. It's most convenient for us and we have heaps of hot water. At 5.30 I queue again for our second lot of milk, and then dash back and queue up again for the children's supper, though lately Miss Thomas has done this for me, as Catherine and Audrey were making the most of my absence and running off and getting lost!

I forgot to say that tiffin is usually beef stew, rice and tea. And supper beef stew, rice and tea, with cabbage, cucumber, beetroot and one or two other vegetables occasionally, beans most often. Occasionally we have a pudding or roast peanuts.

As soon as Catherine finishes supper I pop her into bed and she goes to sleep almost at once. Rosemary goes into the garden to play and Audrey plays on her bed in her own funny little way. She loves to play with tiny things by herself and gets completely lost in a world of her own.

I then go off again to queue for our supper and Ronald and I take it onto our little lawn if the weather is good – it's lovely there in the evening. After supper and washing up, I put down all our mosquito nets and kill off any who look particularly unpleasant. In the morning the little creatures are fat and bursting, it's disgusting.

For washing, washing up, toilets, every single thing we queue and it takes so much of our time. Every morning there's a queue outside the Doctor's office. We spend so much time waiting in queues and as we're usually holding heavy trays, we can't knit or read conveniently.

It doesn't sound as though I do much with my day, but I seem to be busy and on my feet all the time until about 8.30 p.m. and then there's mending and I'm usually so tired and sleepy I can't keep awake to do much. We have a lamp in our cubicle, but it's too dark for working and, anyway, it's hard on the children if we are in while they try to sleep.

There are now three hundred and sixty odd people here and the most that can be housed conveniently is two hundred and fifty, so you can imagine the fun. There's no public room at all, but while the weather's fine we can sit out of doors. The kitchen is much too small to provide meals for such a crowd, so that cooking is a problem. There were thirty seven of us originally, then others were added in May and June. Every available space, suitable or unsuitable, is used for billets.

It's August 5th now and whooping cough is our worry – there's been a terrific lot. Fortunately a mild form, but it means six weeks in Isolation Hospital and last week Catherine and Ian Scott both started coughing so Carrie and I had to go off with them. We were lucky to be able to go with them. Ronald informed the Japanese Commandants Association and he phoned the hospital and eventually, on being promised beds, he rang for pedicabs and we got ready. The two infants played at making mud chocolate potatoes until the cabs were ordered and then, while I changed my frock and put on my armband, Ronald bathed and dressed 'Clack' as she calls herself. It was awful to let her go. Carrie and I both wore dark glasses (fortunately it ***was*** a sunny day) - we felt they would hide a lot! Ian and Catherine were quite perky and very interested in going outside camp again.

The isolation hospital is for foreigners and was British and American. It's now run by the Japanese, but it's got German, Russian, Chinese and J nurses. It's a lovely modern place, spotlessly clean and airy and food is good. Anyway better than here, so we know Catherine will be all right, especially as she has it so mildly. She just cried a spot when I came away, but she was very bright till then. There have been others from here and those who've returned all look well cared for. Poor Carrie now has Seana, Tom and Ian there! She took Tom on Tuesday and her family are all in one room and to our joy she saw 'Clack'. She's in with Morag Campbell, a lovely child of five and a half who lives in the next but one cubicle to us, and with Betty Roggers, another friend of hers who also lives in the 'Bar'. Carrie said she looked well and was overjoyed at seeing someone she knew. I'm thankful she is with Morag because she's very fond of her.

Now of course I'm wondering about Audrey. Rosemary has a cough, but as she's had whooping cough we don't think it can be that. Hope not – I can't bear to lose them all for so long. Just now Catherine's the liveliest of our trio. She's developing into a very vivacious, determined young madam and it's terrible without her. We get a weekly report that's all. We seem so cut off and we miss her terribly, though I'm trying to console myself by thinking it's a chance to go through trunks and do jobs I find almost impossible with her around.

Folk in dormitories are worse off but of course they've no children. All families but about two are in cubicles in this camp. We'd have had a room in most of the other camps. However, we're quite content and happy (not content in one way, but content with our lot while we must be in camp). Ronald thinks it's worse than prison, because in prison you know you're 'in' for so many months or years and here we have no idea. Some people think months, others a year, others five years and so on to a hundred years! From the paper we get, it looks as though the Axis have just about won.

After we'd been here about two and a half weeks Carrie and I both suddenly got sick, sort of flu, and we were up in the sick room together. I hadn't been ill for ages, not since my abscesses. I think normally I wouldn't have knocked up so easily but I'd really worked too hard for several months. It's really quite a strain just living in these conditions. Everyone feels it.

We have a Japanese Commandant and his assistants and three or four Japanese Consular Police – they are quite pleasant[190]. The Police Sergeant was seven years in Changtien (next railway station to Chouts'un!) and knows of Foster Hospital. We see very little of all these, one or two come out and count us at roll-call, but otherwise we're quite free (in bounds).

Our English Commandant is Mr Hutchinson, a Hongkong and Shanghai Bank man from Hankow who was with us all the winter, and his assistant is Mr Newcombe, a BAT man from Hankow who has also been here all the time. Ronald is medical officer with three other doctors, Jim Scott is kitchen manager, Miss Thomas heads the Women's Labour and Su is teaching, so all our people are busy.

Mothers with children of three and under are exempt from camp fatigues but all others have to do their share. It is all arranged by the British. Those who are A1 are mostly in the kitchen, men and women. They do squad duty three or four hours per day. The less fit women do light kitchen helping or else clean toilets, tables etc. The men not on regular kitchen duty all have to do one kitchen fatigue a week. Ronald usually does his 1.00 - 4.30 p.m. on Wednesday or Sunday. Everything

[190] All the Shanghai internment camps, with the exception of Haiphong Road, were staffed by Consular Police. Haiphong Road, which accommodated only men, was staffed by the Gendarmerie, the Japanese military police, and conditions there were much harder than in the other Shanghai camps.

has to be done by ourselves, so we're glad some of the men understand plumbing, electricity and other complicated things.

Lights out is at 10.30, but that refers only to big lights, small lamps in cubicles are allowed later. We all brought in a certain amount of cash, but that has now been taken and put in a Japanese Bank. We have all our purchases of milk, eggs and canteen goods taken off on the office books. We ourselves handle no cash at all. For some time we had no money coming in and had to be very careful. The goods we brought in were getting low but lately 'comfort money' has been sent by the Swiss Consulate and we're allowed to purchase $400 worth of canteen goods per head per month. It sounds a lot but the dollar was $15 to £1 when we came to China and now it's said to be $700! Anyway, that's the cash problem settled.

Our mission decided before camp to order parcels each month. Every 'inmate' is allowed one per month of standard size, so we paid for one for each of our family for six months. They started coming yesterday. It was marvellous to get five all at once and, even though we ourselves had paid for them, it was quite exciting. They contain all the things we need except soap, raisins and fresh fruit. The parcels come in through the Red Cross. A lot of people being Shanghai residents normally have neutral friends to supply their parcels.

Then in addition to parcels we had five Red Cross letters! Great excitement - one from Cambridge written in January, and two from Ilkley (December 42 and February 43), and one from Pan who is still living in Shanghai. (Certain aged people are exempt from camp and living in a 'missionary home'. Mr and Mrs Payne are the only two in our mission.)

Also one from Enid Phillips. We hear now that she has gone to hospital with a crushed foot. Since they came here a year ago, Edward broke his wrist and attended hospital, Rosemary broke her forearm, the two boys were in isolation hospital with chicken pox and now Enid has this bad foot. We were very disappointed at not getting to the same camp. They are at Lunghwa, just about five miles out. There are nearly two thousand people there, including a lot of our friends.

John and Georgie Lewis went to a Shanghai Municipal Council camp[191], he as MO. The Blooms went to the other SMC camp[192], both in central Shanghai. Alice, Jags and Mrs Smith are at Yangchow, a day's

---

[191] Ash Camp. See footnote 188

[192] 404 Yu Yuen Road, formerly the Western District Public School and the Shanghai Public School for Girls.

trip up the river. Tom Allen, Fred Drake and Eric Sutton Smith are at Pootung[193]. We hear through Pan that all are well.

In addition to the letter to her parents, Gwyneth kept a diary during internment in which she recorded the day to day details of life in the camp. From this it is clear that the light tone she adopts in her letter conceals much of the hardship they were experiencing. As well as all the petty irritations of living at such close quarters, and the anxiety the internees must have felt about the future, there were other trials and discomforts. Mosquitoes and rats were a problem from the beginning. There are many entries on the lines of 'mosquitoes very bad', 'Catherine crying with mosquito bites at night', 'still having bad nights, babies, teeth, mosquitoes, rats and mice'. On 5th May 1943, she writes of 'three fat rats on shelf over bed', and the following day contains the indignant entry, 'Watch baby rat chase up and down shelf while we have nineses[194].' It became increasingly difficult to protect themselves and their food against these pests.

The arrival of two hundred extra people at the end of June put additional pressure on the available space. 'Absolute chaos,' wrote Gwyneth, 'Quite impossible to feed or house, or provide toilet facilities. At least 80 without billets. People getting very fed up. Luggage everywhere. Queues very long and hard – one faint at night. Tiffin so late that we had no afternoon.' Eventually accommodation of sorts was found for everyone, but it wasn't just sleeping space that was under pressure. Although, unlike some other camps (and unlike Chouts'un), the Columbia Country Club had running water, eleven flush toilets were hardly adequate for the use of 360 people! Every visit to the toilets or washing facilities entailed queueing, and any time spent there was always in the knowledge that there was a queue waiting outside.

The new arrivals had brought whooping cough into the camp. Ronald, as Medical Officer, pressed the Commandant almost daily for eight weeks to be given a supply of whooping cough vaccine. This was eventually obtained after a report had been made public about the death of a six month old child in Chapei camp. In an effort to prevent a large scale epidemic, a serious attempt was made at first to isolate those who were infected, Catherine, aged only two and a half, and Ian Scott being

[193] Pootung Camp, originally for men only, was located across the Whangpoo River, in buildings once used for storage by the British American Tobacco Company.
[194] The evening equivalent of the morning 'elevenses'.

amongst them. 'Feeling very queer with only two children around and at night kept listening for the cot', wrote Gwyneth in her diary, 'I wonder so much how little Clack is', 'Clack gone two weeks! What a long time it seems. I do wish I could see her.'

Although Gwyneth refers in her letter to the 'cash problem' having been 'settled', access to money continued to be an issue. 'Comfort money' was effectively a loan to internees from the British Government, for which internees' employing organisations in the UK were required to act as guarantors. It was then made available to those in the camps by negotiation between the Swiss Government and the Japanese. Comfort money was subject to the vagaries of the financial market and liable to be stopped altogether at times when the Swiss and Japanese were not able to agree an exchange rate. On another occasion it was stopped because of a dispute about who should pay the hospital fees of the seriously ill who were sent out of camp for treatment.

Between internees, the medium of exchange was generally cigarettes – two packets of cigarettes, for instance, for a pound of sugar, a packet of raisins or a jar of peanut butter. Non-smokers were at an advantage when the occasional parcels from the Red Cross gave them a supply of this valuable currency. But without access to cash funds, it was impossible to purchase goods from the canteen, a facility run on a commercial basis by contract with Chinese traders from outside the camp. As well as being a vital source of supplementary food items, internees were entirely dependent on the canteen for soap, toilet paper and peanut oil (for cooking and for lighting when the electricity failed), none of which the Japanese supplied. Stocks in the canteen varied according to what was obtainable in Shanghai at any one time.

Payment for hospital treatment outside camp remained a matter of anxiety and dispute. Henry Payne, the one member of the BMS exempted from internment on account of his age, often found himself called on in such circumstances. He went to great lengths, at considerable cost to himself, to help whenever he could but the options became more and more constrained as the war went on. On one occasion he appeals on behalf of one of the internees to a Baptist colleague working in Free China, 'The authorities here anxious for us to pay the hospital bill, which will be approx. $10,000. We wonder whether you have any ideas how it could be done?'[195]

---

[195] Rev H Payne, Imperial War Museum 89/9/1

10th August 1943

A year by date since we left Tsinan! What a year! And now the Americans we left behind are down in Shanghai expecting repatriation any day. Only about twenty sick British are to go, so we have no hope at all.

Actually in some ways I don't mind as much now as I did last year. I'm much happier now than I was in the old Club days. Although we've only cubicles and can't go out at all and can only buy canteen goods, yet we have a place of our own. The cubicle is ours to do what we like in and I like having a place that can be 'home', though Ronald thinks it's a pig-stye! It's very difficult to keep tidy with three small children of our own playing in it, and others running in and out as they like.

We have very congenial company which makes a tremendous difference in these close quarters. On one side of us over the 'snack bar' counter are Mr Hutchison and Mr Newcombe. They are most uncomplaining and agreeable neighbours and though they must be tired of hearing our noise, they never tell us. Mr Newcombe has a wife and two small children in America – he's younger than Ronald. Mr Hutchison is a bachelor.

On the other side of us, going along the east wall of the Bar, are Mr and Mrs Craig, Alison 7½, Margaret 3½, LMS[196] mishes from Hankow, Mr and Mrs Campbell and Morag 5½, Church of Scotland mishes from Ichang and Carrie and Jim Scott, David 11, Seana 9, Tom 6, Ian 3. Then on the south side are Mr and Mrs Roggers, George 13, Betty 4, Shanghai residents - he was in the police and she is Russian. They've been here since April 22nd and fit in well with us now. Then Mrs Baker and David 10 - her husband was on a boat on December 8 and is now a prisoner of war. The middle space in the Bar is occupied half by Mrs Clayton and Margaret (18) of the SPG[197] from Tsinan, Mrs McLeod, Kenneth 3 and Marion 1½ - her husband was also on a boat, but got away to India, so she's stranded on her own.

It's quite a pleasant crowd and we live very peacefully considering all things. Some of the other rooms here have all sorts of rows. The bowling alley, where Ronald slept all the winter, now houses 94 people and there are all sorts of difficulties there.

---

[196] London Missionary Society

[197] Society for the Propagation of the Gospel

20th August 1943

Although this is a camp for British there are all nationalities here, English, Scotch, Welsh and Irish, Australian, South African, Canadian, Americans. All pass as English speaking, but many speak very poor English, others quite well. There are many Russians, some with English husbands in camp here, but a whole lot who were married to English men but haven't seen them for years. There are Chinese, Japanese, Indian, Philippines, Portuguese, French, Swiss, Belgian, Dutch, German, Hungarians, Bulgarians, Rumanians, Poles, Lithuanian, Latvian, Estonian and others, all with British passports. In one or two families there is a Dutch father, Russian mother and English speaking children. Lots of families are separated - women who have children by a Russian husband but have since become British, have to come into camp and leave the children outside.[198]

Ronald saw Catherine the other day. He goes out occasionally on medical business to escort some patient to hospital or fetch one back here and when he was at the isolation hospital he went to see Catherine. He said she was thinner and when she saw him she burst into tears and said 'where is my Mummy?' and when Ronald gave her some sweets she gave them back and said 'Give them to my Mummy'! We're hoping to get her home at the end of five weeks as there is a slackening of regulations. Several children have got impetigo in hospital which is a considerable snag, but we can't help it. It's horrid without her.

The latest cases have been kept in camp as the epidemic seemed to have got out of hand and Rosemary has got it again. She had whooping cough two years ago, but I think this attack must be due to her 'run down' condition. She has been poorly off and on for a few weeks and has had nasty styes. She hasn't a very bad cough, no vomiting, but it's distressing for her, and I feel sorry that other people in the room have to listen to it. Audrey so far seems as well as ever, so maybe she will escape.

The place is so crowded that the only public space is a rough wooden verandah around the swimming pool. We have our 'Church' there, also school, lectures, dances and other social activities. The space is so small that the children can only go to school on alternate days, but Audrey attends a kindergarten on fine days in the garden. We're lucky to have such a pleasant garden.

---

[198] Where a British man was married to a Chinese woman, he and any children over 13 years were interned, but his wife was not, unless she herself held a British passport. The family could decide themselves if younger children should be interned.

You'll perhaps think I've forgotten to mention Ronald. Well, I hardly ever see him for more than two minutes. He's on the go all day long and often till late at night and then gets called up too. He is medical officer, Dr Duck a former SMC public health officer is in charge of camp public health. Dr Chapman a Methodist doctor from Hankow and Dr Thomas an American from Ningpo do clinics and other jobs. They are all four pretty busy. The majority of people in the camp were sent here on health grounds and so there's plenty of work for the doctors and some of it is strange work. Ronald usually comes late for meals and is often called away or has someone calling to speak to him two or three times during a meal. Special diets, permission to be excused work, billeting and all sorts of problems like that take up a lot of time. Ronald has certainly had some varied experiences and unusual jobs in the last eight years. How he keeps so patient I can't imagine – some of the women are really the limit!

He gets no time at all to see or play with the children and it's rather amusing when some women make a fuss because their husbands have to do three hour shifts for two days and have the third day free. They say they simply cannot manage, but they are mostly women without children or with only one. I don't know how they think I manage with Ronald away all day and three children to look after. Most people think it's awful to have more than one child, that's bad enough, two is terrible, but really for three there's no expression bad enough. Of all the families here, the Scotts head the list with four children, there are three families besides ourselves with three, a few twos, but nearly all just ones.

From Dr Harold Thomas to Ronald's father

c/o American Baptist Foreign Mission Society
New York
19th December 1943

Mrs Thomas and I have just been repatriated to the United States on the Gripsholm from China, and it is one of my first obligations, as well as pleasure, to sit down and tell you of the great privilege I have had in being associated with your son, Ronald, in looking after the health and welfare of the internees of the Columbia Country Club, Shanghai, where my wife and I lived together with Ronald and his family for four months. It has been one of the richest experiences of our lives.

We parted company with Ronald and the camp on the 19 September, and at that time your son and his sweet family were all in the best of health. I am a physician and also a Baptist. I have been located in

Ningpo, a coastal port south of Shanghai, since 1919 where Mrs Thomas and I began our missionary service. From the outbreak of war with Japan we were able to remain in our own home and at our work for most of the time. In May of this year we received an order from the Japanese Military police to go to Shanghai. We were told that the large assembly centres in Shanghai, the Lunghwa and Chapei camps, were now filled to capacity and that we would be sent to a newly created 'Assembly Centre' at the Columbia Country Club.

When the fifteen of us arrived at the Country Club we were graciously received, after we had passed the guards, by Miss Smurthwaite of your mission, and we were relieved to know that the living conditions were quite tolerable, and that a very congenial group of a hundred and fifty Britishers were in residence. We learned that the internal operation of the camp was carried on by a Camp Representative who had been appointed by the British Residents' Association, and who had the assistance of a medical officer, your son Ronald, who also had been appointed by the BRA, and a committee of seven, elected by the internees.

The Japanese Commandant, Veda, was a very eccentric youngster. He had come to the CCC a few weeks previous to our arrival. He had had a bad record in two other camps and had been shifted here and there by the Japanese Consulate of Shanghai, who have the direct supervision of these internment camps for civilians. It would seem that this Veda must have been related to some influential family in Japan, and that he held his position through political pull. Apparently the Consulate had little power to control or desire to discipline him. When he arrived at the CCC it was his desire to make a large Assembly Centre there and he had requested, over the protests of the General Committee, that two hundred more internees be transferred to this centre. And some two weeks after our arrival at Shanghai that is what took place. Within forty eight hours our census jumped from 140 to 367. General pandemonium ensued. The buildings could easily handle 200 – 240, but with 340 odd there was dormitory space only.

In addition to medical duties I was asked to serve on the Billetting Committee and we were much put to it to maintain any morale with some twenty five folks without billets forced to sleep on cots in corridors and out on verandahs. The new groups coming in from other camps, Lunghwa and Chapei, because Japanese had recommended that this camp would be made a sort of sanatorium where special diets could be obtained, became disgruntled because they found conditions no better than the places they had left and demanded that a new General

Committee be elected. After considerable electioneering, attended by many amusing incidents, which really helped to relieve the tension, practically all of the old committee were re-elected.

The young Japanese Commandant, Veda, did not last very long. The problems of the camp, all of which he had brought upon himself, finally swamped him. The Committee faced with an impossible situation had sent a letter of protest to the Jap consulate, requesting that the Swiss Consulate be informed of the unsatisfactory state of affairs and suggesting that the Swiss conduct an inspection. This letter we found out later was held at the Consulate and was not delivered to the Swiss. A copy of the letter found its way somehow, no-one knows, out to the Swiss and they called the Consulate and asked for inspection of the camp. This was carried out, and it resulted in the final removal of Veda.

One evening we were called out on to the wide Piazza across the Main Building, and there Mr Sano, the new Commandant was introduced. It was a very thrilling moment when this gentleman, perhaps fifty five to sixty years, rather frail of physique, stepped forward and quietly informed us that he had been asked to come and live with us; that he had heard we had been having a difficult time; that he knew nothing about the operation of an Assembly Centre; that he would be glad to do his best to make life as easy as possible. His modest and humble manner were in such contrast to the other bombastic upstart that he won the admiration of all at once, and he was greeted with loud applause and cheering. In the weeks that followed I got to know Mr Sano very well. We had several cases of discipline of internees that arose and taxed the Committee's patience and were a sore grievance to Mr Sano. We came through these difficult times with increased respect for Mr Sano, and as I look back on the camp I can only hope and pray that Mr Sano is still there to guide and direct relationships. I am sure that he will do his level best to secure the maximum comfort for those under his care.

Just two instances to further illustrate his kindly interest. About the 15th September we received word that we were to be repatriated. The orders said that we might take two hundred pounds luggage per person, that we might dispose as we wished of other possessions, but beds (we had been allowed to bring our own) must be turned in to the Japanese army authority. Our next door neighbours, separated by a sheet or curtain, Mr and Mrs Moir, had come into camp from Amoy, where they had been interned from the beginning of the war. They brought no beds with them, and had constructed out of materials found at the Club, crude cots with wood and lathes in lieu of springs. We had promised them that they should have our beds if ever we were repatriated before them. This order from the Japs was disturbing. I took the matter to Mr Sano and explained the condition of the Moirs' beds. A number of other Japs were standing around the room. He said he was sorry that he could not change the order respecting the disposal of the beds, and then, dropping his voice, he said, 'You can put your name on the Moirs' beds, can't you?' This we did, and turned them in, and it's a comfort on these cold nights to think of them with snug warm mattresses beneath themselves.

The last morning all the camp turned out for our last breakfast. Fifteen of us were leaving, nine Americans, five Canadians and one British. Mr Sano appeared at the close of our meal and made a brief speech - told us he appreciated our contribution to the life of the camp, was happy with us because we were going home, knew what it was to be confined to camp (he had been in Consular service in USA at beginning of war, and was repatriated), knew what it was to be looking towards homeland, said he would be thinking of us and that until he heard of our safe arrival in New York he would be daily remembering us in his prayers for our safety.[199]

As to Ronald's work, he is medical officer of the camp and has by his breadth of outlook and reasonableness won a position of honour and respect among the internees, and the Japanese in charge of the camp, and the officials at the Consulate. Great responsibility has been carried by him in keeping in touch with the internees who are in hospital in the city. Through the summer months these averaged about twenty five. As there were some eighty individuals in the camp, definitely invalids, and as many others semi-invalids, there was always a great movement to and from the hospitals. The correspondence involved in arranging for the care these people should receive was considerable, and formed a major part of Ronald's responsibilities. The records of all medical cases he also maintained, keeping them up to date most meticulously.

Ronald is keeping up his chess. When not pursuing the ailments of some patient, or rushing round to get someone off to hospital, he'll be seen with a chessboard and men tracking down some victim. In the tournament run throughout the summer, he led the field by a wide margin! Very likely I have omitted things about Ronald that you would like to know. Both Mrs Thomas and I were very much in love with him

---

[199] One ex-internee remembers a conversation about Mr Sano which took place between a mother and child towards the end of the war, when the Americans had started bombing Shanghai. "Mummy, will the Americans fight the Japanese in Shanghai?" "Quite possibly." "Will our guards have to fight?" "I don't think so." "Well, if the Americans fight against our sergeant, then *I'm* on the side of the Japanese." *Unpublished memoir by Doris Bates.*

– so kind, so sympathetic, so appreciative and yet a veritable rock when standing to maintain some principle!

When our bus arrived to take us to the ship, he entered it with me, a big roomy one for our fifteen, and insisted on sitting there till he was ordered out when the bus started. As he left I expressed to him the hope that some day our American and English Baptist Mission work might be pooled and that we might perhaps find ourselves working together in some institution. And so we parted and it will be a very beautiful day when we have the privilege of meeting again!

The letter from Dr Thomas brought Ronald's parents the first real news they had had of him since August 1942. It was eagerly copied for the benefit of Gwyneth's family, and excerpts were passed on to the families of other missionaries still in Shanghai.

The Red Cross arranged for brief messages ('not over 25 words, family news of strictly personal character') to be conveyed to and from prisoners of war and their families. Ronald and Gwyneth and their parents took advantage of this facility whenever it was available, though information exchanged in this way was painfully out of date when it arrived. Ronald's reply to a message his father wrote at the end of December 1942 did not reach Ilkley until March 1944. The mixture of anxiety and hope experienced by those at home in the face of these long silences comes across in the carefully pruned phrases. 'My dears, no message comes from you' wrote May on April 12th 1943, 'Still looking for your return. Olive spent Christmas in Brazil. Audrey back at University College Hospital. Love from all, Mother.' Another message from her, written January 1944, squeezed the maximum out of her twenty five words, 'Good news of Geoffrey Smart. Ernest engaged. Neville not heard of. Our love to all. Hope meet this year. Welcome news via Wilfrid. Mother. Philippians IV.7'[200]

Censorship of the messages was strict and this in itself contributed to the time it took for the letters to get to their destination: there was a shortage of people to undertake the task of censoring. Simple references made by the children to the number of people sharing their room in the camp were blacked out or cut from the letter forms.

The missionary internees were anxious too for news of the Chinese friends and colleagues they had left behind in Shantung. Pastor

[200] 'The peace of God, which passes all understanding, shall keep your hearts and minds through Christ Jesus.' Letter of Paul to the Philippians, chapter IV verse 7

Chang Szu-Ching, superintendent of the Baptist churches in the province, managed to pass some information by roundabout routes to Henry Payne in Shanghai. The hardship and suffering which the Chinese had endured during the early years of the war with Japan had, if anything, intensified. Guerrilla bands continued to strike out against the occupying forces whenever they could, and their efforts were invariably followed by severe reprisals by the Japanese against local villagers. At the same time, both the occupiers and the guerrillas exacted exorbitant taxes from the local people and commandeered crops and livestock at will. Driven by hunger, an almost continuous exodus of refugees trekked on foot to the unoccupied West.

The news from Pastor Chang was relayed by Mr. Payne to missionary headquarters in London, 'The Chinese pastors have shown a magnificent spirit. In most cases they have elected to stay with their people with no hope of any financial reward. They are fortunate if they receive a little grain to carry home to their wives and children.... Many of them work in the fighting district, and have seen their chapels as well as the homes of many of their congregation burnt down. Three of our pastors have thus lost all they possess.... The pastors have sometimes been afraid to visit people lest it puts too great a strain on the latter who are so hospitable, and yet ashamed to offer nothing but chaff and leaves for food.'[201] *Despite the difficulties, Mr Payne reported that work was being maintained in the schools in Chouts'un and in Pei Chen, enrolments in the latter having increased from under five hundred in 1943 to almost seven hundred by the summer of 1944.*

Also through Henry Payne, Ronald and Gwyneth learned that Connie Allen, en route for Canada by sea, had been trapped in Manila when Japan declared war on the Allies in December 1941. Tom, interned in the Shanghai camp in Pootung, was desperate for up-to-date information about her and the three children.

Gwyneth – Continuation of letter intended for Cambridge and Ilkley but never posted

30th July 1944

Nearly a year since I wrote and we're still living in the same old bar! Isn't it awful? I'm thankful to say we're all well, we've had minor upsets, I had two weeks in the sick room in October with a tummy upset

[201] Rev H Payne, Imperial War Museum 89/9/1

and in February the children had sort of flu colds which kept them in bed a few days. Then in April they all had German measles, fairly mildly fortunately. Since then they've been all right, but Ronald had gastric flu last month and is taking time to pick up. He's so overworked and the heat has been pretty terrific for five or six weeks now. We all feel limp, but I prefer it to the cold. The Medical Department seems to keep busy all the time and Ronald is much thinner and looks so tired all the time. However, we hope that it won't last many more months. Though we keep on hoping that! The days fly by, which is a great blessing.

The winter was rather hard, we had no heating and although it wasn't a particularly cold year, it was bad enough and I suffered a good deal with chilblains. Towards the end of the season our hot water supply was cut off, except for one day a week and I found doing all the washing in cold water pretty nasty! It's quite pleasant now in the warm weather.

I can't go into details of all the events that have taken place, the alarms, rumours, and excitements, but we've had small pleasures, such as birthday parties and so on. In November our comfort money was stopped and we relied on our parcels completely for all extras. The worst blow was the stopping of fresh milk and eggs, but we've kept going and the children have all gained some weight during the year.

We've had lucky days, when the Red Cross sent donated stores, when we each had an American parcel, containing almost forgotten things like butter, cheese, raisins, coffee, pork loaf. We personally have never been reduced to eating dry bread, but many have. We've been careful all along, and in the early days when we had comfort money and parcels, we never ate all we had, but tried to build up a reserve, and this has kept us going all the winter. A couple of months ago when we were getting desperate for milk, our 'frozen' cash was 'un-frozen' and we have had a pint of milk a day which is a help. If children are getting a normal diet milk isn't such a necessity maybe, but here it's very important.

This is a day's menu, and every day is alike.

Brekker cracked wheat, black tea
Tiffin vegetable soup, rice, black tea
Supper stew, rice, black tea

The cracked wheat is so heaving[202] that we don't eat much now, the soup is usually very unappetising, the rice isn't white, and has lots of husks and stones in it. The stew usually contains about two square inches of meat too tough to eat, if we're lucky half a potato, a little cabbage or beetroot. We also get one loaf of bread per head. Anything else, we

---

[202] with maggots

have to provide ourselves, and as the canteen has been stopped since comfort money ceased, most people have had a thin time. It's very difficult to make dainty and tempting meals for children who aren't hungry, as ours aren't in this hot weather.

You'll think we think of nothing but food, but it is certainly a very pressing problem and always the topic of the day. We've had no fresh fruit for nearly a year now, and although we're most thankful for the prunes which have come in our parcels, I personally feel as if I never want to see a prune again after camp. Luckily the children don't tire of them. In the winter we started cooking on a small chattie[203]. We acquired a frying pan and have cooked a good deal, though much less than most people because we've not a lot of time. Most men with two or three children reckon to give a lot of help to their wives, but Ronald is too busy to do much. He often fries egg flakes for the children for brekker while I do inside jobs but when we had bean milk we used it up in pancakes and made them day after day. They were always different but always enjoyed by the children. We've also made scones and sometimes if we're lucky enough to have eggs, we fry them with bread or rice.

The last week or two a Portuguese girl who cooks in the camp kitchen and gets a 'baking day' once a week offered to bake a cake for us if I liked, so of course I jumped at the offer. It's only full time kitchen workers who have chances to bake, so cakes are rare for most of us. You know how many cakes I have made! However, I didn't tell her I wasn't used to making them and I've now made three very successful ones, much appreciated by the family. The bread has been so poor lately, very soggy and sour, that it's nice to have something different to help fill up the cracks.

The rats are terrible now, there are dozens of them in the Bar and they're as bold as can be. Come out in the daytime and at night they make an awful mess. They chew up clothes and pinch food and knock things down. One developed a craving for peanut butter and night after night *unscrewed* the metal top of our bottle! At last we put peanut butter in a trap and it couldn't resist the temptation. So ended that pest. We can't get rats into traps otherwise, they're much too cunning. A dozen or

[203] camp stove improvised from old biscuit tins, lined with mud. 'Their designs were many and various, and their owners were always willing to argue about their merits or otherwise! Fuel was coke thrown out every morning by the kitchen or boiler house, and the ashes were picked over by a large, enthusiastic crowd, for wet or fine, snow or sunshine, coke was an essential in the winter for a little heat as well as for cooking.' A. Barrington Light, from *Through Toil and Tribulation*, Carey Press, London, 1947, p99

so died of poison, but our supply of that is finished, so we have to put up with the rats.

Flies and mosquitoes are also a worry and now ants have got into everything, so food never seems safe.

2nd September 1944

The flies are still a worry and, as there have been a good few cases of dysentery and gastric flu in the last few weeks, I keep feeling anxious about the children. Mosquitoes will be bad again soon and then we'll have malaria around I suppose!

When describing our billet I went off the topic and didn't tell you how we have trunks as tables, seats and walls. We are officially given no furniture, but we were luckier in this camp than elsewhere and each have a small 'locker' for food, which keeps rats out but not ants, and Ronald and I each have a wicker chair. The children sit at table on beds or trunks! Also all down one side of the 'Bar' is a long counter and behind it two big sinks. Here sixty or seventy people wash their dishes, clothes, children, and often themselves, so you can imagine the clatter and chatter that goes on in addition to the noise made by children and rats!

About two weeks ago I'd Mummy's February '44 letter, which mentioned receiving a card from us written November '42! We're always so thrilled with letters. I can't think why we've had no more prisoner of war letters, other people seem to get them through.

Two of our guards were changed the other day and one of the departing ones gave our children a cake of soap each. Very decent, wasn't it? Soap now is almost worth its weight in gold. It's so hard to get and so few people have any left.

Prices are terrific. When we came to China a tin of imported jam was 40 cents, now a similar sized tin of local jam is about 200 dollars, if you can buy it, but malt syrup and all sorts of so-called jams are offered in place of real jam. We've one or two tins of a decent Chinese make left, saving for a special occasion.

During the winter, there were Scotch and English country dances every Friday, and we went. That was the only night in the week I felt really warm. Of course we were a bit slow at it, but enjoyed it very much.

Although the air raid sirens have made a terrific row several nights lately, and there have been all sorts of noises off on occasions, Ronald and I sleep right through them!

Recently the Red Cross has sent us donated clothing. Shoes and vests and pants for children were what we asked for and received, and earlier on I got some wool that way too.

2nd February 1945

Being in bed with a septic toe (result of a chilblain) I think I'd better add a few lines to this – it's very scanty now, with lots of gaps, but it's hard to find time to write.

We're all well, except for my chilblains. Ronald has had boils, and was kept in bed about a week just before Christmas by one upon his knee, but otherwise, thank goodness, we're alright.

We've no heating and hot water on Wednesdays only, so it's been pretty cold. The winter has been unusually severe for Shanghai and started at the beginning of December, earlier than usual. However, it's been amazing how everyone has managed. We've worn outdoor clothes most of the time and, except for hands and feet, it's been much better than anyone would have imagined.

Our second Christmas in camp was really marvellous, considering everything and the children certainly enjoyed it, though they don't realise what they missed. Rosemary can remember Chouts'un Christmases but of course the others don't. I had saved a few oddments for presents, so we managed to give them a stocking each.

Christmas began on December 23rd with the school Nativity Play at 8 p.m. Our three were all in it, the first time they'd stayed up for an evening show. Rosemary had a part and did it very well indeed, she doesn't seem at all self-conscious on the stage. Audrey and 'Clack' were in the children's choir and in 'a crowd'. They both looked like little cherubs in their gaily coloured head gear etc., all made of things in hand. The colouring was very effective and the whole play well done. On Christmas Eve the adult choir gave some carols and community singing, Ronald conducted. It was cut short by an alarm and we had to finish the stockings with very much shaded candles!

The children all came to camp church with us in the morning. The Christmas lunch was one and a half hours late, as the gas all went off that morning and the meal had to be cooked on a coal fire made at the last minute. In the afternoon the children had a big party – each child received sweets and an orange and nuts from the Red Cross and a doll from a 'friend'. In the evening there was a dance. The camp meals weren't anything special, nothing like last year, and still we didn't do badly.

Although we've been receiving comfort money now for six months, the canteen service has been very unsatisfactory. The rise in price of everything is so terrific that the money which a few months back would have kept us in milk, eggs and spreads for a month, is now insufficient even for eggs! Our life has been brightened considerably recently by the arrival of more USA Red Cross Comfort parcels – the excitement has been terrific. We received *four* each, net weight for each person 47lbs. We got butter, cheese, raisins, same as before. It's grand to have something nice for the children.

Rosemary seems quite bright at school and enjoys it. She goes off with great enthusiasm every morning and afternoon and usually gets 'stars' every week. Of course I don't know how she'd do in a big school with more competition, but at any rate she's happy and seems to be getting a good grounding. She and a little girl (an orphan, whose father was Dutch-American and mother Russian) are in with three little boys. It's a nice little class and I'm thankful she's enjoying it so much.

Audrey is in a very mixed class. There are eight of them, one boy and seven girls. Su[204] is her teacher, and has a hard job with such a group of little scatter brained monkeys. However, Audrey seems to be learning to read and do small sums, thanks to Su's untiring efforts, so I suppose it's all right. She's very different from Rosemary, doesn't care much about school and can be a real 'clown' and upset all the others if she's in the mood. Although she's a dreamy little creature, she has a real imp of mischief in her, and gets up to all sorts of fun.

---

[204] Su Smurthwaite of Chouts'un

Clack is very hurt if anyone suggests she is not in the big school – always says she's in the big class, which is really in the upper division of the kindergarten. So far she hasn't a lot of patience with study, but revels in games, singing and things practical. She is still retaining her golden hair and rosy cheeks and everyone remarks on her healthy appearance. She's not at all scared of the big boys, and if they go near her garden, she goes for them and uses her fists or a stick. She has none of her Pa's pacifist principles!

Ronald and I have been doing the Scotch and English country dances again this winter, and when Ronald has time he plays chess.

The winter of 1944, the coldest in Shanghai since 1871, was both severe and protracted. The harsh weather combined with worsening conditions in the camp. The food provided by the Japanese was of much poorer quality than it had been earlier in their imprisonment, there was less of it and supplies were unreliable. Conditions in Shanghai itself were deteriorating. Rice, bread and tea stoppages became more and more frequent. By May 1945, after several weeks without rice, internees were told that rice of any kind was unobtainable in Shanghai: any that was available had been bought up by the military. On days when the bread ration was not forthcoming either, and when main meals consisted of a ladleful of poor quality beetroot, onions or spinach, those without stores of their own had a thin time. As one irreverent camp joker put it, 'Long live our iron rations and God save the man without parcels.'

The consequences of the poor diet are evident in the many references to boils, styes, colds, ear and tummy infections which occur in Gwyneth's diary. 'Rosemary coughing badly – two styes on left and one on right eye – very irritable and uncomfy, poor child'; 'Rosemary much better but several small boils on face and leg'; 'Clack's eyes all swollen, boils on forehead and cheek.'; 'Chilblains on feet better today, hands bad – septic thumb'; 'Audrey forehead boil cut'; 'Ronald's boil worse, knee very inflamed and sore – early to bed with fever. Rosemary's stye burst. Evening black out and lights fail. Take off wedding ring because of chilblains.'

On 21st November 1944, internees had identified, with intense excitement, 'eight silver planes' flying in formation above the Shanghai sky. These were the first of the American planes, and their appearance was a welcome indication that the Allies were closing in. During the next eight months frequent air raids and heavy bombing took place day and night, but these raids, frightening and disruptive as they were, gave hope that the end might be near.

At the end of April, all those housed in the CCC were moved to the former Sacred Heart Hospital in the Yangtze Pu district north of the Whangpoo River, where they were joined by the residents of Yu Yuen Road camp. The hospital was situated in the heart of industrial Shanghai, close to the gas works, power station and several military installations. Until hours before the new occupants arrived, it had been occupied by Japanese troops who left it dirty and filled with rubbish. Having been told of the move only the night before, Ronald and Gwyneth were up at 4.30 in the morning to pack and get ready. Ronald laboured all day with the other men loading lorries with the heavy furniture, and cooking and medical equipment.

Gwyneth and the girls, carrying all that they could, joined the crocodile of women and children who travelled, partly on foot and partly by tram, to the new centre. They were escorted by roaring motor cycles, machine guns mounted on their sidecars, and curious crowds of Chinese gathered to watch them as they walked through the Shanghai streets. They arrived to find a rat-infested building, without sanitation, lighting or cooking facilities. As they struggled to find beds for the night from the pile of luggage in the courtyard, rain poured down and a siren heralded one of the heaviest night bombing raids they had experienced thus far.

Gwyneth's diary entries during these latter months of internment are remarkable, not for their accounts of hardship and discomfort but for the picture they convey of everyday pleasures and supportive friendships. In living conditions where every individual's personal habits and idiosyncrasies had a powerful impact on everyone else's happiness, it would have been easy to focus exclusively on the daily trials and irritations. And where a little more food, a little more space meant such a lot, the instinct to concentrate on one's own needs at the expense of the needs of others would have been hard to resist.

Gwyneth records many small acts of kindness. She writes of times when Miss Thomas helped her with the family washing; when Jimmy Scott queued for their meals because Ronald was laid low with a fever. She writes that, when she was unwell herself, 'Kay brought me coffee.' On occasional afternoons, an unmarried friend, Molly, took care of the children allowing Gwyneth to lie down for a rest on Molly's bed in the comparative quiet of the single women's dormitory. She notes that 'Mrs Davis lent us eiderdown', 'Phyllis curled my hair', and that she was able to embark on some baking 'with Effie's help'.

'Elevenses' and 'nineses' were daily social events when adults gathered in one of the family cubicles for conversation or a game of bridge. Special efforts were made to mark anniversaries and the children's birthdays, and food from the precious Red Cross parcels was carefully hoarded for these occasions. On Catherine's birthday in October, Gwyneth wrote with evident pleasure, 'Clack's birthday. Children awake early, all excitement. Clack so happy and grateful all day. Molly cook us brekker and have it with us. Clack to school – with spade.' And, a month later, Rosemary's birthday seemed equally successful, 'Happy day, lots of homemade but welcome gifts. Afternoon thirteen children to tea party – hilarious. Rosemary to watch country dancing with me.'

They marked the passing of 1944 with a Fancy Dress Party on 28th December and a Variety Show on 31st, toasted the Americans on July 4th, and celebrated St Patrick's Day with a soccer match, the English v 'the rest'. Running through everything, one question was never far from everybody's mind, 'when will it be over?' It was a never failing topic of conversation and subject for speculation: bets were placed, tea leaves and palms were read, dreams were interpreted and rumours abounded.

PART FIVE

A NEW ERA
August 1945 – December 1948

Gwyneth to Cambridge

Eastern Area CAC, Shanghai
23rd August 1945

Our dearest dears

It's impossible to start to tell you all I want to say. We still cannot believe the war is over, but we've been told we can write letters home and they will be despatched by air, so we think our captivity must be nearly over. We are still living in 'Camp' but are allowed out. I've not ventured far yet. Shanghai isn't at all an attractive place, at least in my eyes!

We sent a radio last Sunday which we hope you received. We are all well and longing to get home for a holiday and to see you all. We now get BBC news and we hear that there is to be repatriation for all who wish it, so there is hope that we may be with you before so very long – we'll let you know when to expect us. You'll easily recognise us by our clothes, the same old things we wore ten years ago. The children have had infected prickly heat, but it's cleared up and they're looking much better. Audrey is the least robust at present, but I think they'll all pick up when they get a change of air and better food. We haven't been anything like as badly off as many internees here and elsewhere, but the diet has been almost entirely starchy and we pine for fruit, salads etc. There has been almost no variety. Already we are seeing an improvement since the Swiss took us over a week ago. Eggs, tomatoes and cabbage have been sent in.

You'll know we moved camp at the end of April. It was a terrific business. I can't go into details now, but the effort nearly killed us all. And the summer has been very hot, so that we literally have no energy at all and are tired all the time. Of course, the poor food and short rations have taken it out of the strongest. Rosemary is now 51 inches and weighs 58lbs (our scales are probably a bit out). She's not a big type but looks quite bonny and seems happy and full of energy. She loves school. In CCC school, there were only thirty pupils, and she won more stars for good work than anyone. In the one term here, in a school of over two hundred, she came first in her form and is more than a year younger than the average. Audrey is 46 inches, but only weighs 45lbs. She is rather pale and sits around a lot, but she also thinks school 'peachy fun' and came fourth out of twenty odd pupils. She is in Miss Smurthwaite's class. She is *very* like Ronald in appearance, temperament and character I think.

Catherine is 43 inches and 43lbs – she's lost 2lbs recently with a sore tummy. She is the life and soul of every gathering. She loves 'camp', knows everyone and talks to everyone. When she heard the war was over and we were going out of camp, she said, 'Then can we go to another camp?'! She's always saying she'll do *all* Granny's work, she'll stand in all the queues etc.

This last month we've been living in comparative comfort, in a room of our own at last! For eight months I shared a tiny room with a Mrs Russell and her baby and Ronald was in a men's dormitory. Then for two years we had a cubicle for our family in a room with thirty occupants (six men, seven women, seventeen children ages from new born to fifteen years!), then two months sharing a room with the Scotts. It was ghastly. Our cubicle was very narrow and we could only put up four beds. We had to eat, sleep, wash and play in it and it was only six by twenty three feet. The window was above my eye level and the floor so bad that the legs of the beds made fresh holes nearly every night! Now we've a nice room to ourselves and it's such a relief to be on our own.

If we come home soon, I think our summer clothes will see us through. Rosemary is wearing three dresses made from ones I wore on the trip out ten years ago. I don't think there's much I don't know about economy in clothes! Fortunately I have been able to keep their woollies in fairly good condition, and I hope we have enough winter undies for this winter. Their jerseys will need to be 'ripped' and brought up to date. I'm hoping some kind auntie will lend a hand there. This summer has been trying, but last winter I thought I'd never survive. We had no heating, and hot water only one day a week, other days we washed ourselves, our clothes and our dishes in icy cold water.

I hope the food isn't too much limited by war as we're all longing for more variety. We bought one lb. of peaches the first day we were free. Prices are fantastic, we're spending millions of dollars as we used to spend cents! I wonder how prices are at home. I'm always dreaming I'm shopping with Mother and Kay.

We're longing to know about you all. Today we received letters from you and Ilkley of January '45 and from Polly September '44, and you've done wonderfully in telling me news of folk in your Red Cross letters but there's masses more I want to know. Where is Dray now? It's almost four years since we saw a newspaper or heard BBC news. As for fashions, hair-styles etc we're completely pre-war. I still can't realise that this won't have to pass the J. censor, as all letters have done for eight years. I don't know how many letters I'll have time to write, this special mail is only available for another two days and then there'll be a gap until the regular service starts.

I hope the children won't be disappointed, I've painted a rather rosy picture of England, I think! When I was telling them about English fields with buttercups and daisies, and woods with primroses and bluebells, I said 'you'll be able to pick big bunches' and Clack said, 'But will the Japanese let us?' So you can see what her life had been so far! There's no grass here at all, I pine for English scenery.

Please give our love to everyone – Auntie Nellie, Daisy, Carol, Smarts, Pris, Mary Stephen, and all the others. I hope to see them all soon.

Ronald to Ilkley

Eastern Area CAC, Shanghai
25th August 1945

It is such a long time since I wrote a letter of more than twenty five words that I hardly know how to begin a longer letter. The first thing to say is that we have news of you up to January of this year saying that you were all well then, and as that was nearly at the end of the war in Europe we are hoping that you have all come through well. How thankful we are that it is all over! May we never see another war in all our lifetimes!

We too are all well. The children have come through better than we would have expected. We are thankful that they have suffered no constitutional damage, nor, as far as we can judge, any nervous damage either. We are thankful for their sakes that it has not lasted any longer, and we hope we shall soon be able to bring them home to you and start them off in more normal surroundings again.

I think Gwyneth has had the most trying time of us all. The constant worry about the welfare of the children, the complete lack of privacy during three years of cubicle conditions, anxiety about the children's safety during the recent nearby air-raids, and the physical labour of doing all that needs to be done for three young children, often with very little help from me or from anyone, all these have been as heavy a burden as anyone in the camps has had to carry, and I'm sure it would have driven a less well-balanced woman crazy. I think you will find us both looking thinner and older. Gwyneth has lost 15lbs in weight since our move here from CCC at the end of April. But now that we are free, with opportunities for a more varied diet and with the prospects of a sea voyage ahead of us, I hope that we shall all be looking fit and well and strong again by the time we see you, and we hope that will be soon!

We have no definite news of repatriation yet. At the time of writing this the peace has not formally been signed. But we have already had a visit from a 'humanitarian commission' connected with the American forces in Chungking, who assure us that there is a large number of ships near at hand and that our Government's intention is to get people to their homes at the earliest opportunity.

We have not yet been able to move about freely in Shanghai (distance of the various camps from each other and cost of transportation have been the main obstacles), so we have had no general meeting of our mission group as yet, but we have received visits from visitors from the other camps, and yesterday Gwyneth and I went to the camp where John and Georgie Lewis are and had a good time with them. No doubt a general mission meeting will be arranged in due course. I should imagine that the decision taken would be to leave a small group of people in China, in order to enable the Home Board to keep in close touch with developments in the Chinese Church in the reorganisation that is bound to take place, and to arrange for as many as possible of the remainder who are due for furlough to get home as soon as possible.

At the time of writing I don't know whether it will be considered necessary for a doctor to remain with the small group to be left behind. If it is considered necessary, I imagine that I should be the person to be asked to remain, as Bloom does not intend to return here after furlough. But my own view at the moment is that I could spend my time most usefully for the mission by returning home as soon as possible, rubbing up my extremely rusty knowledge of medicine, and fitting myself as soon as possible to get back to China when it has been decided what personnel will be required and what will be the manner of the new cooperation between the Home Board and the newly organised Chinese Church. Of course I shall be willing to abide by the decision of our mission authorities, but I need hardly tell you that my own wish is to come home with Gwyneth and the children as soon as ever it is possible. I understand that the US Commission is promising people that they will be home before Christmas. That will be none too soon for us! The sooner the better!

It isn't possible in this letter to tell you the full story about our last two and a half years in these Camps. That will have to wait until we are together. It is enough that they are over now and that we still have our health. The worst feature of the CCC camp was the overcrowding and the lack of privacy. Cubicle life in those conditions is almost enough to drive a sane man 'nuts'. And if we had had to depend entirely on the Japanese rations for our food we should have been severely undernourished.

Most of my own time has been taken up with camp Medical Officer's work. At the CCC I was Principal camp MO for the whole period April '43 – April '45. It was quite a heavy job. The camp was designed by the Jap authorities as an invalid centre, because we possessed at the CCC certain so-called amenities not possessed by other Centres. So we were landed with a large bunch of 'crooks, cranks and cripples' from the other Centres, who got rid onto us, in addition to their serious invalids, of a large number of persons who were undesirable for other reasons! Altogether the camp MOs have had a tough time in all the Centres. Ill health has been at a premium in camp. It enabled its owner to get more of the privileges and to escape the hardships of the camps, and the MO's job in deciding which of two deserving invalids should have milk, and which should go without, when only a limited supply was available has given him many a headache – and even much abuse!

But it has had its lighter side too. There was time for Russian and German lessons. I can pick my way through a Russian Testament and a Russian story-book now with the aid of a Dictionary and we have had some good chess too. On Thursday this week the Soviet Club is bringing a team to play our Camp team over six boards. I shall be at Board 1 for our team, but I think I shall lose, because I played at Board 2 for the Shanghai International Club against the Soviets before we were locked up and lost then. But we'll have a good game and a good time.

More of all this in the next letter. We're looking forward so much to being with you all. Our very best love to Will and Florence and Reg and Phyllis and your dear selves.

The realisation that the war was indeed over, that they were no longer captive but free, was accompanied by a never-to-be-forgotten sense of euphoria. Everything that happened in the following weeks took on sharper colours: the entry into the camp of the Swiss consul and the British Red Cross unit; the arrival in Shanghai of the American and then the British fleets; the food parcels dropped by parachute; the celebratory parties; the first ventures out into the streets and to the shops; the reunions with friends in other camps.

As well as the general air of jubilation, small comforts immediately became available. Benevolent individuals in Shanghai sent money gifts to enable the internees to buy extra food or pay for transportation. Gwyneth found she was able to employ someone to help with the heavy washing ('Thank goodness for amahs', she wrote in her diary). Chinese traders were quick to set up stalls inside the camp gates, to which Rosemary was sent to buy eggs for the family for breakfast. On their first outings into Shanghai, Ronald and Gwyneth rejoiced in being able to buy small surprise gifts for the children (a tiny purse, a tin brooch, small wooden sailing boats) which they hid under their pillows at night.

Yet the internees quickly realised that there were no wands to be waved. There were enormous logistical problems to be overcome before they could get home and resume the comfortable and independent lives for which they longed. Once the Japanese were relieved of responsibility for them, decisions had to be made as to who was responsible for their well being and how they were to be fed until such time as the camps could be cleared. After the years of drudgery, there was a natural reluctance on the part of many to keep up with the usual camp chores and various groups of workers abandoned their posts or went on strike. In order to keep track of the rapid changes in personnel, it was decided in some camps that anyone who was absent for more than forty eight hours would no longer be provided with camp meals and accommodation.

Some of those for whom Shanghai was home found that their houses were still occupied by the Japanese military or had been too badly damaged during the war for immediate re-entry. Many had lost their jobs as a consequence of the treaty negotiated between the British and Chinese governments in January 1943, which did away with the Shanghai Municipal Council and Shanghai Municipal Police. Those who had businesses in Shanghai set about trying to pick up the pieces, floundering inevitably amidst the general disruption and widespread shortages.

For the War Office, there were questions about who should be granted free passage back to Britain (not all British passport holders had homes or family in Britain) and whether priority should be given to senior ranks, and civilians holding high office, or to the sick and wounded. Means had to be found to bring ships from India, Singapore and Australia, where the British fleet had been based, to transport the thousands of ex PoWs and internees located in Hong Kong, Shanghai and Japan.

After the years of malnutrition, most were struggling with reduced energy levels and poor health. For weeks after the Japanese surrender, Gwyneth suffered from throat and leg infections, from crippling head and stomach pains. 'Feel weak and head very sore... By night quite done in. No sleep, head so sore.... All day feeling half dead....' All this, just when she wanted to be fit enough to enjoy meeting up once again with Tom Allen, the Lewis and Phillips families, and all their other friends who had been interned in other camps. Suddenly it became urgent, too, to shop and sew and prepare for the return home, which might happen at any time, beyond their control.

Gwyneth to Cambridge

Eastern Area CAC, Shanghai
28th September 1945

One of our fellow 'inmates', who leaves here tomorrow for Hong Kong on the Glenearn, has promised to post this on her arrival home. Kay Campbell and I have lived so near to each other in the last three years, that we hate being separated now, but there's a possibility that we may catch her up at Hong Kong. Anyway, the first post-war repatriation boat is due to leave on the 30th – great thrills all round. I'm sorry in some ways not to be on it, but we are assured the next trip will be better and that we can get on it, so here's hoping! We're sick of Shanghai, and are all packed up, except for last minute additions.

We hear we're to be given double rations for our first two months at home, so we should soon put on the weight we've lost. Ronald has just had another bad attack of 'boils' and we've had flu and tonsillitis, but we've both recovered. We're getting quite good food now the Americans are feeding us, but we're heartily sick of queueing for every meal and then eating off chipped enamelware at a funny little table. The children's manners at table are appalling, so don't expect too much. I hope they'll soon learn when they get into a home again.

Can you imagine the thrill we've all had seeing the British fleet sail up the river? It has been good to see the USA marines and airmen but to see the British, after seeing nothing but Japanese military for so long, was indeed an excitement for us! They're all enjoying themselves very much, and seem to have endless reserves of cash. The children all went to a party on HMS Belfast today. She's the flagship here and the sailors rigged up all sorts of swings and seesaws and gave them a grand time.

Maybe I'll be home before this reaches you! Golly, we're all so thrilled. We've felt pretty homesick recently and are just longing to be in England. Lots of people had 'lovely weeps' when they saw the Allied fleets coming in and we began to feel the war was really over. The great burning question is now, 'What shall we wear to land in?' but as none of us has more than one winter coat and some of us none, that item settles itself easily. 'How shall I do my hair?' isn't quite so simple. But at least the children are all straightforward, and Ronald can keep to his 1935 style.

The Campbells are off tomorrow. So are the Scotts, Miss Thomas and Miss Smurthwaite, so we'll feel a bit lonely, but we hope to catch them up before long. Goodbye then for a very little while. Love from every one of us to you all, Goo.[205]

William Lyttle to Ronald

Shanghai
3.10.45

Dear Dr Still

Before you go from amongst us I wish, on behalf of the Representative, the General Committee of Management and the Residents, to tender you our grateful thanks for the devoted service you have rendered to us during the long period of our internment. You have more than maintained the high standards of your noble profession and by your knowledge, skill and patience have made a big contribution to the health and wellbeing of the Camp.

Knowing you as we do, we realise that you do not desire thanks, nevertheless we feel that a task so nobly done, cannot be allowed to pass without an expression, however inadequate, of the appreciation so deeply and widely felt among all our people. You will carry with you the thanks of the people for whom you have laboured so hard and leave behind you the memory of one who gave all, asking for no return.

Wishing you all good fortune in the years yet to be,

William Lyttle
Vice Representative
Eastern Area Civil Assembly Centre

---

[205] 'Goo' was the family's pet name for Gwyneth

Ronald to Ilkley

On board HMHS Empire Clyde, nearing Hong Kong
Friday evening 26th October 1945

Well, we are really and truly on our way home to you, and can hardly believe it is true! We expect to put in at Hong Kong tomorrow morning and will post this by air mail, so it should reach you in time to let you know that your prodigals are on their way back! Gwyneth sent a letter by one of the passengers on the Glenearn, which left about a month ago, telling you that we hoped to be on the next boat, and perhaps the Glenearn passengers will already have arrived and you may have had messages through them.

We were very disappointed not to come with them. We only left Shanghai last Monday, just ten years and one month since we landed in Shanghai. But anyway, now we are really aboard and sailing westwards as fast as we can in your direction, and we're glad, oh so glad, that we're on our way home to you. We're not sure yet whether we're sailing all the way home on the Empire Clyde or whether we're to trans-ship at Hong Kong on to the Oxfordshire. And we don't know which port we shall dock at when we reach home, though we hear that some repatriation boats from the Far East have docked at Southampton. Anyway, look out for us, dears, at one of the British ports, either on the Oxfordshire or the Empire Clyde sometime before Christmas.

We don't know what will be the best arrangement whereby we can see you all as soon as we can. All we know is that we want to see you *all* and be with you all as soon as we can. Lots of things may affect the arrangements that we are able to make – things like your own health and holiday plans, the arrangements we make for the children's schooling and so on – so perhaps we cannot make final plans until after we have arrived in England. But so far as we are able to judge at present, perhaps it will be best if we go first of all to Cambridge, and if we only arrive, as seems likely, a short while before Christmas, to spend Christmas in Cambridge and to travel north to you for the New Year. What do you think, dears? I know that you will long for us to come as soon as ever we can to you, and you know that that is what I want too, but I know that you will unselfishly want Grannie and Grandpa Johnson to see their grandchildren as soon as they can, and we will bring Rosemary and Audrey and Catherine to see you all and their cousins as soon as we can after that. Poor dears! I'm afraid it will be a terrible invasion for you when we do come and you'll be tired of your noisy grandchildren, if not of your noisy children! But I know you'll try to put up with us, as well as to put us up.

Just one thing, we're fairly well supplied with clothes. The Red Cross has done wonders for us and we shall have all the clothes we really need when we arrive, so don't go spending your precious coupons on clothing for us because we have really been well taken care of since we have been released.

Gwyneth to Cambridge

HMHS Oxfordshire
7th November 1945

I cannot realise that we are really on the way at last! I've been looking forward to this so long. We expect to land at Southampton about December 7th. The ship is HMS Oxfordshire, so you can make enquiries maybe. We have no real idea about transport at home now or about anything else but we've been told we'll get to our homes as soon as possible after landing. Of course we'd love to have someone to welcome us at the first possible spot. Maybe Southampton is out of the question in these days, especially with uncertainty of time of docking, but perhaps London. Anyway, if it suits you we hope to come to Cambridge first for Christmas and then go up to Ilkley for the New Year, but we cannot make definite plans till we arrive. We're travelling under the Navy and it's not certain what will happen when we land, but we'll get in touch at the earliest possible moment.

I don't know how you'll be able to cope with five of us. I can assure you we're well accustomed to living at close quarters, five in a room and so on. I'm afraid you'll have a fit when you see our luggage if it gets home intact. Do you think you can possibly find a spot where we can park ten trunks? It sounds awful but it's all our belongings and if possible we'd like to bring them all to Cambridge. We had only twelve hours' notice to pack up at the end so we've had to pack things in a rather unsatisfactory manner and will want to go through everything at the earliest opportunity. Any hope of getting them into No 8[206], shed or house?

Don't worry about us. We're being well fed, fresh fruit at last and plenty of milk and eggs, more than we can cope with. Ronald looks a different man from a month ago, and I'm eating a terrific amount. You'll think we've been doing pretty well when you see Rosemary,

[206] 8 de Freville Avenue, Cambridge.

Audrey and Catherine. We've had issues of clothing from the Australian Red Cross, they've been marvellous, so we are really alright. We're wondering how we'll find you. Reports are so conflicting but I suppose you're still in de Freville. We'll try and send word as soon as we land and will come straight home when able. It's very vague but I know you'll understand.

We're bringing two camp beds and mattresses and as soon as our trunks arrive we've blankets, pillows and everything, but I imagine we may need to depend on hand luggage at first. Anyway, we'll be thankful to be home and if you can manage to fit us in somehow that's all that matters. The children are quite easy and settle down happily in new surroundings. Catherine asks about a dozen times a day 'Is England a boat?' They take all this without turning a hair, climb up to their top berths as if they'd always been used to double decker beds. There are sixty five in our ward so you see we're used to publicity.

I feel so excited about getting home, shall probably weep buckets when I do arrive! Rosemary, Audrey and Catherine are all wearing dresses made out of ones I wore on the trip out in 1935! My winter coat I had then, too, and the two small fry will arrive in their old red coats. Rosemary wears a brown coat I made from my summer coat of 1932 and one of Kay's India dresses of '29 is still going strong with alterations, so you'll recognise us. We have additions too of course, in fact we're quite well clad for these days.

Gwyneth to Cambridge

HMHS Oxfordshire
16th November 1945

We are due in Aden early tomorrow. Yesterday we passed Socotra, near enough to see land clearly and last night we could see the lighthouse on the north east tip of Africa, so we feel we're making progress, though it's a slow trip. We are all doing well in the food line, and the children are fine, but even so, we'll be relieved when we're home. So far the weather has been wonderful. The next few days will be hot and then the cold, which I dread, though I don't think it can be worse than last winter.

We keep getting rumours as to when and where we'll land, but no one seems to know for certain what will happen. We understand that the arrival of repatriation ships is broadcast so you'll probably hear all about it when the time comes. We'll need to wait where we land for ration books and identification cards. I can imagine you shutting the door in our faces if we turn up without such articles!

There are lots of Australian magazines on board and, what spare time I have, I'm devouring every word – we feel so completely cut off. It's four years now since we had regular letters and I'm dying to know so much about everything at home. You'll have to be patient with our ignorance! also with our camp manners! I'm afraid the children are not exactly models, though on the whole they're pretty good. It's grand for them on board, the sun is so hot and yet not too overpowering. They stay on deck from 8.00 - 12.00 and from 1.00 - 6.00, so they have plenty of fresh air. I think we were saved in camp by the sunshine, so few days when the children were kept in by the weather. I'm thinking of putting Catherine on a farm, plenty of hard work and fresh air seems to appeal to her. Ronald is in a ward on C deck and has a port-hole near his bed, so he spends a lot of time down there studying. He's had so little time for it in camp.

They tell us that we're feeding far better than we shall at home. There's plenty of butter, and other things that maybe you don't get at home, but after the food in camp whatever you provide will seem good. Also what we *long* for is to live in a home, not an institution. Always to do everything in public becomes rather trying, and the children get very fed up with never having anywhere to play undisturbed.

What news is there of Polly? Any hope of a complete family reunion? Is Dray free to come home much? And what is Kay doing? I keep wondering about so many people, the Aldens, the Lockharts and lots of Cambridge friends.

We'll have to settle Rosemary in school, and Audrey too, though Rosemary is the more urgent. Audrey by the way is almost toothless at the top. Fortunately you'll see the type of baby tooth we grow as Catherine still has her complete set. Their teeth have all suffered I'm afraid. Rosemary's new ones have already started to decay. It's thanks to Miss Thomas that the kids have enough clothes for the winter, as she has helped a terrific lot, unpicking outgrowns and reknitting. She also helped me with washing on many occasions when I was particularly busy.

I wonder if you ever got any of the Red Cross letters Rosemary wrote you – she couldn't understand why the replies were so long delayed!

Please don't worry about our arrival, or overdo yourselves in preparing. We don't want to cause you any more trouble than is absolutely necessary. Just to be home with you is all we want. We are used to arriving in a bare room and having to settle down and do everything ourselves, putting up beds and so on, so we're not fussy.

It's too late to write to Gibraltar if you've not done so yet, but you could send a line to wherever we dock, if you hear the day before of our expected arrival – just to let us know if you can put us up. Love to all, Goo

PS Is your telephone number still the same?

Kay to Gwyneth

8 de Freville Avenue, Cambridge
Phone 54197
14th November 1945

Dearest Goo, Ronald and little sprats,

Yesterday we had G's letter written in Shanghai and brought home by Kay Campbell. Were we thrilled to see your fist on the familiar blue envelope?! Then this morning we heard from Ilkley that R's airmail letter from Hong Kong had reached them. Like you, we can hardly believe you are really on the way!! We cabled to Hong Kong to the address you sent us, and Mother posted to the ship but the PO is delightfully vague about addresses and so on.

We're glad to know you'll be coming to us first and propose to stay over Christmas.

You'll see I've put on the phone number!

Yesterday we had four Red Cross messages from you, January 45 and February 45, the latter were from the children. We were glad to have them.

Blanco[207] is the only one here who eats off enamel ware! He'll love the children, but he *does* bark, so be prepared!

Tons of love to all from all of us, Kay

Gwyneth to Kay

HMHS Oxfordshire
27th November 1945

Yours of 14th and Mother's of earlier received at Aden and Suez. More than welcome! Glad the idea of an invasion doesn't completely overwhelm you. I had better warn you – the noise of our 'dear sweet little angels' is pretty terrific at times, but I'll do my best to keep them under! They're all thrilled outwardly about Blanco, but secretly I think

[207] Kay's Sealyham dog

they all feel scared stiff. They've had no pleasant contact with dogs or cats yet, so don't be disappointed if Audrey jumps on the nearest table or chair at the sight or sound of him! I'm glad they're to have the opportunity of becoming used to animals.

The trip was very pleasant at first, but is beginning to be a bit tiring now, and the weather has changed from summer to winter in one day. So with no public lounge, we either rush up and down the deck, or sit huddled up in rugs, or else I stay down and repack. At Suez we had a marvellous reception, Band to welcome us, free teas and fruit and clothing for all. RAPWI and NAAFI did us well. (We've no idea what most of these sets of initials stand for and don't like to show our ignorance by asking, so don't be alarmed if we shower questions at you all day long.)

I'm sorry we missed Geoffrey Smart, but thankful he's all right. There are so many families I've no news of. I'm just longing to know if they're safe and sound.

The latest is that we arrive in Liverpool. I'm sorry I've not just the right garments for 'les enfants' (influence of visiting French port Algiers!). I'd hoped for them to be dressed just right, and now they're all 'bits' and 'pieces' and my colour schemes are all wrong. But beggars can't be choosers and I'm thankful to have warm clothes, let alone the children alive and well. One day I hope to go to a really decent shop and buy really nice clothes for the kids – they're nice ones now, but they don't go together.

Only four more days to Liverpool. Gosh, I'm getting thrilled, shall probably weep buckets to celebrate our arrival. I'll rave if they delay us long at Liverpool but I can see no hope of getting our baggage sorted for days, so don't get too optimistic!

The kids are absolutely full of energy. They completely exhaust me, so don't expect anything meek and mild, and their manners at table are *appalling* – please be patient. I'm dying to see what you think of them. Catherine is just like a wild puppy, so she and Blanco should hit it off! Audrey is definitely a clown, and Rosemary very much a little schoolgirl, and very friendly with everyone. They've all small appetites so don't expect much in that line. We've only been in a private house about three times since we left our home three and a half years ago. We shall probably feel lonely at first, after being in a crowd so long.

On December 4th, almost six weeks after leaving Shanghai, the Irish coast came into view and excitement on board was intense. There was a scramble to get on deck as the ship neared land and then, after what seemed an age, eased into the docks at Liverpool. Ronald's brother, Will, was amongst the excited crowd on the quayside and the children strained to get their first glimpse of their uncle. They were able to go ashore that evening with Will, but had to return to spend the night on board.

By early on the morning of December 6th, disembarkation was underway. Ronald and Gwyneth and the children packed into the crowded 10.15 train to Euston, where Dray was waiting. She travelled with them on the last leg of the journey to Cambridge, and the family – John and May, Ronald and Gwyneth, Rosemary, Audrey and Catherine, and their aunts Kay and Dray – sat together for the first time around the kitchen table in de Freville Avenue.

Two days later Ronald travelled to Ilkley to see his parents, but was back in Cambridge for Christmas celebrations with the Johnsons. On the 27th, the whole family headed north by train to spend a few days in Ilkley.

Gwyneth to Cambridge

Cowpasture Road, Ilkley
30th December 1945

I'm sorry I didn't write yesterday but it was really impossible. The train didn't leave till after 12.00 on Thursday and stopped at every station to Kettering. However, we had ten minutes to wait for the London train. When it arrived it looked hopeless, but we managed to push and shove (priority for mishes of course!) and eventually all got in, wedged fast in an upright position, and stayed like that till the next big station, where we pushed a bit harder and got next the luggage rack and lifted Audrey and Catherine up. They sat there acting the fool, singing all funny ditties and making daft remarks which seemed to amuse the surrounding company. (Audrey's umbrella was well to the fore all the time, and I narrowly escaped losing an eye several times!) After about one and a half hours or perhaps more, we got two seats and then at Sheffield we were all sitting.

We were about half an hour late in Leeds, but the Ilkley train was also delayed, so we caught it. It got held up by ?engine trouble at Guiseley and we eventually arrived at 8 p.m. Our luggage was no trouble at all, and we were able to get porters to give it a shove on to trains for us. The children were perfectly happy and cheerful all the way, except during the wait at Guiseley when they did become a little impatient. Mr and Mrs Still and Margaret met us at the station and we were soon up at the house. We had supper at once and got the children into bed by about 9.30. They are all rather tired and irritable still. They've had so many changes and recently met so many new people that it's not surprising.

Yesterday we had brekker at about 9 a.m. and then Ronald and I took the children up to feed the ducks at the Tarn. Will, Florence and Geoffrey arrived about 11.00 and we had a Christmas 'Tub', presents for all. In the afternoon Mr and Mrs Greenwood and their two sisters came and we had games, tea, games, supper. The infants were all madly excited of course, and on the whole behaved fairly well, though I had several anxious moments when I was on the alert to prevent explosions between Audrey and Catherine! I got them all into bed by 8.30 which wasn't bad considering. Tonight it's 8.15 and they are still not asleep. However, I hope they'll settle soon.

This morning we climbed to the Cow and Calf[208] and they were very thrilled. They ran up and down and climbed the rocks and loved it. Rosemary had a grand time with Margaret. She really is very thrilled to be with other children again. She's so very sociable. Afterwards I went with Mrs Still to try to get something with our coupons but the shops were mostly still shut, so we'll try again.

I've not told you how much we appreciated the warmth of our welcome home, and all the preparations you had all made. It was a wonderful homecoming and quite came up to expectations, and exceeded them too. We had thought about it so often. I especially always had it in mind. Whatever happened in camp I was always determined to hang on, so we could get home. I longed so much for the children, too, that they should have an opportunity of becoming acquainted with English home life. I noticed lots of things you had done and planned, even though I didn't comment on half of them. I'm only sorry that you had to work so hard on our behalf, and sorry, too, that you'd been starving so long, also on our behalf!

I shouldn't say there is an absolute *shortage* of food here – shall we say rather *small* rations. So far in two days I've seen on the table two large chickens, a big joint of beef and a turkey, and in the pantry is a roast goose and another fowl awaiting our attentions. Of course there have been cakes, puddings and pies and occasional snacks just to keep us going, and cups of tea in between to keep us from becoming too

[208] Cow and Calf rocks, Ilkley

devastated by hunger.[209] Catherine has managed to have a taste of every dish appearing at any meal!

I see that the 'China get-together' is now developing into a big public 'Welcome' meeting, but it's at 7 p.m. so I shall have to leave after the tea (I can't bear to miss that of course!)

PS Catherine evidently can't cope with two Grannies – she keeps calling Mrs Still 'auntie'.

It was at the 'China get together', held in London on January 15th, that Ronald and Gwyneth met up once again with Tom and Connie Allen, and heard for the first time about Connie's three and a half years in Manila, her imprisonment there with the three children, and their dramatic rescue by the Americans when they liberated the Philippines in February 1945.

After the excitements of the first reunions, Ronald and Gwyneth's priorities were to arrange schooling for the girls and to find somewhere for the family to stay during their furlough in England. Through a friend, they were able to rent a small unfurnished cottage in Little Abington, near Cambridge, and Rosemary, Audrey and Catherine commenced their formal schooling. Ronald applied himself enthusiastically to updating his medical and surgical knowledge, and was kept busy speaking at church meetings all over the country, sharing information about the mission and the Chinese church.

In China, the end of the war with Japan had brought into prominence once again the rift between the Nationalists and the Communists. In the autumn of 1945 skirmishes between the two factions had occurred with increasing frequency on or near the railway from Tsinan to Tsingtao, and by October Shantung was engulfed in fighting on a large scale. By the following July, the struggle for control of the country had developed into all-out civil war.

A small group of Baptist missionaries returned to Chouts'un early in 1946. There they found that the mission property, and particularly the hospital, had been thoroughly looted and was practically in ruins. Fred Drake wrote urgently to the Mission House in London, requesting help with the medical work in Shantung. 'The hospital (in Tsingchou) has reached the point when some assistance is necessary if it

---

[209] The generous amount of food was almost certainly supplemented by gifts from members of Ronald's father's congregation, all anxious to provide a warm welcome to the returning internees.

is to be maintained. It is the only mission hospital in these parts that has survived the war, and that because of the place won for it in the hearts of the people by Dr Ching and his staff ... Dr Ching stated quite truly that he has been strained to the utmost during the past years and earnestly hoped that a colleague could be sent to relieve or release him.'[210]

Cutting short his furlough in response to Dr Ching's call for help, but leaving Gwyneth and the children behind in Little Abington, Ronald set out once again for China. Travelling by sea, he arrived in Hong Kong on December 4th. A small Chinese vessel took him from there to Tsingtao and he made the last part of the journey by train to Chouts'un.

From Ronald's diary

25th December 1946

Arose at 6 a.m. in the Chinese inn at Weihsien. Breakfast of shao-ping and then caught the 7.24 train. Made good speed and were at Tsingchou by 9.30, Changtien by 11.45 and at Chouts'un prompt to time by 12.33.

At the station no-one to meet me, Chou Taifu and others having been there twice the day before and our second wire having been misread as 17.30 and not 12.30. One of the station guards now familiar, and one in the baggage room. Hired two carts and set off on foot for 'home'. Now beginning to snow quite heavily.

Arrived at the hospital gate to find it blocked up and made my way to the newly made gate, west of the original one. Everyone gone to church for the Christmas Day service but by the time the carts were unloaded, our old dear Kao Ta Ko was back and met me with as much apparent joy as I felt in seeing him. Chatted with him over cup of tea, then went round the compound and looked over the property.

Then to Dr Chou's and found him and Mrs Chou with a little daughter, Li-li, just one year old. On the way back saw Kao Yueh-t'an and rickshaw puller Kao, and had pao-tzes with Kao Ta Ko.

---

[210] Letter from F S Drake to C C Chesterman, File CH/16 BMS Archive, Angus Library, Oxford

Ronald to Dr C C Chesterman[211], BMS 92 Gloucester Place, London

c/o English Baptist Mission, Tsinan

14th January 1947

Dear Dr Chesterman

I have delayed writing to you until now, in order to be able to give you some idea of the state of our Mission hospitals in Shantung, and also partly in the hope that I might be able to report some actual progress.

Since I arrived in Chouts'un on Christmas Day I have made visits to Tsingchoufu and Tsinan. At Chouts'un, the foreign nurses' bungalow is now in good shape, having been repaired along with four small rooms at the West end of the Men's Ward in the main hospital building. These rooms can serve as offices, or even as a temporary residence if need be, during repairs to the rest of the property. Electric light has been installed, and the local current is fair.

While passing through Tsingtao I was informed by Dr Han Li-min that the Provincial Health Departments had funds available for the repair of Mission Hospitals. I therefore made an appeal on behalf of the Foster Hospital to the Director of the Shantung Provincial Health Department. He told me that he had $400 million at his disposal for the whole province, of which he had instructions to devote $40 million to Mission hospitals and of this sum he has given us $25 million for the Foster Hospital. Dr Wang, Medical Director of CNRRA[212] for the province, informed me that the Foster Hospital has been recognised by the Government Health Administration, and by CNRRA, as one of the four one hundred bed hospitals in the Province, and this should entitle us to receive a proportionate share in the allocation on CNRRA supplies.

We have obtained recent estimates for the repairs at Chouts'un. The estimated total cost of repairs to the hospital premises, but not including furnishings, light fittings, nor heating apparatus, is about $180 million. We have timber on the compound to the value of $10 million, and I am hoping, on my visit to Tsingtao this week to be able to get a donation of flour from CNRRA to meet the cost of labour. We can therefore see our way to completing the repairs to the outpatient building, with a small balance in hand towards the larger task of repairs to the main hospital building, and these should be completed during April.

---

211 Secretary with responsibility for medical aspects of BMS work at that time.

212 Chinese National Relief and Rehabilitation Administration, an off-shoot of the United Nations Relief and Rehabilitation programme, sourced predominantly with American money.

At Tsingchou, the hospital buildings present a pleasingly whole and complete appearance, as compared with the ruins at Chouts'un, but here too there is much to be done. Inside the hospital there is much need for help. During the war years the situation has become so difficult that standards have been seriously lowered. Stores of linen and equipment, especially enamelled ironware, have dwindled to nothing and urgently need replacement. The buildings, too, while they have not suffered to the same extent as the Chouts'un plant, are now in need of extensive attention. I hope that I may be successful in obtaining some help from CNRRA for this purpose.

At Cheeloo the main and urgent need seems to be for nurses. Staff and equipment are available in sufficient quantity, but work is being held up and wards remain closed because of a lack of nurses. At present only one men's ward and one children's ward are open, the women's and midder blocks being unable to open. The shortage of nurses is general throughout the country, probably because no training of students went on in occupied China during the war. The re-opening of the Nursing School is an urgent immediate need.

The political future of the Province remains doubtful but it is beginning to seem certain that a major armed clash between the government and the Communist forces must occur early this year, and Tsingchou may quite likely be near the centre of the battlefield. This situation, and the high cost to the mission of maintaining work in China in present conditions, makes the decision as to how far and how rapidly we should rush the work of reconstruction and rehabilitation a difficult and serious one. At the same time, there is a great need for experienced missionaries in all departments of the work which is felt and very generally expressed by Chinese colleagues.

I shall be glad if you will let me know the amount of the financial allocations for 1947 for the Chouts'un and Tsingchou Hospitals as soon as possible, and I know that I need not urge you to make them as generous as possible. In the meantime I shall do my best to secure what help we can get from the various relief organisations in Tsingtao and Shanghai.

I am proceeding back to Shanghai via Weihsien and Tsingtao tomorrow and shall get back to Shantung as soon as possible, returning probably about February 10th.

Ronald's prediction of an imminent clash between Nationalist and Communist armies proved correct. During the early months of 1947 a major campaign was fought out in central Shantung, culminating in mid May in the overwhelming defeat and virtual annihilation of the Nationalist forces in the province. It proved impossible to go ahead with repairs to the hospital in Chouts'un, or to re-establish a missionary presence there.

Anxious to put his medical skills to use, Ronald went first to Tsingtao, where he worked for several months in the Lutheran hospital, and then to Cheeloo University Medical School in Tsinan, where he was appointed acting hospital superintendent and head of the department of Obstetrics and Gynaecology. By the middle of 1948, Tsinan and Tsingtao were the only areas in Shantung remaining under Nationalist control. It was evident that it was only a matter of time before the Communists established themselves as the national government and the presence of foreign missionaries would thereafter serve as an embarrassment to Chinese Christians.

When, in late August 1948, Ronald wrote to Gwyneth in Little Abington saying that he would shortly return to England for furlough, the news was joyfully received by the family. His mother wrote at once, 'To think that this Sunday is your last in Tsinan makes our life quite different. We do thank God for the good news so long awaited, and hardly dare think of it lest some snag should come. There will be those who are sorry this is your last Sunday in hospital and in the church and we are sorry for them left behind in such unsettled conditions, but we can't help thinking too of a brave wife and loving girls who haven't seen you for two years and for their sakes and our own we cannot but be glad. Soon we shall be able to say, 'All news when we meet'! Until then, God have you in His safe keeping.'

In the weeks that followed his return to England, Ronald and Gwyneth were greatly exercised as to the consequences for their own future of the changed situation in China. By the end of the year, they felt compelled to make a fresh decision.

Ronald to his father and mother

Little Abington, Cambridge
10 p.m. 31st December 1948

It is just twenty years ago this month since I wrote to you from Cambridge, telling you that I wanted to be a medical missionary. Now, since I am home from China this last time, Gwyneth and I have been feeling that we must make another and a different decision. We haven't made any final decision yet, and don't feel that we can do so until we have been able to consult with you, but we want you to know the way in which we are feeling to be led just now.

During these past days I have felt that it would not be right to postpone making a decision about whether I return to China in the coming Autumn or not, for several reasons. If I should decide not to return, the Cheeloo staff should know of the decision as soon as possible, because they will have to make arrangements for my place to be filled by someone else. Also, I should be required to give the BMS six months' notice of resignation, and that would mean that, if I were not to return to China in the autumn, the coming January Committees would be the latest opportunity for me to resign giving the requisite notice. And, if my resignation meant that I had to look out for another job, and if finding another job should mean that we would have to leave Little Abington, then for the children's sake we ought to try to make the move in time for them to go to their new school this coming September.

So it seems to me as though we ought to decide quickly whether I should try to return to China this autumn, or whether I should ask the Society to allow me to resign. It seems to us that there are four possibilities:

(1) That I should return to China alone, leaving Gwyneth and the children in England as last time.

(2) That Gwyneth and I should go back to China together and that we should try to find guardians for the children.

(3) That Gwyneth and I should return to China with one, two or all three children, and

(4) That I should resign from the Society

Of these, the first would involve a family separation for the greater part of the next ten years. Apart from our disinclination from these prolonged separations, I feel quite sure that this would involve asking Gwyneth to carry too big a burden, and one that she should not be asked to carry, and to some extent I feel that there are things that I can do in the upbringing of the children when I am with them, that I could not do for them if I were away for these long periods.

The second alternative is difficult, because we do not feel it is fair to put the responsibility of the three children's future on other persons. Guardianship is especially difficult in these days of shortages and restrictions and besides we feel that the children need the care and supervision of parents, if possible. I know that some of our colleagues whom we most admire find it possible to leave their children with guardians, but I think I can only feel that I am not as they are, and that our circumstances are not quite parallel with theirs.

About (3), I think the present China situation is too uncertain to justify us in taking the children back to it. Both Rosemary and Audrey will need home education within the next three to five years, and there will be no suitable educational facilities for them in China so this does not seem a right solution.

I have been very reluctant to consider the possibility of resigning. It would mean giving up what I hoped might be a life work, turning back after putting my hand to the plough. In many ways it would feel like letting down good colleagues, both Chinese and foreign, and would seem very much like 'quitting' just at a time when I was most needed, and just at a time when I was growing to be useful.

But although I do not like to think of resignation, the more I think over the problem, the more I feel led to the conclusion that I can really do no other. I have tried to feel sure that whatever answer came to me should be a God-given one. I think that I do have that feeling of assurance, and I think that if I were to resign, although it would be with regret, yet it would be with the conviction that it was God's will and that I can do no other.

Now, Mother and Father dears, I do not want this letter to cause you any anxiety or worry. I shall need to write to the Society in good time before their Committees beginning on January 17th, and I shall be glad to have a letter from you, when you have time to write, just telling us what you feel. Just write down whatever you have in your hearts that you want to say, and that will be the best guide to us in making our decision. Do not think anxiously, either, about what we shall do if I resign from the BMS. We have no prospects in mind at present, but we are not worried about that. I am sure that, if it seems to be the right thing to do for me to resign, some suitable appointment will be available before long. The first thing to do is to feel sure that the decision we take about resignation is the right one.

But if I were not on the active list of the Missionary Society, and if I had to undertake some kind of medical practice at home, I hope I should still be on the active list of workers for the Kingdom at home. I don't think that any of your children could feel loyal to you, unless they were doing their best to "seek first the Kingdom", and Gwyneth and I would want you to feel assured that, even if we had to give up our work in China, we intend to do our best for the Church at home.

I won't write more now, except to send you the loving wishes of us all for the New Year. We hope that we may have many opportunities of seeing you in it.

POSTSCRIPT

Gwyneth & Ronald *(first & third from left)* in the 1960s, with Iain & Kay Campbell with whom they shared so much during their internment in Shanghai.

Having resigned from the Baptist Missionary Society in 1949, in September that year Ronald took up the new post of Student Health Officer in the University of Leeds. He remained there until his retirement in 1973 when he and Gwyneth moved to St Andrews. Her sudden death early in 1974 left him to face retirement alone.

It had become impossible to maintain any contact with friends or colleagues in China following the setting up of the People's Republic of China in 1949, but in the early 1980s students from mainland China began appearing in very small numbers at British universities. Through a chance contact with a student in Edinburgh, Ronald was once more put in touch with former colleagues at Tsinan. It was as a result of these contacts that he received, to his great joy, the following letter (the original in Chinese) from Kao Ta Ko's son, Kao Yen Tsing.

Kao Yen Tsing to Ronald

Chouts'un
5th May 1984

Dear Uncle[213] Still

When I received the photograph of you and your family, I took it for my father to see. My father was so pleased that he burst into tears, tears of heartfelt joy.

I should have replied to you earlier, but did not do so, partly because I cannot write in English, and partly because I wanted to send you a photograph of our family. Up until now the family has not been all

[213] Chinese form of address for a respected senior family friend

at home together at the same time, so I have not been able to do this. Please forgive me.

Twice you have visited our village, and a deep friendship has grown between you and my father, a friendship sealed by this photograph which has come all this distance across the sea. It is only a thin piece of paper, but I count it more precious than a thousand tons of gold.

When my father learned that auntie[214] had died, he sighed heavily and began to weep. Seeing the strength of his emotion, I wrote these words in her honour, 'She came from a thousand miles away, leaving with us a lasting impression of her beauty - a gentle, gracious, humble, wise and discerning person. Though she is now unable to accompany uncle into his old age, the happiness and contentment derived from the time they shared together will remain with uncle for ever.'

My father has been remembering, too, that your wish to rebuild the hospital was unfulfilled when you returned to your homeland. He reflected that you and he together had hoped to fulfil this great ambition. Now your heads are white and this dream cannot be realised, but you have your families to enjoy and in the evening of your days can smile as you remember past times. When I told my father of the possibility that you might come to China he broke into a smile. I hope very much that time may come soon.

Dear uncle, my father has one son, three daughters, five grandsons, one granddaughter, seven nephews and six nieces. My mother has already died, at the age of 82. You would certainly be glad to see all these, would you not? My father has been ill for six years & bed-ridden, but he can take food five times a day. His sight and hearing are good and he still has all his teeth. I myself am sixty years old. I studied a little medicine and at present still live in Chouts'un, but shortly expect to return to our home village with my father, because of his great age.

I hope very much that you will be well enough to come to China. After you receive this letter, if possible please convey our good wishes to Mr Harris and his family.

With all kind regards to you all, Kao Yen Tsing

Ronald made detailed plans to return for a third time to China in autumn 1985 but he died that year on the 5th June, before he was able to realise them.

---

[214] Gwyneth

ACKNOWLEDGEMENTS

My greatest debt in producing this volume has been to my parents who wrote the original letters, and to my grandparents who faithfully preserved every communication from China. The effort on all their parts to keep in touch, despite enormous difficulties, was nothing short of prodigious – and the faithful service of the Post Office authorities, in England and in China, in managing to deliver such a remarkable percentage of the mail entrusted to them during the turbulent war years, is hardly less noteworthy. Getting to know my parents afresh through the letters has been a particularly happy experience for me.

It has also given me great pleasure, in the course of this project, to revisit scenes from my childhood. In Jinan (Tsinan), I have been made wonderfully welcome, and have been helped in innumerable ways, by Gaoyan, the daughter of one of my father's colleagues at Qilu (Cheeloo); by Zhang Yumei, a graduate of the nursing school at Foster Hospital[215], who died in December 2006 in her 87th year; and by Zhou Mao Cheng, another colleague of my father from Qilu, whose own father was a pastor of the church at Zhoucun (Chouts'un) in the 1930s and 1940s. Qi Luyuan and Songhong Pearl, good friends from Qingdao (Tsingtao), took me to visit Miss Manger's cottages, still standing on the cliffs above the beach, and also accompanied me on a memorable visit to the hospital and mission buildings in Qingzhou (Tsingchou). In Shanghai, Wang Zhao Zhen entertained me most graciously and escorted me to see the site of the former Sacred Heart Hospital, where my family was interned in the last months of the war in 1945.

Research into the historical background to the letters was made possible partly by a grant from the Carnegie Trust for the Universities of Scotland, and I am glad to be able to acknowledge their valuable support. I am grateful, too, to the librarians and archivists who facilitated my work, Sue Mills, Andrew Hudson and Julian Lock at the Angus Library at Regent's Park College, Oxford, Rod Suddaby and his colleagues at the Imperial War Museum, and Margaret Acton of the Centre for the Study of Christianity in the Non-Western World, Edinburgh. I acknowledge with thanks the graciousness of the Baptist Missionary Society in allowing me to quote from documents for which they hold copyright, and the Imperial War Museum to use photos from their wonderful archive.

---

[215] Zhang Yumei can be seen, standing 6th from left, in the photograph of the nurses' graduation ceremony in 1941.

The formidable typing skills of Jane Gough, who, along with my daughter Clare, typed a large part of the original letters, got the project off to an excellent start. Clare later provided the maps and played a major part in formatting the final text. Without her care and expertise the end product would have been much poorer. David Roche's contribution in helping to prepare the photographs was also most valuable.

Julia Prescott nobly read almost the whole one million words of the unedited letters, and John Morgan-Wynne, Wayne Thomas and Gill Tritter read subsequent versions. I thank them all for their interest and for their thoughtful comments. Very many others have provided me with most welcome information, encouragement and suggestions. I hesitate to try to draw up a comprehensive list for fear of inadvertently overlooking someone, but I must mention help with a medical reference from Jennifer Felderhof, editorial advice from Brian Hollingworth, lexicographical advice and meticulous proof reading from Lucy Hollingworth, suggestions about publication from John Lloyd, and help with modern Chinese place names from Wang Yueh-hua. The combined efforts of Gaoyan, Professor Liu Ping and Professor Zheng Zhao Li of Fudan University enabled me to add a Chinese title to the book cover in Professor Zheng's fine calligraphy. My thanks go also to John Ewing for allowing me to use a photograph from his family collection.

My sister, Rosemary Hollingworth, has been invariably generous in response to my questions or requests for help and I have benefited greatly from her ideas, critical acumen, and practical support. Her encouragement and that of my younger sister, Catherine Ewing, have been important factors in keeping me going during the work. My husband, Robin, and daughters, Clare and Judith, have encouraged me from the beginning by their enthusiasm for the project and their faith in my ability to carry it through. I am more grateful than I can say for this, and for their significant practical help in all kinds of ways.

Audrey Salters
October 2007

APPENDIX 1

Modern (Pinyin) equivalents of Chinese place names

Wade Giles	Pinyin
Amoy	Xiamen
Canton	Guangzhou
Changtien	Changdian
Cheeloo	Qilu
Chefoo	Yantai
Chouts'un	Zhoucun
Chungking	Chongqing
Foochow	Fuzhou
Hankow	Hankou
Hong Kong	Xianggang
Hopei	Hebei
Hsuchow	Xuzhou
Huang Ho	Huang He
Moukden	Shenyang
Nanking	Nanjing
Paoting	Baoding
Pei-chen	Binzhou
Peitaiho	Beidaihe
Peking/Peiping*	Beijing
Pootung	Pudong
Poshan	Boshan
Shansi	Shanxi
Shantung	Shandong
Shensi	Shaanxi
Shih chia chuang	Shijiazhuang
Sinchou	Xin zhou
Swatow	Shantou
Szechuan	Sichuan
Taichow	Dai Xian
Techow	Dezhou
Tientsin	Tianjin
Ting Hsiang	Dingxiang
Tsangchow	Cangzhou
Tsinan	Jinan
Tsingchou/Tsingchoufu	Qingzhou
Tsinghua University	Xinhua
Tsingtao	Qingdao
Tsouping	Zouping
Weihsien	Weifang
Whangpoo	Huangpu
Wuting/Wutingfu	Huimin

* Peking, meaning 'Northern capital', was renamed Peiping ('Northern peace') after Nanking was made the national capital by Chiang Kai-shek in 1928. The two names tended to be used more or less interchangeably by foreigners during the 1930s and 40s.

APPENDIX 2

Index of Baptist Missionaries referred to in the letters, with dates when they served with the BMS in China

Allen, Connie *née Greening*	1931-1951
Allen, T W (Tom)	1931-1951
Bain, Miss J M	1937-1940
Bethell, Dr S E	1920-1936
Black, Adam	1923-1951
Bloom, Dr C V	1931-1946
Broomhall, Dr B C	1904-1932
Clow, Dr Ellen (Nellie)	1928-1948
Clow, Dr J Menzies	1929-1951
Dart, R H P	1925-1954
Dawson, S R	1936-1946
Drake Frederick S	1914-1952
Drake, S B	1886–1910
Elder, A C and Mrs	1940-1953
Emmott, H A	1924-1950
Ennals, S W	1899, killed 1900
Flowers, Dr Wilfred S	1928-1949
Flowers, Mrs Annie *née Irvine*	1929-1949
Franklin, Miss K M	1905-1943
Glasby, Miss B	1924, killed 1938
Greening, A E	1897 - 1936
Harris, James S (Hu)	1908-1948
Harris, Mrs Mabel *née Moore*	1911-1948
Henderson Smith, John	1935-1949
Hickson, Miss G M	1924-1947
Ingle, Agnes (Nan) *née Ferguson*	1919-1940
Ingle, Dr Lawrence M	1919-1940
Jagger, Miss Amy (Jags)	1938-1950
Jasper, Ceridwen *née Lloyd*	1937-1946
Jasper, V J	1936-1946
King, Dr Gordon	1927-1940
King, Miss Mary *(Mrs Mudd)*	1935-1952
Lewis, Mrs Georgie *née Menzie*	1939-1947
Lewis, Dr J	1909, died 1916
Lewis, Dr John	1938-1947
Lewis, Mrs Nellie *née Turner*	1911-1948
Logan, Miss M (Logie)	1909-1940
Lower, T E,	1902-1928, 1932-1938
Madge, E G T	1935-1951
Manger, Miss Jessie	1908-1938
Natten, Miss W *(Mrs Gunn)*	1934-1952
Pailing, Mrs Muriel *née Coombs*	1916-1946
Pailing, William P (Bill)	1914-1946
Payne, H (Pan)	1905-1947
Phillips, Edward	1924-1951
Phillips, Mrs Enid *née Gibbon*	1927-1951
Price, F W	1911-1947
Scott, Carrie *née Prentice*	1931-1951
Scott, Jim	1929- 1951
Smurthwaite, Miss A (Su)	1920-1950
Stonelake, H T	1906-1940
Tait, Dr Ruth	1924-1950
Thomas, Miss Margaret	1909-1946
Turner, J J	1883-1920
Watson, Miss F M	1920-1951
Watson, Dr J R	1884-1923
Wheal, Miss Alice	1926–1949
Williamson, H R (Wei)	1908–1939
Wood, Miss F M,	1908-1937
Wyatt, Dr H G	1925, killed 1938

APPENDIX 3

Maps

For modern placename equivalents, see Appendix 1

(i) China in 1935, showing the 3 provinces (Shantung, Shansi & Shensi) where BMS missionaries were located

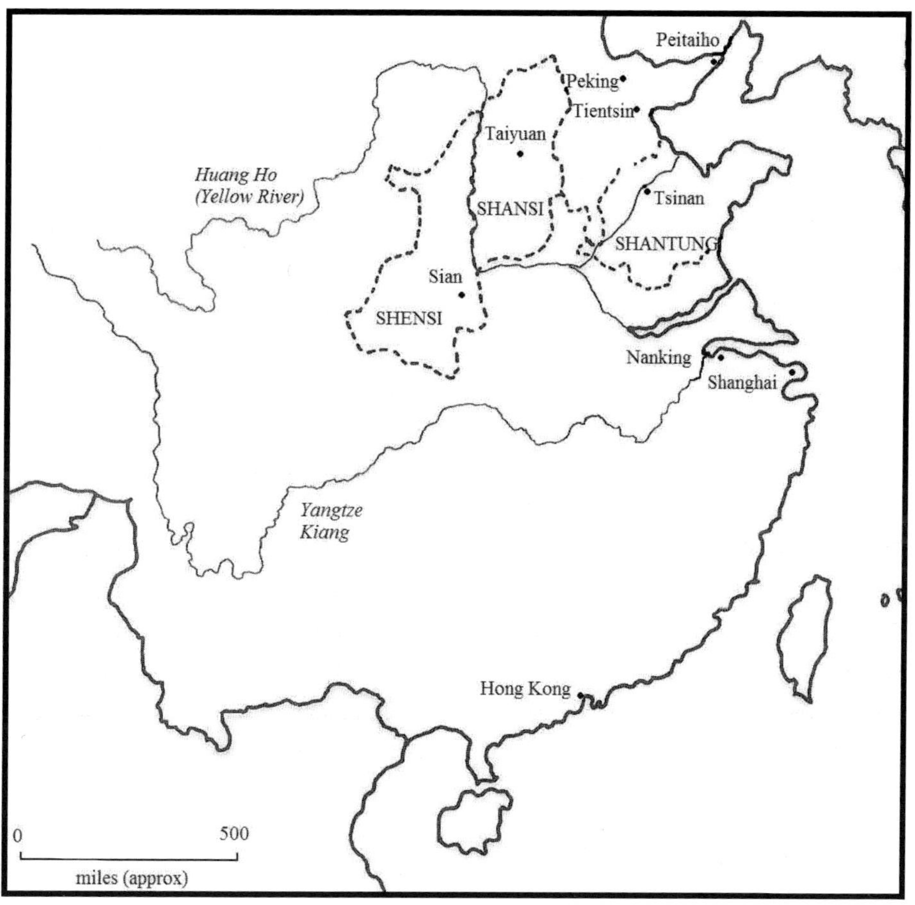

(ii) Shantung Province in the 1930s & 40s

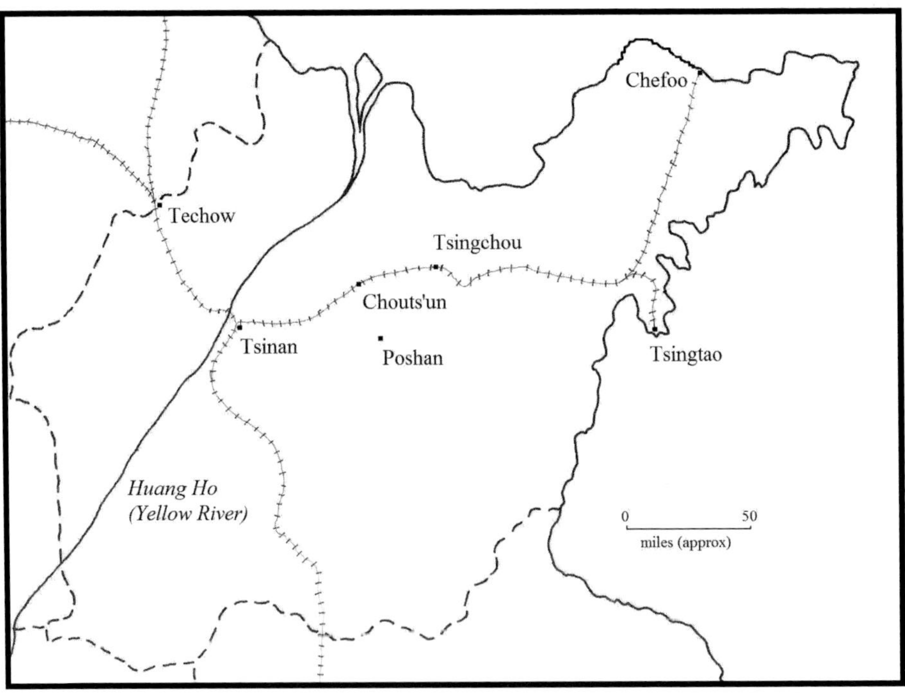

--- Province border
++++++ Railway line

AUDREY SALTERS was born in Japanese occupied China and spent three years as a child in internment in Shanghai. She graduated in English language and Literature from the University of Oxford, and undertook post-graduate study at the London School of Economics and the University of Edinburgh. After a career in social work and social work education, she has retired and lives with her husband in St Andrews.